REVELATION

A Book of Promises

REV
ELA
TION

A Book of Promises

GREG LAURIE

HARVEST MINISTRIES ✕

Riverside, California

Revelation: A Book of Promises

International Standard Book Number: 978-1-61754-016-5

Cover design: Josh Huffman

Please address requests for information to:
Harvest Ministries
6115 Arlington Avenue
Riverside, CA 92504

Library of Congress data

1 2 3 4 5 6 7 / 24 23 22 21

CONTENTS

Introduction

I think we're all very aware of the fact that our world is in turmoil right now.

There's a sense of fear in the air, due in part to this global pandemic that was supposed to have come and gone but just seems to keep going with new strains and no real end in sight. We hear daily news about COVID-19, the vaccine, and vaccination rates, and new words have entered our regular vocabulary, such as *self-isolation, social distancing, community spread, herd immunity,* and even *mask shaming.*

Meanwhile, our cities here in the United States are in turmoil, with violence and murder rates rising dramatically.

As we see all the things that are going on, it causes us to wonder, "Are these signs of the times? Are these the things the Bible told us to be looking for, things that signal the return of Christ?"

Yes, they are.

Jesus likened end times events, or the signs of the times, to "birth pangs." They're what we might call labor pains. When a baby is close to being born, the mother's labor pains get closer and closer together. In the same way, the Bible tells us that as we get closer to the Lord's return, we'll see the signs closer and closer together, alerting us to the fact that His return is near.

We could look at these signs almost like dominoes. If you were to line up multiple dominoes closely together and then knock over the first one, the rest would fall down in rapid succession. That is what the last days events are like.

But the first domino has not yet fallen. It is my opinion that the next event on the prophetic calendar is the Rapture (I have a lot to say about that event in this book, so read on), but the Rapture has not yet taken place.

I do believe that we're in the last days. Therefore, it's important that we understand what is happening around us.

In chapter 13 of Romans, the apostle Paul wrote, "This is all the more urgent, for you know how late it is; time is running out. Wake up, for our salvation is nearer now than when we first believed. The night is almost gone" (verses 11–12 NLT).

We need to understand the times we're living in, and there's no better book to explain that to us than the book of Revelation.

God doesn't want to conceal these things from us. Rather, He wants to reveal them to us. Bible prophecy is not given to scare us; it is given to prepare us. Bible prophecy is not given to inflate our brains; it is given to enlarge our hearts.

There's more to this book than prophetic subjects such as Armageddon, the Antichrist, and the mark of the Beast. Before Jesus addresses the future, He has a lot to say to the church, to His followers.

Interestingly, Revelation is the only book of the Bible with a built-in blessing, which we find in verse 3 of chapter 1: "Blessed is he who reads and those who hear the words of this prophecy, and keep those things which are written in it; for the time is near."

Studying the book of Revelation also unlocks the mystery of history. We see that God is in control, and things are moving according to a master plan. This isn't being decided by people in power, whether it's people in government or tech or any other people, wherever they are. God is ultimately in control. And He sees the future as accurately as we see the past.

Revelation brings sense to our suffering as well. What do you say to someone who has suffered tragedy or who's grappling with a disability? What do you say to someone who has lost a loved one, someone who's weeping from grief? You say this is not God's final plan. It's in Revelation that God tells us that He will wipe every tear from our eyes. There will be no more death or sorrow or crying or pain. All these things will be gone forever. When I read the book of Revelation, I realize that God is going to resolve all things in the end.

The primary focus of Revelation, however, is Jesus Christ. Revelation gives us the only physical description of Jesus Christ in the New Testament, and it's largely symbolic.

Therefore, give your attention to who Jesus Christ is, because He is the very center of the book of Revelation, and He's the very center of Bible prophecy in general. As Revelation 19:10 tells us, "For the essence of prophecy is to give a clear witness for Jesus" (NLT).

Jesus is the centerpiece and star of the book of Revelation. And He should be the centerpiece and star of our lives as well.

THE OBJECTIVE OF REVELATION
The unveiling of Jesus Christ

THE OUTLINE OF REVELATION

I. The things that are seen (Chapter 1)
II. The things that are (Chapters 2–3)
III. The things that will take place after this (Chapters 4–21)

REVELATION

A Book of Promises

Part One

THE THINGS THAT ARE SEEN

CHAPTER ONE

Your Password to Unlocking Revelation

Blessed is he who reads and those who hear the words of this prophecy, and keep those things which are written in it; for the time is near.
(Revelation 1:3)

IN THIS CHAPTER

- The book of Revelation shows, or uncovers, what is to come in our world and in the heavens.
- Jesus is the star of Revelation and its main theme.
- Revelation was given from Jesus through the angel to the apostle John.
- Three prerequisites for the special blessing promised in the book of Revelation
- Seven things the book of Revelation gives us

A number of years ago we took our granddaughter Stella to her first 3-D movie. It was one of those computer-animated films, and she had never seen anything like it. When we put the glasses on her, she saw those objects appearing to move straight at her, and it frightened her. She started crying.

As it turned out, her mom and her grandmother sat with her in the lobby while I stayed and watched the rest of the movie. I was thoroughly engrossed and didn't want to leave.

Of course, 3-D is a special effect. It's not real, but it *seems* real. It almost feels as though you're looking into another dimension.

The book of Revelation is a bit like putting on those 3-D glasses. What we see in the pages of this book, however, isn't conjured up in some Hollywood studio or special effects lab; it's real. This last book of the Bible enables us to look beyond the physical realm into another world, another dimension. It's the supernatural realm of Heaven and Hell, of angels and demons, of God and Satan.

Revelation also allows us to glimpse realities that are outside of time, in the eternal realm. It reminds us that our God lives in that eternal reality and isn't bound by the pages of a calendar, the hours in a day, or the hands on a clock. He has no yesterday or tomorrow, because it's all just a continuum to Him. That being so, God can look at the future with as much clarity and accuracy as you and I might look at the recent past. In fact, more so, because I don't recollect the past accurately. I will jumble up the details and get events switched around.

God, however, has perfect recollection and perfect foresight. When He says that a certain event will happen, it's as though it has already taken place. From our point of view, time seems to stretch on and on, but God isn't affected at all by the duration of time. As Peter noted, "A day is like a thousand years to the Lord, and a thousand years is like a day" (2 Peter 3:8 NLT).

> **GOOD TO KNOW**
> It's worth noting that two-thirds of the Bible is prophecy—and one-half of those predicted events *have already taken place.*

When God predicts the future, it isn't as though He's going out on a limb or taking a risk. He knows that future already; with Him, it's already an established fact. He doesn't just predict the future; *He has been there.* In fact, He's there right now, just as much as He is with us in the present moment.

Revelation is a book that dares to predict the future many, many times over. Yet strangely, it's often a neglected book in the New Testament. They will chase after unfounded and wild conspiracy theories, yet they will neglect the Word of God that predicts the future, not once, not twice, but *hundreds* of times with 100 percent accuracy.

The Bible is the one and only book that we can completely trust.

It's worth noting that two-thirds of the Bible is prophecy—and one-half of those predicted events *have already taken place.* So, if half of these events have happened just as God said they would, then we have no reason to doubt that the remaining prophecies will happen as well.

Part of what has discouraged people from delving into the book of Revelation is the fact that much of it is written in figurative language. Many of the predictions that God gave John to record were so far removed from his understanding and the language of his day that he had to use symbols, metaphors, and other techniques to communicate what he was witnessing.

For instance, how would you describe a nuclear war (if John was indeed doing that—and he may have been) if you lived in AD 90? There was no precedent for such a concept. In fact, black powder wasn't invented until the ninth century after Christ, and dynamite didn't appear on the scene until the mid-1800s. So how do you describe a thermonuclear exchange between nations?

Revelation speaks of the power of one man to deny people the ability to buy or sell without his "mark." That sounded so implausible and futuristic, even fifty years ago. But today with current technology, such a system could be up and running in short order.

GOOD TO KNOW

Revelation means "the unveiling." The very title of the book promises that those who seek understanding will find it.

We read in the book of Revelation about an army numbering two hundred million, marching toward the final battle, the Battle of Armageddon. When John recorded that number, there weren't even two hundred million people on the planet. At the time of this writing, there are well over seven billion. And there is one nation (as we will see) that can field an army of two hundred million *this afternoon.*

Even so, many people shy away from reading and studying the book of Revelation because they don't think it's understandable, or they imagine it to be far too complex to get a handle on.

I beg to differ.

Revelation means "the unveiling." The very title of the book promises that those who seek understanding will find it. Taken as a whole, the book *reveals* more than it conceals.

THE UNVEILING

The book of Revelation shows, or uncovers, what is to come in our world and in the heavens. It reminds me of a car show, where they have a new model under a covering. And then, as the lights and music come up, they pull that piece of fabric away, and everyone gets their first look at that carefully designed car.

What does Revelation uncover or unveil? Actually, many things. But it certainly reveals the spirit world, the realm of angels and demons. We also learn about great cataclysmic events in store for the planet, including the Great Tribulation and the Battle of Armageddon. Within the pages of this book, we learn about the coming Antichrist and his henchmen.

But the primary objective of this last book in the New Testament isn't to reveal the Antichrist; it is to reveal the Christ.

It is the unveiling of Jesus Christ.

Jesus is the star of the book and the main theme.

In Revelation 1:5 He is the faithful witness and the firstborn from the dead. In verse 8 He is the Alpha and Omega, the One who was, who is, and who is to come, the Almighty! There are eight references to Jesus in Revelation 1 alone.

GOOD TO KNOW

The primary objective of Revelation isn't to reveal the Antichrist; it is to reveal the Christ. Jesus is the star of the book and the main theme.

Another thing about this book that I find amazing is that it comes with its own outline. Oftentimes when we teach a book of the Bible, we take time to determine the outline of the book so we can break it into sections and make it more understandable. Revelation, however, comes with its own outline in Revelation 1:19: "Write the things which you have seen, and the things which are, and the things which will take place after this."

So there are three sections to Revelation.

> (1) *The things that are seen.* That is what John describes in chapter 1 as he views the resurrected and glorified Christ, who is in complete control of all that is about to happen.

(2) *The things that are.* This is a reference to the seven churches we will read about in Revelation 2 and 3. This section not only describes seven real and functioning churches of that day, but it also gives penetrating insight into the church of today.

(3) *The things that will take place after this.* These are the future events found in chapters 4 to 22. And this simple, three-point outline essentially gives us a quick flyover of the contents of the book.

DELIVERED BY ANGELS, RECORDED BY JOHN

Another unique thing about Revelation is that it's the only book that was delivered by an angel. In Revelation 22:16 we read, "I, Jesus, have sent My angel to testify to you these things in the churches."

In fact, Revelation is full of angels from beginning to end. Angels appear in every chapter of Revelation, with the exception of chapters 4 and 13. We read about them again and again.

The book we will be considering together, however, was given from Jesus through the angel to the apostle John.

Within the twelve disciples, John was part of that inner group of three who often accompanied the Lord on special missions. Peter, James, and John were there when Jesus was transfigured and stood with Moses and Elijah on the mountaintop, and His face and clothing shone like the sun. John was there in the Garden of Gethsemane when Jesus prayed, "Nevertheless not My will, but Yours, be done" (Luke 22:42).

And to his eternal credit, John stood boldly at the foot of the cross after our Lord had been crucified. While the others made themselves scarce or went into hiding, John stood there in plain sight, keeping watch on that dreadful day. Maybe that was one of the reasons Jesus gave him the mission of caring for His mother. One of the last words of Jesus

GOOD TO KNOW
Revelation is the only book that was delivered by an angel. It was given from Jesus through the angel to the apostle John.

from the cross was when He looked down at John, standing next to Mary, and said to him, "Behold your mother!" The Bible tells us that "from that hour that disciple took her to his own home" (John 19:27).

After getting news that Christ's tomb was open and empty, John and Peter both ran to the scene, and John got there first. When John looked in, he saw that the tomb was empty and noticed the bandages that had been wrapped around the body of Christ. But now the body was gone. We read that he saw that and believed, while presumably Peter saw the same thing but walked away, wondering what it was all about.

John seemed to be a little more spiritually perceptive than the others—perhaps because he was always so close to the Lord, calling himself "the disciple whom Jesus loved." On one occasion, we read of John leaning his head on Jesus' chest as they were reclining at a meal, so as not to miss a single word. After Christ had risen from the dead, calling out from the shore to the disciples in a fishing boat on the lake, it was John who realized that it was Jesus and exclaimed, "It is the Lord!" (John 21:7).

GOOD TO KNOW

John wrote his gospel that we might believe, his epistles that we might be sure, and the book of Revelation that we might be ready.

John had a close, loving relationship with Jesus. It makes sense that God would give him the privilege of writing the last book of the Bible. From the pen of this apostle we have five books of the New Testament: the fourth gospel, three epistles, and the book of Revelation. He wrote his gospel that we might believe, his epistles that we might be sure, and the book of Revelation that we might be ready.

EXILED ... BUT NOT ALONE

John received the revelation from Jesus during a time of punishment and exile on the island of Patmos.

When you read the word *island*, don't think of Catalina or Maui.

Patmos is a tiny, rocky island in the Mediterranean—cold, windy, and barren. This was an era when the church was under intense persecution in the

Roman Empire. It started with the emperor Nero and continued through other emperors—most notably Diocletian. Many believers were losing their lives in those days, and a pall of menace and uncertainty hung over the young church of Jesus Christ. Families were being torn apart as believers were arrested, imprisoned, tortured, or put to death in coliseums.

So, they exiled the aged John to this distant place, never expecting to hear from him again, but God had other plans. On that rugged, windswept little island, God gave to the elderly apostle the incredible revealing of the future that became the book of Revelation.

GOOD TO KNOW
John received the revelation from Jesus during a time of punishment and exile on the island of Patmos, a tiny, rocky island in the Mediterranean.

In many ways Revelation reads like an action-packed thriller. If you love novels, then you will love this book. It has drama, suspense, mystery, warfare, and horror. It contains rebellion, unprecedented economic collapse, and the ultimate war of all history. But despite these ominous occurrences, it throbs with joy and hope. Best of all, it comes to a glorious climax where sin and death are banished forever, and God's adopted sons and daughters live with Him forever.

In Revelation 21:3–4 we read,

> Behold, the tabernacle of God is with men, and He will dwell with them, and they shall be His people. God Himself will be with them and be their God. And God will wipe away every tear from their eyes; there shall be no more death, nor sorrow, nor crying. There shall be no more pain, for the former things have passed away.

Revelation reminds us that we win in the end. You can't have a better happy ending than that.

A SPECIAL BLESSING: THREE PREREQUISITES

There is a special blessing promised in the book of Revelation for the person who reads, hears, and keeps the words of the book. No other book in the Bible promises such a blessing:

> "Blessed is he who reads and those who hear the words of this prophecy, and keep those things which are written in it; for the time is near." (Revelation 1:3)

There are three prerequisites to receive the promised blessing.

(1) You must read it. By the way, the Greek term used here for *read* means to read it *out loud.* Have you ever tried reading the Scriptures out loud in your devotional time? Sometimes the Word comes to us with more power when we hear it with our ears in addition to simply forming the words in our minds. It isn't just a matter of reading, however; it's a matter of hearing.

GOOD TO KNOW

There is a special blessing promised in the book of Revelation for the person who reads, hears, and keeps the words of the book.

(2) You must hear the words of the prophecy. Jesus would often say, "He who has ears to hear, let him hear!" If you were to read this book simply as a great work of literature, which it is, or a mere religious writing, you wouldn't necessarily get that much out of it. But if the Holy Spirit opens your spiritual eyes and ears to see and hear what God is saying, it can make all the difference in the world.

(3) You must keep it. The Scripture speaks of *keeping* the truths that are written in this book. In other words, I apply these truths to my own life, my own situation, and my own daily experience. If I do that, then this book will motivate me to live a godly life and make

me ready to meet the Lord. *The reason we want to learn about the future is to help us to live rightly in the present.*

Let's dive right in to chapter 1.

"WHAT YOU SEE, WRITE IN A BOOK"

The Revelation of Jesus Christ, which God gave Him to show His servants—things which must shortly take place. And He sent and signified it by His angel to His servant John, who bore witness to the word of God, and to the testimony of Jesus Christ, to all things that he saw. Blessed is he who reads and those who hear the words of this prophecy, and keep those things which are written in it; for the time is near.

John, to the seven churches which are in Asia:

Grace to you and peace from Him who is and who was and who is to come, and from the seven Spirits who are before His throne, and from Jesus Christ, the faithful witness, the firstborn from the dead, and the ruler over the kings of the earth.

To Him who loved us and washed us from our sins in His own blood, and has made us kings and priests to His God and Father, to Him be glory and dominion forever and ever. Amen.

Behold, He is coming with clouds, and every eye will see Him, even they who pierced Him. And all the tribes of the earth will mourn because of Him. Even so, Amen.

"I am the Alpha and the Omega, the Beginning and the End," says the Lord, "who is and who was and who is to come, the Almighty."

I, John, both your brother and companion in the tribulation and kingdom and patience of Jesus Christ, was on the island that is called Patmos for the word of God and for the testimony of Jesus Christ. I was in the Spirit on the Lord's Day, and I heard behind me a loud voice, as of a trumpet, saying, "I am the Alpha and the Omega, the First and the Last," and, "What you see, write in a book and send it to the seven churches which are in Asia: to Ephesus, to Smyrna, to Pergamos, to Thyatira, to Sardis, to Philadelphia, and to Laodicea."

Then I turned to see the voice that spoke with me. And having turned I saw seven golden lampstands, and in the midst of the seven lampstands One like the Son of Man, clothed with a garment down to the feet and girded about the chest with a golden band. His head and hair were white like wool, as white as snow, and His eyes like a flame of fire; His feet were like fine brass, as if refined in a furnace, and His voice as the sound of many waters; He had in His right hand seven stars, out of His mouth went a sharp two-edged sword, and His countenance was like the sun shining in its strength. And when I saw Him, I fell at His feet as dead. But He laid His right hand on me, saying to me, "Do not be afraid; I am the First and the Last. I am He who lives, and was dead, and behold, I am alive forevermore. Amen. And I have the keys of Hades and of Death. Write the things which you have seen, and the things which are, and the things which will take place after this." (Revelation 1:1–19)

WHAT DO WE LEARN FROM CHAPTER 1?

Revelation reveals that the events of the last days are closely linked together.

Verse 1 speaks of "things which must shortly take place." A better translation might be, "What must speedily happen."

Some might respond, "Speedily happen? Are you kidding me? Wasn't this book written two thousand years ago? God must be a little on the slow side when it comes to getting things done."

But let's take a minute to understand John's words here. He wasn't speaking of events that would happen quickly in his own lifetime. Rather, he was referring to how quickly those events would move forward once they began.

In other words, once the first domino falls, the rest will fall in rapid order.

Revelation speaks of Jesus Christ revealing Himself to us.

Verse 5 speaks of "Jesus Christ, the faithful witness." In the book of Revelation, Jesus reveals Himself to us. And who better? Who is a better source on you than you? Who is a better source on Jesus than Jesus?

In Luke 24:13–27 the risen Christ spoke with two discouraged disciples as they returned home to Emmaus following the crucifixion and death of Jesus in Jerusalem. They not only were grieving the loss of their Lord and Friend, but they also were completely confused about what had just happened. They had completely misunderstood what Jesus the Messiah was supposed to accomplish during His time on Earth. To put it simply, they had it all wrong.

As the three men walked the four miles to the little town of Emmaus, Jesus spoke to them about Jesus—though at that point they didn't even recognize Him. Jesus pointed out all the Scriptures that alluded to His suffering, death, and resurrection.

There is no better expert on Jesus than Jesus Himself. If the book of Revelation is nothing else, it's a portrait of Jesus, a "selfie" of God, if you will. And in this book, He reveals Himself in unprecedented ways.

Notice also that He is the *faithful* witness. Not every witness is faithful, and right now we need a trustworthy source. Sometimes people will stretch the truth, speak all around the truth, or tell an outright lie. People are coming unhinged with crazy conspiracy theories they find online, along with fanciful, weird ideas about what's going on. Sometimes they'll even take Bible truths and hijack them or attach other things to them. We need to distance ourselves from all this and approach it in a clearheaded way, seeing what the Bible says about our future.

We have no better source to help us than Jesus Christ. The witness of Jesus Christ to Himself and to the events to come is a faithful witness. It's true. It's authentic. You can count on it.

Not only does Jesus tell us the truth, but He does so with love.

I love that phrase in verse 5: "To Him who loved us." A better translation would be, "To Him who keeps on loving us." Sometimes we may think we have to do certain things or adhere to certain standards to merit the love of God. But that isn't true. God just loves you, and He always will love you. The love of God is consistent, and it is persistent. He says, "Yes, I have loved you with an everlasting love; therefore with lovingkindness I have drawn you" (Jeremiah 31:3).

What a contrast the love of God is to the so-called "love" of our culture. Our world loves you when you are young and beautiful; God loves you when you are old and not so attractive. Our world loves you when you are famous and a celebrity; God loves you when you are unknown and a complete nobody. Our world loves you when you are rich and powerful; God loves you when you are penniless and weak.

Our world loves the extraordinary; God loves the ordinary—people like you and me. And God has demonstrated this love for us in a tangible way. Jesus said, "Greater love has no one than this, than to lay down one's life for his friends" (John 15:13).

GOOD TO KNOW

The witness of Jesus Christ to Himself and to the events to come is a faithful witness. You can count on it.

Jesus showed His love by dying for us, which brings us to Revelation 1:5: "[He] . . . washed us from our sins in His own blood." Notice this is in the past tense. In other words, it is *done*. He has washed you from your sins. God has forgiven you through Christ for all the wrong you have done.

Revelation tells us repeatedly that Jesus is coming back.

Verse 7 of chapter 1 says, "Behold, He is coming with clouds, and every eye will see Him." This great truth of the return of Christ appears in more than five hundred verses throughout the Bible. It has been estimated that one out of every twenty-five verses in the New Testament refers to the Second Coming.

This gives us hope in a hopeless world. There may not be very many hopeful or positive developments in the news today, but God says there is hope: Jesus is coming back. In fact, the Bible refers to this as "the blessed hope" (Titus 2:13).

What does it mean when it says that Jesus is "coming with clouds"? It might simply refer to the fact that He will come again in the sky and the air. Jesus said, "For as lightning that comes from the east is visible even in the west, so will be the coming of the Son of Man" (Matthew 24:27 NIV).

Then again, the clouds spoken of in this passage may refer to clouds of people. Hebrews 12:1 says that we are "surrounded by so great a cloud of witnesses." This reference to clouds in Revelation 1:7 may be speaking of the fact that when Jesus returns to the Earth, He will bring His church with Him. Colossians 3:4 tells us that "when Christ who is our life appears, then you also will appear with Him in glory."

GOOD TO KNOW

An estimated one out of every twenty-five verses in the New Testament refers to the Second Coming.

What goes up must come down. We who will have been raptured from Earth before the Tribulation will return with Jesus to Earth—millions and millions of us—in His awesome Second Coming.

Revelation says that all the world will see Him and know Him.

Verse 7 says that "every eye will see Him," including those who pierced Him. The Jewish people will become aware of the fact that Jesus was and is their long-awaited Messiah. Zechariah 12:10 says, "They will look on [Him] whom they pierced. Yes, they will mourn for Him as one mourns for his only son."

Revelation reveals Jesus as God incarnate.

In verse 8 we read, "I am the Alpha and Omega, the Beginning and the End . . . who is and who was and who is to come, the Almighty."

Can there be any doubt? Clearly Christ is saying here that He and the Father are equal.

Through the years, some have maintained that Jesus never actually claimed to be God and that it was all an invention of His followers. But that isn't true.

Jesus did claim to be God and to be equal to God the Father—here and in a number of other places in the Scriptures. Jesus accepted worship on multiple occasions—and this was after saying, "Worship the LORD your God, and Him only you shall serve" (Matthew 4:10).

Jesus claimed to be God because He is God. Referring to Himself as "the Alpha and the Omega" is another way of saying that He is the beginning and the end. Alpha and Omega are the first and last letters of the Greek alphabet. So it would be like Christ saying, "I am the A and the Z. I am the beginning and the end."

This reminds us that what God starts, He will finish. God, in contrast to me, always finishes what He begins. I am notorious for starting big projects that I don't complete, because I get bored or distracted. But God isn't that way. He will finish the work that He has begun in your life (see Philippians 1:6), and He will finish His work in this world that He has created.

Some imagine that God just wound up the universe like a clock and walked away from it. No, He has been involved in His creation from the beginning, and He will stay involved because He loves all of us so much. Yes, humanity has marred this planet with its rebellion and sin, but God will soon make things right. When it comes to the history of Planet Earth, He is last word, the beginning and the end, the Alpha and Omega.

GOOD TO KNOW
Jesus claimed to be God because He is God.

John says in verse 10 that he was "in the Spirit on the Lord's Day." That may have meant it was Sunday. The early church met on Sunday because that was the day Christ rose from the dead. Then again, John may have been referring to "the day of the Lord," which, of course, hasn't happened yet. It was almost as though John had been placed in a time machine back in the first century and was whisked forward into the future. He was catapulted into the twenty-first century, or perhaps beyond, saw all of these amazing phenomena, and then sought to describe it in the language of his day.

And so, as all of this was happening, verse 12 says that John "turned to see the voice that spoke with [him]."

I hope that we all will do that as we study this book together. We want to see Jesus revealed, and we want to hear what He has to say.

We all know people who study biblical prophecy like it was an academic exercise or even a hobby, obsessing over maps and news accounts and prophetic charts. Are you one of those people? I've listed a few indicators below to help you determine whether you might be obsessed with Bible prophecy.

- You know you're obsessed with Bible prophecy if barcode scanners make you worry about the mark of the Beast.

- You know you're obsessed with Bible prophecy if you never buy green bananas.

- You know you're obsessed with Bible prophecy when you can name more signs of the times than Ten Commandments.

- You know you're obsessed with Bible prophecy when you refuse a tax refund check because it's in the amount of $666.

- You know you're obsessed with Bible prophecy when you always leave the top down on your convertible in case of the Rapture.

Granted, some go overboard, becoming so obsessed with Bible prophecy that they seem to miss the point altogether. We never want to miss the essential message of the book of Revelation: the unveiling of Christ. The more we hear about the imminent return of our Lord to Earth, the more it should motivate us to lead more godly lives. As John wrote in 1 John 3:2–3, "Yes, dear friends, we are already God's children, right now, and we can't even imagine what it is going to be like later on. But we do know this, that when he comes we will be like him, as a result of seeing him as he really

GOOD TO KNOW

We never want to miss the essential message of the book of Revelation: the unveiling of Christ.

is. And everyone who really believes this will try to stay pure because Christ is pure" (TLB).

One of the benefits of understanding Bible prophecy, then, is that it will motivate you to live a pure life. It also will stir you to reach others with the gospel, knowing the time for such sharing is short.

Instead of finding yourself in some kind of holy huddle where it's all about you and me getting to Heaven, it will cause you to want to bring others along, too. As 2 Peter 3:14–15 says, "Dear friends, while you are waiting for these things to happen, make every effort to be found living peaceful lives that are pure and blameless in his sight. And remember, our Lord's patience gives people time to be saved" (NLT).

It's amazing to me how some people can dig into the nitty-gritty details of Bible prophecy and yet remain unmoved in their hearts.

It reminds me of King Herod's theological scholars in Jerusalem when the wise men rode into town. The visitors from the East asked Herod about the birth of the One who would be called the "King of the Jews." Herod called in these biblical experts, and they said, in essence, "Oh yeah, it's right here in the book of Micah. The Messiah will be born in Bethlehem."

So the wise men basically said, "Thanks for the tip" and went off to Bethlehem to find the Messiah.

Why didn't Herod go? Why didn't the scholars go? How is it they could see something so momentous so clearly in the Scriptures and not make the ten-mile journey to experience it for themselves? How is it they could believe the Bible but not want to worship the newborn King? This just shows how you can study all the details of these things and draw all kinds of complicated diagrams but have your heart remain as cold as a stone.

Revelation gives the only physical description of Jesus in the New Testament.

John had what must have been an overwhelming encounter with the risen, glorified Christ and did his best to capture what he saw. He spoke of "One like the Son of Man, clothed with a garment down to the feet and girded about the chest with a golden band. His head and hair were white like wool, as white as snow, and His eyes like a flame of fire; His feet were like fine brass, as if refined in a furnace, and His voice as the sound of many waters; He had in His right hand seven stars, out of His mouth went a sharp two-edged sword, and His countenance was like the sun shining in its strength" (verses 13–16).

It's a symbolic description. We don't think that fire literally was shooting from His eyes or that His feet were made of brass, and so on. But these descriptive terms speak of His wrath, His righteousness, His justice, and His power.

Nevertheless, there is something about that depiction of His eyes shooting flames. Jesus was indignant over something. He saw something happening, and He was going to deal with it.

John made eye contact with Jesus, and it must have been pretty frightening. Whenever I meet someone, I like to look them in the eyes. I'm always suspicious of people who won't make eye contact or who stare at their feet or over your shoulder while you're trying to talk to them.

But Jesus stepped in close. He made eye contact. His eyes were shooting fire, and He began speaking some very important words.

Revelation reveals that Jesus is the One who decides who lives and dies.

We don't decide who lives and dies. He does.

In verse 18 Jesus said, "I have the keys of Hades and of Death." In other words, He alone possesses the key of authority over death. No one can die apart from His divine permission. By the way, I'm so glad that Jesus has those keys and I don't. (I always keep several sets of keys because I'm constantly losing them.)

I love verse 17. Jesus laid His hand on John, who was down on the ground, quivering like a mound of JELL-O. Then He said, "Do not be afraid; I am the First and the Last. I am He who lives, and was dead, and behold, I am alive forevermore. Amen. And I have the keys of Hades and of Death" (verses 17–18).

In other words, "John, it's Me. Don't be afraid. I am in control of your life."

That's good to remember, isn't it? No matter what happens to us, no matter if our world seems to turn upside down, He is in control of our lives. He is the

Beginning and the End, and He is *our* beginning and *our* end. He was there when we were born, He was there when we were born again, and He will be with us when we draw our first breath of air in Heaven.

THE PATMOS IN YOUR LIFE

Remember where John was when he experienced these things and wrote these words? He was on Patmos, which is a barren little island, thirty miles in circumference, out in the middle of the Aegean Sea. This was no tropical paradise; it was a place of extreme isolation. Yet in this place of lonely exile and banishment, John saw and heard amazing things. This was a place of extreme isolation. Yet in this lonely exile and banishment, John saw and heard amazing things.

GOOD TO KNOW

The Patmos experiences of your life may become times of great spiritual insight and growth for you.

Maybe you are on your own little island of Patmos right now. In other words, you feel imprisoned by life's circumstances. You may be living in an unhappy marriage. You may be confined to a sick bed, a hospital room, or a prison cell. It can feel pretty lonely sometimes. But God can work in these Patmos experiences of your life. In fact, they may become times of great spiritual insight and growth for you.

As God revealed Himself to John, He wants to reveal Himself to you. He wants to reveal Himself to you when you get back the medical report that says things don't look so good, when the divorce papers arrive in the mail, when the business goes belly up, when someone you've trusted has hurt you or let you down, when your parents divorce, or when your child runs away.

You can turn from God in rebellion, or you can turn to Him in prayer.

There are many times when we would like to get off the island on which we find ourselves. We pray that the Lord would release us from our exile, our loneliness, our isolation. But the reality is that we can learn and experience things in those places that we could not learn or experience anywhere else.

We don't want that island of Patmos.

We don't want that thorn in the flesh.

We don't want that storm.

We don't want that trial.

We don't want that hardship.

We don't want that tragedy that has crashed into our peaceful world.

But through these hardships God comes near. That is why Paul was able to say about his own "thorn in the flesh" (probably some irritating, painful physical affliction), "So now I am glad to boast about my weaknesses, so that the power of Christ can work through me. That's why I take pleasure in my weaknesses, and in the insults, hardships, persecutions, and troubles that I suffer for Christ. For when I am weak, then I am strong" (2 Corinthians 12:9–10 NLT).

Are these the words of a crazy man? No, they are the words of a man who learned that God Himself comes very near in times of hardship and tears. Maybe it's because we listen more and pay better attention to Him. Maybe it's because we lean on Him harder when our own knees are weak, and in so doing, we find ourselves more stable than ever before.

If you are in such a place right now, God wants to come near you as He came near to John. And through your tears and weariness and disappointment, you will hear a voice that says, "Call to Me, and I will answer you, and show you great and mighty things, which you do not know" (Jeremiah 33:3).

THREE TAKEAWAY TRUTHS

- Revelation reminds us that we win in the end.
- Jesus is the Beginning and the End, and He is *our* beginning and *our* end.
- We can learn and experience things in trials and hardship that we could not learn or experience anywhere else.

Part Two

THE THINGS THAT ARE

CHAPTER TWO

What Jesus Thinks of the Church

"Remember therefore from where you have fallen; repent and do the first works, or else I will come to you quickly and remove your lampstand from its place—unless you repent."
(Revelation 2:5)

IN THIS CHAPTER
- God's objective in the book of Revelation is not to conceal but to *reveal.*
- Three ways Jesus' letters to the churches are relevant today
- Jesus' message to the church of Ephesus
- Six qualities of a person who loves God
- The three Rs of returning to God

The word *revelation* means "unveiling."

In the book of Revelation, God unveils a supernatural dimension beyond what our earthly eyes normally see. It is the world of God and Satan, angels and demons, Heaven and Hell. We are swept into an eternal realm where time as we know it no longer exists.

In Ecclesiastes 3:15, Solomon wrote these intriguing words:

> Whatever was, is.
> Whatever will be, is.
> That's how it always is with God. (MSG)

In other words, our God, who lives in the realm of eternity, sees the past, present, and future at the same time. He speaks of the future with as much certainty as He does the past, because He sees the whole continuum at once. As we noted in the last chapter, God isn't going out on a limb when He speaks of the future, because He has already been there. In fact, He is there right now, just as surely as He is with us in this present moment.

THE KEY TO THE FRONT DOOR

God's objective in the book of Revelation is not to conceal but to *reveal*. In the very first chapter of the book, God gave us a key to understanding what follows.

Speaking of keys, I usually carry around a big wad of them. Most of the time when I need a particular key to open a lock, I fumble through *all* of the keys before I get to the one I need. It's always the last one! But as Adrian Rogers has pointed out, the golden key to the book of Revelation is hanging on "the front door," in the first chapter, in plain sight. You really can't miss it.

In Revelation 1:19 we read, "Write the things which you have seen, and the things which are, and the things which will take place after this." The three sections of the book of Revelation, then, could be described like this:

1. The things you have seen.

2. The things that are.

3. And the things that will take place after this.

We have already covered "the things you have seen" in the previous chapter, where the apostle John saw the resurrected and glorified Christ with all power and authority in Heaven and Earth. This is the "unveiled" Lord Jesus who has complete control over all that happens or will happen.

Now we approach the section we will call "The Things That Are."

HOW THE LETTERS TO THE SEVEN CHURCHES SPEAK TO US

On the barren island of Patmos in the Aegean Sea, somewhere between modern Turkey and Greece, John received a stunning revelation of the future that remains as valid today as it was when it was first set down on a scroll over two thousand years ago.

These messages from Jesus to the seven churches in Asia speak to us on at least three levels.

They speak to us practically.

Jesus wrote to actual, functioning churches of John's day. There really were local congregations in Ephesus, Smyrna, Thyatira, Pergamos, Sardis, Laodicea, and Philadelphia. In fact, a postal route of that day would have stopped at all seven locations. Again, these were real churches filled with real believers facing real and daunting challenges.

> **GOOD TO KNOW**
>
> The word *revelation* means "unveiling." God's objective in the book of Revelation is not to conceal but to *reveal*.

They speak to us prophetically.

Within these seven letters, many commentators through the years have seen the whole story of the church unfold, with each of the seven churches representing an era of history. Sadly, it is more of a regression than a progression. Jesus starts with an apostolic church and ends up with an apostate church. We begin with Ephesus, where the church is in danger of leaving its first love, and we end with the church of Laodicea, where Jesus is on the outside, trying to get back in again.

They speak to us personally.

These words of Jesus to the churches may also be read as personal letters to each one of us, because as Christians we are members of the church, His body.

THE CORRESPONDENCE BEGINS

"To the angel of the church of Ephesus write,

'These things says He who holds the seven stars in His right hand, who walks in the midst of the seven golden lampstands: "I know your works, your labor, your patience, and that you cannot bear those who are evil."'" (Revelation 2:1–2)

Jesus is speaking to the representatives of the churches in Revelation 2. The seven stars are identified as the seven messengers of the church. Some translations speak of these messengers as angels. So either He was addressing an angel representing a church or, if you take the word *messenger* at face value, He may have been speaking to the pastor of that church. I lean toward the latter view and believe that Jesus most likely was speaking to the pastors of these seven congregations. The churches are also represented as golden lampstands, reminding us of our Lord's words in Matthew 5:15–16: "Nor do they light a lamp and put it under a basket, but on a lampstand, and it gives light to all who are in the house. Let your light so shine before men."

Beginning with the church of Ephesus, Jesus at first commends them and then adds a serious word of caution:

"I know your works, your labor, your patience, and that you cannot bear those who are evil. And you have tested those who say they are apostles and are not, and have found them liars; and you have persevered and have patience, and have labored for My name's sake and have not become weary. Nevertheless I have this against you, that you have left your first love. Remember therefore from where you have fallen; repent and do the first works, or else I will come to you quickly and remove your lampstand from its place—unless you repent." (Revelation 2:2–5)

What did Jesus mean when He said, "You have left your first love"?

If you are married, think back to the time when you first met your husband or wife to be. You wanted to impress this person, right? So if you are a guy, you actually took a shower, ironed your clothes, and splashed on some cologne. In my dating days, I favored the cheaper colognes like Jade East, Hai Karate, or Old Spice. And yes, I probably used way too much, and you could smell me coming for a block.

Most of us tried to be on our best behavior on that first date. If you're a guy, maybe you took your special girl to a nice restaurant, opened the door for her, and made some pleasant conversation with her. If you're the lady on this date, you probably said nice things to him, affirmed him, and actually laughed at his lame jokes.

As the courtship developed, however, leading to engagement and marriage, subtle things began to change. As they say, "The honeymoon is over." Maybe you're not as polite or kind or attentive to your partner as you once were. Maybe you're not as careful with your words. You begin to forget about the little courtesies and kindnesses you used to do to help, please, or encourage your loved one.

Slowly, your relationship starts changing. Instead of being attentive to one another, you begin taking each other for granted.

This same sad process can happen in your relationship with God. Remember when you first gave your life to Jesus Christ and how exciting it was to realize that your sins had been forgiven—washed clean out of your life? Remember how the wall of bitterness came crashing down and that vast, aching void in your life was filled with God Himself? Can you recall that flood of joy and peace that swept through your soul?

As you learned that you could pray, simply talking to God about all your hopes and dreams and fears, it overwhelmed you to realize that you could stay in conversation with Him all day long, no matter where you were or what you were doing.

I remember praying my first prayer as a brand-new Christian. I'd been given a little paperback New Testament called *Good News for Modern Man* and had almost worn it out. I saw the big, fancy Bibles that others were carrying around, and I wanted one like that. I wanted a "real" Bible. So I walked into a Christian bookstore to see what they had. I remember being blown away by the beautiful leather covers, the gold pages, the ribbons, and all the rest of it. I found a Scofield cross-reference King James study Bible that I really liked but couldn't afford.

Leaving the store and standing outside on the sidewalk, I remember the very words I said to the Lord: "Okay, God, here is my first prayer. Would You please provide me with a Bible?"

I didn't tell anyone I had prayed that prayer, but before the day was over, I got a phone call from my grandmother (I called her Mama Stella).

"Greg," she said, "I heard that you became a Christian."

"Yes," I told her, "I did."

"Well," she said, "*I want to buy you a brand-new Bible.* You go find the nicest Bible you can, and I will buy it for you."

Yes! My very first prayer had been answered within hours! You can't believe how excited and happy that made me feel.

Speaking of the Bible, do you remember when God first began speaking to you through the pages of His Book? Did it dawn on you (as it did me) that you had found the user's manual for life that you had always been looking for? Do you remember the excitement of having the Holy Spirit speak directly to your needs as you opened the Bible and began reading it for yourself? It made so much sense! It spoke to so many areas of your life.

Maybe, like me, you began to carry it around with you, not caring who saw you, who laughed at you, or what anyone said about you. You learned that it was okay to write in your Bible and mark it up as different passages began to jump out at you and speak to you in a fresh way. Rather than nibbling here and there on Scriptures, you began taking them in with great gulps.

And going to church? If you were like me, you loved it! Something was going on at the church I attended almost every night of the week during those exciting days of the Jesus Movement, and I didn't want to miss any of it. If there didn't happen to be a church service on a particular night, I would plug into a home Bible study somewhere. I just couldn't get enough of it. And if I couldn't find a group meeting somewhere, I took advantage of the cutting-edge technology of the day: teaching tapes on cassette! I could listen to Pastor Chuck Smith and others whenever I wanted to. My appetite for God's Word seemed to have no limits.

Sharing my faith just came naturally. I looked for opportunities to talk about Jesus and what He had done for me. I kept my eyes open for people to talk to. My relationship with Christ just sort of bubbled up in all my conversations.

Was that the way it was with you when you first came to Christ? Is that the way it is now? Or have things changed? Is the honeymoon over? Have you left your first love?

Yes, you still pray (when you think of it), and you say still say grace over a meal (most of the time). No, it may not be like it used to be, but . . . God understands, right? After all, you're so busy these days with so many responsibilities.

And Bible study? Yes, you still read the Bible . . . now and then . . . here and there. No, you don't carry the Bible around like you used to. You don't want to be perceived as a fanatic or a freak for having a Bible in your classroom or workplace.

As far as sharing your faith goes, you used to do that. But you were a lot more zealous in those days. Now you're more laid-back. You believe in what you like to call "lifestyle evangelism." In other words, "If I live a good life, work hard, and try to be a good husband or wife, dad or mom, that will be an example to others, and people may come to me and occasionally ask me about my beliefs." (Not that they ever have, but they *might*.)

So things have changed a little bit in your life. You're a Christian, yes, but you don't "wear it on your sleeve" anymore. You're a little cooler. More subtle. More subdued. More laid-back. You blend in a little better with your surroundings.

What has happened to you? I think it's the same thing that happened to the church of Ephesus. You are beginning to leave your first love.

"I KNOW"

Notice how aware Jesus was—and is—of what's happening in His church:

> "These things says He who holds the seven stars in His right hand, who walks in the midst of the seven golden lampstands." (Revelation 2:1)

He walked in their midst. He walks in *our* midst. He walks in the midst of the churches in your city. It isn't just "church," it is *His* church. He is a part of it. He gave His life for it. He cares passionately about what happens *in* the church, *to* the church, and *through* the church. The church today has a great number of critics but no equals. If you want to encounter Jesus, then you must be a part of His church.

Jesus begins His letter by saying, "I know" (2:2). He knows what is happening. He knows what is taking place on the surface and what is happening under the surface, in the hearts and minds of His people. *He knows.* Jesus is always aware of what transpires in the lives of His redeemed people.

GOOD TO KNOW

The church in Ephesus was originally pastored by the apostle Paul himself. Later, the apostle John stepped in as pastor.

The church in Ephesus was originally pastored by the apostle Paul himself. Later, the apostle John stepped in as pastor. Can you imagine having Paul and John as two of your first pastors? (How would you like to follow those guys as the *next* pastor?) What a launch this church had! And there was still some strength and vitality in this local congregation. Jesus took note of the positive things taking place in the church before speaking some words of caution and correction.

By the way, that is an excellent way to talk to someone whom you might need to confront. Always start with the positive—and mean it! Express appreciation for the good things before you begin your critique.

"Hey, you know what? I've noticed how hard you work, how you take this job seriously and want to do your best. I really appreciate your dedication. But I just wanted to bring a couple of things to your attention."

Jesus begins by commending the Ephesian believers for the many things they were doing *right.* For instance . . .

They were a hardworking church.

For starters, the church of Ephesus was a very active church. Jesus said, "I know your works, your labor, your patience." This word for *works* could be translated, "You work to the point of exhaustion." These believers weren't just workers; they were dedicated, diligent workers. They gave the best of their labors to the Lord, and you have to appreciate that.

The eyes of Jesus—"eyes like a flame of fire"—don't miss a thing. Perhaps you've been working hard and pouring out your heart in service to the Lord, but nobody ever seems to notice, comment, acknowledge your work, or even say a simple thanks. Yes, that may be discouraging, and the situation may not be ideal, but remember that Jesus is aware of everything you do for Him. He says, "I know."

When others get the attention, acclaim, or awards and your contributions are seemingly ignored, remember they are not ignored by Him. In Matthew 6 He says, "But when you give to someone in need, don't let your left hand know what your right hand is doing. Give your gifts in private, and your Father, who sees everything, will reward you" (verse 3–4 NLT).

So these Ephesian believers worked hard and put in the hours. And Jesus said, "I know."

They were an enduring church.

The Lord of the church said to them, "I know your works, your labor, your patience."

The word *patience* means "to bear up under a load." Now what does this mean? What was the "load" they carried?

It probably means they lived right in the midst of a pagan city that was known for its idolatry and false gods. It was actually something of a tourist destination for people who wanted to worship at the temple of Diana, one of the wonders of the ancient world. People from across the Roman world came to see this architectural marvel and worship before these magical, mystical gods and goddesses.

Ephesus had the original magical mystery tour and was thronged with idolaters and revelers. The mere fact that a strong church existed in Ephesus at all was amazing in itself. In the middle of a city renowned for its wickedness, here was a group of believers earnestly and loyally serving the Lord. They were an enduring church, working with great patience in a difficult environment.

And Jesus had said, "I know."

They were a discerning church.

In verse 2, Jesus said to them, "You cannot bear those who are evil." *The Message* says it this way: "You can't stomach evil, . . . you weed out apostolic pretenders." They were surrounded by false doctrines and what we might today call New Age mysticism. But these church leaders had their heads screwed on right. They knew right from wrong and took pains to warn and equip their people.

When Paul took his final leave from the church of Ephesus, praying on a beach with the church elders before he boarded a ship, he gave them this warning:

> "I know that false teachers, like vicious wolves, will come in among you after I leave, not sparing the flock. Even some men from your own group will rise up and distort the truth in order to draw a following. Watch out! Remember the three years I was with you—my constant watch and care over you night and day, and my many tears for you." (Acts 20:29–31 NLT)

So the church had been warned, and they had been doing a good job in keeping the wolves at bay and equipping the sheep.

That's why it's so important to get good teaching and to know how to study the Bible for yourself. You need to be a discerning believer. Far too many Christians are naïve and gullible. In 1 John 4:1, the apostle says, "Dear friends, do not believe everyone who claims to speak by the Spirit. You must test them to see if the spirit they have comes from God. For there are many false prophets in the world" (NLT).

Despite all of these good and admirable qualities, however, the church at Ephesus had a subtle but serious problem. It was a problem so understated and difficult to see that most people probably hadn't noticed the change in this church.

But the Lord did.

Jesus, who walks in the midst of the church, saw it and told them the truth: they no longer loved Him as they once did.

Please notice that Jesus does not say, "You *lost* your first love." Sometimes we hear people say that. "I lost my first love." But that's not true. You don't *lose* love, you *leave* it.

If you lose something, you don't know where it is. I lose stuff all the time. I even lose things in my car and can't find them. (*Oh my goodness, there's that burrito I lost two months ago! It's not looking so good now!*)

Leaving, however, is different. If I *leave* something and walk away, I know where it is and can come back to it if I choose. Jesus said to them, "You have left your first love." Or as another translation puts it, "You don't love me . . . as you did at first" (NLT).

GOOD TO KNOW

Ephesus was a pagan city known for its idolatry and false gods. It was actually something of a tourist destination for people who wanted to worship at the temple of Diana, one of the wonders of the ancient world.

What does this mean? It probably means their devotion had turned to duty. They had motion, but they had lost the emotion. They had substituted labor for love, work for worship, perspiration for inspiration, and the joy of walking with Jesus for a grim, set-your-jaw adherence to the forms and norms of the Christian life. These Ephesian believers had been so busy maintaining their separation from the world that they were neglecting their adoration of the Savior.

You might ask, "Is that really such a big deal? What's wrong with being hung up on duty? It's not like murder or stealing or adultery."

Yes, it *is* a big deal because of what it leads to. It starts you off in the wrong direction, away from the heart of God.

Think of it like this. You could be in great shape outwardly, but if you have heart disease, then you're in big trouble. Years ago, I knew a man who was really strong and loved to boast about his strength. He was one of those somewhat annoying guys who would flex his arm all the time and say, "Feel this. Feel my muscle!" Or he might say, "Look at these abs, man!" He would go down on the floor and do multiple push-ups just to show how fit he was.

And then sadly one day, I got the news that this very fit man had died of a massive heart attack. So even though he was in peak shape outwardly, his heart was diseased. As it turned out, for all his boasting, he was living on borrowed time.

In the same way, we can do all of the right things outwardly and yet have a heart issue, a soul issue. And if there is a breakdown in your heart, it will affect every area of your life.

"YOU HAVE FALLEN"

Jesus said, "I have this against you, that you have left your first love. Remember therefore from where you have fallen" (2:4–5). When you start to drift from a love relationship with Christ, you are in the process of backsliding. It may be a slow, subtle motion, but it is a backslide nonetheless.

Let's trace this dynamic in the life of David, Israel's first king.

Scene 1

When we are first introduced to David in the Scriptures, he is a young shepherd out in the fields with his dad's flock, practicing his slingshot and composing beautiful worship songs to God. This is a young man who loves the God of Israel with all his heart. That is why the Bible describes him as "the sweet psalmist of Israel" (2 Samuel 23:1) and "a man after [God's] own heart" (1 Samuel 13:14).

Scene 2

David faces off with a nine-foot-six-inch Philistine named Goliath—and brings the freakish giant down with a sling and a stone, becoming the hero of Israel.

Scene 3

David is the rightful king of Israel, but the paranoid King Saul doesn't want to give up his throne and hunts David up and down the land as though he were a wild animal. David, however, never responds in kind, never retaliates, and never kills Saul, even when he has the opportunity, fearing to do harm to "the Lord's anointed."

Scene 4

After Saul perishes in battle, David finally ascends to the throne, rules over the land, and is beloved by his people. His reign is righteous, kind, and wise. David is a worshiper, a warrior, a musician, a poet, and a king, all in one package.

Scene 5

Somewhere in his middle years, David is on his rooftop, kicking back when his troops are in battle and when he should be leading them. He's taking a little time off—not only from the battle, but apparently from God, too. From his vantage point on the palace roof, he sees a beautiful woman bathing herself, lusts after her, learns she is the wife of Uriah (one of his best warriors) but brings her up to his chambers anyway and has sex with her. When Bathsheba becomes pregnant, David tries to cover up his sin instead of confessing it before God. Ultimately David has Uriah put to death by devious and cowardly means, and he marries Bathsheba, thinking he has effectively covered up his sin.

How could such a thing happen? How in the world do you go from worshiping God in the wilderness to murdering a man and taking his wife?

Well, it didn't happen overnight.

David had left his first love, and this was the result.

When David finally became king and moved into a palace, life became much easier for him. He was no longer living hand-to-mouth in the wilderness and running for his life from Saul. Once that conflict ceased, however, David let his life slip into neutral spiritually. We don't read of his worshiping the Lord or playing his harp or creating hymns and songs of praise. It was only a matter of time until he lost that intimate relationship with God—and found himself doing things he never would have dreamed of doing years before.

HAVE YOU LEFT YOUR FIRST LOVE?

You may be saying, "What do you mean by that? I'm not sure that I understand what it means to love God in the first place."

Let me give you some quick takeaway points on what loving God is all about.

A person who loves God will want to be with God.

A person who loves the Lord desires to have personal communion with Him. It's just like being married. When you are in love with someone, you look for every excuse to be with that person. I've been married for almost fifty years, and I love to spend time with my wife. We just like being together and don't enjoy spending time apart from one another. When you hear of a married couple spending less and less time together and even taking separate vacations, you know that problems are beginning to develop. It shouldn't be that way. People who love each other want to be in each other's company, sharing life together.

In the same way, people who love God want to walk with God through the day and be with Him. In Psalm 63 David wrote, "O God, You are my God; early will I seek You; my soul thirsts for You; my flesh longs for You in a dry and thirsty land where there is no water. . . . When I remember You on my bed, I meditate on You in the night watches. Because You have been my help, therefore in the shadow of Your wings I will rejoice. My soul follows close behind You" (verses 1, 6–7).

A person who loves God will love the things that God loves.

We know what God loves by what He has declared in His Word. The psalmist says, "Oh, how I love your law! I meditate on it all day long" (Psalm 119:97 NIV).

If you love God, then you will love the Bible, the Word of God. You will want to hear the Word, read the Word, and think about the Word through the day and even on your bed at night.

You will love God's people, His sons and daughters.

You will love lost people who need the Lord.

If you love God, then you will love what He loves.

A person who loves God will hate what God hates.

Psalm 97:10 says, "You who love the LORD, hate evil!" God hates sin, and we should do the same. Romans 12:9 says, "Abhor what is evil. Cling to what is good." But here is the problem: sometimes we find ourselves fascinated by certain aspects of evil. We are drawn to it, perhaps first as an observer but later as a participator. Don't do it! Run from evil. Don't flirt with sin. Don't have tea with the Devil. Don't even communicate with him.

A person who loves Christ will love other Christians.

First John 3:14–15 says, "If we love other Christians, it proves that we have been delivered from hell and given eternal life. But a person who doesn't have love for others is headed for eternal death. Anyone who hates his Christian brother is really a murderer at heart; and you know that no one wanting to murder has eternal life within" (TLB).

You might find yourself in a situation where you're in church, singing about how much you love God, when someone walks in that you really don't even like. In fact, you hate that individual. That's a big problem! You can't love God and hate your brother at the same time. The Scriptures make that fact abundantly clear.

A person who loves Christ will long for His return.

Shortly before the end of his life, the apostle Paul wrote to Timothy, "And now the prize awaits me—the crown of righteousness, which the Lord, the righteous Judge, will give me on the day of his return. And the prize is not just for me but for all who eagerly look forward to his appearing" (2 Timothy 4:8 NLT).

Does it ever cross your mind?

Do you ever wake up in the morning with the thought, "Today could be the day"? Do you ever crawl into bed at night and remind yourself, "Jesus could come for me before my alarm clock rings in the morning"?

Do you think about the rapture of the church? Do you think about His Second Coming, when He will finally set our world to rights? If you do, then it's an indication that you love Him and long for His return.

A person who loves Christ will keep His commandments.

Jesus said in John 14:21, "He who has My commandments and keeps them, it is he who loves Me. And he who loves Me will be loved by My Father, and I will love him and manifest Myself to him."

In other words, you can't claim to love God and then go out and break His commandments left and right.

Imagine that I walked up to you and said, "I want you to know that I love you."

And maybe you would reply, "Wow, Greg. Thank you. I love you, too."

But then, before I left, imagine that I slapped you right across the face. How would you feel? Yes, you would be shocked, perhaps, that a pastor would do such a thing.

Holding your stinging face, you might say, "Hey! What in the world? . . . That really hurt! Why did you do that?"

Imagine that I put my face in my hands and replied, "I don't know, I don't know! I don't know what came over me. Would you please forgive me?"

"Well, . . . yes," you might say. "My ear is still ringing, but yes, I do forgive you."

"Thank you so much!" I reply. And then I promptly punch you in the stomach.

As you're trying to catch your breath, I moan out loud, "Oh man, what am I doing? I am so sorry! Why did I do that? Can you forgive me?"

"Let me get my breath first," you gasp. "I don't know what's going on, but yes, Greg, I forgive you."

Before the words are barely out of your mouth, however, I punch you in the face and knock you off your feet.

What would the result be? Besides having me locked up as a psycho (for my own good), you would be ready to run the other way if I ever said "I love you" to you again. Why? Because no sane person would say that he loves you and then treat you in such a shameful way.

But what about our relationship with the Lord? How would it work for me to say, "Oh Lord, I love You so much," and then sit down to look at pornography on the Internet? How can we tell Him, "I love You, Jesus" and then turn away from a brother or sister with hate in our hearts?

Can we say that we love the Lord but then go ahead and divorce our husband or wife for no valid biblical reason?

Can we say we love God but then launch a lawsuit against a fellow believer?

If you do those things, then you're proving that you don't love God at all.

That's not my opinion; that is what He says.

THE THREE Rs OF RETURNING TO YOUR FIRST LOVE

Maybe you've recognized yourself in some of the scenarios I've just described. Maybe it has begun to dawn on you that you don't love Jesus as much as you once did. Is there any hope for you? Is there any alternative for you?

Yes. Absolutely.

God wants you back. Jesus wants you to recover the love that you once had for Him. To accomplish that in your life, He gives you the three Rs of returning to your first love in Revelation 2:5: "Remember therefore from where you have fallen; repent and do the first works."

Here, then, are the three Rs:

- Remember

- Repent

- Repeat (do the "first works" again)

First, remember. Remember from where you have fallen. That means taking some time to think back on your life. Can you remember a time when you were closer to God than you are today? *Remember* that time. Think about it. Was it a year ago? Ten years ago? Six months ago? Call that time of your life to mind again and consider what it was like.

Second, repent. To repent means to change something. Change your mind. Change your pattern. Change your behavior. Change your schedule. Change your attitude. Get back to those things you were doing before, when your love for Jesus was more vibrant and alive.

Third, repeat. Let's imagine that you are having trouble in your marriage and things aren't the way they used to be. Okay, so what did you do when things were better?

Maybe I'm talking to a man here, and he says, "Well, we used to spend more time together."

So do it again. Make it happen.

Or maybe he would say, "I used to tell my wife she was beautiful."

Maybe a wife would say, "I used to affirm my husband."

And you've stopped doing those things? Start again! Sure, it might seem a little awkward at first, but it won't after a while.

Go back to what you used to do that kept the love fires burning. Think of ways to make each other happy.

"But we don't *feel* it anymore," you might say.

Who cares whether you feel it or not? Just do it. Don't wait for the feelings, because emotions come and go. *Do* romantic things and the romance will return.

So let's bring this to our relationship with God. Do the "first works" again. Were you memorizing more Scripture verses then? Do it again.

Were you listening to more praise and worship music in those days? Tune in again.

Were you spending more time with other believers? Get connected again. Plug into a good church. Join a Bible study. Get into a small group.

Were you looking for opportunities to share your faith? Open your eyes! They're still there. Initiate some conversations. Ask God for openings.

Were you listening to teaching cassettes in those early days? Get on your computer or phone and download some messages from a trusted Bible teacher.

Go back and do the things you used to do and then watch how that flame will be rekindled in your heart!

It comes down to this. If you love God with all of your heart and with all of your soul and with all of your mind and love your neighbor as yourself, then everything else will fall into place—all of those other troublesome details of life.

A FINAL WARNING

Someone might say, "Well, this is a fascinating chapter, but I'm not really all that interested in making changes in my life."

If that is the case, then you need to pay attention to our Lord's warning at the end of verse 5:

> "Remember therefore from where you have fallen; repent and do the first works, or else I will come to you quickly and remove your lampstand from its place—unless you repent."

The primary application here is to the church. A lampstand in the book of Revelation is a symbol of the church, and this is a reminder that no single church has a guarantee that it will continue on indefinitely. The church of Jesus Christ will march on until the end, and Jesus said that even the gates of Hell will not prevail against it. No individual or government ever will stop Christ's church, no matter how hard or how brutally they try. Most individual congregations, however, have a certain life span.

I have seen churches—huge, cavernous buildings once filled with people who were hungry for the Word of God—that now sit empty. Not long ago I was in New York City and saw a church building that had been turned into a nightclub. That was a place where God used to be worshiped, and now it's a place where other things are worshiped. In Wales, the home of the great Welsh Revival, you can see old stone churches that are now stuffed full of hay and being used as barns. How sad!

GOOD TO KNOW

The seven stars are identified as the seven messengers of the church. Some translations speak of these messengers as angels. A lampstand in the book of Revelation is a symbol of the church.

If a church—*any* church—neglects God's Word, stops loving Him as they did at first, stops influencing and impacting lives for Jesus, and begins to compromise on the truth, it is in danger of losing its light in a community. The Lord of the church may remove its lampstand. But when that happens, God raises up another church and another church. And He always will.

If you lose your love for Jesus, it's only a matter of time until you lose your light.

This is true on a personal level as well. You can lose the radiance and beauty of Christ in your life if you continue to compromise and neglect your walk with Jesus Christ. You no longer will be the light that you once were in your school, in your family, at work, or in your neighborhood.

In His Sermon on the Mount, Jesus said, "You are the salt of the earth; but if the salt loses its flavor, how shall it be seasoned? It is then good for nothing but to be thrown out and trampled underfoot by men" (Matthew 5:13).

What good is salt that has lost its flavor? Can you make it useful again? No, you throw it out and people walk all over it. It's worthless.

What good is noncarbonated Coke? For that matter, what good is decaf coffee? Some time ago I went to get coffee with a friend who ordered a low-fat, decaf latte. I turned to him and said, "Why? Why don't you just order an empty cup and *pretend* to be drinking a latte? All the fun is gone. What good is it?"

I think there are some noncarbonated Christians out there—believers who are flat and have lost their fizz. Or maybe you could call them decaf disciples—deeply in need of stimulation.

To another of the seven churches Jesus wrote, "I see right through your work. You have a reputation for vigor and zest, but you're dead, stone-dead" (Revelation 3:1 MSG).

The love for Jesus fades away . . . then the light is removed. The reputation might be the last to go, but it eventually fades as well.

The good news is this: it doesn't have to be that way. Jesus gives us the opportunity to return to Him with a full heart—and to experience full restoration.

THREE TAKEAWAY TRUTHS

- If you want to encounter Jesus, then you must be a part of His church.
- If you lose your love for Jesus, it's only a matter of time until you lose your light.
- If you love God with all of your heart, all of your soul, and all of your mind and love your neighbor as yourself, then everything else will fall into place.

CHAPTER THREE

Jesus' Words to Suffering Christians

"Do not fear any of those things which you are about to suffer....
Be faithful until death, and I will give you the crown of life."
(Revelation 2:10)

IN THIS CHAPTER
- Jesus' commendation of the believers in Smyrna
- Why Christians can expect persecution
- Encouraging words from Jesus for those who are suffering
- How believers should respond to persecution
- Six things to remember when you're suffering

Jesus called the church in Ephesus back to their "first love."

He commanded them to *remember* the love relationship with Him that they once had, to *return* to those loving actions they once practiced, and to *repeat* them.

So here's the question: If I get back to my first love, if I am walking with Jesus as I ought to and experiencing a rekindling of my passion and love for Him, what can I expect from the world?

Applause?

Congratulations?

Pats on the back and words of affirmation?

No, what I can expect is persecution.

Real love always costs something. When you truly love someone, there always will be some suffering involved. If any harm comes to them, you hurt for them and with them. If they are attacked, you defend them vigorously. If they are taken from you, you mourn deeply.

It is the result of love. Love will cost you.

In his book *The Four Loves*, C. S. Lewis wrote these words: "To love at all is to be vulnerable. Love anything and your heart will certainly be wrung and possibly broken." [1]

In the same way, if you love Jesus and let that be known, you will pay a price. People will attack you for no other reason than your love for Him.

Jesus Himself predicted it when He said, "If the world hates you, remember that it hated me first. The world would love you as one of its own if you belonged to it, but you are no longer part of the world. I chose you to come out of the world, so it hates you. . . . Since they persecuted me, naturally they will persecute you. And if they had listened to me, they would listen to you" (John 15:18–20 NLT).

This is the very dynamic that was playing out in the church of Smyrna in Revelation chapter 2.

A TOUGH PLACE TO BE A CHRISTIAN

"And to the angel of the church in Smyrna write,

'These things says the First and the Last, who was dead, and came to life: "I know your works, tribulation, and poverty (but you are rich); and I know the blasphemy of those who say they are Jews and are not, but are a synagogue of Satan. Do not fear any of those things which you are about to suffer. Indeed, the devil is about to throw some of you into prison, that you may be tested, and you will have tribulation ten days. Be faithful until death, and I will give you the crown of life.

"He who has an ear, let him hear what the Spirit says to the churches. He who overcomes shall not be hurt by the second death.""" (Revelation 2:8–11)

This is the shortest of the seven messages Jesus gave to these churches. It's also interesting to note that Jesus had no critical words for them. He simply commended them and encouraged them.

As I've already noted, Smyrna was an actual congregation in Asia Minor. At this particular time, Smyrna, along with Ephesus, was a center of paganism and false worship. In fact, Smyrna—known for its loyalty to Rome—was renowned for the worship of Caesar. It was almost like a contest among the occupied territories of Rome as to who would have the privilege of building a special shrine to Caesar. And as it turned out, Smyrna won the contest. As a result, they were known for their emperor worship and for declaring, in effect, "Caesar is Lord."

The believers in Smyrna, however, refused to say, "Caesar is Lord."

Instead they would say, "Jesus is Lord."

And that was an offensive, countercultural message in that city.

Smyrna, then, was a tough place to be a Christian. If you took a stand for Jesus Christ, you would almost certainly pay a price. In verse 9 Jesus said to them, "I know your works, tribulation, and poverty." Why were they experiencing poverty in a prosperous seaport? It was because of their stand for Jesus. When some of the citizens of Smyrna found out that a shopkeeper was a Christian and didn't believe in worshiping Caesar, they would take their business elsewhere.

It's not unlike what happened to the Jews in Germany during the rise of Hitler. It started off with people refusing to frequent Jewish-owned businesses. And then the Gestapo came in and wrote *Juden* or *Jew* on the window of the business, sternly warning potential customers away. Jews were forced to wear yellow armbands, further identifying them as enemies of the state. Before long, the Jewish businesses were vandalized and burned down—right before Jews were rounded up and sent off to concentration camps.

That's what it was like in Smyrna. Someone would find out that you were a believer, and they would say, "We don't want to give our business to you—and

> ## GOOD TO KNOW
> Jesus had no critical words in His message to the church in Smyrna. It is the shortest of His seven messages to the churches.

we are reporting you to the authorities!" As a result, poverty descended on the Christian community, right in the midst of the city's prosperity.

The believers also were slandered. Again, in verse 9 Jesus said to them, "I know the blasphemy of those who say they are Jews and are not, but are a synagogue of Satan." Lies were being told about the believers. The blasphemy Jesus spoke about here wasn't as much against God as it was against God's people.

It may be small comfort in the heat of the moment, but when someone is forced to make up outrageous lies about you because they can't find any inconsistencies in your character or actions, that is a wonderful thing. In this passage, Jesus commends His slandered people, telling them, "Be faithful until death, and I will give you the crown of life" (verse 10).

GOOD TO KNOW

Smyrna, along with Ephesus, was a center of paganism and false worship. Smyrna was known for its loyalty to Rome and renowned for the worship of Caesar.

At this time Jesus wasn't giving them happy news about their future on Earth. He didn't tell them to think positive. He told them to stay faithful. Why? Because He knew that even more suffering was coming their way.

And so it did. The believers of Smyrna, as well as many of the Christians in Rome itself, suffered greatly for their faith. Thousands upon thousands of Christian men, women, and children were put to death simply because they would not say, "Caesar is Lord." Roman historian Tacitus wrote this tragic record about what happened to them:

> As they died they were further subjected to insult. Covered with hides of wild beasts, they perished by being torn to pieces by dogs; or they would be fastened to crosses and, when daylight had gone, burned to provide lighting at night. Nero had offered his gardens as a venue for the show. [2]

Imagine how horrible this was. The emperor Nero began to tyrannize the church of Jesus Christ, but the persecution actually intensified under Diocletian. But it didn't work out so well for Rome, did it?

When we visit sites in the old Roman world today, what do we go to see? Ruins. We visit the wreckage and remains: a column here, a viaduct there, a piece of Roman road appearing and then disappearing under turf or drifting sand.

But the church of Jesus Christ? It is alive and well, all over the world. Jesus said the gates of Hell will not prevail against His church (see Matthew 16:18). Today, we name our sons after apostles and our dogs after Roman emperors.

Instead of destroying the church, these Roman emperors actually strengthened it. The persecution had a purifying effect, as nominal, half-hearted believers left the church. Those would-be believers departed from the faith when there were no economic or social advantages of being identified as followers of Jesus. But truly committed Christian men and women pressed on, going from strength to strength.

So God used the persecution of His people, which had been meant for evil, to advance His kingdom. Nevertheless, it was terribly difficult and heartbreaking for those who endured it.

PERSECUTION THEN . . . AND NOW

Sometimes when we read things like these, we find ourselves saying, "I'm sure glad that I didn't live back then!"

The truth is, even to this present day, there are thousands of "Smyrnas" around the world. Countless thousands of men, women, and children are still being persecuted, imprisoned, tortured, raped, flogged, sold into slavery, and killed because of their loyalty to the name of Jesus. It has been estimated that since the early church was formed to this present day, millions and millions of Christians have been martyred.

Violent persecution of God's people hasn't stopped; it continues even as you read these words. The Bible declares it clearly: "Everyone who wants to live a godly life in Christ Jesus will be persecuted" (2 Timothy 3:12 NIV).

That is a promise from the Word of God . . . but it's not one that we usually claim. We like to lay hold of promises of provision and protection. When is the last time you said, "Now Lord, You promised in Your Bible that if I live a godly life, I will be persecuted. So bring it on, Lord!"

No, we don't pray that. Who wants to be persecuted? The people of Smyrna didn't want it, and we don't, either. No sane person does. Nevertheless, if you are living a godly life, persecution will come—in some form or another.

HOW SHOULD I RESPOND TO PERSECUTION?

So how should I react when persecution comes my way? Jesus gives us this word in the Sermon on the Mount: "When you are reviled and persecuted and lied about because you are my followers—wonderful! Be happy about it! Be very glad! for a tremendous reward awaits you up in heaven" (Matthew 5:11–12 TLB).

GOOD TO KNOW

It has been estimated that since the early church was formed to this present day, millions and millions of Christians have been martyred.

Why are we persecuted? Because righteousness is confrontational. And by this I don't mean that it's necessarily because of anything you say. Your very presence can get under people's skin. The simple fact of your faith in Jesus puts you on the radar screens of others. It bothers them a little (or a lot). It makes them uneasy or sometimes hostile. So simply living for the Lord in our day-to-day lives eventually will bring about some persecution.

Let me just add one proviso here. Jesus said, "Blessed are those who are persecuted for righteousness' sake" (Matthew 5:10).

He *didn't* say, "Blessed are those who are persecuted for *being obnoxious*." Or, "Blessed are those who are persecuted for *being self-righteous*." Or, "Blessed are those who are persecuted for *being holier-than-thou*."

May I be very candid for a moment? Some Christians—or people who claim to be Christians—are just plain strange. Some believers are just a real downer to be around. A nonbeliever might say, "I saw the most magnificent sunset last night."

And the Christian replies, "'Love not the world, neither the things that are in the world. The world passes away and the lusts thereof.' Praise God." (And by the way, that verse is not referring to Earth, but to the "world system" under the control of Satan, who is the "god of this world." The believer can and should enjoy the wonders of creation.)

"You know what?" that other individual might reply, "You're kind of weird, aren't you?"

I'm not saying don't stand your ground. I'm not saying don't speak up for what is true. I'm just saying, whenever possible, be *nice* about it. Be civil. Be polite. Be thoughtful. Be kind. Be winsome.

How was Jesus known when He walked this earth? He was known as a friend of sinners. We might think that sounds like a compliment now, but it wasn't meant as a compliment then. Some members of the religious Jewish leadership establishment were appalled that Jesus would hang out with "lowlifes." No, He never compromised—this was our holy God, in the flesh. But He loved these outcasts, this off-scouring of society, and what's more, they *knew* that He loved them. They were drawn by that love, just like moths are drawn to a Coleman lantern in the middle of night in the wilderness.

We need to love people in the same way. Since we're going to be persecuted, let's be persecuted for the right reasons.

"WHAT GOOD ARE THESE TRIALS?"

Have you ever found yourself wondering, "Why do these difficulties have to happen to me? What possible benefit could there be in all this?"

Maybe you've heard the story of how fresh fish retailers were having difficulty shipping codfish from the East Coast to the West Coast. By the time the fish filets arrived at their destination, they were mushy and no longer firm. They tried sending the cod live, but the fish inevitably would die before they arrived.

Then someone had a bright idea. They experimented with putting catfish, the mortal enemies of codfish, into the tanks. From then on, the cod arrived fresh and frisky because they had spent the entire journey running from the catfish.

GOOD TO KNOW

When Jesus walked this earth, He was known as a friend of sinners.

Sometimes God will put a catfish in our tank. We may find ourselves praying, "Lord, why do I have to have such an obnoxious neighbor?" Or maybe, "Why do I have to be seated in my classroom next to this antagonistic person?" Or perhaps, "Lord, why do I have to have this family member who always harasses me and gives me such a hard time?"

Maybe God has placed a catfish in your tank to keep you on your toes. (Or should I say on your fins?) Maybe He has placed you in a situation that won't allow you to slip into a sleepy complacency but will keep you alert and fully dependent on Him.

If you are discouraged by your suffering or hardship, Jesus offers some encouraging words.

Jesus is eternal.

In verse 8, Jesus opened His message to the brokenhearted believers in Smyrna with these words: "These things says the First and the Last, who was dead, and came to life."

In chapter 1, verses 17 and 18, He said, "Do not be afraid; I am the First and the Last. I am He who lives, and was dead, and behold, I am alive forevermore."

In other words Jesus was saying, "Remember this: I am eternal. I always have been, I always will be, and whatever is happening to you right now is only temporary, because you who have believed in Me are eternal. You, too, are immortal. You will spend eternity in My presence. So whatever your suffering is, remember that it won't last forever!"

In 2 Corinthians 4:17 Paul says, "For our present troubles are small and won't last very long. Yet they produce for us a glory that vastly outweighs them and will last forever!" (NLT).

Jesus knows all about it.

Jesus Himself said that He knows about our suffering. In verse 9, He said to the Smyrna church, "I know your works, tribulation, and poverty." The word used here for *know* doesn't just mean that He knows by watching. The word also implies that He knows because He has passed through the same thing

Himself. He was saying, "You're hurting. You're suffering. I know. . . . I have suffered, too."

When you find yourself dealing with any kind of stress or pain, it's a real comfort to talk with someone else who has been there, someone who has faced the same things that you are facing. There may be people who haven't experienced your particular trials, and they may be very caring and sympathetic. They try to relate to you, but they really can't. But then you talk to someone who says, "I know," and you learn that they really do. Believe me, it makes all the difference when someone has passed through the fire that you're still enduring, and somehow they came out of it alive. That's a helpful thing to know. They are able to comfort you with the comfort that they themselves have experienced (see 2 Corinthians 1:3–7).

Jesus doesn't give the suffering believers in Smyrna a long sermon or some worn-out platitudes. He really didn't have a lot to say to them. But what He did say is very, very significant. He said, "You're suffering. I know. I understand. I've been there, too. I am with you."

Suffering won't last forever.

I recently read a piece by Joni Eareckson Tada in which she wrote about the paralyzed man who had been lying by the pool of Bethesda. The man had been an invalid for thirty-eight years. The Gospel of John says that "when Jesus saw him lying there, [He] knew that he already had been in that condition a long time" (John 5:6). Jesus spoke to him, eventually healing him.

What Joni pointed out was that even though Jesus is eternal, has lived forever, and will live forever, He acknowledged that for this man, thirty-eight years as an invalid was "a long time."

He understands that. He knows. But He also reminds us that even though our sufferings seem to go on and on, they won't. They will be over soon. There will be a beginning, a middle, and an end to them, and that will be that. He told the people in Smyrna, "Indeed, the devil is about to throw some of you into prison, that you may be tested, and you will have tribulation ten days" (2:10).

That is ten days . . . not eleven, and not one hundred. The suffering would come, yes, but it would also go.

So maybe as you're going through a hardship in your life, you find yourself inclined to pray, "Oh God, You've just got to get me out of this thing. You've got to airlift me out of this situation." But the Lord says, "I know your situation, and My grace is sufficient for you. I am eternal. I am in control. There will be an end to this. You need to persevere. It won't last forever."

History records ten waves of persecution that hit the early church, and some commentators believe this is what Christ was alluding to when He said, "You will have tribulation ten days." I don't know if that was the case or not, but I know they were persecuted. Jesus, however, told them He was watching the clock, so to speak. There was a time limit on their suffering.

He says the same thing to us in our disappointments and heartaches: "I am in control. I am with you. I am sovereign."

Jesus has a plan.

In verse 10 Jesus said, "The devil will throw some of you into prison to test you" (NLT).

Jesus knew this would happen, He had a plan, and the Devil's intentions would not supersede His plan.

GOOD TO KNOW

History records ten waves of persecution that hit the early church. Commentators believe this is what Christ was alluding to in Revelation 2:10.

Why do bad, sorrowful, hurtful things happen to us? I don't know. We can be sure the Devil is behind some of it. But remember that whatever Satan proposes, if it happens in our lives, then God permitted it.

The story of Job is a perfect example of this. You'll remember that Satan came before the Lord and essentially said, "Let me have some time with Job, this favorite of Yours. Let's see what he's really made of."

And God could have said, "Back off, Devil! You leave Job alone."

But for some reason He didn't.

The Lord, who loved Job, allowed Satan to cruelly oppress Job for a time. God had a wise purpose in it, though Job never did learn that purpose. The problem with Job is he never read the book of Job!

In the same way, God will allow certain trials and tests in our lives. The Devil may intend to harm us or destroy us with those trials, but God will allow the suffering to refine us instead. I'm so thankful for Romans 8:28 and its assurance that "God causes everything to work together for the good of those who love God and are called according to his purpose for them" (NLT).

So Jesus reminds the believers in Smyrna (and us) that events aren't out of control, even when they *feel* out of control. He has a plan.

Jesus is loving and will reward faithfulness.

In verse 10 Jesus also said, "Be faithful until death, and I will give you the crown of life."

As in a number of Roman-controlled cities, Smyrna had an arena where athletic events took place. Everyone in Smyrna, then, knew all about running races and winning crowns. We're not talking here about the great, heavy, gold-encrusted crowns like the queen of England might wear on occasion. This probably referred to a crown of laurel leaves, woven together, which they would give to the winner in an athletic event. It was an award, and it had great significance in that culture. Jesus was saying to the suffering believers, "I have a crown waiting for you. Not a crown of laurel leaves, but a crown of *life*."

The New Testament speaks of multiple crowns. There is a "crown of rejoicing," which is apparently given to those who lead other people to Christ. There is a "crown of righteousness," which is promised to those who love the appearing of the Lord.

But in this passage Jesus offers the crown of life. In fact, He was saying to the church at Smyrna, "I will give it to you." He was telling them, "You have faced suffering. You have endured persecution. Many of you will be martyred. But I have a reward waiting for you just around the corner. It won't be long."

This reward, the crown of life, is also promised to the person who resists temptation and endures personal suffering. In James 1:12 the apostle says,

"Blessed is the man who endures temptation; for when he has been approved, he will receive the crown of life which the Lord has promised to those who love Him."

All of us face temptations, and it can be difficult to stand up to them when they come our way. Temptations will come and, in the moment, they may be hard to resist. You've been in that place, just as I have. You find yourself swayed by some desire you know to be displeasing to God. And you resist, quoting the Word of God, seeking to yield to the Holy Spirit, and telling the Devil to leave you alone.

The Tempter is saying to you, "You idiot. This is the greatest opportunity ever! Go for it."

But you stand firm, and after a while the temptation passes. When it does, you experience a sense of relief and joy. You say, "Thank You, Lord, for helping me to pass that test!"

A reward awaits those who have endured temptation, but it is also for those who have endured suffering.

Maybe this applies to you as you read these words. You may have family problems . . . marital problems . . . physical problems . . . financial problems. Maybe you've recently lost a loved one or had some bad news from the doctor. Whatever it is, you are suffering, and it doesn't seem fair to you.

You may not even verbalize it, but sometimes you can't help thinking, "Josh and Brittany aren't suffering. . . . Joe doesn't seem to have any problems. . . . Everything seems to go right for Emily. . . . Ryan always lands on his feet. . . . Why do I have to go through this? Why does my family have to endure this?"

The Lord would say to you, "Don't worry about them. You just be faithful and follow Me. The suffering won't be forever, and at the end of it, I will reward you with gifts beyond your imagination."

"Don't fear the second death."

In closing, the Lord said to Smyrna, "He who has an ear, let him hear what the Spirit says to the churches. He who overcomes shall not be hurt by the second death" (2:11).

What is the second death? It means spending eternity separated from God in Hell. A nonbeliever effectively dies twice, while a believer only dies once.

For the nonbeliever, life on Earth on this side of eternity is like a living death. The apostle Paul even said that she "who lives for pleasure is dead even while she lives" (1 Timothy 5:6 NIV). The Bible tells us that before we were saved, we were "dead in trespasses and sins" (Ephesians 2:1).

Those outside of Christ "live" in a state of spiritual death. When you don't know the Lord, you chase after everything this world has to offer. And you may as well, because this world is as good as it ever will get for the nonbeliever. For the believer, however, this Earth with all its troubles and woes is as bad as it gets. For us, the best is yet to come.

If you are a nonbeliever, then you will die twice. You endure a deadness in life while you live, and after that, you will face eternal separation from the Lord of life.

If you are a believer in Jesus Christ, however, you only die once. Yes, there is physical death. But then you will live forever. You could sum it up this way: Born once, die twice. Born twice, die once.

The second option is better—better now, and better forever.

THREE TAKEAWAY TRUTHS

- Historically God has used the persecution of His people to advance His kingdom.
- As Christians we're going to be persecuted, so let's be persecuted for the right reasons.
- Jesus knows what we're going through, and there is a time limit on our suffering.

CHAPTER FOUR

The Compromising Church

"I know your works, and where you dwell, where Satan's throne is. And you hold fast to My name. . . . But I have a few things against you."
(Revelation 2:13–14)

IN THIS CHAPTER

- How the Devil's plan to destroy the first-century church backfired
- Jesus' words of commendation and warning for the church in Pergamum
- Two problems for Pergamum: the Nicolaitans and Balaam
- Why compromise for the Christian is a big deal
- A special promise for the believer who avoids the compromised life

I heard a story about a man who went out hunting with his rifle and suddenly found an old brown bear in his sights.

As he took aim and began to squeeze off a shot, the bear lifted his paw and said, "Excuse me. Isn't it better to talk than to shoot? Why don't we try to negotiate the matter?"

"Well . . . okay," the hunter said, lowering his rifle. "I guess I'm open to that."

"Good," said the bear. "Now tell me. What is it exactly that you want?"

"What I want more than anything else," the hunter replied, "is a fur coat. I'm really cold out here in these woods."

"Now we're getting somewhere," said the bear. "Maybe we can reach a compromise, because what *I* am looking for is a full stomach."

So the hunter leaned his rifle against a tree and walked into the woods with the bear. A little while later the bear emerged alone, licking his lips, with the negotiations successfully concluded. The hunter got his fur coat, and the bear got a full stomach.

That's how compromise works. Someone usually ends up with the short end of the deal.

In this chapter we will be considering what the Lord had to say to the church of Pergamum (sometimes called Pergamos), a congregation that was engaged in compromise.

SATAN'S PLAN B

In our last chapter, we considered the Lord's words to the church of Smyrna, the suffering church. Looking down through the centuries and millennia of history, we noted how literally millions of believers have given up their lives for their faith in Jesus Christ.

That evidently was the Devil's Plan A from the beginning. He reasoned that if he could stop the church cold in Jerusalem in the first century, the whole party would be over, and the movement would die in its tracks.

But it didn't work out that way. In fact, the Devil's plan backfired. Here is how it happened.

Prior to His ascension, Christ said to His disciples, "Go into all the world and preach the gospel" (Mark 16:15). Have you ever noticed that the first two letters of the word *gospel* are *g-o*?

He had told them to go, but they didn't go—or at least not very far. The fledgling church of Jesus Christ enjoyed the comforts of home in Jerusalem, savoring all of that sweet fellowship. The Holy Spirit had been poured out on the day of Pentecost, the believers were having this great little holy huddle, and no one really wanted to break ranks and leave town with the Good News. Wouldn't there be time later to launch out on all of this missionary stuff? No one felt an urgency necessarily to get started right away.

And then along came Saul of Tarsus, who brought the gift of urgency.

Saul was on fire in his vendetta against the followers of Jesus, hunting down Christians like wild animals throughout Jerusalem and from city to city.

After Stephen was arrested and stoned to death, we read in the book of Acts that "at that time a great persecution arose against the church which was at Jerusalem; and they were all scattered throughout the regions of Judea and Samaria, except the apostles" (Acts 8:1).

The bad news was that a great wave of persecution hammered and harassed believers in Jerusalem. The good news was that as the Christians scattered, they took the message of Christ with them, and the gospel spread like wildfire on those reliable Roman roads across the entire Roman world. So instead of destroying the church through persecution, the Devil actually helped to establish and strengthen the church. Historically the church always has been stronger when it has been persecuted than when it has been patronized.

The Devil, however, evil as he certainly is, is no fool. Instead of merely trying to crush the church, he also launched a plan to effectively *join* the church. In Pergamum and later in Thyatira, we see the servants of Satan beginning to infiltrate the ranks of the church. Jesus had predicted this very tactic in His parable of the wheat and the weeds:

GOOD TO KNOW

Historically the church always has been stronger when it has been persecuted than when it has been patronized.

"The Kingdom of Heaven is like a farmer sowing good seed in his field; but one night as he slept, his enemy came and sowed thistles among the wheat. When the crop began to grow, the thistles grew too.

"The farmer's men came and told him, 'Sir, the field where you planted that choice seed is full of thistles!'

"'An enemy has done it,' he exclaimed.

"'Shall we pull out the thistles?' they asked.

"'No,' he replied. 'You'll hurt the wheat if you do. Let both grow together until the harvest, and I will tell the reapers to sort out the thistles and burn them, and put the wheat in the barn.'" (Matthew 13:24–30 TLB)

Initially, those little thistle sprouts looked just like wheat sprouts. You couldn't really tell the difference. In the same way, the Devil recognizes that he needs to infiltrate the church with false teaching and false believers. Satan says, "I'm going to come up with my own versions of these Christian teachings and try to confuse people with fakes, imitations, and substitutes."

So are there fake Christians? Yes, there are. But take note of this: it is not necessarily my job to figure out who the fakes are; it's my job is to make sure that I'm not one of them.

Here is what the resurrected Lord Jesus wrote to the church of Pergamum:

"These things says He who has the sharp two-edged sword: 'I know your works, and where you dwell, where Satan's throne is. And you hold fast to My name, and did not deny My faith even in the days in which Antipas was My faithful martyr, who was killed among you, where Satan dwells. But I have a few things against you, because you have there those who hold the doctrine of Balaam, who taught Balak to put a stumbling block before the children of Israel, to eat things sacrificed to idols, and to commit sexual immorality. Thus you also have those who hold the doctrine of the Nicolaitans, which thing I hate. Repent, or else I will come to you quickly and will fight against them with the sword of My mouth.

'He who has an ear, let him hear what the Spirit says to the churches. To him who overcomes I will give some of the hidden manna to eat. And I will give him a white stone, and on the stone a new name written which no one knows except him who receives it.'" (Revelation 2:12–17)

"WHERE SATAN HAS HIS THRONE"

Pergamum at that time was the capital and cultural center of Asia. The city was built on a rocky hill with a view of the Mediterranean. It was renowned for its magnificent library that housed two hundred thousand rolls of parchment.

Many cities have an iconic structure or building that immediately identifies them to the world. In San Francisco, it's the Golden Gate Bridge. In Seattle, it's the Space Needle. St. Louis has its giant arch, and New York City has the Statue of Liberty and the Empire State Building. In Pergamum, the picture that would have dominated all the postcards in all the souvenir shops was a huge, throne-shaped altar dedicated to Zeus. It was regarded as one of the Seven Wonders of the Ancient World.

Other gods were worshiped in the city as well, including Dionysus and the snake god Asclepius, also known as "the savior god." People would come to the snake shrine from around the world to worship this god and seek healing for their illnesses. In the temple itself, nonvenomous snakes would slither around the floor and crawl over the supplicants who were lying there. If you were touched by a snake, it was believed, you might be healed from what it was that troubled you. What a creepy place that would have been! It sounds like an Indiana Jones movie.

Besides these, there was also a great temple erected for the worship of Caesar Augustus. Augustus means "of the gods," and by this time the Caesars not only were accepting worship, but they also were demanding it.

Pergamum, then, was a very dark place. And there was a church of Jesus Christ right in the middle of it.

In verse 13, Jesus spoke of Pergamum as the "city where Satan has his throne" (NLT). In other words, the place was so much to Satan's liking that he hung his hat there (if the Devil has a hat).

God is omnipresent, which means that He is always everywhere at the same time. Satan, however, can only be in one place at one time. And in this particular era of history, he felt right at home in Pergamum.

GOOD TO KNOW

Pergamum was the capital and cultural center of Asia, renowned for its magnificent library that housed two hundred thousand rolls of parchment.

Have you ever noticed how some cities seem more wicked than others? Have you ever been in a city or a section of a city where the spiritual atmosphere felt heavy or oppressive? Maybe you drove through the city, and when you were finally through it, out on the open road, you breathed a sigh of relief and felt that sense of oppression slip away. Some cities have even tried to capitalize on being on the edge or over the edge. Las Vegas likes to call itself Sin City and projects that image to the world. They spent millions promoting the now-famous tagline "What Happens Here, Stays Here."[3]

GOOD TO KNOW

Jesus spoke of Pergamum as the "city where Satan has his throne."

In other words, "Come here and do whatever evil you like, and no one will ever know."

I'm aware there are some vital, vibrant churches in Las Vegas, filled with Christians who love the Lord and want nothing more than to shine their light for Jesus in a dark place. It was the same in Pergamum. There were some strong believers who were hanging in there and serving the Lord in spite of all kinds of opposition. Jesus acknowledged those dedicated followers and commended the ones who held fast to His name.

Are you in a spiritually dark place right now? Maybe you recently came to Christ, and you're the only Christian in your family. Whenever the family gets together, you're the one who catches all the flak, and it seems as though everyone is against you. They may even be angry with you for going against the family identity and becoming a follower of Jesus.

Maybe you're in a neighborhood or apartment complex surrounded by godless people. Then again, you might be working in a place where your supervisors or fellow employees constantly harass you for your faith.

Know this: Jesus is fully aware of the challenges, pressures, and temptations you face at this very moment. He understands (more completely than you ever could) the atmosphere where you live, work, or go to school.

Notice again in verse 13, where He says, "I know where you live" (NIV). He knew these believers were living in a hellhole and were trying to hold on to their faith. Jesus said, in effect, "I know that your city is messed up. You live under the shadow of giant idols and pagan altars. You have people worshiping snakes and rolling around on the floor with them. You've got people bowing down to worship Caesar, a mere man. You have temple prostitutes walking the streets, trying to entice people into their temples to do horrible things. And yet you are serving Me right in the midst of it all. I am aware of that."

Jesus went on to say, "You hold fast to My name, and did not deny My faith even in the days in which Antipas was My faithful martyr, who was killed among you, where Satan dwells" (verse 13).

We don't know a lot about Antipas. Church tradition tells us that his persecutors put him inside a bronze bowl and heated it up until he literally roasted to death. No one is sure how he died, but we know that he was a martyr for the name of Christ.

Antipas refused to worship Caesar and refused to utter the words *Kurios Kaiser*, or "Caesar is Lord." If he had said those words, putting just a little incense on Caesar's altar, he would have been allowed to go home.

But he wouldn't do that, even if it meant a terrible death.

Was Antipas being foolish? Was it really such a big deal to say those two little words? Did he really have to be tortured and die for his faith?

The life and death of Antipas says, "Yes, it is a big deal. A very, very big deal, because the words that you say really matter."

We've spoken of Antipas. But how about Cassie Bernal? Remember her? On April 20, 1999, at Columbine High School, two boys who were armed to the teeth made their way through the campus, targeting those who, among other things, believed in Jesus Christ. When they confronted Cassie Bernal, they asked her, "Do you believe in God?"

> **GOOD TO KNOW**
> Antipas refused to worship Caesar and was a martyr for the name of Christ.

Knowing full well what they intended to do, Cassie answered yes, and they shot and killed her.

Her parents later posted one of Cassie's favorite verses on her website:

> Now I have given up on everything else—I found it to be the only
> way to really know Christ and to experience the mighty power that

brought him back to life again, and to find out what it means to suffer and to die with him. So whatever it takes, I will be one who lives in the fresh newness of life of those who are alive from the dead (Philippians 3:10–11 TLB).

What would you have done if someone had held a gun to your face and said, "Do you believe in God?"

Words do matter, don't they?

It's like when you stand before a judge, put your hand on a Bible, and say, "I swear to tell the truth, the whole truth, and nothing but the truth, so help me God." You are truthful in your testimony, and you don't perjure yourself in a court of law—because words matter.

Maybe you once stood before a pastor and your friends and family in a church, and you looked at that man or woman across from you and said, "I do" or "I will." Those words matter very much.

Maybe it was when temptation came knocking at your door, and you reached up for help from God, stood strong, and said, "I won't do this."

Cassie Bernal paid the ultimate price for refusing to deny the name of Jesus. So did Antipas.

And we can never forget the nine believers who were mercilessly shot to death during a Bible study at the Mother Emanuel AME Church in Charleston, South Carolina, on June 17, 2015.

Not long after, another unspeakable tragedy unfolded on November 5, 2017, this time at the First Baptist Church in Sutherland Springs, Texas, where 26 people, including an unborn child, were brutally gunned down (with another 20 injured) at a Sunday morning service.

In the aftermath of these horrific crimes, news stories emerged of survivors and grieving family members still standing firm in their faith—and even finding forgiveness for the perpetrators.

The church in Pergamum stood firm as well, holding on to their faith in spite of strong opposition. Again, Jesus commended them. But He also had some words of warning.

THE WAY OF COMPROMISE

"But I have a few things against you, because you have there those who hold the doctrine of Balaam, who taught Balak to put a stumbling block before the children of Israel, to eat things sacrificed to idols, and to commit sexual immorality. Thus you also have those who hold the doctrine of the Nicolaitans, which thing I hate. Repent, or else I will come to you quickly and will fight against them with the sword of My mouth." (Revelation 2:14–16)

So who were the Nicolaitans? Their founder was Nicolas, possibly one of the seven who had been chosen to be a deacon in the early church, along with Stephen. But apparently Nicolas fell away from the faith, became apostate, and began to lead people astray. Some have speculated that Nicolas was telling people they could offer sacrifices in the pagan temple and engage in acts of immorality and still be Christians. And because he was one of the original deacons of the church of Jerusalem, his opinion carried a lot of weight, and people were willing to follow him. As a result, a movement grew up around him, and these followers of Nicolas became known as Nicolaitans.

The basic Nicolaitan philosophy that was endangering the church of Pergamum is still a danger to us today. It's the idea that you can engage in sin, live pretty much as you please, and still be a Christian. "After all," this philosophy says, "God will understand. Your sins are forgiven and your position in Christ is secure."

What is the biblical response to that view? Romans 6:1–2 says, "Well then, should we keep on sinning so that God can show us more and more of his wonderful grace? Of course not! Since we have died to sin, how can we continue to live in it?" (NLT).

This doctrine of the Nicolaitans is sometimes referred to as antinomianism. It's the philosophy of Christian liberty gone amuck. Maybe you've heard words like these from your nonbelieving (or even Christian) friends: "Hey, do you have to be so intense all the time? Does it always have to be *the Bible this* and *the Bible that*? Can't you just relax a little? Can't you kick back, have a few drinks, and have a little fun for a change? Okay, so you mess around sexually with that girl or that guy. So what? God will understand. God will forgive you. You're still a Christian, and He still loves you."

Not long ago I was talking to someone who was living in disobedience to God, and I told him that he shouldn't go that way.

"Well," he said to me, "God knows my heart."

"Exactly," I said. "And that is the problem! The Bible says [in Jeremiah 17:9] that the heart of man is 'deceitful above all things, and desperately wicked.' Your heart is sinful, God knows it, and that is no excuse to deliberately disobey Him."

Needless to say, he was not thrilled by my answer.

That's the essence of what the Nicolaitans taught. What harm is a little idolatry or a little immorality? You're not going all in—you're just playing around a little.

But this is how compromise always works. Those little things turn into big things. As Solomon once put it, the little foxes in the vineyard destroy the grapes. We tell ourselves, "I can handle this. What's it going to hurt? It's just a little flirtation. A little peek at pornography. A little taste of this or that. A little venting against my spouse or my kids. A little fudging on my income tax. Where's the harm?"

The harm is that we *can't* handle "a little sin." None of us can. It always will, inevitably, lead to more and more.

No one ever suddenly falls away from the faith. It's the little things: the little compromises, the little fantasies, the little cutting of corners, and the little rationalizations that eventually send someone over the edge. And then they lose control and say, "I don't know how this happened to me!"

The Old Testament's Samson is a perfect example. He was known for his great acts of physical strength. We usually think of him as some perfectly sculpted muscle-man with bulging biceps and washboard abs. But the Bible never says that. What it says is that the Spirit of the Lord would come upon him, enabling him to do the mighty things that he did. We really don't know what he looked like, other than the fact that he had long hair. He had taken the vow of a Nazarite, a man who was set apart for God, and part of that vow was that you never allowed your hair to be cut.

No one could take down Samson on the battlefield. One day, lacking another weapon, he picked up a bone off the ground and killed a thousand Philistine soldiers. Another time, he picked up the gates of a Philistine city, put them on his shoulders, and carried them for miles (which was probably a very effective cardiovascular workout). Samson was unstoppable.

So the Devil looked at him and reasoned, in effect, "Okay, I've got to change tactics. I can't beat him on the battlefield . . . but I think I can get him in the bedroom."

It finally dawned on Satan that Samson was a he-man with a she weakness. So he sent along a woman named Delilah to do to Samson what no mighty warrior had ever been able to do.

Samson had first walked down this lustful path with a prostitute. Later he ended up in a relationship with the deadly Delilah.

Delilah (whose name, by the way, means "delicate") came along and said, "Please tell me where your great strength lies, and with what you may be bound to afflict you" (Judges 16:6).

The nerve of this woman! You at least have to give Delilah credit for being up front with her intentions. Samson, however, just laughed it off. He wasn't worried. He must have said something like, "Afflict *me? You?* Little Miss Delicate? Hey, I kill Philistines for fun and tackle lions for my morning exercise. You don't worry me one little bit."

After giving her a couple of false stories, he essentially told her, "A razor never has touched my head. If you shave my head, I will be like any other man."

"Really? Great! Now why don't you take a little nap with your head in my lap?"

So he fell asleep in her lap (which was an insane thing to do) and woke up with no hair on his head. The Philistines came, and this time he couldn't toss them across the room like little rag dolls. They bound him, gouged his eyes out, and eventually tied him to a flour mill, where he ground their grain like an ox. Later they brought him into one of their big temples to mock and laugh at him.

You say, "But Greg, wait. I know how that story worked out. In the end, Samson prevailed. He put his arms against those foundational pillars and pushed them aside, causing the temple of the Philistines to collapse. They all died."

Yes, I know. And Samson died with them.

What would have happened if he would have obeyed God? What might have he become if he had been careful to stick with his vows and allowed the Holy Spirit to use him to the fullest? The world never will know. Samson thought he could handle his lust. But when the crucial moment came, he couldn't handle it at all. He wasn't anywhere near as strong as he thought he was. He took the bait and paid the price. The Devil got Samson—hooker, line, and sinker.

So don't tell me that you can play with sin and keep things under control. Don't tell me how strong you are or how many years you've known the Lord and why these little things won't bring you down.

Compromise is the Devil's most effective tactic. If you could look in the Evil One's tool kit, compromise would be the tool that's more used and worn than any other. And why not? It keeps right on working for him.

Have you ever seen a baby rattlesnake? They're actually kind of cute. They are miniature versions of the adult snakes, with their tiny little fangs and itty-bitty rattles. But make no mistake about it: those cute little snakes can still kill you. And that is how it is with sin in our lives. Little sins morph into big ones—and faster than you might imagine. So don't lower your guard and fall for the trap of compromise. It will start you on a downhill slide that may be very difficult to stop.

When did this world start becoming more attractive to you than the Christian life? Did it start when you decided that you would mow the lawn instead of going to church? Or maybe when you decided to dissolve your marriage because of "irreconcilable differences"? Or maybe it was when you got more excited about the latest movie than what you found from reading God's Word.

Whatever it was, wherever it started, the old emptiness has returned. Because slowly but surely you have been compromising and going in the wrong direction. You're not hearing from God anymore—and it is not because God doesn't want to talk to you. It is because you have effectively cut off communication with Him.

I heard a story about a massive redwood tree out in the middle of some forest here in California. It had stood tall for four hundred years, surviving countless earthquakes, storms, floods, and fires. Yet one day, without warning, this massive tree came crashing down with an impact that shook the earth. And nobody knew why. No one had laid an axe to it, and no bolt of lightning had torn it asunder. On closer examination, however, they discovered why this ancient tree had fallen.

Tiny beetles had worked their way into the trunk and had eaten away at its life-giving fibers, weakening its mighty bulk from the inside out. What the lightning and wind could not do, the insects did.

In the same way, Satan seeks to bring Christians down through a steady drone of small, seemingly insignificant temptations.

We may even be fighting Satan on one front while on another front, we're making an alliance with him without even realizing it. We may pride ourselves on the fact that "I don't do this" or "I would never do that." In the meantime, however, we may be lowering our guards and compromising in another area of life that no one else sees or knows about. And in so doing, we are putting our spiritual lives in peril.

In Revelation 2:14, Jesus puts His finger on yet another danger area at the Pergamos fellowship.

THE DOCTRINE OF BALAAM

"You have there those who hold the doctrine of Balaam." (2:14)

We understand what the Nicolaitans' problem was: they were trying to live in two worlds. What, then, is the "doctrine of Balaam"? Actually, it is very similar.

You may remember the story of Balaam in Numbers 22–24. There was a king of Moab named Balak who hated the Jews and wanted to wipe them out. After thinking about it for a while, he decided the best plan would be to have God Himself curse them. He went out and found a prophet named Balaam and offered him big money to call down curses on the children of Israel as they were passing through the wilderness on the way to the Promised Land.

So it appears Balaam was a for-profit prophet.

After finally accepting the job (in spite of a few reservations), Balaam loaded up his donkey and headed out to the wilderness to bring curses on God's own people, the people whom He loved. Then, as Balaam was riding along, his donkey suddenly stopped in its tracks, refusing to go any further. At this point, Balaam experienced a little road rage and began beating the animal. The donkey went a little further and stopped again, this time ramming Balaam's leg up against a wall. Again the angry prophet began beating the poor animal.

Why was this happening? Because the donkey had more sense than the fool on its back. The donkey clearly saw an angel of the Lord with a drawn sword—and you don't ever want to mess with an angel, no matter who you are. And if that angel happens to have a sword out at the ready, then you'd really better put on the brakes.

That's what this donkey did, and it made Balaam angry. Why? Because he couldn't see the angel; all he saw was a stack of Moabite money in his future.

What happened next has to be one of the strangest and funniest incidents in the entire Bible. Here's how it reads from the book of Numbers:

> This time when the donkey saw the angel, it lay down under Balaam. In a fit of rage Balaam beat the animal again with his staff.
>
> Then the Lord gave the donkey the ability to speak. "What have I done to you that deserves your beating me three times?" it asked Balaam.
>
> "You have made me look like a fool!" Balaam shouted. "If I had a sword with me, I would kill you!"
>
> "But I am the same donkey you have ridden all your life," the donkey answered. "Have I ever done anything like this before?"

"No," Balaam admitted.

Then the LORD opened Balaam's eyes, and he saw the angel of the LORD standing in the roadway with a drawn sword in his hand. Balaam bowed his head and fell face down on the ground before him.

"Why did you beat your donkey those three times?" the angel of the LORD demanded. "Look, I have come to block your way because you are stubbornly resisting me. Three times the donkey saw me and shied away; otherwise, I would certainly have killed you by now and spared the donkey." (Numbers 22:27–34 NLT)

Now here is what is amazing to me. Yes, the donkey spoke. But without missing a beat, Balaam talked back to it! Doesn't that seem a little unusual? Finally, the angel made himself visible to Balaam as well. He said, in essence, "Your donkey had more sense than you. It's a good thing you stopped, or I would have killed you."

Now, any clear-thinking individual would have changed course after being rebuked by a talking donkey and an angel with a sword. But not Balaam. He simply figured out another way to get the job done. He smelled money, and he dreamed up a compromise.

So he went to King Balak and basically said, "I can't curse these guys, or I'll get into big trouble. But I want the money, so check out this plan. You get your best-looking Moabite women to go down there to Israel's camp and seduce those young Israeli boys. Get those young men to follow the Moabite women into their tents and to worship the Moabite gods. And then, when they're worshiping those false gods of Moab, God will judge His own people, and the job will be done for you."

Balak liked that plan, and that is exactly what happened. (The Bible tells the sad story in Numbers 25.)

The sin of Pergamum, then, just like the sin of Balaam, was the toleration of evil. It's the idea of calling yourself a Christian but living any way that you want to. These are people who want to go to Heaven but live like Hell in the meantime.

Once again, it comes back to the issue of compromise. It is the process of gradually weakening your spiritual life until you wake up one day and find yourself doing the very things that you once condemned and hated.

So is there a way out of this? Thankfully, there is.

THE WAY OUT

"Repent, or else I will come to you quickly and will fight against them with the sword of My mouth.

"He who has an ear, let him hear what the Spirit says to the churches." (2:16–17)

Jesus had commended them for holding fast to their faith and standing strong, even under the threat of martyrdom. But then He clearly identified the problem: They had been influenced by the Nicolaitan faction and the doctrine of Balaam to think they could live in two worlds—that they could call themselves Christians but live any way they pleased. And Jesus was telling them, "You'd better change your heart and change your ways, because those views eventually will destroy you."

The truth is, of course, that even committed Christians sin, making mistakes and taking falls. It's not a question of being perfect, because no one is. Nevertheless, you can live as a dedicated follower of Christ, doing your best (with God's help) to honor the Lord with your life, while at the same time acknowledging your weakness and your need to depend on the Holy Spirit's help to live the Christian life. Or, you can follow the path of compromise, living outwardly as a Christian but indulging in sin when you feel like it, telling yourself that it will be okay because God will forgive you.

The thing is, He will. But that doesn't remove the *consequences* of your sinful words and actions. For instance, let's say that you get drunk, get behind the wheel of your car, and get arrested for a DUI. But then you repent and ask God to forgive you. Will He do it? Yes, He will. But you still will pay a fine or spend time in jail for breaking the law.

Just because we confess a sin and receive God's cleansing doesn't mean that we will somehow skip the repercussions of our actions. As the old saying goes, some believers want to sow their wild oats but then pray for a crop failure. The Bible, however, is very, very clear about this. The apostle Paul wrote, "Don't be misled—you cannot mock the justice of God. You will always harvest what you plant. Those who live only to satisfy their own sinful nature will harvest decay and death from that sinful nature. But those who live to please the Spirit will harvest everlasting life from the Spirit" (Galatians 6:7–8 NLT).

So yes, God will forgive you. And eventually He even will work all things together for good in your life, as it says in Romans 8:28. But that doesn't mean you will dodge all the consequences. You still will face the natural outcomes of your sins.

Maybe at some point you said, "I'm sick of this marriage. I'm tired of my husband (or tired of my wife). I'm going to divorce my spouse and remarry someone else." Then later, you repent of what you did and seek God's forgiveness. Will He forgive you? Yes, He will. But for the rest of your life, you will have to deal with the repercussions of what you foolishly or impulsively did. You will have to deal with the turmoil and unhappiness of a blended family, the awkward or hostile relationships, the incredible financial toll, and all the stress, regret, and sorrow you have brought on yourself and your loved ones—perhaps for generations.

We reap what we sow. But that is also true in a positive sense as well as a negative one. It is also true of faithful Christians who walk daily with the Lord, who have honored their vows, set a strong example for their children, and refused the path of compromise. They, too, will reap what they sow. Galatians 6:8 reminds us that "he who sows to his flesh will of the flesh reap corruption, but he who sows to the Spirit will of the Spirit reap everlasting life."

They will have a marriage that will give them joy in their declining years, they will have their family around them, and they will see their legacy of loving

Jesus being passed on from generation to generation. And they will realize that the Word of God and the Spirit of God has kept them safe and protected them from devastating harm.

Will there still be hard and difficult times—times when tragedy strikes and the tears flow? Yes, there will be those times. But the Bible says that "Even in darkness light dawns for the upright" (Psalm 112:4 NIV).

"HIDDEN MANNA"

There is a special promise for the person who avoids the compromised life. Look at the Lord's words in chapter 2, verse 17: "To him who overcomes I will give some of the hidden manna to eat. And I will give him a white stone, and on the stone a new name written which no one knows except him who receives it."

What is the hidden manna? As you may recall, when the Israelite nation left their slavery in Egypt and were making their way through the wilderness toward the Promised Land, God provided food for them every day, which was waiting outside their tent doors. It was called manna—a supernatural, heavenly substance. The psalmist called it "the bread of angels" (78:25 NIV). It tasted wonderful and provided the Lord's people with complete nutrition. And here the Lord was saying, "To him who overcomes I will give some of the hidden manna to eat."

Manna is bread right out of Heaven.

I don't know about you, but if you put a luscious dessert in front of me, I can usually resist it. But if you put freshly baked bread in front of me, I can't resist it. I love hot bread, right out of the oven, slathered with butter.

God says, "I will give you the freshest bread, like the Israelites had in the wilderness, but even greater and better than that."

In the gospel of John, Jesus identified Himself as "the bread of God" that has come down from Heaven (see John 6:30–40). Jesus was saying, "I will give Myself to the person who follows Me and who trusts in Me. I will satisfy you beyond anything you could ever imagine or dream or conceive. I will give you the hidden manna and the white stone."

What is the white stone? The Bible doesn't say. It could have been something given to athletes in those original, first-century Olympic games. Perhaps it was like a ticket or a pass allowing the athletes to enter the feast of celebration after the competitions.

Whatever it might have been, the Lord was saying to us here, "If you follow Me, obey My Word, and walk with Me through the hours and days and years of your life, then I will satisfy your deepest needs. I will be there for you. I will personally give you the golden ticket to the wedding feast of the Lamb. You will be My special guest and live with Me forever."

What pleasure on Earth could possibly compare with that?

Not one.

THREE TAKEAWAY TRUTHS

- The basic Nicolaitan philosophy that endangered the church of Pergamum is still a danger to us today.
- No one ever suddenly falls away from the faith. It's the little compromises that eventually send a person over the edge.
- There is a special promise for the person who avoids the compromised life.

CHAPTER FIVE

A Sick and Dying Church

"I know your works, love, service, faith, and your patience; and as for your works, the last are more than the first. Nevertheless I have a few things against you. . . . But hold fast what you have till I come."
(Revelation 2:19–20, 25)

IN THIS CHAPTER

- How to know when you're spiritually dying
- A prescription for the spiritually dying
- What's good and bad about tolerance
- Five signs of a dead church
- Who will (and won't) be at the Great White Throne judgment
- How to be sure you're ready for Christ's return

Ruth Bell Graham once observed that "the definition of a bore is someone who, when asked how they are feeling, will actually tell you."

Have you ever met someone who was obsessed with being sick?

It's almost as though they *look forward* to coming down with something. And if they do, they relish telling others about all the gory details. It reminds me of an epitaph I read about on the tombstone of a hypochondriac: "I *told* you I was sick."

You've met people like that, of course—people who love to talk about their multiple aches and pains and all that is wrong with them.

I'm certainly not one of those people. I'm one of those stubborn guys who hates going to the doctor and never wants to admit that he's sick. Sometimes, however, when your symptoms become overwhelming, you have to go see those people in the white coats whether you want to or not. You have to find out what's going on in your body.

I heard a true story about a woman in Seattle who went to the emergency room with nonstop nausea and vomiting. After doing a series of tests on her, the doctors discovered that the woman had eaten a tube sock. (That's one of those really thick cotton socks that people pull on when the weather gets cold.)

When confronted with this fact, she acknowledged it was true, saying, "I have a nervous habit of eating half a sock each evening." (Hmm. Maybe she ought to try a mug of Ovaltine instead.)

In the second and third chapters of Revelation, we will consider two very sick churches, one in critical condition (Thyatira) and the other on life support and almost dead (Sardis). While these are letters from Jesus to two sick and dying first-century churches, they are also words to sick and dying believers, because the church is made up of individual men and women.

How did these churches get to this point?

Probably in the same way that a person does. It starts with some uncomfortable symptoms that get worse and worse. The days pass, one thing leads to another, and before long the sick person is on his or her deathbed.

So how can we tell when a church is dying? Or more to the point, how can we tell if we are spiritually dying? And if we do find ourselves on a spiritual deathbed, is there a way we can be revived?

The answer, thank God, is a resounding yes.

THYATIRA . . . A CHURCH ON THE CRITICAL LIST

"And to the angel of the church in Thyatira write,

'These things says the Son of God, who has eyes like a flame of fire, and His feet like fine brass: "I know your works, love, service, faith, and your patience; and as for your works, the last are more than the first. Nevertheless I have a few things against you, because you allow that woman Jezebel, who calls herself a prophetess, to teach and seduce My servants to commit sexual immorality and eat things sacrificed to idols. And I gave her time to repent of her sexual immorality, and she did not repent. Indeed I will cast her into a sickbed, and those who commit adultery with her into great tribulation, unless they repent of their deeds. I will kill her children with death, and all the churches shall know that I am He who searches the minds and hearts. And I will give to each one of you according to your works.

"Now to you I say, and to the rest in Thyatira, as many as do not have this doctrine, who have not known the depths of Satan, as they say, I will put on you no other burden. But hold fast what you have till I come. And he who overcomes, and keeps My works until the end, to him I will give power over the nations—

'He shall rule them with a rod of iron;

They shall be dashed to pieces like the potter's vessels'—as I also have received from My Father; and I will give him the morning star.

"He who has an ear, let him hear what the Spirit says to the churches."" (Revelation 2:18–29)

What is amazing about this church in Thyatira is that they started well but then went into a steep decline. Before correcting them, however, the Lord spoke words of commendation, saying (in another translation), "I know your deeds, your love and faith, your service and perseverance, and that you are now doing more than you did at first" (verse 19 NIV).

So this was a growing church, and there was more growth in the end than in the beginning.

It's great to have a good beginning and a good ending, but if you have to have one or the other, the best thing is to finish well. Sometimes we may not have a great launch in our walk with

GOOD TO KNOW

The church in Thyatira started well but then went into a steep decline.

Christ. Maybe we started following Jesus later in life and had to work through a number of personal issues that had accumulated over the years. Or maybe, quite honestly, we have thrown away some precious years chasing after silly, empty things.

Here's the good news: if you come to your senses now, you can still get back in the race and finish well. That is a better scenario than starting into the Christian life like a rocket ship off the launching pad, only to crash and burn later in life. Your best days should not be behind you; they should be in front of you.

Sometimes someone my age or older will come up to me and say, "Hey, Greg, remember the old days? The Jesus Movement? Those were great days, weren't they? The Lord was really working in those days."

They are referring, of course, to a genuine American revival back in the late sixties to the early seventies known as the Jesus Movement. I came to Christ at that time (1970, to be exact), and I thank God for it. In fact I wrote a book about it, titled *Jesus Revolution*.

But sometimes what I want to say is, "Yes, they were incredible days. But now there is today!"

Certainly, the Lord was working fifty years ago. But He is working today, too. I think of the Lord's words to Israel through Isaiah: "Forget the former things; do not dwell on the past. See, I am doing a new thing! Now it springs up; do you not perceive it?" (Isaiah 43:18–19 NIV).

I may be excited about what the Lord did in my life yesterday, but what I'm really looking forward to is what He will do in and through me today and tomorrow, if He gives me tomorrow.

Some people want to live in the glories of the past. They look back on old methods, old patterns, and old, familiar ways of doing things and say, "It was better back then—back in the good ol' days."

But Jesus was saying to the church at Thyatira, "You're doing more now than you used to. Your latter works are better than your earlier ones." That is a good thing! That's something that should be true of every believer. Yes, ten years ago was good and last year was amazing, but *this* is the year when God will do something special and unexpected in and through our lives. We should be experiencing constant growth in Christ.

So what happened at Thyatira? They were making excellent headway but then began to drift off course. It's a warning for all of us. In Hebrews 2:1, the writer says: "So we must listen very carefully to the truth we have heard, or we may drift away from it" (NLT).

How true! In fact, *the very moment you begin to neglect your growth in Christ, you will begin to drift away from Him.*

A WORD ABOUT "TOLERANCE"

In the last chapter we read about the church at Pergamum, which was beginning to compromise with sin. But here in Thyatira they were tolerating open sin.

It's interesting to me how Jesus used that word *tolerate*. In Revelation 2:20 He said, "I have this against you: You *tolerate* that woman Jezebel, who calls herself a prophet. By her teaching she misleads my servants into sexual immorality and the eating of food sacrificed to idols" (NIV, emphasis added).

Tolerance. Isn't that the watchword of the day? Our culture will forgive almost anything except intolerance. And many people outside of Christ think that Bible-believing Christians are intolerant and bigoted.

I disagree. All of the strong Christians that I know are in fact very tolerant people. Here is what I mean: true Christians have a worldview that comes from our study of the Scriptures and from our faith in Jesus Christ. We genuinely believe these things to be true. As a result, when we talk to someone who isn't a believer, we try to convince and persuade them. We want them to believe in Jesus like we do.

What happens, then, when someone says, "I don't agree with you"?

Do we assault them physically if they don't embrace Christ? Of course not. Do we scream in their faces? No, we don't do that, either. Do we attempt to cancel

> **GOOD TO KNOW**
>
> The church of Thyatira tolerated gross sin in their midst, and Jesus was effectively saying to them, "I am intolerant of your tolerance."

and silence them on social media? Not at all. We lovingly say, "I disagree with your view, and I will pray for you. I hope that you come to your senses someday."

We tolerate their decision, even though we disagree with it.

But the tolerance being pushed by today's contemporary culture is very different. People say to Christians, "You have no right to say that your version of truth is any better than anyone else's version of truth." Therefore, you should accept and embrace what *they* believe, just as you embrace what you believe. And if you don't, you are intolerant.

I have found the most intolerant people of all to be those who talk most about so-called tolerance. They not only want to forbid me from saying that I disagree with a certain point of view, but they want me to endorse that point of view as well.

If I don't, then I'm written off as intolerant or narrow-minded.

Nowadays, if you don't agree with popular opinion, you have a phobia.

To take a stand on a moral issue is defined as hate.

Holding to certain convictions is branded as bigotry.

Truths the church has believed and held for centuries are regarded as discriminatory.

The church of Thyatira certainly had an issue with tolerance. They tolerated gross sin in their midst, and Jesus was effectively saying to them, "I am intolerant of your tolerance. I am intolerant of this sin. You are allowing sexual immorality into the ranks of My church, and I won't stand for it."

JEZEBEL

> "You tolerate that woman Jezebel, who calls herself a prophet."
> (verse 20 NIV)

Was Jesus speaking here of a woman literally named Jezebel, or was He using the name as a metaphor for wickedness? The Bible doesn't really tell us.

In the Old Testament, Queen Jezebel, the wife of Israel's King Ahab, was an extremely wicked woman. We know that she underwrote 850 false prophets in the land, put to death the true prophets of the Lord, and taught that immorality really wasn't a serious issue. This historical Jezebel ultimately was thrown from a window and eaten by dogs in the courtyard below.

In the words of the great theologian Frank Sinatra, "The lady was a tramp."

So here, perhaps, we find the Lord saying to the church of Thyatira, "You are guilty of tolerating sin on the level of Queen Jezebel, and I am aware of that."

In verse 18, Jesus described Himself like this:

> "These things says the Son of God, who has eyes like a flame of fire, and His feet like fine brass."

Having His feet like fine brass speaks of refinement and of judgment. Having eyes like a flame of fire means that He sees everything—and that this is making Him angry.

It must have been an amazing thing during our Lord's earthly ministry to look into His eyes. Yes, He was a man, but He also was God. And when you looked into those eyes, you were looking at God in human form. How awesome that would have been!

In the Gospels we read how He would look at people with a penetrating glance. In fact, He could see right through them. When He called Matthew the tax collector, we read, "He saw a man named Matthew sitting at the tax office. And He said to him, 'Follow Me'" (Matthew 9:9). A better rendering of that verse would be, "Jesus looked right through Him and said, 'Follow Me.'"

We know that after Peter's third denial of the Lord in the courtyard of Caiaphas, Jesus made eye contact with His erring disciple. The text says, "The Lord turned and looked straight at Peter" (Luke 22:61 NIV).

Jesus didn't just look at people; He knew what they were thinking. And when He would expose their thoughts, it would completely freak them out.

"Why are you thinking this right now?" He would say.

And they immediately understood that He could look into their very thoughts, reading their unspoken words (see Matthew 9:4).

Here in Revelation, the look of the resurrected and glorified Jesus Christ is like twin laser beams, cutting right through everything. And the Lord is saying to this church, "I am intolerant of this sin. You cannot be Christians and try to live in two worlds."

In Thyatira, immorality was taking place in the lives of those who professed to be believers. The Bible has some strong warnings for those who believe that God will "tolerate" this sin. In Galatians 5 we read,

> When you follow the desires of your sinful nature, the results are very clear: sexual immorality, impurity, lustful pleasures, idolatry, sorcery, hostility, quarreling, jealousy, outbursts of anger, selfish ambition, dissension, division, envy, drunkenness, wild parties, and other sins like these. Let me tell you again, as I have before, that anyone living that sort of life will not inherit the Kingdom of God. (verses 19–21 NLT)

This is a stern warning, and none of us should miss it: if you live an immoral lifestyle without repenting, you will not go to Heaven.

In Revelation 22:15 it speaks of those who do not make it into Heaven, saying, "Outside the city are . . . the sorcerers, the sexually immoral, the murderers, the idol worshipers, and all who love to live a lie" (NLT).

GOOD TO KNOW

Queen Jezebel, the wife of Israel's King Ahab, underwrote 850 false prophets, put to death the true prophets of the Lord, and taught that immorality really wasn't a serious issue.

There are no exceptions to this. I have had people who are not married come up to me and say, "We are having sex outside of marriage, but God told us it was okay."

"Really?" I will say. "How did He do that?"

"He just spoke to our hearts."

And I will reply, "No, He didn't. I don't know who it was who spoke to your heart, but it wasn't God, because God would never contradict His Word. And 1 Thessalonians 4:3 says, 'God's will is for you to be holy, so stay away from all sexual sin'" (NLT).

In Revelation 2:22, Jesus gives a strong warning to those who would live in immorality: "Indeed I will cast her into a sickbed, and those who commit adultery with her into great tribulation, unless they repent of their deeds."

This verse seems to be saying that if you continue to live this way, you will be left at the Rapture. This fits in with other verses that warn us to be watching and ready as we await the Lord's return.

In Luke 12 Jesus speaks of the wicked servant who thinks that his master is delaying his return and begins to party, get drunk, and abuse the other servants. Jesus says that the master will return and cut that person off.

In Matthew 24:40, He says that "two men will be in the field: one will be taken and the other left."

There will be people who thought they were Christians that will be left when the Lord returns. How tragic it would be to be left!

Now we shift gears and find out what happens to the sick church that refuses to listen to the Lord's rebuke. They end up as a dead church.

SARDIS . . . THE DEAD CHURCH

"And to the angel of the church in Sardis write,

'These things says He who has the seven Spirits of God and the seven stars: "I know your works, that you have a name that you are alive, but you are dead. Be watchful, and strengthen the things which remain, that are ready to die, for I have not found your works perfect before God. Remember therefore how you have received and heard; hold fast and repent. Therefore if you will not watch, I will come upon you as a thief, and you will not know what hour I will come upon you. You have a few names even in Sardis who have not defiled their garments; and they shall walk with Me in white, for they are worthy. He who overcomes shall be clothed in white garments, and I will not blot out his name from the Book of Life; but I will confess his name before My Father and before His angels.

"He who has an ear, let him hear what the Spirit says to the churches."" (Revelation 3:1–6)

The First Church of Sardis looked really impressive—on the outside.

Have you ever had the opportunity to see a television or movie set? It's never the way it appears on the screen. Instead of being striking or imposing, it seems smaller and more fake. That beautiful three-story building may just be a painted façade, propped up by pieces of wood.

That's a picture of the church in Sardis. They had an outer shell that was very impressive, but it was nothing more than smoke and mirrors. The inner fire was gone, burned down to ashes.

It reminds me of a downtown local church that caught fire. The pastor stood and sadly watched as the fire department vainly tried to beat the blaze back. Then another man came and stood alongside the pastor, watching the conflagration. The pastor looked at him and said, "I've been inviting you to come to this church for as long as I can remember, and you've never come. Yet here you are on this night. Why?"

Without taking his eyes off the flames, the man said, "Pastor, this is the first time in all of those years that this church has been on fire."

Sardis looked good, but something was missing.

They had a name and reputation, there was no shortage of money, and the place buzzed with activity. Outwardly it had every indication of a church on the move.

But Jesus reveals things that no one else sees.

GOOD TO KNOW

The church in Sardis had an outer shell that was very impressive, but it was nothing more than smoke and mirrors.

It's a reminder to us that the way we might evaluate a "successful" church is different from the way that God does. Our measure of success probably includes how many people attend, how big and beautiful the facilities are, or the quality of their music and sound system. And those are all desirable features to have in a church. But Jesus sees things differently. And the church at

Sardis wasn't measuring up to His standards—which are really the only standards that count.

In Revelation 3:2 He says to them, "I have not found your works perfect before God." That word *perfect* might be better translated "complete" or "fulfilled." In other words, "You have not fulfilled your purpose before God."

What, after all, is the purpose of a church? Is the objective just to become larger, with lots of people everywhere? It has to be more than that.

As far as I can see in my study of the Scriptures, the church has a threefold objective: upward, inward, and outward. To put it another way, the church is here to exalt God, edify the saints, and evangelize the world.

But there are churches that are not fulfilling their purpose, and Sardis is an example of such a church.

Did they pray in Sardis? I would imagine they prayed quite dutifully—perhaps even with eloquence. But their prayers went no higher than the ceiling. Why? Possibly because they were more interested in the form of the prayer than in the One to whom it was addressed.

> **GOOD TO KNOW**
> The church has a threefold objective: exalt God, edify the saints, and evangelize the world.

Did they listen to sermons? No doubt they did. But they were more focused on the skill of the orator than on the message itself.

Did they worship? I would imagine so. They may have even had the first-century equivalent of a full-blown orchestra and a massive choir. But they were more concerned with how it sounded than the One to whom it was directed.

If you ever visit our church in Southern California, I hope that you don't come to listen to our worship band; I hope that you leave thinking about the amazing God whom we worship.

I hope that you wouldn't leave our midst saying, "What a great sermon." I would rather that you walked out saying, "What a great Savior we have."

How can you tell if a church is dying?

In his excellent commentary on Revelation, Pastor Chuck Swindoll points out five marks of a dead church. [4]

1. A dead church worships its past.

Maybe some of the old-timers can relate inspiring stories of miracles, conversions, and changed lives "back in the early days."

That's okay as far as it goes. But we have to move on. We can rejoice in what God did twenty, thirty, or forty years ago. But what about now? God doesn't want us to live in the past—even a glorious past. A living church lives in the present and plans for the future.

2. A dead church is inflexible and resistant to change.

Sometimes in the church we are flexible where we should be inflexible and inflexible where we should be flexible. In other words, we should be inflexible in the essentials. We come together to worship God and to study the Word. There's no need to change those essential priorities.

But there are other areas where we ought to be flexible: things like music and worship styles, which change with the years. People get very sensitive about these things.

"Well," someone will say, "I prefer this style—it was what I was raised on, and I don't like anything else. Your style offends me, and it probably isn't even valid."

But this is an area where we ought to be flexible rather than rigid and unbending.

Some people don't like it when churches embrace new technology and resist or drag their feet over changes. I remember back in the mid-1990s when our church put up our first video screens. Some people were upset about it. Some even said, "We're leaving the church over this! We don't come to church to watch TV."

But it's different now. When I speak these days, I notice some of these same people looking at the screens more than me, though I am standing right in front of them. The fact is the video draws you in closer, making it more intimate. I only wish they had invented HD technology when I was in my thirties. Now every blemish is on display.

I remember hearing Christians being critical of churches having websites. Now everyone has them. My point is these new technologies are like a massive, updated Roman road system that opens up the world to us. We ought to use and leverage every technology platform: radio, television, film, the Internet, as well as social media like Facebook, YouTube, Twitter, Instagram, TikTok, and new ones as they emerge.

This is an area in which we need to remain flexible. But there are also areas in which we must remain inflexible. For instance, the church must always be a place where God's Word is taught and the gospel is proclaimed. The church must always be a place where the Lord is glorified through prayer and worship. We cannot "flex" in those areas. They are non-negotiables.

3. A dead church has lazy leadership.

Complacency and lethargy set in as the church slips into spiritual cruise control, not wanting to do anything new or even rethink the way things are done.

I can think of some methods and practices and programs in our own church—things we have done the same way for years—that probably need to be reexamined. There are ways of doing things that used to work but haven't worked very well for years.

But we've always done it that way!

Yes, but we don't need to anymore. Local churches need to be constantly evaluating, considering, and weighing options, keeping in mind the big picture of what they were called into their communities to do.

4. A dead church neglects youth.

If they aren't careful, aging congregations can so please themselves that they fail to reach the next generation. And that, my friend, spells death.

We started Harvest Christian Fellowship when I was just 20 years old. In fact, we had so many young people coming on Sunday nights that we started a Sunday morning service as an outreach to "older" people—those over thirty!

Sometimes a worship pastor will want to introduce a style of music and will be told, "The older people won't like that."

Yes, but the younger people might like it very much—and maybe the older saints just need to flex a little.

5. A dead church lacks evangelistic zeal.

If new converts aren't coming into the church, then it's only a matter of time until that church stagnates and becomes spiritually dead. New believers are the lifeblood of the church. We should want them . . . pray for them . . . embrace them . . . encourage them . . . minister to them in every way that we can.

REMEDY FROM THE GREAT PHYSICIAN

What, then, should a dead church do? For that matter, what should a believer who has slipped into a deadened state do?

In this passage the Great Physician gives His advice for a complete spiritual recovery. And by the way, it doesn't do you any good if you go to the doctor and then neglect to do what he or she tells you to do. You have to follow the physician's directions if you want to see improvement in your condition.

I heard about a man who went to see his doctor on a return visit and said, "Doc, it's been one month since my last appointment, and I *still* feel miserable."

"Hmmm," the doctor said. "Did you follow the instructions on the medicine that I gave you?"

"I sure did, Doc," came the reply. "The bottle said, 'Keep tightly closed,' and that's what I've done."

"That's true," the doctor said. "But keep reading, and it will tell you what to do *next*."

You have to listen to the Lord and then do what He says. You'll never recover if you keep tightly closed up and refuse to respond to the Lord. In fact, Jesus tells us exactly what we need in our lives. It's found in the way He presents Himself to the church. He says, "This is the message from the one who has the sevenfold Spirit of God and the seven stars" (Revelation 3:1 NLT).

These symbols were identified for us in the first chapter of Revelation. The seven spirits (or sevenfold Spirit of God) are symbols of the Holy Spirit in His fullness. What Jesus was saying, then, is that dead churches and comatose believers *need the power of the Holy Spirit* in their lives.

Let's imagine that you just purchased a new car. For almost a week-and-a-half, you drive it around happily, enjoying that new car smell and all the features of your shiny new ride. But then—suddenly and inexplicably—your car sputters, chugs to a stop, and cannot be started again.

Resourceful person that you are, you call a tow truck and have the car towed back to the dealer where you purchased it. "Hey," you say with indignation, "you guys sold me a lemon! It doesn't run anymore."

The salesman asks to see your keys, turns on the ignition, and notices the fuel light is glowing orange on the instrument panel.

"Umm, just a question," the salesman says, "but did you ever put gas in this car?"

"Gas? No. I . . . thought it was electric."

"No. It's not electric. It has a gasoline engine. That means you need to *refuel* your car."

GOOD TO KNOW

The seven spirits (or sevenfold Spirit of God) in Revelation 3:1 are symbols of the Holy Spirit in His fullness.

It's a simple analogy, I know, but let's compare that scenario to the Christian life. You've been charging around all week, full of energy and joy, and then find yourself sputtering and stalling out. Maybe you've even come to a complete standstill. So here is the question: Have you refueled lately?

You need to be filled with the Holy Spirit.

That is not just a onetime event! Ephesians 5:18–19 says, "Be filled with the Spirit, speaking to one another in psalms and hymns and spiritual songs." In the Greek language, however, that term *be filled* could be translated "be *constantly* filled with the Holy Spirit." Be filled over and over again, and get those refills from God.

It's interesting that this "be filled" verse comes in the context of a discussion on marriage and the family, where the apostle Paul is speaking about men and women, husbands and wives, fathers and mothers. In context, then, God's Word is saying that if you want to be a good husband . . . a good wife . . . a good parent . . . then you need to be filled and constantly refilled with the Holy Spirit. We need God's help to do everything that He has called us to do and to be all that He has called us to be.

Jesus goes on to give His three-part prescription for spiritual renewal:

> "Be watchful, and strengthen the things which remain, that are ready to die, for I have not found your works perfect before God. Remember therefore how you have received and heard; hold fast and repent. Therefore if you will not watch, I will come upon you as a thief, and you will not know what hour I will come upon you." (Revelation 3:2–3)

WAKE UP!

The New King James term is "be watchful," but "wake up" is probably a better translation.

I recently got back from an international trip with a severe case of jet lag. I don't do well with jet lag. Some of the people I travel with move through the time zones and just seem to adapt and roll with it.

I wish I could.

I will have jet lag for up to a week before I actually adapt. The sad thing is that many of my trips last for one week. Just as I get myself reoriented, it's time to fly back and start all over again. If you've experienced it, then you know that jet lag isn't like normal tiredness. At your new destination, you get up really, really early (according to your body clock) and then you start hitting the wall around 2:00 in the afternoon.

I usually will go for a triple espresso, but it only lasts for a couple of hours. By 5:00 p.m., I'm beyond tired. I can't even put sentences together (which is inconvenient when I have to preach in the evening). Just when I really need to function well, I can hardly function at all.

I read an article not long ago that said sleep-deprived people are just as dangerous on the road as drunk drivers. In fact, the effects are nearly the same.

So the word of the Lord to a lethargic church or a comatose believer is, "Wake up. Get your spiritual eyes open—*fast*. Your life in Christ depends on this. Snap out of it!"

STRENGTHEN WHAT REMAINS

The Greek word translated "strengthen" means to stabilize that which is frail. In other words, there is still something good here: a spark, a flicker, a glowing ember. *Strengthen* that.

Have you ever seen a movie where someone is bending over a person who has been ill or injured and is close to death? The person ministering to the victim keeps saying, "Stay with me now! Don't leave me!" This scene in Revelation 3 is similar. The Great Physician is leaning over this church and saying, "Stay with Me! Don't leave Me! You can do this! There's still hope."

BE READY FOR THE LORD'S RETURN

Verse 3 says, "Therefore if you will not watch, I will come upon you as a thief, and you will not know what hour I will come upon you."

A thief doesn't make an appointment or announce when he is coming. Otherwise, he wouldn't be a very good thief. Even so, it would be nice, wouldn't it? You get a text that says, "I'm going to rob your home around 2:00 a.m. tomorrow morning. Just a little heads-up."

It would be a considerate thing to do, because then you could have a little reception committee waiting for him.

But thieves don't do that. They come unexpectedly. They hit when your back is turned or you're away on a trip or you're distracted. Jesus was saying, "That is the way I will come—like a thief!"

As Christians who are walking with the Lord, we're happy that He might come at any moment. We don't fear or dread His coming because we are ready and waiting for His return. But if we aren't right with God, He will come like a thief, and there is an element of dread or danger in that. What is your attitude toward His return? It will speak volumes about where you are spiritually.

The apostle John speaks of potential reactions to Christ's return. In 1 John 2:28 he says, "And now, dear children, remain in fellowship with Christ so that when he returns, you will be full of courage and not shrink back from him in shame" (NLT).

If you are right with God, you will be filled with courage as you await His return. If you aren't right with God, you will find yourself shrinking back in shame at the thought of His sudden return.

THE BOOK OF LIFE

As Jesus wrapped up His letter to the church at Sardis in Revelation 3, He concluded with this very important—but often misunderstood—message: "He who overcomes shall be clothed in white garments, and I will not blot out his name from the Book of Life; but I will confess his name before My Father and before His angels" (verse 5).

The Bible clearly teaches that God has a book. It goes by a number of names. It is sometimes called the Book of Remembrance, containing the names of those who fear the Lord and think on His name. Sometimes it's simply called the Book. At other times it is referred to as the Lamb's Book of Life.

According to Revelation 20, one day at the Great White Throne judgment, the *books* (plural) will be opened, and the dead will be judged by the things written in the books. And then a Book (singular) will be opened, which is the Book of Life. And whoever's name is not found written in the Book of Life will be cast into the lake of fire (see verse 15).

No Christian will be present at the Great White Throne judgment; it is for nonbelievers only. At that time they will be judged out of the books.

But the big issue—in fact, the greatest question in your whole existence—is whether or not your name is written in the Book of Life. No matter what else you may experience or achieve in the course of your years on Earth, that is the question that will determine your destiny.

You might have your name written on a church register, which in the end really doesn't matter. What matters is whether your name is written on Heaven's register.

On one occasion in the Gospels, the disciples were elated and excited because they had been able to cast out demons by the power of God. Jesus, however, said to them, "Do not rejoice in this, that the spirits are subject to you, but rather rejoice because your names are written in heaven" (Luke 10:20).

I know that my name is written in the Lamb's Book of Life. When was it written there?

I have no idea.

Has it always been written there because God knew I would believe? Or was it penned into the pages on the day I received Christ as my Savior?

I don't know. I just know it's there.

In this passage, God promises the victorious Christian that He will not blot out his or her name. In fact, the statement "I will not blot your name" in the Greek language is a double negative. It's as though Jesus were saying, "I will never, by any means, blot out his name."

The believer who walks with God need not fear for his or her salvation. In fact, in this passage Jesus declares that He not only will refrain from blotting out the name of that believer, but He will speak it aloud—confess it—before God the Father and the angels of Heaven: "He who overcomes shall be clothed in white garments, and I will not blot out his name from the Book of Life; but I will confess his name before My Father and before His angels" (Revelation 3:5).

Jesus says, in effect, "I will stand up for you in Heaven."

In a related statement, Jesus said in Luke 12:8–9, "Also I say to you, whoever confesses Me before men, him the Son of Man also will confess before the angels of God. But he who denies Me before men will be denied before the angels of God."

Often not confessing Him can be a way of denying Him. Let me illustrate. Let's say you are in a conversation with a group of nonbelieving friends, and the talk turns for a moment to issues of life and death.

Someone says, "To tell you the truth, I don't even know if I believe there is a God."

And another says, "I certainly don't think there is a final judgment—or a Heaven or a Hell."

Everyone is weighing in with his or her opinions, and then they turn to you. They say, "What do *you* think?"

Let's imagine your response is something like this: "I really don't know. It's all so controversial. . . . I don't really like to get into politics or religion anyway."

May I be blunt with you? In effect, you just denied the Lord.

I'm not saying here that you have to insert the name of Jesus in every conversation or be obnoxious about it. But I am saying that when one of those divine setups happens, when a door suddenly opens and you have the opportunity to speak about your faith in Jesus Christ, you need to walk through that door. Confess Him before men, Jesus says, and He will confess you before the Father and the angels.

Is your name written in the Book of Life?

Does the thought of the sudden return of Jesus Christ to this Earth fill you with dread—or with joy and anticipation?

Maybe you have been tolerating known sin in your life. It began, perhaps, with "just a little compromise," but the Lord Jesus has shown you clearly that all your rationalizations won't stand before the One whose gaze penetrates like fire.

This chapter about two first-century churches, one dying and the other almost dead, may serve as a wake-up call.

If you have ears to hear, then listen to what the Lord of the church is saying to you right now.

THREE TAKEAWAY TRUTHS

- The moment you begin to neglect your growth in Christ is the moment you'll start to drift away from Him.
- Your attitude toward Christ's return speaks volumes about where you are spiritually.
- Jesus says that if you confess Him before men, He will confess you before the Father and the angels.

CHAPTER SIX

Jesus' Message to Last Days Believers

"I know your works. See, I have set before you an open door,
and no one can shut it; for you have a little strength,
have kept My word, and have not denied My name."
(Revelation 3:8)

IN THIS CHAPTER
- The church of Philadelphia is a picture of the last days church.
- Jesus had unqualified commendation for the church of Philadelphia.
- We are the generation that could see the return of Jesus Christ.
- Jesus is the One who opens and closes doors.

Think for a moment about the last time you went through an illness.

Remember those little telltale signs? Maybe there was a spot in your throat that suddenly began to feel a little sore. You started sniffling and maybe clearing your throat every couple of minutes. You began feeling a little lethargic and tired.

And then the realization hit: "Oh good grief, I'm getting sick."

Maybe you got a little worse and felt nauseated. Your head began to throb. You didn't want to eat or talk to anyone. You just wanted to lie there. So you were stuck in your bed or on the couch for a day . . . and then two days . . . and then three days. You began to wonder if you were ever going to get better.

Then one morning you woke up and your appetite had returned a little. You felt some strength returning to your body, so you jumped out of bed, showered, and got dressed. Maybe you went out to exercise or went back to work.

But it was too soon! Before long, you felt weak again, and your head began to throb. That's when you realized you were better than you had been, but you weren't back to full speed yet.

That is the picture of the church as Jesus sees it in the last days. It is not a super church; it's a church that has been sick but is returning to life. It is the church making a comeback, the church being revived. It is the church of the last days.

In Revelation 3, Jesus identified it as the church of Philadelphia.

HIGH MARKS

Jesus could not say enough nice things about this church. In contrast to His loving but firm words of correction to the churches of Pergamos, Thyatira, and Sardis, Jesus had unqualified commendation for the church of Philadelphia.

More than that, I believe that in Revelation 3:7–13 we have the words of Jesus to the last days church. In other words, us. I believe we are the generation that can indeed see the return of Jesus Christ. All the more reason to pay careful attention!

In our last message we looked at the church of Sardis that was on life support and nearly dead. But now suddenly we see signs of life. The church is springing back in a place called Philadelphia.

SIGNS OF LIFE

"And to the angel of the church in Philadelphia write,

'These things says He who is holy, He who is true, "He who has the key of David, He who opens and no one shuts, and shuts and no one opens": "I know your works. See, I have set before you an open door, and no one can shut it; for you have a little strength, have kept My word, and have not denied My name. Indeed I will make those of the synagogue of Satan, who say they are Jews and are not, but lie—indeed I will make them come and worship before your feet, and to know that I have loved you. Because you have kept My command to persevere, I also will keep you from the hour of trial which shall come upon the whole world, to test those who dwell on the earth. Behold, I am coming quickly! Hold fast what you have, that no one may take your crown. He who overcomes, I will make him a pillar in the temple of My God, and he shall go out no more. I will write on him the name of My God and the name of the city of My God, the New Jerusalem, which comes down out of heaven from My God. And I will write on him My new name.

"He who has an ear, let him hear what the Spirit says to the churches.""" (Revelation 3:7–13)

What does Jesus have to say to the church of the last days?

JESUS HAS GIVEN US AN UNPRECEDENTED OPEN DOOR

"He who opens and no one shuts, and shuts and no one opens."
(Revelation 3:7)

In the New Testament, the phrase *open door* usually refers to opportunity. In 2 Corinthians 2:12, for instance, the apostle Paul says, "When I came to Troas to preach Christ's gospel, . . . a door was opened to me by the Lord."

In Acts 14:27 when Paul and Barnabas gathered the Antioch church together to report on their missionary journeys, "they reported all that God had done with them, and that He had opened the door of faith to the Gentiles."

In the same way we should pray that the Lord would open such doors in our lives as well. In Colossians 4:3–4 the apostle specifically asks, "Pray for us, too, that God will give us many opportunities to speak about his mysterious plan concerning Christ. That is why I am here in chains. Pray that I will proclaim this message as clearly as I should" (NLT).

As we look at the unprecedented opportunities before us, we need to bring our A game and take all this very seriously. We make a big mistake if we rest on our laurels and become preoccupied with past opportunities and yesterday's victories.

I've had the opportunity to proclaim the gospel in large-scale evangelistic events since 1990 and more recently through our cinematic crusade, *A Rush of Hope*. And we have seen more than 600,000 professions of faith.

Even so, as we undertake these events each year, we never say, "It went well last year. We don't have to worry about this year." No! Every year should be like our first year, because it could easily end up being our last year.

Every opportunity should be taken seriously. Every open door should be treasured.

Often, I'm afraid, we believers end up thinking mostly about ourselves—our comforts, our desires, our goals—and not thinking about others, both in the body of Christ and outside the faith. We forget the fact that we are blessed to be a blessing.

Jesus was saying to the church of Philadelphia—and I believe to us today— "Listen . . . I have opened the door. I've got the keys."

Now *that* is a relief. (If I had them, they would be lost by now. I am always misplacing keys.)

Here's the point: Once a door is open, we need to walk through it, remembering that we are living at a critical time in human history. As Charles Dickens wrote in *A Tale of Two Cities,* "It was the best of times, it was the worst of times."

The same could be said for the twenty-first century. In some ways it certainly is the worst of times. I can't think of any era of our nation's history that has been darker morally and spiritually than right now. Things that were only hinted at just fifteen years ago are being enacted today by our national and state governments, right before our

GOOD TO KNOW

In the New Testament, the phrase *open door* usually refers to opportunity.

very eyes. There's no other way to describe it: our contemporary culture in the United States has grown very dark and is becoming even darker by the day.

On the other hand, it is the best of times because we have unprecedented opportunities to bring the gospel to our generation.

Let's think about the local application of the message of Christ to the church of Philadelphia. They were an actual, functioning church. The congregation

GOOD TO KNOW
We have unprecedented opportunities to bring the gospel to our generation.

wasn't a large one, and they certainly didn't have the fame and publicity of Sardis. However, though their numbers were small, their potential was great. At this particular time in history, a number of events and situations had lined up to enable this church to reach many people.

What were this church's advantages?

Pax Romana *was in place.*

Pax Romana refers to the "peace of Rome." It was an era of peace in the world that was enforced by the powerful Roman armies. This enabled the first-century Christians to go practically everywhere and preach.

The Greek language removed barriers.

Secondly, the Romans had established Greek as the official language of the empire. The Romans, though they had conquered Greece, had become enamored with all things Greek. They adopted their philosophies, their form of government, their gods, and even the beautiful and descriptive Greek language. As a result, that language went everywhere, removing barriers of understanding.

The Roman roads carried the gospel.

Over the years of their rule, Rome built a network of excellent roads across its empire, enabling the free flow of commerce, communication, and military power. But those same Roman roads all carried the gospel of Jesus Christ. Apostles, teachers, missionaries, and countless Christians traveled those highways, spreading the Good News across the known world.

Philadelphia became something of a gateway to the east, and that strategic geographic location enabled the believers in that city to reach many cultures and people groups.

Everything was in place for Philadelphia to have a huge impact for Christ. As Jesus had said, "See, I have set before you an open door."

And so it is with believers today, the church of what must surely be our world's last days. Through modern technology, we can accomplish things we never could have accomplished before. Television and the Internet have made the world a much smaller place, and in many ways we speak a common cultural language.

GOOD TO KNOW

When the Lord opens a door, it is very important that you go through it.

In recent years, our Harvest Crusades have had amazing international audiences through live views or viewings of archived versions.

Since the pandemic, we started an exclusively online service that we call *Harvest at Home,* which is viewed by 300,000 people on any given weekend. And literally thousands are coming to Christ as we extend an invitation to do so at the end of each message. In one year alone, we saw well over 100,000 professions of faith in Christ from people watching online.

God will open doors of opportunity for you personally as well, if you ask for them. Maybe there was something you always wanted to do that you have (to this point) never been able to do. Then suddenly a door opens to you from the Lord. *When that door opens, it is very important that you go through it.*

Sometimes we have plans that we've cherished for our lives. From ages seven to seventeen, my goal in life was to be a professional cartoonist. I had my own little world of cartoon characters and stories, and I was ready to go. In fact, some of my cartoons had already been published while I was still in my teens. I was corresponding with different cartoonists, including Charles M. Schulz, who wrote gracious letters to me and sought to encourage me. In a sense, I was locked into that goal, that passion. It's what I saw myself doing for the rest of my life.

Then, unexpectedly, I became a Christian at age seventeen.

"No problem," I thought to myself, "I'll just be a Christian cartoonist." And that's what I did for a time, working in graphic design and cartooning. Before long, however, I discovered that God had gifted me with an ability to share the gospel. Just that quickly, I had a new passion. Beginning on the streets, and then in front of groups of people, I would preach about salvation in Christ. Soon I was traveling with various Christian bands, bringing messages to even larger audiences.

Was God calling me to be an evangelist? I certainly thought so at the time.

In the early 1970s, I went to see Billy Graham preach at a crusade in San Diego. While I lived with my grandparents, I had seen Billy preach many times, watching him on the old black-and-white television with the rabbit ears antenna on top.

When I finally saw Billy preaching in person, I thought, "This is what I want to be. This is what I want to do."

Of course I never dreamed I would preach in a stadium to thousands of people like Billy Graham, but that's what I wanted—someway, somehow—to do with my life. I wanted to preach evangelistic messages to people.

But God closed the door on that desire at that particular time of my life, and He opened a door in another area that hadn't been in my thoughts and plans at all. In Riverside, California, He gave me the opportunity to start a Bible study for young people. As the study grew, some people started calling me "Pastor Greg"—though I tried to discourage them from that.

As time went on, however, I began to realize that God was indeed calling me to be a pastor. As a result, I set aside my aspirations to be an evangelist and accepted that God had called me in a different direction.

Twenty years later, God reopened the door to evangelistic crusades. We began to do our Harvest events in Southern California and have kept it up ever since.

That's the way it is with the Lord. Sometimes He will gently but firmly close a door in our lives—only to suddenly open it again at a time and place of His own choosing.

If you have recently experienced a closed door, remember this: God only closes one door to open another. Just because a door is closed right now doesn't mean it always will be closed. In fact, it might open at another time. So just be faithful with what the Lord has set before you right now. As Jim Elliot once said, "Wherever you are, *be all there*. Live to the hilt every situation you believe to be the will of God." [5]

Jesus is the One who opens and closes doors. In Revelation 3:7 we read, "These things says He who is holy, He who is true, 'He who has the key of David, He who opens and no one shuts, and shuts and no one opens.'"

When God opens a door, no one can shut it.

In Acts, chapter 12, we read the account of the apostle James being martyred by King Herod with the sword. Then Peter was arrested, and it looked like he was next up for Herod's executioner. The church, however, prayed passionately for his release.

GOOD TO KNOW

Just because a door is closed right now doesn't mean it always will be.

As the church prayed, God dispatched an angel to Peter's prison cell and the shackles fell off Peter's arms and legs. And then we read this:

> So Peter left the cell, following the angel. But all the time he thought it was a dream or vision and didn't believe it was really happening. They passed the first and second cell blocks and came to the iron gate to the street, and this opened to them of its own accord! So they passed through and walked along together for a block, and then the angel left him. (Acts 12:9–10 TLB)

I love that. The heavy iron gate leading to the street opened on its own. The angel didn't push on the gate. It just opened, and Peter and his heavenly escort walked right through.

Note that two things happened here: (1) the Lord opened the door, and (2) Peter walked through it.

There are some things that only God will do and some things that only we can do. God will open a door, but He isn't going to force us to walk through. He won't force us to say what we don't want to say or take advantage of opportunities that we refuse to grasp. The question is will we go through the open door and do what God has called us to do?

GOD HAS GIVEN US ENOUGH STRENGTH TO DO WHAT HE HAS CALLED US TO DO

In verse 8 of Revelation 3 He says to the church of Philadelphia, "You have a little strength." That wasn't a negative comment but a commendation of the church's strength. He was saying, in effect, "You guys are making a comeback. You're doing pretty well. So now listen to Me: you have all the power you need to do what I call you to do."

When Jesus gave the Great Commission, He said, "All authority has been given to Me in heaven and on earth. Go therefore and make disciples of all the nations" (Matthew 28:18–19). In Acts 1:8 He said, "You shall receive power when the Holy Spirit has come upon you; and you shall be witnesses to Me."

The divine authority is there. The power is there. And consider this: sometimes when you have "a little strength," you can be stronger. The fact of the matter is that sometimes when you have a little strength, you can do more than if you had much strength. Why? Because a gifted, confident, super-talented person might say, "God, I'm the person for the job. I've got all the skills and experience I need. So I ask that You go ahead and use me now."

And the Lord effectively replies, "I don't know. . . . I'll get back to you on that."

Then there is someone else who might pray, "Lord, I know that I don't bring a lot to the table, but I will go where You want me to go, and I will do what You want me to do."

And the Lord says, "I can work with that."

God delights to use men or women who see their weakness, see their inadequacy, and lean on Him for strength and wisdom. It's not that God can't use talented people, because He does. But the Bible tells us over and over again how God uses humble people who depend fully on Him rather than on themselves.

The apostle Paul had the unique experience of being caught up to Heaven and returning to Earth. Following that experience, the Lord sent Him a painful thorn in the flesh to keep him from becoming conceited and self-inflated. We don't know what that thorn actually was. It might have been some kind of physical infirmity that came as a result of one of his many beatings.

Whatever it was, it kept Paul humble and dependent.

Here is what he wrote about that to the church in Corinth: "Three different times I begged the Lord to take it away. Each time he said, 'My grace is all you need. My power works best in weakness.' So now I am glad to boast about my weaknesses, so that the power of Christ can work through me. That's why I take pleasure in my weaknesses, and in the insults, hardships, persecutions, and troubles that I suffer for Christ. For when I am weak, then I am strong" (2 Corinthians 12:8–10 NLT).

So here is the church of Philadelphia. It was not a super church but a church that was returning to life and strength and beginning to make an impact.

What more could we hope for than that? We've never been promised that Christianity will convert the whole world prior to the return of Christ. Even Jesus said, "When the Son of Man comes, will he find faith on the earth?" (Luke 18:8 NIV). But we know that operating in the power of the Holy Spirit, we will make an impact.

And so it was with the church at Philadelphia. They were making a comeback and getting back to their roots. They weren't as strong as they once were, but they found themselves standing before an open door. Maybe the church of Philadelphia didn't have the wealth and influence of Laodicea or the rich history and heritage of Sardis. But they had Jesus, and that was enough. They may have had little strength, but they were trusting in a great God. And that's an unbeatable combination.

GOOD TO KNOW

God uses humble people who depend fully on Him rather than on themselves.

THEY WERE KEEPING HIS WORD AND NOT DENYING HIS NAME

"You . . . have kept My word, and have not denied My name." (Revelation 3:8)

We're living in an era of our nation's history when many people don't know the first thing about the Word of God. The Bible, however, specifically warns that one of the signs of the end times will be a profusion of false teachers, false prophets, false apostles, and even those who work "lying wonders" (see 2 Thessalonians 2:9). In other words, if ever there was a time when we needed a better grip on the truths of the Bible, it is now.

Years ago C. S. Lewis gave this warning: "If you do not listen to Theology, that will not mean that you have no ideas about God. It will mean that you have a lot of wrong ones."[6] The awakened believer in the church of the last days not only keeps or guards God's Word but also spreads it. Some Christians treat the gospel like some people treat their four-wheel drives. They take them to the car wash regularly, accessorize them with all the latest gear, and protect them with the best antitheft devices. But they never actually do any off-roading in them. They wouldn't think of getting them dirty.

People treat the gospel the same way. They talk about the gospel, analyze the gospel, debate the gospel, get into arguments about the gospel, and defend the gospel. But the gospel wasn't meant to be locked away in a safe place; it was meant to be *used*. We need to preach the gospel and take it as far as we can.

Jesus commended the church of Philadelphia for guarding the faith, but He also told them, in effect, "You guys go through that open door of opportunity I have set before you. Don't miss that."

Jesus also said, "Freely you have received, freely give" (Matthew 10:8). What God has been so faithful to give us, we must be faithful to give out to others.

But please take note of this: if we are keeping His Word and guarding it and proclaiming it as we go through open doors of opportunity, we can expect to face opposition.

WHEN WE KEEP AND PROCLAIM HIS WORD, THE DEVIL WILL OPPOSE US

"Indeed I will make those of the synagogue of Satan, who say they are Jews and are not, but lie—indeed I will make them come and worship before your feet, and to know that I have loved you." (Revelation 3:9)

Satanic opposition is confirmation that you are on the right track. Spiritual opportunities are always met with opposition and obstacles. Wherever God has His church, Satan has his chapels and synagogues.

This phrase *the synagogue of Satan* is used twice in Christ's message to the seven churches, once in His letter to Smyrna, the suffering church, and again in this message to Philadelphia. It's also worthy to note that these were the only two churches out of the seven that the Lord commended. This reminds us that when we are on the right track and pursuing the Word of God, the Devil always will rise up to oppose us.

GOOD TO KNOW

Satanic opposition is confirmation that you are on the right track.

It's also interesting to note that the opposition came from religious people. It was that way for the apostle Paul as well. Some of his most ardent critics and enemies were religious Jews. They weren't true Jews honoring the God of Abraham, Isaac, and Jacob; they were blinded by their religion and became bigoted, mean, hateful, and destructive.

Yes, religion can do that.

I never try to defend "religion." As a follower of Jesus Christ, I don't consider myself "religious." There is a big difference between what the world regards as religion and a true and living faith in God through Christ.

Be very careful about criticizing or opposing those who preach the gospel. If you do, you will find yourself on the wrong side of the debate. There always will be critics of those who proclaim Christ, and sometimes those critics will come from within the church—or perhaps the so-called church. Are they true Christians? I don't know. That's up to God to decide. But here is what I do know: whenever I am doing the work of God, there will be opposition. And if there *isn't* opposition, I begin to wonder if I'm doing something wrong.

I know very well that if we're really on the right track, there will be an outcry against what we're doing. The criticism, the cynicism, and the opposition will surely come. It is a confirmation that we are doing the work of God.

But here is the problem. If we go on and on with an in-house debate about how and when to share the gospel, we may very well miss open doors of opportunity. Vance Havner used to say that if we don't stop using our sickles on one another, we're going to miss the harvest.

In Luke 10:2 Jesus said, "The harvest truly is great, but the laborers are few." And I might add this: the harvest truly is great, and the critics are many. The harvest truly is great, and the observers are many. But the actual laborers, those who are truly doing the work, are few.

JESUS PROMISED TO KEEP US FROM THE GREAT TRIBULATION

"I also will keep you from the hour of trial which shall come upon the whole world, to test those who dwell on the earth." (Revelation 3:10)

As followers of Christ, we certainly will have our share of trials, tribulations, and even tragedies. But there is a difference between those and what the world will face in the Tribulation. The essence of the Lord's message to the church living in the last days is twofold: "I come quickly" and "I will keep you from the hour of trial."

For two reasons, I believe verse 10 refers to the seven-year time span we call the Great Tribulation. First, Jesus said it will come upon "the whole world." In other words, it will be a global event. Second, Jesus called it "the hour of trial." It is a trial that will last for a specific period of time: seven years.

It is my belief that this Tribulation period can't even begin until the church is caught up to meet the Lord in the air at the event we know as the Rapture. Why do I believe that? Because 2 Thessalonians 2:6–8 says,

And now you know what is restraining, that he may be revealed in his own time. For the mystery of lawlessness is already at work; only He who now restrains will do so until He is taken out of the way. And then the lawless one will be revealed, whom the Lord will consume with the breath of His mouth and destroy with the brightness of His coming.

These verses tell us that right now, the restraining force in the world is the Holy Spirit, working through the church of Jesus Christ. True Christians will stand up for what is right and speak up about what is wrong. It is Spirit-filled Christians who are restraining the evil in our world. But once we are caught up to meet the Lord in the air, that restraint will be removed, and the Antichrist will emerge on the world scene.

Some suggest that the Holy Spirit Himself will be removed from the world at this time, but I disagree with that point of view. Why? Because people will come to Christ during the Great Tribulation—millions of them. In fact, there will be a great revival. This tells me that the Holy Spirit still will be at work, drawing people to faith in Jesus Christ.

GOOD TO KNOW

It is Spirit-filled Christians who are restraining the evil in our world.

I don't think we should be wasting our time speculating about the Antichrist or watching for his appearance. Instead, we should be focusing on Jesus as we await His return.

Jesus said, "I will keep you from this hour." And the Greek word translated "keep" means "to keep from" or "to keep out of." Because genuine believers have persevered and kept His Word, Jesus promised to keep them from the specific time when God will pour out His wrath on the world.

We use the word *rapture* to describe the moment when Jesus instantly will draw all believers out of this world to meet Him in the air. Some have said, "The word *rapture* isn't even in the Bible." Perhaps not. But the event is certainly in the Bible. Jesus will remove His bride, the church, before that great judgment begins.

The fact is that you can't find a single instance in the Scriptures where God pours out His judgment on believers and nonbelievers alike. The book of 2 Peter specifically points out that God spared Noah and his family and saw them safely inside the ark before the judgment came. As the rain came down, the ark went up. It was the same when Abraham's nephew Lot was rescued from Sodom and Gomorrah with his family. God would not let His wrath rain down on those evil cities until Lot and his family were taken out and put on the road to safety. (Read that whole dramatic account in Genesis 19.)

Then Peter goes on to say in 2 Peter 2:9, "The Lord knows how to deliver the godly out of temptations and to reserve the unjust under punishment for the day of judgment." And then in 1 Thessalonians 5:9 we read, "For God did not appoint us to suffer wrath but to receive salvation through our Lord Jesus Christ" (NIV).

If you are a Christian, then you will be caught up to meet the Lord before this period begins. If you are not a Christian, then you will be left on Earth to face the Great Tribulation.

And trust me on this. You don't want to be around for that.

LAST DAYS BELIEVERS NEED TO HOLD THEIR COURSE

"Behold, I am coming quickly! Hold fast what you have, that no one may take your crown." (Revelation 3:11)

Because of the imminent return of Jesus for His church, believers must hold fast. A true believer will be a faithful believer. Colossians 1:22–23 says that God "has reconciled you to himself through the death of Christ in his physical body. As a result, he has brought you into his own presence, and you are holy and blameless as you stand before him without a single fault. But you must continue to believe this truth and stand firmly in it. Don't drift away from the assurance you received when you heard the Good News" (NLT).

Hold your course. Don't drift away.

Why is that important? Because the Bible warns that in the end times, there will be an apostasy, or a falling away. The Bible says, "the Holy Spirit tells us clearly that in the last times some will turn away from the true faith; they will follow deceptive spirits and teachings that come from demons" (1 Timothy 4:1 NLT). But if I will hold my course and keep the faith, God makes this promise to me: no one will take my crown.

Take my crown? What crown? What does that even mean? Most of us don't walk around

GOOD TO KNOW

When the New Testament speaks of crowns, it is speaking of rewards.

wearing crowns . . . unless you happen to be a little girl. My experience with granddaughters has taught me that all little girls want to be princesses with crowns and sparkly scepters. What is it with that? I think it's in their DNA.

When the New Testament speaks of crowns, however, it is speaking of rewards. Remember what Paul wrote in the last days of his life?

> I have fought the good fight, I have finished the race, I have kept the faith. Now there is in store for me the crown of righteousness, which the Lord, the righteous Judge, will award to me on that day—and not only to me, but also to all who have longed for his appearing. (2 Timothy 4:7–8 NIV)

That is just one of the many biblical references to a crown or heavenly reward.

After the Rapture and before the Second Coming—when we are in Heaven during those seven, dreadful years on Earth—there will be judgment. This isn't the Great White Throne judgment we read about in Revelation 20. That judgment will be for nonbelievers only. Before that happens, there will be a judgment for believers, when eternal rewards are given out. You almost could call it a celestial rewards ceremony. Paul explains it like this:

> But on the judgment day, fire will reveal what kind of work each builder has done. The fire will show if a person's work has any value. If the work survives, that builder will receive a reward. But if the work is burned up, the builder will suffer great loss. The builder will be saved, but like someone barely escaping through a wall of flames. (1 Corinthians 3:13–15 NLT)

Tragically, some will have little to show for their lives and their years on Earth, while others will have a great deal to show. Doesn't that make you want to redouble your efforts to glorify God with the time that you have on this Earth?

You might say, "Well, Greg, I don't really care about all of that reward business. All I care about is getting to Heaven."

Really? On that day when I stand before Jesus, I would like to have something to show for the life that He entrusted to me. Not that I could ever pay Jesus back for all He's done for me. I couldn't do that in a trillion years. Nor could you. But I'd like to be able to say, "Lord, You were so good to me through the years of my life. Here are just a few things that You enabled me to do for you, and I hope You are pleased. I wanted people to know about You. I wanted to walk through those open doors of opportunity that You set before me."

> **GOOD TO KNOW**
> It is possible to have a saved soul and a lost life.

Did you know that it is possible to have a saved soul and a lost life? Yes, you gain Heaven through the grace of Jesus Christ and by His blood that was shed for you. But what do you have to show for the years that He gave you? What do you have to show for the talents and gifts and opportunities that He entrusted to you?

Jesus closed with these words in Revelation 3:13: "He who has an ear, let him hear what the Spirit says to the churches."

The Greek language puts this verse in the present tense, which means that you could translate it like this: "Here is what the Spirit is saying *today*." These words are more current than tomorrow's newspaper.

They are from God to you. Right now.

He is saying, "I want you to hear this. I want you to do this. I want you to be faithful to Me. I want you to keep My Word. I want you to proclaim My Word. I want you to go through those open doors of opportunity and hold to your course. I want you to show faithfulness to Me, and as you do, I will keep you from the hour of tribulation coming upon the earth."

THREE TAKEAWAY TRUTHS

- We make a big mistake if we rest on our laurels and become preoccupied with past opportunities and yesterday's victories.
- Spiritual opportunities are always met with opposition and obstacles.
- Jesus wants us to go through open doors of opportunity and hold our course.

CHAPTER SEVEN

The Church That Made Jesus Sick

*"I know your works, that you are neither cold nor hot. I could wish
you were cold or hot. So then, because you are lukewarm, and
neither cold nor hot, I will vomit you out of My mouth."*
(Revelation 3:15–16)

IN THIS CHAPTER
- The seven churches of Revelation were actual churches in actual places.
- Laodicea was a prosperous city, known for its commercial life.
- Lukewarmness makes Jesus sick.
- God disciplines those whom He loves.
- Jesus stands and knocks at the door of our lives.

Most things that we eat are generally good when they're hot or cold. There are very few that you would serve lukewarm. Coffee and tea, for example, are great when they're hot. And both are delicious when they're icy cold. Milk is the same way. And then there's fish. I like it hot off the grill. I also love sushi, which is cold.

But who wants to eat room-temperature sushi that's gone mushy or a grilled filet that's cooled off? And who prefers barely warm coffee, tepid tea, or lukewarm milk? It's almost enough to make you sick.

Lukewarmness makes Jesus sick, too. In fact, it's enough to make Him want to throw up. That's how the church of Laodicea made Him feel, and we're about to find out why.

We've been looking at the messages of Christ to the seven churches of Revelation, which were actual churches. But they also represent states of the

Christian life. They represent certain churches that are around today. And they might even represent individual Christians.

Jesus began by addressing the church of Ephesus, the church that was leaving its first love (2:1–7). He commended this church for their hard work and their discernment. But a problem was developing. They were in danger of leaving their first love. This is where the breakdown began that was fully realized in the six other churches. To the church of Ephesus Jesus said, "Remember therefore from where you have fallen; repent and do the first works" (verse 5).

With these words, Jesus gave us the three Rs of getting right with Him: remember, repent, and repeat.

Next was the church of Smyrna, the persecuted church (2:8–11). Jesus brought words of encouragement to this church as they suffered persecution for their faith. He didn't have any critical words for the church of Smyrna. Rather, He promised them a crown for their faithfulness.

If you're suffering for your faith, Jesus promises that you, too, will be blessed. You will receive a reward.

The third church was Pergamos, the compromising church (2:12–17). I think the Devil operates by the old adage that says, "If you can't beat them, join them." In a sense, Satan joined the church of Pergamos. This was a church that he had infiltrated. We need to know that the Devil is evil, but he isn't stupid. He's been honing his craft for a long time. The church of Pergamos was compromising and turning to sin.

That brings us to the fourth church, the church of Thyatira (2:18–29). We could call this the corrupt church, because compromise had run its full course and immorality was rampant. What was winked at in the church of Pergamos was fully tolerated and in many ways, embraced, in the church of Thyatira.

That's always how sin works. It starts small and then gets big. It starts with a little issue and then metastasizes and spreads through the system like cancer, showing itself in so many ways. Jesus warned the church of Thyatira that if they didn't repent, they would go through the Tribulation period.

Then we come to the church of Sardis, the dead church (Revelation 3:1–6). That which was sick in Thyatira was pretty much dead in Sardis. But out of this came two streams: the church of Philadelphia and the church of Laodicea.

Philadelphia was going through open doors of opportunity. They were coming back to life. The church of Philadelphia was full of passion and fire.

Finally we have Laodicea, the seventh of the seven churches. Laodicea was in full compromise. In fact, this church was so messed up that Jesus was on the outside, trying to get back in. And it's to this church that Jesus actually says, in so many words, "You make me sick."

LAODICEA...THE LUKEWARM CHURCH

"And to the angel of the church of the Laodiceans write,

'These things says the Amen, the Faithful and True Witness, the Beginning of the creation of God: "I know your works, that you are neither cold nor hot. I could wish you were cold or hot. So then, because you are lukewarm, and neither cold nor hot, I will vomit you out of My mouth. Because you say, 'I am rich, have become wealthy, and have need of nothing'—and do not know that you are wretched, miserable, poor, blind, and naked—I counsel you to buy from Me gold refined in the fire, that you may be rich; and white garments, that you may be clothed, that the shame of your nakedness may not be revealed; and anoint your eyes with eye salve, that you may see. As many as I love, I rebuke and chasten. Therefore be zealous and repent. Behold, I stand at the door and knock. If anyone hears My voice and opens the door, I will come in to him and dine with him, and he with Me. To him who overcomes I will grant to sit with Me on My throne, as I also overcame and sat down with My Father on His throne.

"He who has an ear, let him hear what the Spirit says to the churches."'" (3:14–22)

Some churches make Jesus sad. Some churches make Jesus angry. And some churches make Him sick. This is one of those.

Laodicea was a thriving commercial center.

Laodicea was an actual place with an actual church. As the banking center of Asia, the city was noted throughout the Roman province of Asia for its great wealth and commercial life. Laodicea was the most prosperous of the seven cities in which the seven churches of Revelation were located. In fact, the ruins of many of the large, beautiful homes in Laodicea are still visible today in some cases. Some of them even may have been owned by Christians.

GOOD TO KNOW

Laodicea was an actual place with an actual church.

The city also had a flourishing clothing industry. A particular breed of sheep was raised in the area, and clothes made from the animals' glossy black wool were sold exclusively in Laodicea.

It also was known for its medical practice and specifically for eye salve, which was exported throughout the Greco-Roman world.

So Laodicea would have been a desirable destination for many people. It was sort of like having the corporate headquarters for the Bank of America, Gucci, and the Mayo Clinic all in one location.

The church of Laodicea was blind to its spiritual condition.

Jesus, however, had some tough words for this church. He was saying, "I'd rather you be hot. I'd rather you be cold. But if you're lukewarm, it turns my stomach."

That's a pretty harsh thing to say.

You might tell someone, "You broke my heart" or "I'm really upset with you." But if you say, "When I see you, I want to vomit," does it get any worse than that?

Yet that is exactly what Jesus is saying.

While the church of Sardis was a cold, dead church and the church of Philadelphia was hot, alive, and vital, the church of Laodicea was neither cold nor hot. It was merely lukewarm.

By the way, archaeologists have discovered a fascinating fact about this city. They didn't have a local water supply, so the city obtained water through an aqueduct from the hot springs at Hierapolis, some six miles away.

If you were staying in a hotel in Laodicea and turned on the tap to get a cold drink of water, you'd probably spit it out because it was lukewarm. From traveling that distance, the hot water would partially cool down, becoming nauseating and repulsive.

GOOD TO KNOW

Lukewarm people are blind to their own spiritual condition.

Lukewarm people are often the last to know they are lukewarm. Notice what Jesus says in verse 17: "You say, 'I am rich. I have everything I want. I don't need a thing!' And you don't realize that you are wretched and miserable and poor and blind and naked" (NLT).

They think they are good, but they are blind to their own spiritual condition. They can't even see their own spiritual state.

One of Hans Christian Andersen's most well-known stories, "The Emperor's New Clothes," is about a prideful emperor whose main concern was his wardrobe. So he hired two weavers who claimed they made beautiful cloth that was only visible to those who were fit for the office they held or to those with good character.

But in reality, these guys were slackers. They only pretended to do the job. When the emperor wanted to check on their progress, he obviously didn't want to risk being embarrassed if he couldn't actually see the cloth. So one by one, he sent some of his officials to see how the work was going.

However, none of them wanted to admit they couldn't see it, which would mean they were unfit for their offices. So each of them pretended they could see the weavers' cloth, and they brought back glowing reports to the emperor.

Eventually the day came for the emperor himself to see the beautiful fabric the weavers had made. The imposters pretended they were holding up garments when they actually were holding nothing at all. And to make matters worse, the officials feigned admiration for the invisible clothing. The emperor, embarrassed that he was the only one who couldn't see what the weavers had done, acted as though he could see it too. Then he commissioned them to make him a new suit from the fabric, which he would wear in a procession through the capital city.

On the day of the procession, the king walked out of the palace completely naked, thinking that he was in a beautiful garment. As he walked through his kingdom, all the people bowed before him, not wanting to state the obvious. The only exception was a child who pointed to him and said, "But the Emperor has nothing at all on!" [7]

Finally the emperor realized that he had been deceived.

The lukewarm church of Laodicea was like that emperor. They were saying, "I'm rich. I have everything I want. I don't need a thing!"

But Jesus says, in effect, "Actually, you're in big trouble. You have the shame of your own nakedness." Then He tells them to buy gold refined in the fire. He's saying, "Think about your souls. Think about your spiritual life."

Jesus said these things because He loved this church. Look at His words in verse 19: "I correct and discipline everyone I love" (NLT).

God's discipline is motivated by love.

There are a lot of ways we can express our love. The most obvious is saying, "I love you." By the way, don't forget to say that to your husband or wife, your mom or dad, or your son or daughter. Just tell them that you love them. It means a lot.

But there are other ways to show love too. If someone I love was running toward the street and a car was headed their way, I might yell at them to stop or even grab them and yank them back. That might seem a little abrupt. But that is love, too, because I'm trying to protect them from harm.

Or, if I see someone doing something that's self-destructive, I might bring it to their attention and hopefully convince them to stop what they're doing. That, too, is a form of love.

If you're a parent, you don't just indulge your children and give them whatever they want, do you? (That's the job of a grandparent.) As a parent, you have to be responsible. You teach your children manners and how to have respect. And when they do something wrong, you may even discipline them.

God does the same thing. The writer of Hebrews tells us, "'For the Lord disciplines those he loves, and he punishes each one he accepts as his child.' As you endure this divine discipline, remember that God is treating you as his own children" (verses 6–7 NLT).

The passage goes on to say, "If God doesn't discipline you as he does all of his children, it means that you are illegitimate and are not really his children at all" (verse 8 NLT).

You only discipline your own children. You don't discipline someone else's children, though at times you'd probably like to.

And if you are a child of God, then He will discipline you too. Let me explain. If you're a Christian, then God has given you a conscience, and the Holy Spirit will speak to you through that conscience. When you start to do something wrong, the Lord will say, "Don't do that" or "Apologize for that" or "Don't cross that line." He is there helping you, because He deals with the ones He loves in that way.

On the other hand, if you say that you're a Christian, but you can do things like go out and party, get drunk with your friends, and have sex with your boyfriend or girlfriend without remorse, it tells me something. It says to me that you're not a Christian.

Of course, I can't say who is or who isn't a Christian. But I will say this. If someone can live in sin without any pang of conscience, it indicates to me that he or she isn't a Christian. If you're without discipline, then you're a fatherless child. God doesn't discipline someone who doesn't belong to Him. But He does discipline those whom He loves.

I love how David wrote of the Lord in Psalm 23, "Your rod and your staff protect and comfort me" (verse 4 NLT).

So if you were to tell me, "Greg, every time I cross the line, every time I start to compromise, the Lord really convicts me," that is a good thing. God just said, in so many words, that He loves you.

He also loved the church of Laodicea. That is why He told them the truth about their real condition.

GOOD TO KNOW

If you are a child of God, then He will discipline you.

WHAT'S YOUR TEMPERATURE?

We have an overly sensitive smoke alarm in our house, which I've had to pull off the wall a couple of times. But I keep putting it back, because I know that it's better to have an overly sensitive smoke alarm than one that doesn't work.

Like my smoke alarm, if your conscience is sensitive and responsive, then that is a very good thing.

So here's my question for you: What is your spiritual temperature right now?

According to the Bible, there are only three options. You can be boiling hot. You can be icy cold. Or, you can be miserably lukewarm.

Hot

The word *hot* Jesus used in verses 15 and 16 comes from the Greek word *zestos*, which means "boiling hot." The Bible tells us in Romans 12:11 to be "fervent," or hot, in spirit. *The Message* puts it this way: "Don't burn out; keep yourselves fueled and aflame."

Acts 18:25 describes a preacher named Apollos as "being fervent in spirit."

The apostle Paul reminded Timothy to "to fan into flames the spiritual gift God gave you" (2 Timothy 1:6 NLT). And that's what we should do when we're starting to cool down spiritually.

If you have a fire at home that you build with actual logs, you feed the fire to keep it going. The same is true of our spiritual lives. When we find ourselves cooling down, we need to fan the flames and feed the fire. We do that by hearing the Word of God. When you attend church on the weekend or are in a Bible study small group, you're feeding the fire. When you open up the Word of God every morning, you're feeding the fire. And when you listen to music that honors the Lord and have fellowship with other Christians, you're feeding the fire.

You may remember the story of the two discouraged disciples on the road to Emmaus after Jesus had been crucified. They thought He was dead and gone forever. But of course He was alive, and He joined them on the road incognito. They just thought He was a stranger, but He happened to be a stranger who knew the Word of God very well.

As they walked along, Luke's Gospel tells us that "Jesus took them through the writings of Moses and all the prophets, explaining from all the Scriptures the things concerning himself" (24:27 NLT).

At the end of their journey, they said, "Didn't our hearts burn within us as he talked with us on the road and explained the Scriptures to us?" (verse 32 NLT).

If you want to keep your heart hot and stay on fire for God, then fill it with the Word of God every day and night.

Cold

The second spiritual temperature Jesus mentions is cold. He says to the Christians in Laodicea, "I know all the things you do, that you are neither hot nor cold. I wish that you were one or the other!" (Revelation 3:15 NLT).

Cold is pretty much the spiritual temperature of nonbelievers who have no interest in God. They're as cold as ice. Their heart is like a rock, and they have no interest in spiritual things. They don't want to hear about what Jesus has to say.

In fact, the Bible tells that one of the signs of the last days is that "sin will be rampant everywhere, and the love of many will grow cold" (Matthew 24:12 NLT).

Believe it or not, it's better to be cold than it is to be lukewarm. We might think that lukewarm isn't as good as hot, but it's better than cold.

No, it actually isn't.

The British theologian G. Campbell Morgan wrote, "There is more hope of the man outside the church . . . than for the man within the church who is near enough to its warmth not to appreciate it, and far enough away from its burning heat to be useless to God and man. [There is a] greater chance for the heathen who has not heard the Gospel than for the man who has become an evangelized heathen."[8]

There could be someone sitting in a bar right now, nursing their fourth beer, feeling miserable and without any sense of direction in life. I suggest that person potentially could be closer to the kingdom of God than someone who's sitting in church.

GOOD TO KNOW

Believe it or not, it's better to be cold than it is to be lukewarm.

Understand, I'm not saying that we should start going out to the bar for beer after church. Here's what I am saying. Someone at a bar could be looking at their life, assessing it, and thinking, "I hate my life. I've made so many bad decisions. I need to do something drastic. I need to get right with God."

Although their spiritual temperature is cold, they're at least contemplating their current state.

Lukewarm

On the other hand, there can be someone sitting in a church service who's completely bored. They're checking their social media or texting a friend or just daydreaming. Maybe they're at church because someone pressured them to go. But they're just looking forward to getting it over with.

Here's the problem: they're evangelized nonbelievers.

They might be thinking, "I go to church. I'm good."

Maybe—if they're listening and putting into practice what they're hearing. But if they're going to church and not putting what they hear into practice, they can turn lukewarm.

Someone might say, "Greg, I'm a Christian, but I don't want to be perceived as fanatical. I don't want to make anyone uncomfortable with what I believe. I don't want to come off too extreme or overboard."

Do you know what Jesus' reaction is to that kind of thinking?

It makes Him sick. Remember, He said, "But since you are like lukewarm water, neither hot nor cold, I will spit you out of my mouth!" (Revelation 3:16 NLT).

Jesus didn't say that He wants us to be crazy or fanatical. But He does want us to be on fire and committed. You can do that in a relatively sane way. You can become a very dedicated person—a very committed person—without making it weird.

So don't disconnect and say, "Well, that is some church that existed two thousand years ago." Not only can there be a lukewarm church, as we saw from this passage, but there can be lukewarm individuals as well.

THE REMEDY

Here's the remedy Jesus prescribed for the church of Laodicea: "Therefore be zealous and repent" (verse 19 NLT). This could be literally translated, "Let them repent at once and irrevocably. Let them continue always to be fired with zeal."

If you're living in two worlds, if you're doing things that a Christian should not do and have no remorse, here's what God is saying to you: Quickly repent.

Why quickly? Why not repent in a week or a month?

Do it immediately, because if you're lukewarm spiritually, then you're seriously ill and need to take action *now*. If you continue in this state, you could get an irreparably hardened heart.

Hebrews 3:12–13, addressed to believers, warns about this: "Be careful then, dear brothers and sisters. Make sure that your own hearts are not evil and unbelieving, turning you away from the living God. You must warn each other every day, while it is still 'today,' so that none of you will be deceived by sin and hardened against God" (NLT).

The idea is to act on this right away.

When Jesus knocks, you need to answer.

Let's not forget that contextually, Jesus was speaking to people in the church when He said in verse 20, "Behold, I stand at the door and knock. If anyone hears My voice and opens the door, I will come in to him and dine with him, and he with Me."

However, there's nothing wrong with quoting this to nonbelievers, either. I do it all the time.

In the first century, dinner was a big event. They didn't come home and watch Netflix. They didn't play video games or constantly check their smartphones. The big event was being with family and friends.

So when Jesus said, "I will come in to him and dine with him, and he with Me," He was saying, "I want to take time with you. I want to hang out with you. I want to have long moments with you. I want you to open your heart to me. And I'm going to open my heart to you."

In our fast-food culture, we don't do this like other generations did. We're in a rush. We often eat our food on the go. So the idea of a long meal might be lost on us. But that was the culture of the time.

The Bible tells us, "But as many as received Him, to them He gave the right to become children of God, to those who believe in His name" (John 1:12). When you become a Christian, you really do invite Jesus to come into your life.

He really does come and live inside you.

I heard about a mother who was explaining to her daughter that Jesus comes and lives in our hearts. So the little girl put her ear up against her mother's chest and listened carefully. Then she looked up and said, "Mom, right now I think He's in there making coffee."

So yes, Jesus lives inside every Christian, but every Christian needs to enter into deeper fellowship with Him.

Would Jesus feel at home in your heart?

Let's imagine for a moment that you're about to enjoy a late-night snack when you hear a knock at your door. You look to see who it is, and you realize it's Jesus. But you don't necessarily want to be interrupted at the moment. And you really don't want to share your snack. So you just go back to what you were doing. How do you think Jesus would react to that?

I hope that instead you would run to the door, open it, and pull Him in.

But some people might leave the door closed.

Think about how Jesus spent time with His disciples. They would have meals together, and He shared important truths with them over those meals.

Jesus is saying, "That is what I want. I want to come in and have fellowship with you."

The apostle Paul prayed for the Christians in Ephesus "that Christ may dwell in [their] hearts through faith" (3:17). The word *dwell* in the original language is a compound word that basically means to live in a house. So Paul was saying, "I pray that Christ is at home in your heart—not just as a guest but as a person who lives in that place."

Do you think that Jesus is at home in your heart right now?

In his book *My Heart—Christ's Home*, Robert Boyd Munger illustrates this idea with a fictional story of Christ coming to his actual house. As Jesus walked in and looked around at the pictures on the wall and the books and magazines in the room, the author writes, "As I followed his gaze, I became uncomfortable. Strangely enough, I had not felt badly about this room before, but now I was embarrassed."[9]

Let's go back to the idea of Jesus actually showing up at your house. But this time you let Him in. Would you feel uncomfortable if Jesus knew your browsing history or what movies you've been watching? Would that bother you? If so, maybe you should rethink those things. That is the idea of Christ being at home in your heart. He's the Lord there. He is ruling there, and you're having fellowship with Him. He's welcome there.

GOOD TO KNOW

To not say yes to Jesus is to say no.

That wouldn't describe the heart of someone who is lukewarm. They don't want Jesus in their lives in that kind of way.

When Jesus is knocking and we don't answer, that is our way of saying, "Go away." The problem is that people think Jesus always will be knocking. They think there always will be that opportunity.

Maybe.

Or maybe death will come suddenly, and they won't even have a moment to get right with God.

Maybe their heart will get so hard by saying no to Him again and again that they just won't care anymore.

You don't want that to happen.

Before I became a Christian at age 17, there were moments in my life when Jesus was knocking. I can remember certain experiences from my childhood when I sensed God and my need for Him. But I didn't know how to get into a relationship with Him until someone explained it to me.

Maybe you can look back on your life and think of times like that. Maybe it was a close brush with death or the unexpected death of a loved one that was a wake-up call of sorts. Maybe you heard the gospel and came close to committing your life to Jesus Christ, but you didn't take that next step.

Jesus gives this promise to those who quickly repent and open their hearts to Him: "To him who overcomes I will grant to sit with Me on My throne, as I also overcame and sat down with My Father on His throne" (3:21).

In the Scriptures a throne is a symbol of authority and conquest. As Christ conquered the world and the Devil and was exalted at the Father's right hand, so, too, will the conquering Christian be honored. As Christ shares God the Father's throne, the Christian will share Christ's throne.

I don't know what this means exactly. But I do know that after those of us who have put our faith in Jesus Christ leave this world and go to Heaven, one day Heaven will come to Earth. The Bible says that we who have served the Lord will rule and reign with Him. We'll have responsibilities. And we'll also receive rewards for our faithful service to Him. It's an amazing thing to know that as we allow Christ to rule in our lives now, He will allow us to rule with Him someday.

But right now, this is your moment to get right with God.

Is Jesus standing on the outside of your life, trying to get in?

To not say yes to Him is to say no. To not invite Jesus in is to turn Him away.

So what do you want to do? Would you like Him to come in and forgive you of your sin? Would you like Him to take residence inside of you?

Then you need to open the door of your heart. And by the way, you can only open it from the inside. That means Jesus won't kick it in. He won't forcibly enter. No, He will wait until you hear His voice and open the door.

Only you can do this. Only you can invite Jesus in. And He will come in. He will get rid of the junk that you don't want in your life, and He will replace it with things that are far better.

But best of all, He will live inside of you and make His home with you. You never will be alone again. And you never will regret that decision.

THREE TAKEAWAY TRUTHS

- When you're spiritually lukewarm, often you're the last to know it.
- If God disciplines you, it's because you're His child and He loves you.
- Jesus wants to enter into fellowship with you, but you must invite Him in.

Part Three

THE THINGS THAT WILL TAKE PLACE AFTER THIS

CHAPTER EIGHT
What Heaven Will Be Like

After these things I looked, and behold, a door standing open in heaven. And the first voice which I heard was like a trumpet speaking with me, saying, "Come up here, and I will show you things which must take place after this."
(Revelation 4:1)

IN THIS CHAPTER
- Why the rapture of the church is a source of hope for all believers.
- The Rapture is separate and distinct from the Second Coming.
- What John saw in the third heaven
- Heaven is aware of events that transpire on Earth.
- How God calls believers to live in expectation of His return

Years ago on the opening night of one of his crusades in a certain city, Billy Graham was walking the streets, looking for a post office where he could mail a letter to a friend.

He saw a young boy standing on a street corner and approached him.

"I was wondering," he said, "if you could tell me where the post office is?"

The boy pointed it out. "It's right over there, sir."

Billy thanked him and thought it would be a good opportunity to invite this boy to that night's crusade. "I hope you will come to the stadium tonight," he said, "and I will tell you how you can find your way to Heaven."

The little boy looked at him for a moment and said, "How would you know the way to Heaven? You don't even know the way to the post office!"

I don't know whether that story is true or not, but it makes a point.

If we belong to Jesus Christ, we can be sure of this: one day we will make our departure to Heaven in one of two ways. It will be by death, or it will be when the Lord Jesus comes for His church at the Rapture.

REVELATION: A BOOK OF PROMISES

Revelation 4 gives us a picture of that great event. The third chapter of Revelation ended with a closed door. Jesus stood outside the church of Laodicea, trying to get in: "Behold, I stand at the door and knock. If anyone hears My voice and opens the door, I will come in to him" (verse 20).

The fourth chapter, however, begins with a door *opening*.

And it opens right into Heaven itself.

"AFTER THESE THINGS"

> After these things I looked, and behold, a door standing open in heaven. And the first voice which I heard was like a trumpet speaking with me, saying, "Come up here, and I will show you things which must take place after this."
>
> Immediately I was in the Spirit; and behold, a throne set in heaven, and One sat on the throne. (Revelation 4:1–2)

John begins his words in verse 1 with the phrase *after these things*.

The natural question, then, is after *what* things?

As we have already discovered, the book of Revelation is unique in that it comes with its own outline. In Revelation 1:19, Jesus told John to write:

- the things you have seen (Revelation 1),

- the things that are (Revelation 2–3), and

- the things that will take place after this (Revelation 4–22).

In the first section, John saw the resurrected and glorified Christ, with all power and authority in Heaven and Earth ("the things you have seen").

In the second section, we saw the messages of Jesus to the seven churches in Asia, obtaining at the same time a flyover of church history ("the things which are").

Beginning with Revelation 4, we enter into the third section of the book ("the things which will take place after this").

After what?

After the things that pertain to the church. With the beginning of Revelation 4, I believe the church has finished its work on Earth and has been called up to Heaven. I also believe that the open door into Heaven, which John entered after hearing a heavenly voice say, "Come up here," pictures the rapture of the church.

In verse 1 we read, "The first voice which I heard was like a trumpet speaking with me." Now where have we heard about a trumpet before? Over in 1 Thessalonians 4:16–17, the apostle Paul writes some of the most stirring words in all the New Testament: "For the Lord Himself will descend from Heaven with a shout, with the voice of an archangel, and with the trumpet of God. And the dead in Christ will rise first. Then we who are alive and remain shall be caught up together with them in the clouds to meet the Lord in the air. And thus we shall always be with the Lord."

The sound of the trumpet, then, brings us to the topic of the Rapture. And whenever you raise this topic, questions inevitably follow. Let's take a look at a few of them.

QUESTIONS ABOUT THE RAPTURE

What is the Rapture?

Author Mark Hitchcock defines it like this: "The Rapture of the church . . . is the intersection of two events: the resurrection of the dead, specifically only believers, and the transformation of living believers. They will all be immediately together in Jesus' glorious presence, and He will escort them to heaven to live with Him forever." [10]

Is it true that the word *rapture* isn't in the Bible?

Yes, but neither is the word *Trinity*, and we know that the Bible teaches the truth of the triune God. For that matter, even the word *Bible* isn't in the Bible— but it doesn't mean that we should stop using the word.

In 1 Thessalonians 4:16–17, as we just read, the apostle Paul teaches that "the dead in Christ will rise first. Then we who are alive and remain shall be *caught up* together with them in the clouds to meet the Lord in the air" (emphasis added).

The Greek word for "caught up" is *harpazo*. It is used thirteen times in the New Testament and means "to take forcibly," "to snatch," or "to catch up." That is what the Rapture is. The Lord will snatch up His church off Planet Earth in the blink of an eye.

Why is there a Rapture?

In the context of 1 Thessalonians 4, Paul was addressing believers in Thessalonica who were concerned about loved ones who had already died. They were thinking, *If my loved one died, does that mean he or she missed the Rapture?* Some people in that church were deeply concerned about this, bordering on grief and despair. And that's why Paul, as a good pastor-teacher, brought them teaching about the Rapture to comfort their hearts and give them a better perspective.

GOOD TO KNOW

The Greek word for Rapture is *harpazo* and means "to take forcibly," "to snatch," or "to catch up."

In verse 13 he said, "And now, dear brothers and sisters, we want you to know what will happen to the believers who have died so you will not grieve like people who have no hope" (NLT).

In other words, "Guys, don't panic about this. I don't want you to worry or to grieve. Be comforted. You most certainly *will* see your loved ones again. Let me inform you. Let me tell you how it will take place."

After he made this statement about the Rapture, Paul then said in verse 18, "Comfort one another with these words."

Thoughts of the Rapture *ought* to be a comfort—and a deep well of hope and joy for every believer. Try to imagine how it will be. You will be going about your business one day when suddenly—in a moment so rapid it can't be measured—you will be caught up into God's presence and reunited with your loved ones. Best of all, you will be face-to-face with Jesus Himself.

The Lord Himself spoke of this event in John 14:2–3: "In My Father's house are many mansions; if it were not so, I would have told you. I go to prepare a place for you. And if I go and prepare a place for you, I will come again and receive you to Myself; that where I am, there you may be also."

When He said "receive you to Myself," that could be literally translated "take you by force."

In 1 Corinthians 15:51–52 Paul added some more details to this future event. He said, "Behold, I tell you a mystery: We shall not all sleep, but we shall all be changed—in a moment, in the twinkling of an eye, at the last trumpet. For the trumpet will sound, and the dead will be raised incorruptible, and we shall be changed."

It's that fast.

In Matthew 24:40–42, Jesus spoke again of the Rapture when He said, "Then two men will be in the field: one will be taken and the other left. Two women will be grinding at the mill: one will be taken and the other left. Watch therefore, for you do not know what hour your Lord is coming."

Are there other examples of "rapture" in the Scriptures?

One example that comes to mind is Enoch. In Genesis we read how he was suddenly caught up into Heaven. The book of Hebrews says this about that moment: "It was by faith that Enoch was taken up to heaven without dying—'he disappeared, because God took him.' For before he was taken up, he was known as a person who pleased God" (11:5 NLT).

In Genesis 5:23–24, we're told that "Enoch lived 365 years, walking in close fellowship with God. Then one day he disappeared, because God took him" (NLT). Apparently Enoch and the Lord would take walks together quite frequently. Then one day the Lord may have said to His friend, "You know, Enoch, today we're a little closer to My house than yours. Why don't you come home with Me?" So Enoch woke up on one shore and went to bed on another. He went right into God's presence, caught up to meet the Lord.

GOOD TO KNOW

Elijah did not die a natural death but was caught up suddenly into Heaven.

A similar (if more dramatic) thing happened to the prophet Elijah at the end of his time on Earth. He did not die a natural death but was caught up suddenly into Heaven. The book of 2 Kings, chapter 2, tells us that Elijah and Elisha, who was to carry on Elijah's ministry, were walking together and talking when suddenly a chariot of fire appeared, drawn by horses of fire. It drove between them, separating them, and Elijah was carried by a whirlwind into Heaven.

In the New Testament book of Acts, we have another example in Philip. He was raptured as well (so to speak), although in his case, it was more horizontal than vertical. At the Lord's instructions, Philip had witnessed to an Ethiopian man who had been riding through the desert in his chariot. When they came to some water, the man wanted to receive the Lord and be baptized. Philip baptized him, and then in Acts 8:39–40 we read, "Now when they came up out of the water, the Spirit of the Lord caught Philip away, so that the eunuch saw him no more; and he went on his way rejoicing. But Philip was found at Azotus. And passing through, he preached in all the cities till he came to Caesarea."

By the way, the word used here to describe Philip being caught away is *harpazo*. So Philip was raptured *sideways*, finding himself in Azotus, about thirty miles away from where he was! (I wish I could do that in Los Angeles. It would be so good to cross the city without getting on the freeways.)

You might say the Lord Himself was raptured into Heaven. After Jesus finished His public ministry, died on the cross for the sins of the world, and rose from the dead, He was taken up, or *caught up*, into Heaven. The Bible uses the same word, *harpazo*, in Acts 1:9:

> Now when He had spoken these things, while they watched, He was taken up, and a cloud received Him out of their sight.

When is the Rapture?

I don't know.

And by the way, neither do you.

Neither does anyone.

A few years ago a California preacher predicted the date of the return of Christ, and his organization spent millions plastering the date on billboards. As it turned out, he was wrong. Then he adjusted his date and was wrong again. Finally he had to admit that he was wrong the whole time.

No one knows the date, as the Lord Jesus clearly stated: "But about that day or hour no one knows, not even the angels in heaven, nor the Son, but only the Father" (Matthew 24:36 NIV).

Having established the fact, however, that no one knows the precise day or hour of the Rapture, it must also be noted that *it could happen at any time*. It could happen today. It could happen tonight. It could happen before you finish reading this sentence. And it will happen in a moment so rapid, you can't even measure it in human time.

In 1 Corinthians 15:52 Paul tells us that it will happen "in a moment, in the twinkling of an eye, at the last trumpet." The Greek word translated "moment" in this verse is the term *atomos*, from which we get our word *atom*. The idea being conveyed here is that this is something so small, it can't even be divided.

You just leave one time frame and enter into another, with no sense of movement.

Before we ascend, however, the dead in Christ will go up before us. Some find this confusing. Aren't those who have died in Christ already in Heaven? How is it that they will ascend in the moment of the Rapture?

Here's the answer: believers who die are immediately with the Lord. 2 Corinthians 5:8 speaks of being absent from the body and present with the Lord. What kind of bodies do believers in Heaven have right now, then, if they are waiting for their bodies to be resurrected at the Rapture?

We don't know the answer to that.

Is there some sort of intermediate body before those in Heaven receive their resurrection body?

The Bible doesn't say.

When the dead in Christ rise again, will they literally burst out of their graves? It would seem that is the case.

What happened in Matthew 27:51–53, however, might be a prototype of such an occurrence. You may remember that after Jesus died on the cross, supernatural events began to happen, including an earthquake:

> Then, behold, the veil of the temple was torn in two from top to bottom; and the earth quaked, and the rocks were split, and the graves were opened; and many bodies of the saints who had fallen asleep were raised; and coming out of the graves after His resurrection, they went into the holy city and appeared to many.

This account seems to picture the actual opening of graves and a bodily resurrection of God's people.

What's the difference between the Rapture and the Second Coming?

Sometimes people lump these two occurrences together. Nevertheless, according to the Bible, they are two separate events.

Both could be described as the Lord's return, but at the Rapture, Jesus comes in the air, calling His church to meet Him in the clouds. In the Second Coming He returns to Earth. The Rapture will happen in an instant. It will come quickly, like "a thief in the night" (1 Thessalonians 5:2). In the Second Coming, however, He will come "with clouds, and every eye will see Him" (Revelation 1:7).

In the Rapture He comes before judgment; in the Second Coming He returns with judgment.

GOOD TO KNOW

In the Rapture Jesus comes before judgment; in the Second Coming He returns with judgment.

BACK TO JOHN ON PATMOS

On the lonely island of Patmos, John the apostle had just heard the Lord speak to the church of Laodicea, saying that He stood at their door, knocking and offering this invitation: "If anyone hears My voice and opens the door, I will come in to him and dine with him, and he with Me. To him who overcomes I will grant to sit with Me on My throne, as I also overcame and sat down with My Father on His throne" (3:20–21).

As he was recording these words, a door was suddenly opened into Heaven, and he was hurtled into the presence of God:

> Immediately I was in the Spirit; and behold, a throne set in heaven, and One sat on the throne. And He who sat there was like a jasper and a sardius stone in appearance; and there was a rainbow around the throne, in appearance like an emerald. Around the throne were twenty-four thrones, and on the thrones I saw twenty-four elders sitting, clothed in white robes; and they had crowns of gold on their heads. And from the throne proceeded lightnings, thunderings, and voices. Seven lamps of fire were burning before the throne, which are the seven Spirits of God.
>
> Before the throne there was a sea of glass, like crystal. And in the midst of the throne, and around the throne, were four living creatures full of eyes in front and in back. The first living creature was like a lion, the second living creature like a calf, the third living creature had a face like a man, and the fourth living creature was like a flying eagle. The four living creatures, each having six wings, were full of eyes around and within. And they do not rest day or night, saying:
>
> "Holy, holy, holy,
> Lord God Almighty,
> Who was and is and is to come!"
>
> Whenever the living creatures give glory and honor and thanks to Him who sits on the throne, who lives forever and ever, the twenty-four elders fall down before Him who sits on the throne and worship Him who lives forever and ever, and cast their crowns before the throne, saying:

"You are worthy, O Lord,

To receive glory and honor and power;

For You created all things,

And by Your will they exist and were created." (Revelation 4:2–11)

We are seeing a heavenly scene, and John is in the third heaven.

According to the Bible, there are three "heavens." In 2 Corinthians 12, Paul states that he "was caught up to the third heaven . . . whether in the body or out of the body I do not know, God knows" (verses 2–3). He went on to say that he was "caught up into Paradise and heard inexpressible words, which it is not lawful for a man to utter" (verse 4).

So what are the three heavens? The first heaven is the sky—the atmosphere and clouds. The second heaven is everything in the cosmos—all that lies beyond Earth's atmosphere, including the moon, the sun, the stars, and the galaxies. The third heaven is the dwelling place of God Himself.

In the early years of the space race with the Soviet Union, a Russian astronaut orbiting our planet mockingly reported that he had looked through the window of his spacecraft but didn't see God.

That's because he was peering into the second heaven, not the third. If he had taken off that cosmonaut suit for one minute, I guarantee you that he would have seen God really fast.

Is this third heaven beyond the galaxies, then? Would we ever be able to develop a telescope that looks into it? No, and I don't think physical distance is the problem. In fact, I think the third heaven may be closer than we realize. It might even be all around us, unseen. Remember when Elisha's servant was allowed to see the heavenly armies surrounding the town of Dothan (see 2 Kings 6:17)? All it took was opening his spiritual eyes to see.

GOOD TO KNOW

The third heaven is the dwelling place of God Himself.

Whatever it is or wherever it is, the third heaven is the dwelling place of God Himself. And John found himself caught up into that glorious scene.

WHAT DID JOHN SEE IN THE THIRD HEAVEN?

He saw the Lord seated on His throne.

> And behold, a throne set in heaven, and One sat on the throne. And He who sat there was like a jasper and a sardius stone in appearance; and there was a rainbow around the throne, in appearance like an emerald. (Revelation 4:2–3)

Sardius and jasper were used to describe the Lord. These, interestingly, were the first and last stones on the breastplate of the high priest. In Revelation 21 the jasper stone is described as being crystal clear, or diamond-like. The sardius stone is blood red, like a ruby. John said the appearance of the Lord "was like" these precious stones, which was the closest he could come to describing what he saw. First-century Greek was an amazing language, but any language has limitations when you are attempting to describe something this awesome.

He saw twenty-four elders.

> Around the throne were twenty-four thrones, and on the thrones I saw twenty-four elders sitting, clothed in white robes; and they had crowns of gold on their heads. (4:4)

Who are these elders? They could be angelic beings, but I doubt that. Others think they might be representatives of both the Old and New Covenants, perhaps twelve patriarchs from the Old Testament and twelve apostles from the New Testament. Then again, the twenty-four elders may be representatives of the New Testament church who have received their crowns. The word used here for "elders" is a word from which we get our English word *presbytery*, which speaks of eldership or leadership. That word is never used to describe angels, only men.

The elders wore "crowns," which come from the Greek word *stephanos*, a word that speaks of a reward given for faithful service. We could compare it to winning a medal at the Olympics. So it isn't a crown like the ornate headpiece worn by a king or queen. It's more like an award for faithfulness.

We find these crowns in several places in the New Testament. Jesus promised "the crown of life" to the church of Smyrna because of their suffering (Revelation 2:10). James wrote that if we endure temptations and trials, God will give to us "the crown of life" (James 1:12). In 2 Timothy 4:8 Paul told his young disciple that "the prize awaits me—the crown of righteousness, which the Lord, the righteous Judge, will give me on the day of his return. And the prize is not just for me but for all who eagerly look forward to his appearing" (NLT).

I have a friend who has run in numerous triathlons and Ironman events and has the ribbons and medals to show for it. I dared him to wear them publicly. I said, "Put all of your medals on and go walk around."

"No," he said, "I'm not doing that. It would seem boastful."

Maybe I was just envious because I've never won a medal for anything.

Could it be that we imagine Heaven this way? Do we visualize all of those high achievers—those whom God has blessed in an extraordinary way—walking around with hundreds of medals or multiple crowns? Then they meet you on one of those streets of gold, and you have your one tiny purple ribbon for just showing up.

No, I don't believe Heaven will be like that at all. Note that in Revelation 4:10, the elders cast all their crowns at the Lord's feet.

I love that. It's as though they are saying, "I didn't win this to boast. I didn't receive this just to say, 'Look how much I have done.' Lord, here is my crown, here is my reward, here is my life. I give it back to You."

He saw ominous storm warnings.

> And from the throne proceeded lightnings, thunderings, and voices. Seven lamps of fire were burning before the throne, which are the seven Spirits of God. (Revelation 4:5)

These are all symbols of judgment in the Scriptures. From the safety of Heaven, John can see that a storm is brewing on Earth. That storm will be unfolding in the Great Tribulation, but believers will be safe in God's arms, in the sanctuary of Heaven.

Didn't Jesus promise that?

Remember what He said to the church in Philadelphia in Revelation 3:10: "Because you have kept My command to persevere, I also will keep you from the hour of trial which shall come upon the whole world, to test those who dwell on the earth."

The church, the bride of Jesus Christ, will not go through the Great Tribulation. We will have *tribulations*, yes, and Jesus promised those also. But we won't be on Earth to face the outpouring of God's wrath on a world that has rejected His Son.

I remember a summer storm when we were visiting North Carolina a number of years ago. Seemingly out of nowhere, dark clouds rolled in, thunder began to rumble, and lightning flashed all around. We were sitting in rocking chairs on the porch of a hotel, being entertained by the storm.

GOOD TO KNOW
Because of the Rapture, the church will not go through the Great Tribulation.

It would have been a different situation altogether if we had been wandering around out in an open area somewhere—especially with all the lightning strikes. So it's one thing to see a storm from a safe place, and it's another thing completely to find yourself in the middle of a storm.

We will see the Tribulation storm on Earth from the vantage point of Heaven.

Which brings up another question.

Are Those in Heaven Aware of Events on Earth?

I believe that we will be aware of at least some events.

There are two extreme viewpoints on this topic. One extreme is that people in Heaven are in effect peering over the edge and watching everything we do. The other extreme is that residents of Heaven are completely unaware and oblivious to what you might be going through on Earth.

I don't agree with either of those views.

Some would say, "If the redeemed in Heaven spend all their time watching events on Earth, how could they enjoy the wonders and joys of 'My Father's house'?" In a number of passages, however—passages we will explore later in this book—it seems that some in Heaven are indeed aware of what is transpiring on Earth.

In Heaven we will have *perspective*. For that reason I think we will know *more* in Heaven in our glorified state than we know on Earth. I think we will have memories and be aware of earthly doings, but with God's perspective on it all.

WORSHIP IN HEAVEN

Awestruck, John watched what was going on around him in Heaven, trying to take it all in. He saw magnificent angelic creatures worshiping. He saw the twenty-four elders falling down in worship. He heard their worship cries and songs and wrote down the lyrics.

Heaven will be all about worship. And why not? Why shouldn't we engage in unbridled worship? We will know all things. All of our questions will be answered. All of our pain will be removed. All of our tears will be dried. So we will be worshiping.

For some people that sounds a little boring—as though Heaven were one long church service.

Not at all.

Yes, we will be worshiping, but we will be doing much more than that. We also will be busy doing God's work, moving through the new Heavens and the new Earth at the speed of thought. Revelation 22:3 says, "His servants shall serve Him." Revelation 7:15 says that we will be before the throne of God, serving Him day and night.

So yes, Heaven is a place of rest.

I don't know about you, but I can only rest for so long. Some people say they can't wait to retire. I ask them, "What are you going to do?"

"Golf."

"Then what?"

"Fish."

"Then what?"

"Sleep in."

"Then what?"

"Umm . . . travel."

"Then what?"

"Umm . . . golf and fish some more."

Now *that* sounds boring to me. I can understand taking some time off and traveling a little or pursuing certain activities—golf, surfing, fishing, or whatever. But then, after you're recharged, it's time to get back to work.

Use your free time for the Lord. Use it in volunteer service doing something good for other people. You and I have been put on this earth to glorify God, not to just please ourselves.

Heaven will be a place of rest, certainly. But it will be far from boring. We can't even begin to conceive of the activities and opportunities the Lord has lined up for us. What did Paul say to the Corinthians? "No mere man has ever seen, heard, or even imagined what wonderful things God has ready for those who love the Lord" (1 Corinthians 2:9 TLB).

Because He Is Coming Soon

Both the Bible and events in our contemporary world point to a soon return of Jesus Christ for His own.

So what are we supposed to do in the interim?

When that California pastor predicted the day of Jesus' return, people did some pretty crazy things. Some divorced their mates. Others ran up huge credit card bills, believing they would never have to pay them.

But that's not how God wants us to respond.

Remember Enoch? What did he do?

He walked with God.

What does it mean to walk with God? Walking speaks of effort, regular motion, and consistency. The Bible doesn't say that Enoch *sprinted* with God.

They simply walked together through life, one step at a time. And the Bible says that we are to do the same. The apostle Paul said, "Walk in the Spirit, and you shall not fulfill the lust of the flesh" (Galatians 5:16). And again, "As you therefore have received Christ Jesus the Lord, so walk in Him, rooted and built up in Him and established in the faith, as you have been taught, abounding in it with thanksgiving" (Colossians 2:6–7).

Personally, I don't care much for running, but I try to get out and walk every day. I listen to a podcast while I'm walking, or some Bible teaching. But I love to walk. People tell me that if I ran, I would lose more weight. Perhaps I would. But I would also be more miserable. When it comes to the Christian life, I don't want to sprint and then collapse. I want to keep a good, steady walking pace that will keep me moving along.

Enoch walked with God, and that's my goal in life too.

In the Old Testament book of Amos, we read, "Can two walk together, unless they are agreed?" (Amos 3:3). In other words, if we're going to walk together, then let's walk *together.* I usually walk fast, which presents a problem when I walk with my wife, because her pace is slower.

The idea of walking together is that we need to accommodate our pace to one another. And it's the same in our walk with God. We shouldn't lag behind Him or run ahead of Him. We let Him set the pace.

Sometimes He might say, "Step it up a bit, Greg. I've got something for you to accomplish today."

At other times He might say, "Slow down a bit, Greg. I want to show you something. Stay with Me."

That's the goal: staying with Him and living in harmony with Him.

That verse from Amos that I quoted above could be better translated, "Can two walk together unless they have made an appointment?" The Hebrew word implies a meeting at a fixed place at a fixed time.

Can you imagine being late for an appointment with God?

Have you ever made time in your schedule to meet with someone, and they come strolling in 15 minutes late?

"Sorry, man. It's the traffic."

Or maybe, "Sorry, something came up."

Or maybe they don't even offer an explanation. They just plop down and start talking. That's a little bit offensive, isn't it? It shows a disregard for your time and the priorities you might have on your schedule.

My friend Bob Shank likes to say, "Early is on time, on time is late, and late is never acceptable."

Can you imagine being late—or not showing up—for an appointment with God? When you think about who He is and what He has done for us, maybe the best idea would be showing up fifteen minutes early.

The lesson here is to set and keep an appointment with God every day of your life. Start the day in the Word, listening to His Holy Spirit. Start the day in prayer, spreading out your schedule before Him, seeking His counsel, and giving Him thanksgiving and praise. Think of Him. Focus on Him. Commit your life to Him afresh.

This is what it means to walk in harmony with Him.

And if this is the day I go to Heaven, fine. If it's tomorrow, great. If it's thirty years from now, that's up to Him, and it's not my concern.

One day, when our life on Earth ends and we enter eternity, every one of us will have a face-to-face meeting with our Creator. You might think you know when that day is or imagine that you have a pretty good idea.

But you don't. Only God does.

So always be ready.

THREE TAKEAWAY TRUTHS

- At the Rapture, believers have the comfort and hope of seeing their loved ones again.
- Heaven is not in the least boring; it's a place of activity and excitement.
- We should not await Christ's coming with flippancy but with faithfulness.

CHAPTER NINE

Why We Were Created

*And every creature which is in heaven and on the earth and under
the earth and such as are in the sea, and all that are in them, I
heard saying: "Blessing and honor and glory and power be to Him
who sits on the throne, and to the Lamb, forever and ever!"*
(Revelation 5:13)

IN THIS CHAPTER

- What the Bible says about the meaning of life
- The identity and worthiness of the Lamb
- Why Jesus came to Earth to die on a cross
- God hears and stores every prayer of His people.
- How a worship service in Heaven can inspire us on Earth

An elderly man was speaking to a young student about his future goals. "Tell me, son," the older man said, "what are your plans after you graduate from law school?"

"Well," the younger man replied, "I would like to get a job with a good firm and start making some money."

"All right. That sounds good. Then what?"

"I—well, I'd like to get married."

"Very good. Then what?"

"I would like to start a family, have some children, put my kids in good schools, and have enough money to eventually get a vacation home somewhere in the sunshine."

"Okay. Then what?"

"Well . . . then after I've worked for however-many years, I could maybe come to a point where I could retire. If my wife and I are in good health, maybe we could travel—see the world a little."

"All right. Then what?"

"Maybe we would have grandchildren. I've heard that grandchildren are more fun than children."

The older man smiled. "Yes, that's true. But then what?"

"Umm . . . I guess just pass my money on to my children, hoping they'll have as comfortable of a life as I've had."

"Yes, and then what?"

"Well," the young man said, "I guess I will die."

And the older man said, "Yes. *Then* what?"

Then what?

Then comes eternity.

Far too often we think of this life as being everything and don't give much, if any, thought to the next life. In reality, however, this is the before life and then comes the afterlife. You might even say this life is a warm-up act for eternity, with so much more to come.

It's very important that we know why we are here on Earth, because if we don't, we could easily waste our lives. The old cliché continues to be true: If you aim at nothing, you'll hit it every time.

So, then, why do we exist? Why are we here? Why did God create us in the first place? We find the answer in Revelation, chapters 4 and 5.

WHAT IS THE PURPOSE OF LIFE?

I have an iPhone with a feature on it called Siri.

It allows you to ask a question out loud, and you get an answer from some database somewhere. But the answer is in a woman's voice, and her name is Siri.

I could, for instance, push a button and ask Siri where I could get a good cup of coffee. Siri will go to work with the built-in navigational device in my phone and come up with a list of coffee places that are nearby.

The other day I decided to go a little deeper with Siri and ask her a philosophical question.

"Siri," I said, "what is the meaning of life?"

"I can't answer that right now," she said. "But give me time and I will write a play in which nothing happens."

What?

I asked her again. "Siri, what is the meaning of life?"

Siri replied, "I don't really know, but I think there is an app for that."

I gave it one more try, and Siri answered, "All evidence to date points to chocolate."

Somebody, somewhere, had programmed some snappy replies into Apple's database. But Siri's answers really weren't any worse than how other people answer that question.

A poll was taken among Americans where the question was asked, "What is the purpose of life?" Sixty-one percent of the respondents said that the main purpose of life is "enjoyment and personal fulfillment."

We might expect such an answer from nonbelievers who don't have God's perspective on things, but when the same question was asked of "born-again" Christians, the results were pretty close to the same: 50 percent of those who were asked stated that the purpose of life is enjoyment and self-satisfaction.

Is that true? Is that the purpose of life for us as followers of Jesus Christ? Do we exist for personal enjoyment and self-satisfaction?

No, it is not true. Far from it. To find the genuine answer to this question, we have to go to the Scriptures. One statement of the Bible's answer can be found in the scene that unfolds before us in Revelation 4.

ELDERS AND ANGELS

The apostle John had been banished to the island of Patmos. It was there he was swept up into the vision that comprises the book of Revelation. At the beginning of chapter 4, John was suddenly hurtled into Heaven, caught up into the very presence of God. Using the language of his own day, he did his best to describe the indescribable.

In verses 2 and 3 John saw the Lord seated in Heaven, resplendent in glory, with an emerald rainbow encircling His throne. In verse 5 we read that "from the throne came flashes of lightning and the rumble of thunder" (NLT). These seem to be ominous storm warnings from the throne of God, indicating that serious trouble is coming to Planet Earth.

From verse 6 to the end of the chapter, John tried to describe some magnificent angels caught up in the worship and praise of God:

> And in the midst of the throne, and around the throne, were four living creatures full of eyes in front and in back. The first living creature was like a lion, the second living creature like a calf, the third living creature had a face like a man, and the fourth living creature was like a flying eagle. The four living creatures, each having six wings, were full of eyes around and within. And they do not rest day or night, saying:
>
> "Holy, holy, holy,
> Lord God Almighty,
> Who was and is and is to come!"
>
> Whenever the living creatures give glory and honor and thanks to Him who sits on the throne, who lives forever and ever, the twenty-four elders fall down before Him who sits on the throne and worship Him who lives forever and ever, and cast their crowns before the throne, saying:
>
> "You are worthy, O Lord,
> To receive glory and honor and power;
> For You created all things,
> And by Your will they exist and were created." (Revelation 4:6–11)

It's difficult for us to wrap our minds around the passage we just read. (It must have been difficult for John, too.) The book of Revelation, however, is full of references to angels. In fact, there are seventy-one such references, more than in any other book of the Bible.

Why is that?

For one reason, Revelation is a glimpse into the next dimension, the supernatural world.

According to the Bible, two worlds coexist: the natural and the supernatural. We live and move in a familiar physical world, but we are surrounded at all times by the spiritual world.

Right now as you read the pages of this book, if you are a Christian, you need to know that there are literally angels all around you. How do I know this? The Bible says that "the angel of the LORD encamps all around those who fear Him" (Psalm 34:7). The book of Hebrews assures us that all angels are "ministering spirits sent to serve those who will inherit salvation" (1:14 NIV).

GOOD TO KNOW

The book of Revelation has over seventy-one references to angels, more than in any other book of the Bible.

There are also fallen angels, or demons, who inhabit this spiritual realm. In Ephesians 6 we read there are principalities and powers, both good and evil, with different rankings and different powers. The apostle Peter tells us that Christ has "gone into heaven and is at the right hand of God," with "angels and authorities and powers having been made subject to Him" (1 Peter 3:22).

Clearly there are rankings in the angelic realm. We know this because one such ranking would be *archangel*. There is only one angel who has that title in the Scriptures, and that is Michael. The word *archangel* occurs just twice in the New Testament. In both instances it is used in the singular and preceded by the definite article *the*, as in *the* archangel. Michael, then, clearly seems to be the heavyweight angel of angels, and he has a very special privilege. When the Rapture happens, we read in 1 Thessalonians 4:16 that "the Lord Himself will descend from heaven with a shout, with the voice of an archangel, and with the trumpet of God. And the dead in Christ will rise first."

The first time that you ever hear Michael's voice may be in the moment when you are called out of this life with believers from all over the world to meet the Lord in the clouds.

And then there is Gabriel. We don't know whether Gabriel is an archangel, but he, too, has been given awesome privileges. Gabriel unrolled the scroll of the future for the prophet Daniel. It was also Gabriel who appeared to Zacharias and revealed that he would have a son in his old age, whose name would be John and who would be known as John the Baptist. And it was Gabriel who was given the privilege of announcing to that little peasant girl named Mary, in Nazareth, that she would be the mother of the Messiah.

I'm guessing that last announcement was an angelic assignment that every angel wanted in on, but the privilege was given to Gabriel. It was his role. The other angels had their opportunity, too, however, when they lit up the sky with their announcement of the birth of Jesus to the shepherds. Luke tells us that "suddenly there was with the angel a multitude of the heavenly host praising God and saying: 'Glory to God in the highest, and on earth peace, goodwill toward men!'" (2:13–14).

I spoke of Gabriel's announcement to Mary as "his" role. For whatever reason, all angels in the Bible are presented in the masculine, rather than the feminine, form. It may be conventional wisdom to speak of angels as feminine: *she sings like an angel,* or *she is as pretty as an angel.* But in reality, angels always appear as men. It's just the way it is.

In addition to the named, high-ranking angels, Michael and Gabriel, the Bible also speaks about cherubim and seraphim. They are described in Ezekiel 1:5 and also in Ezekiel 28. God sent cherubim to guard the tree of life in the Garden of Eden after Adam and Eve ate of the forbidden fruit. We read in Genesis 3:24 that after He drove our first parents out of the Garden, "the Lord God stationed mighty cherubim to the east of the Garden of Eden. And he placed a flaming sword that flashed back and forth to guard the way to the tree of life" (NLT).

Why did He do that?

So that Adam and Eve never would be able to eat of the tree of life, enabling them to live forever in a fallen state. One thing is for sure: you never want to mess with an angel who carries a sword.

In Isaiah 6:1–4 we read about seraphim before the throne of God. Isaiah writes,

It was in the year King Uzziah died that I saw the Lord. He was sitting on a lofty throne, and the train of his robe filled the Temple. Attending him were mighty seraphim, each having six wings. With two wings they covered their faces, with two they covered their feet, and with two they flew. They were calling out to each other,

"Holy, holy, holy is the Lord of Heaven's Armies! The whole earth is filled with his glory!"

Their voices shook the Temple to its foundations, and the entire building was filled with smoke. (NLT)

In a similar scene in Revelation 4:11, the twenty-four elders reveal to us why we exist and why we are on Earth: "You are worthy, O Lord, to receive glory and honor and power; for You created all things, and by Your will they exist and were created."

So why do I exist? Why was I created?

I exist to bring God glory and pleasure.

Someone needs to alert Siri—and Google too, while you're at it. Even Alexa should be told.

I don't exist to bring *myself* glory and pleasure. In fact, if I live for pleasure, I will never find it. In 1 Timothy 5:6 Paul writes that "she who lives in pleasure is dead while she lives." The fact of the matter is that living for pleasure is one of the least pleasurable things a person can do. It has been said the best cure for hedonism is an attempt to practice it. If you've ever deliberately set out to live for pleasure and pleasure alone, then you will know what I am talking about.

I'm reminded of Freddie Mercury, who was the lead singer of the rock band Queen. Queen has sold over 150 million records—and some estimates go as high as 300 million. A movie was

GOOD TO KNOW

Why do we exist? To bring God glory and pleasure.

also made about him and his band. They are best known for their hit song, "Bohemian Rhapsody." So the young men in this band were awash in fame and fortune. From a worldly point of view, they had it all, and Freddie Mercury spent his life in the pursuit of pleasure. One of his friends, Elton John, said of Freddie that he was the only person he knew who could out-party him. Freddie's appetites, he said, "were unquenchable."

In an interview Freddie Mercury was quoted to say, "Excess is a part of my nature. To me, dullness is a disease. I need danger and excitement. . . . Straight people bore me stiff. I love freaky people." [11] Suffice it to say that he did not deny himself anything, sexually or materially. But it didn't turn out well for Freddie. In fact, it never does for people who pursue such a path. As time went on, Freddie realized that by becoming a star, he had effectively created a monster.

"The monster is me," he said. "I can't blame anyone else. It's what I've worked for since I was a kid. . . . Success, fame, money, sex, drugs—whatever you want. I can have it. But now I'm beginning to see that as much as I created it I want to escape from it. I'm starting to worry that I can't control it, as much as it controls me." [12] Eventually Freddie lost his fight with the monster. In 1991 he died at age forty-five from complications due to AIDS.

Speaking of the "monster" reminds me of a statement God made to Cain, way back in the beginning of human history. God saw trouble developing in Cain's heart and issued a warning to this son of Adam: "Watch out! Sin is crouching at the door, eager to control you. But you must subdue it and be its master" (Genesis 4:7 NLT).

Sin is like a crouching beast, ready to pounce, ready to control you. And if your aim is to live for pleasure, then the beast, the monster, will have its way with you, just as it did with Freddie Mercury. Again, living for pleasure never will bring pleasure.

Living for God, however, will bring you great pleasure as a side effect. You won't gain it by seeking that pleasure, but by seeking Him. The Bible tells us in Psalm 16:11, "In Your presence is fullness of joy; at Your right hand are pleasures forevermore."

If we live for the glory of God, then we will fulfill the very purpose for which we were created—and that will bring true peace and satisfaction to our lives. In Isaiah 43:7 the Lord says, "Everyone who is called by My name, whom I have created for My glory; I have formed him, yes, I have made him."

Ephesians 1:11 tells us that "because of what Christ has done, we have become gifts to God that he delights in, for as part of God's sovereign plan we were chosen from the beginning to be his" (TLB).

In 1 Corinthians 6:19–20, the apostle Paul reminds us, "Do you not know that your body is the temple of the Holy Spirit who is in you, whom you have from God, and you are not your own? For you were bought at a price; therefore glorify God in your body and in your spirit, which are God's."

In 1 Corinthians 10:31 the Bible says, "Whatever you do, do it all for the glory of God" (NLT).

So here is my question for you: Are you living for God's glory, or are you living for your own? If you can't pursue a particular direction or engage in a particular activity and do it for the glory of God, then you shouldn't be doing it. You and I should be able to write "hallowed be Your name" over any pursuit we have in life.

Can you write that over your marriage right now?

Can you write it over your career and business ethics?

Can you write it over your leisure-time activities?

Can you write it over your online searches?

Whatever your vocation, you can pursue it for the glory of God. If you are a builder, build for the glory of God. If you are a mother, be one for the glory of God. If you are a musician, play for the glory of God. Whatever you do, do it for the glory of God. That is why you are here. And if you do so, you will know God's pleasure.

As I said earlier, life is preparation, or the warm-up act, for eternity. We were made by God and for God, and God wants us to practice on Earth what we will do forever in eternity. And what is that?

Let's look into Revelation, chapter 5, for the answer.

"WHO IS WORTHY?"

And I saw in the right hand of Him who sat on the throne a scroll written inside and on the back, sealed with seven seals. Then I saw a strong angel proclaiming with a loud voice, "Who is worthy to open the scroll and to loose its seals?" And no one in heaven or on the earth or under the earth was able to open the scroll, or to look at it.

So I wept much, because no one was found worthy to open and read the scroll, or to look at it. But one of the elders said to me, "Do not weep. Behold, the Lion of the tribe of Judah, the Root of David, has prevailed to open the scroll and to loose its seven seals."

And I looked, and behold, in the midst of the throne and of the four living creatures, and in the midst of the elders, stood a Lamb as though it had been slain, having seven horns and seven eyes, which are the seven Spirits of God sent out into all the earth. Then He came and took the scroll out of the right hand of Him who sat on the throne.

Now when He had taken the scroll, the four living creatures and the twenty-four elders fell down before the Lamb, each having a harp, and golden bowls full of incense, which are the prayers of the saints. And they sang a new song, saying:

> "You are worthy to take the scroll,
> And to open its seals;
> For You were slain,
> And have redeemed us to God by Your blood
> Out of every tribe and tongue and people and nation,
> And have made us kings and priests to our God;
> And we shall reign on the earth."

Then I looked, and I heard the voice of many angels around the throne, the living creatures, and the elders; and the number of them was ten thousand times ten thousand, and thousands of thousands. (Revelation 5:1–11)

What an amazing scene! But what is this mysterious scroll with seven seals? It's important for us to understand this because we don't know very much about scrolls these days. Scrolls were the forerunners of books—and I suppose digital books as well. Back in the first century, everything was written on parchment or scrolls that you could roll and unroll. And everything that was written on those scrolls had to be written by hand.

Everyone in that day who read about a scroll with seven seals would know that this was a very important document. For instance, the wills of the Roman emperors Vespasian and Caesar Augustus were secured with seven seals. For such a document, a scribe would get out a long roll of parchment and start writing. After of period of time, he would stop, roll the parchment enough to cover his words, and at that point seal the scroll with wax. Then he would write again and seal, and he would repeat this until he was finished. This would ensure that the document on the scroll would be read a portion at a time. You would have to break open the seal, read, then break open the next seal, read some more, and so forth.

Also at this time, if a Jewish man was required to forfeit his land and possessions, the losses would be listed on a scroll that had been sealed seven times. The conditions to purchase back the land and possessions were written on the outside of the scroll.

GOOD TO KNOW

John's readers would all have understood that a scroll with seven seals indicated a very important document.

Coming back to verse 1, we read, "I saw in the right hand of Him who sat on the throne a scroll written inside and on the back, sealed with seven seals."

The moment had the attention of Heaven. Everyone was looking at that scroll. While I can't speak with absolute certainty here, I believe the scroll is effectively the title deed to Earth.

Humanity lost this title deed in the Garden of Eden, when our first parents ate of the forbidden fruit. From that moment on, Satan basically has had control of this planet. That is why the Bible describes him as "the god of this world" (2 Corinthians 4:4 NLT), the "ruler of this world" (John 12:31), and "the prince of the power of the air" (Ephesians 2:2).

Satan is behind all of the evil, corruption, and wickedness of our world. In one sense he's the one who is calling the shots and running the show. So Jesus came to Earth to purchase back that which was lost in the Garden of Eden. And Jesus knew the only way to do so was by His death on the cross in fulfillment of prophecy.

This theme played out in a dramatic way during the temptation of Jesus in the wilderness. You may remember that, after a series of other temptations, the Evil One showed Jesus all the kingdoms of the world in a moment of time and then made this amazing statement: "I will give you all these splendid kingdoms and their glory—for they are mine to give to anyone I wish—if you will only get down on your knees and worship me" (Luke 4:6–7 TLB).

Here is what's so amazing. Jesus never refuted this statement of Satan's! If it were false, He certainly would have. But He didn't contradict the Devil's assertion because it was true. Even though Satan is known as the "father of lies," he sometimes tells the truth. And in this case he was. He was saying, in effect, "Jesus, both of us know that I hold the title deed to Earth. Both of us know that it is under my control."

Of course Jesus replied, "You shall worship the LORD your God, and Him only you shall serve" (verse 8). Our Lord would have nothing to do with this.

But why did Satan even try this line? Why would this even be a temptation for Jesus? *Because Satan was offering a shortcut to Christ, a way to bypass the cross.* Satan was saying, "Listen, Jesus, I can give You what You want without going through all of that. Accept my offer, and there will be no cross, no scourging, no crucifixion, no bearing the sins of the world, no separation from the Father. I'll give it all to You on a silver platter—if You'll just worship me."

Jesus would have none of it because He knew there was only one way for the goal of redeeming humanity to be accomplished, and that was through His death on the cross.

All of this has a direct bearing on what was happening in Revelation 5. I believe in that moment, the title deed to Earth was being held up in front of all the eyes of Heaven.

Here is this scroll. Who is worthy to open this scroll?

No one stepped up. No took the scroll or even looked at it, and there was a great silence—broken only by the sound of the apostle John, crying his eyes out because no one was worthy to do this.

Really? Think of all the heavy hitters in Heaven: Abraham. Moses. Job. David. Jeremiah. Elijah. The apostles.

But no one was worthy.

No one reached for that scroll.

Suddenly there was an answer:

> But one of the elders said to me, "Do not weep. Behold, the Lion of the tribe of Judah, the Root of David, has prevailed to open the scroll and to loose its seven seals." (Revelation 5:5)

Jesus, the Lamb of God, appeared. And as soon as God's Son took hold of that seven-sealed scroll, everything changed. Heaven went from weeping to worshiping.

I love this scene.

Sometimes people say there is no crying in Heaven. In fact, the word used for John's weeping in this passage means "weeping profusely." So apparently there are some tears in Heaven.

Why did John weep?

I don't know the full answer to that. Somehow it broke his heart that no one in Heaven was worthy to open the title deed to Earth. And then Jesus came and took the scroll Himself. And it was time to worship!

The elders seem to set the tone in this worship service, getting everything rolling. This reminds us that one of the great pastimes of Heaven is simply worshiping the Lord. That is why we need to keep in practice right here on Earth. Verse 8 says, "And the twenty-four elders fell down before the Lamb, each having a harp, and golden bowls full of incense, which are the prayers of the saints."

So not only does God keep our tears in a bottle (see Psalm 56:8), but He also keeps our prayers in a bowl. Nothing is wasted. God never throws your prayers away. He stores them for you. Some prayers are answered immediately, while others are kept in heavenly storage for an answer to come later.

We all experience times when life just doesn't seem fair. Things happen in our lives that simply don't make sense. We say, "Why didn't God answer my prayers?"

He will.

He will answer your prayers in His way, for His glory, in His time.

Someday when we are in Heaven, standing beside God's throne, we will see that golden bowl full of prayers being brought forth and will realize that God heard every one of our prayers. We also will realize that His answers are far, far better than what we asked for in the moment.

We will see how God took a particular hardship or tragedy or inexplicable event and used it in a long chain of circumstances to produce a result. And that result will be the most complete answer to prayer that we can imagine, and it will bring God glory—which is the ultimate reason for our very existence.

I love the fact that Jesus is presented as both "Lion" and "Lamb" in Revelation 5. What is more impressive than a ferocious lion? Have you ever been up close and personal with a lion? Have you ever heard a lion roar?

GOOD TO KNOW
God never throws your prayers away. Some prayers are answered immediately, while others are kept in heavenly storage for an answer to come later.

Years ago I was in Ethiopia, speaking at a pastor's conference with Franklin Graham and Dennis Agajanian. We took some time to visit a zoo, and what I remember is there was hardly anyone working there. If we had wanted to, we could have hopped over one of the fences to get closer to the animals. (Not that we would have wanted to.)

In one of the cages was the most underfed lion I have ever seen. He looked almost half-dead sitting over in the corner of the enclosure. You could walk right up to the bars of the cage, and Dennis, for some reason known only to him, started shaking the bars.

The lion sprang at us with a great roar.

It may have been a scrawny, underfed lion, but it was still a lion! And if I'd had hair, it would have been standing on end.

At the same time, what is more meek, weak, and lowly than a little lamb?

The way I see it is like this: Jesus, with all His might and power, became as submissive as a lamb before those who condemned Him, abused Him, and put Him to death. He could have easily escaped that terrible situation. He could have easily overpowered Pilate and the Roman garrison with single word.

But He didn't do that.

He submitted as a lamb and became the Lamb of God.

This reminds us of the Jewish Passover and the requirement to slay a lamb for the feast. But it wasn't to be just any lamb; it was supposed to be an unblemished lamb—a perfect, beautiful lamb. What's more, the Israelites were to take that lamb into their home for four days before they slaughtered it. Why? So they would become attached to it. If you had a lamb in your house for four days, it would become like a little pet.

And when John writes about Jesus as a lamb in this chapter, he uses a term that means "a pet lamb." The last time I was in Israel, I had the opportunity to hold a little lamb out in a pasture. They really are adorable and very vulnerable.

But God required them to slit the throat of the lamb to which they had grown attached. Why would He require such a thing?

Because sin hurts. There is a cost to sin, and most of us look at it far too casually.

Slaughtering the innocent pet lamb gave them a picture of the perfect, sinless Lamb of God who would die on a cross for the sins of the world.

In Heaven on this very day, the Lamb still bears the scars of that crucifixion on His body. It's moving to think that we will be reminded of what

Jesus did for all eternity. Every time we see the marks on His body, we will be reminded of how we got to Heaven in the first place and have a fresh reason to praise Him.

In Revelation 5:13 we read about a universe-wide praise service that breaks out after the Lamb of God is proclaimed worthy to open the scroll. Joyous worship breaks forth from every imaginable dimension:

> Then I heard every creature in Heaven and earth, in underworld and sea, join in, all voices in all places, singing:
>
> To the One on the Throne! To the Lamb!
> The blessing, the honor, the glory, the strength,
> For age after age after age. (MSG)

Okay, everybody . . . all together now . . . Earth, under the earth, the sea, under the sea, and every corner of God's realm, praise to the Lamb!

Again, we can practice right now for that day. We can tune up for eternity by giving praise to Jesus wherever we are and in whatever we may be doing. That is the core reason for our existence. That is why we are here.

Remember that conversation Jesus had with that woman at the well in John, chapter 4? She had been married and divorced five times and was living with a guy. Jesus said to her, "Whoever drinks of this water will thirst again" (verse 13). He used that well as a metaphor for life.

In effect He was saying to her, "Let Me tell you something, lady. Men will never fill the deepest needs of your life. That is why you've gone back to the well five times. You always will thirst. You always will be unsatisfied. But if you drink of the water that I give you, you never will thirst again."

Then He went on to say that "God is Spirit, and those who worship Him must worship Him in spirit and in truth" (verse 24). In fact, He told her that God was *looking* for such people to worship Him.

God is looking for people who will figure out why He gave them life and placed them on Earth. If you live for pleasure, as I wrote earlier, you never will find pleasure. You will be like the woman at the well in Sychar, drinking and drinking but never, ever satisfied.

Like Freddie Mercury, many today are wasting their lives by chasing empty fantasies. But if you will put God first in your life and live in relationship with Him through the Lord Jesus Christ—the great Lion and Lamb who became our Savior—and if you seek to bring glory to that wonderful name, then you will find the very reason you were created.

THREE TAKEAWAY TRUTHS

- Living for our own pleasure will never satisfy; living for God's glory does.
- Whatever our vocation, we can bring God glory with our day-to-day lives.
- We will be worshiping the Lamb in Heaven, so we might as well start now.

CHAPTER TEN

The Four Horsemen of the Apocalypse

And I looked, and behold, a white horse. He who sat on it had a bow; and a crown was given to him, and he went out conquering and to conquer.
(Revelation 6:2)

IN THIS CHAPTER
- The beginning of the Great Tribulation
- What to make of the four horsemen of the apocalypse
- How the Antichrist emerges onto the world scene
- God gives people every opportunity to repent and turn to Him.
- Three things Christians can do to equip themselves for spiritual battle

In his book *Storm Warning*, Billy Graham wrote, "Horses are among the most beautiful and intelligent animals of God's creation. But the four horses and their riders in John's vision are anything but beautiful. They are terrible and terrifying. In my view, the shadows of all four horsemen can already be seen galloping throughout the world. I not only want to look at these four symbols of events yet to come, but also put an ear to the ground and to detect their hoofbeats, growing louder by the day." [13] The distant rumble of those hoofbeats is sounding more and more like thunder. You don't even have to put your ear to the ground to hear them.

It's getting very, very close.

Think about what has happened—think how the world has changed—in just the last three decades. The computer age has dawned with global access, allowing people to get information on demand from everywhere.

China has emerged as a global economic and military superpower. Tensions and wars continue to break out in the Middle East, revolving around Jerusalem. A global pandemic or modern day "plague" took thousands of lives around the world. And we have unprecedented violence in the streets of America.

Meanwhile, Israel seems more hated and isolated than ever.

It is exactly as the Scriptures predicted it thousands of years ago. This is precisely how the Bible *said* it would be in the end times. It all unfolds before us here in the book of Revelation.

You might say the real action of this book is right here, in Revelation 6:1–19. This is in many ways the heart of the book. These verses contain twenty-one judgments that will be unleashed on the world during the seven-year period of the Great Tribulation.

THE FOUR HORSEMEN

In the book of Revelation, we have three distinct series of future judgments. We have seven seals. We have seven trumpets. We have seven bowls. Each series of seven describes unique events that will take place during the Tribulation period. The first of these four seal judgments is the four horsemen of the apocalypse.

In the last chapter as we considered Revelation 5, we were shown a seven-sealed scroll in the right hand of God, which may very well have been the title deed to Earth. John the apostle wept bitterly because there was no one in Heaven who was found worthy to take the scroll and open its seals. And then One emerged who was like a Lamb that had been slain. A heavenly voice told John that "the Lion of the tribe of Judah, the Root of David" (verse 5) had triumphed and was able and worthy to break the seals and open the scroll.

It was Jesus, and with the title deed of Earth in His hand, He began to break the seals, one by one:

> Now I saw when the Lamb opened one of the seals; and I heard one of the four living creatures saying with a voice like thunder,

"Come and see." And I looked, and behold, a white horse. He who sat on it had a bow; and a crown was given to him, and he went out conquering and to conquer.

When He opened the second seal, I heard the second living creature saying, "Come and see." Another horse, fiery red, went out. And it was granted to the one who sat on it to take peace from the earth, and that people should kill one another; and there was given to him a great sword.

When He opened the third seal, I heard the third living creature say, "Come and see." So I looked, and behold, a black horse, and he who sat on it had a pair of scales in his hand. And I heard a voice in the midst of the four living creatures saying, "A quart of wheat for a denarius, and three quarts of barley for a denarius; and do not harm the oil and the wine."

When He opened the fourth seal, I heard the voice of the fourth living creature saying, "Come and see." So I looked, and behold, a pale horse. And the name of him who sat on it was Death, and Hades followed with him. And power was given to them over a fourth of the earth, to kill with sword, with hunger, with death, and by the beasts of the earth. (Revelation 6:1–8)

The Great Tribulation, which will last for seven years, begins with the rider on a white horse.

Normally when we think of a rider on a white horse, we expect him to have a white hat. In the old westerns, the guy with the white horse wearing the white hat was always the good guy. The bad guy, on the other hand, rode a black horse and wore a black hat.

In this particular case the rider on the white horse isn't a good guy by any stretch of the imagination. In fact, he is the Antichrist.

Because Christ is seen in Revelation 19 riding a white horse, some have been confused about this first rider. In Revelation 19:11–12 we read, "Now I saw heaven opened, and behold, a white horse. And He who sat on him was called Faithful and True, and in righteousness He judges and makes war. His eyes were like a flame of fire, and on His head were many crowns."

That is Jesus Christ, returning to Earth in triumph and glory. The rider on the first horse of the four horsemen of the apocalypse, however, is the Antichrist. He is masquerading as the Messiah, even to the point of wearing a crown. The rider in Revelation 19, however, wears *many* crowns.

Revelation 6 parallels Matthew 24. Revelation 6 is like a bird's-eye view of the entire Tribulation period. It's like watching a movie when the camera pulls way back, and we see the whole scene we've been watching, now from high in the air, giving us the big picture. Then, as we travel further into the book of Revelation, we get a variety of close-up shots of events that Revelation 6 deals with in a broad way.

Matthew 24, also known as the Olivet discourse, is also a big-picture view of end times events as well. The disciples had come to Jesus on the Mount of Olives and said, "Tell us, when will these things be? And what will be the sign of Your coming, and of the end of the age?" (verse 3). Jesus went on to give them a brief chronology, or overview of the events that would one day take place on Earth.

The first thing He said to them was, "Take heed that no one deceives you. For many will come in My name, saying, 'I am the Christ,' and will deceive many" (verses 4–5). That is what we see in the overview of Revelation 6. Right away, the Antichrist emerges on the scene.

THE ANTICHRIST

The prefix *anti* in Antichrist means "against." But it also means "instead of." So is the Antichrist *against* Christ, or is he there *instead of* Christ? The answer is both. He offers himself as an alternative to Christ—or as Christ Himself to the undiscerning. And He certainly is opposed to the Lord.

Contrast the rider of Revelation 6 to the rider of Revelation 19. The Antichrist in Revelation 6:2 has a bow but no arrows; the rider on the white horse in Revelation 19 wields a mighty sword. The Antichrist wears a victor's crown, of the sort that would be won in an athletic competition, while Jesus Christ in Revelation 19 wears many crowns. The Antichrist initiates war; Jesus Christ comes back with His armies to put an end to war. The Antichrist initiates the Great Tribulation; Jesus Christ ends the Great Tribulation.

The Antichrist has many aliases. He is called the man of sin, the son of perdition, the little horn, the wicked one, the prince that is to come, the one who makes desolate, and, of course, the beast. But most of us simply know him as the Antichrist.

If he were to appear today, would we recognize him? Would he be dressed head-to-toe in black, with sinister sunglasses and steam rising off him? Probably not. In fact, he will be attractive and charismatic, suave and intelligent,

GOOD TO KNOW

The prefix *anti* in Antichrist means "against." But it also means "instead of."

with a magnetic personality. If Satan ever had a son, this is him. The only man who probably would even come close to him in wickedness would be Judas Iscariot.

There are over one hundred passages in the Bible that detail the origin, nationality, career, character, kingdom, and final doom of the Antichrist. It's obvious that the Bible has quite a bit to say about him.

You might be surprised to learn that many Americans believe there is an Antichrist. A poll was taken among the readers of *U. S. News & World Report* some time ago, and 49 percent of the readers believe there will be an Antichrist at some point in the future. That surprised me. Almost half of Americans believe there will be an Antichrist. I wonder if even more people would believe Antichrist is coming if the poll were taken today.

In a similar *Newsweek* poll, 19 percent of Americans said they believe the Antichrist is on Earth right now. And in that same poll, nearly half of those who accept Bible prophecy believe the Antichrist is alive right now.

Is he? Is the Antichrist alive at this moment, somewhere on Earth?

No one can answer that authoritatively, but I think that it is entirely possible. The Scriptures tell us that he will rise to power as a world leader at an economically difficult time. He will be able to accomplish what no president, prime minister, king, or world leader has ever done: bring about global economic stability and worldwide peace.

Isn't that what everyone wants right now?

We want a solution to all these festering global issues we face, including stagnating economies and ceaseless world turmoil. I've heard the term *war weary* used numerous times on the news. People are tired of all the conflict and turmoil and bloodletting. Could someone actually rise to power who could accomplish world peace?

The Antichrist will do that and more. He will be hailed as the greatest peacemaker who ever lived. He probably will win the Nobel Peace Prize and no doubt will have his face plastered on the cover of *Time* magazine as its person of the year. Nevertheless, this satanic superman will be drawing his power from the Evil One himself. And the "peace" that he brings to the world will be nothing more than a cruel deception.

A master of deception, he will become arrogant and turn violent, destroying many without warning. Eventually, he will even take on the King of kings in battle, but he will be broken.

The Antichrist, however, will be able to do something that no one else has ever pulled off before. He actually will bring peace in the Middle East. Most likely he will bring an end to global terrorism. Somehow, he will broker a deal with the Muslim nations and the state of Israel. We know that one way he will win the heart of the Jewish people (or at least some of them) will be by rebuilding their temple.

When you look at the skyline of Jerusalem today, you don't see a temple as you would have in Solomon's or Jesus' day. In fact, you might see a building with a large gold dome on it. That is the Dome of the Rock, a holy site to Islamic people around the world.

According to the Scriptures, however, the Jewish temple will be rebuilt on its original site. The original temple, erected by Solomon, was destroyed by the invading Babylonian armies. The second temple, rebuilt in the time of Ezra, was later expanded and beautified by King Herod. Ultimately, that temple also was destroyed by Titus and the Roman legions in AD 70. It has not been rebuilt since.

Where will the Antichrist get such ability to accomplish such things? The Bible tells us that he will draw it from the Devil himself. Revelation 13:2 says that "the dragon [Satan] gave the beast his power and his throne and great authority" (NIV).

Yes, it all sounds very bleak. But God never loses control for one moment, and the days of Satan and his Antichrist are numbered.

Verse 2 says the Antichrist "had a bow; and a crown was given to him." Who will give him that crown? Who will give him permission to have his short-lived reign of deception and terror on Earth?

GOOD TO KNOW

The Antichrist will be able to do something that no one else has ever pulled off before. He will bring peace in the Middle East.

The Lord will. In fact, Satan can do nothing without the express permission of God. Remember the story of Job and how the Devil came with his onslaught against the servant of the Lord? Before the Evil One could lay a glove on righteous Job, he had to first obtain permission from God.

The Antichrist will come with his agenda, which will be allowed for a time, and he will emerge as a great peacemaker, a man of benevolence, a leader with solutions.

And then it will be revealed who he really is. Antichrist is not a peacemaker. He is a troublemaker.

The Scriptures call that moment of revelation "the abomination of desolation."

In Matthew 24:15–16 Jesus said, "So when you see standing in the holy place 'the abomination that causes desolation,' spoken of through the prophet Daniel—let the reader understand—then let those who are in Judea flee to the mountains" (NIV).

The abomination of desolation will take place after the Antichrist rebuilds the temple for the Jews. There will be three-and-a-half years of global peace and economic stability.

Then he will show his true colors.

The apostle Paul writes of the Antichrist,

> Don't be fooled by what they say. For that day will not come until
> there is a great rebellion against God and the man of lawless-
> ness is revealed—the one who brings destruction. He will exalt
> himself and defy everything that people call god and every object
> of worship. He will even sit in the temple of God, claiming that he
> himself is God. (2 Thessalonians 2:3–4 NLT)

The Message puts it like this: "He'll defy and then take over every so-called god or altar. Having cleared away the opposition, he'll then set himself up in God's Temple as 'God Almighty.'"

This is how dictators take control. They come in with acts of benevolence and then, when they get what they want, the rest comes. For instance, when Rome first came into power, the Caesars didn't demand worship. Rome was not only ruled by a Caesar, but also by the Roman senate. As time passed, however, these Caesars began to deify themselves, declaring themselves to be gods and demanding worship from the people.

That is why many Christians lost their lives in the early days of the church. They refused to say, "Caesar is Lord."

In Germany, Hitler followed a similar path. He rose to power in terrible economic times, when Communism was running rampant. He spoke of returning the fatherland to its roots and spoke of the glories to come for the nation of Germany. They were a people of destiny, he told them, and he would bring that about. And in the early years, he did help Germany's economy. But then he began to show his true colors. Soon the faith of the people of Germany was replaced by Nazism, which was a faith in and of itself. And then Hitler began to enact what was described as the "Final Solution," which was his desire to wipe the Jewish people off the face of the earth.

Dictators rarely show all their cards when they first come into prominence. But after they get a firm hold on the levers of power, they reveal their true nature. That is what the Antichrist will do. The other wicked dictators who have ruled on Earth are just prototypes of what is to come.

THE COUNTERFEIT TRINITY

The Antichrist will set up his own false religion. He will have a religious leader working alongside him called the "false prophet." Revelation 19:20 reveals their end: "Then the beast was captured, and with him the false prophet who worked signs in his presence, by which he deceived those who received the mark of the beast and those who worshiped his image. These two were cast alive into the lake of fire burning with brimstone."

Just as surely as there is a holy Trinity—Father, Son, and Holy Spirit—so we have an "unholy trinity" in the book of Revelation. We have the Antichrist masquerading as Jesus Christ, the Holy Spirit being replaced by the false prophet, and the Devil himself wanting to be in the place of God.

That's the job he has always wanted. And in the book of Revelation, for a time, it appears the devil is in control. But he's not.

This "faith"—this religion of the Antichrist—seems to be a combination of many belief systems, intertwined with the occult. That is why any move toward a one-world religion always concerns me. People will say, "Let's have interfaith prayer services. We can have a Christian pray, followed by a Muslim, a Hindu, and a Buddhist. Isn't that beautiful? We all will coexist. After all, aren't we all praying to the same god?"

No, we are not.

The Bible says, "The LORD our God, the LORD is one" (Deuteronomy 6:4). There is only God. The true God is the One who loved us so much that He sent His Son, Jesus Christ, to be our Savior. This is the living God who is revealed in the pages of the Bible.

GOOD TO KNOW

Just as surely as there is a holy Trinity, so we have an unholy trinity in the book of Revelation. We have the Antichrist masquerading as Jesus Christ, the Holy Spirit being replaced by the false prophet, and the Devil himself wanting to be in the place of God.

Of course, nowadays people will say things like, "I'm not into organized religion, but I am into spirituality. I consider myself a spiritual person."

So, what are you into exactly? Disorganized chaos?

When someone says this, they are really saying, "I make it up as I go along. I take a little of this and a little of that—whatever suits me and my lifestyle. That is my faith."

Will that be the essence of the Antichrist's religion—a little of this and a little of that? Perhaps it will, because somehow people of different creeds and backgrounds will be buying into what he is selling.

I think the only person who will not be tolerated in this new "tolerant" religion will be the person who believes that the Bible is the Word of God. There will be a great persecution of Christians, which may begin before the Antichrist actually comes on the scene. In fact, the apostle John told us that "every spirit that acknowledges that Jesus Christ has come in the flesh is from God, but every spirit that does not acknowledge Jesus is not from God. This is the spirit of the antichrist, which you have heard is coming and even now is already in the world" (1 John 4:2–3 NIV).

The Antichrist will have an "ABC" religion: Anything But Christ.

Paul added that one of the signs of the end times will be an apostasy, or a falling away from the truth of the Scriptures. He wrote, "The Spirit clearly says that in later times some will abandon the faith and follow deceiving spirits and things taught by demons. Such teachings come through hypocritical liars, whose consciences have been seared as with a hot iron" (1 Timothy 4:1–2 NIV).

The apostle later stated that "the time will come when people will not put up with sound doctrine. Instead, to suit their own desires, they will gather around them a great number of teachers to say what their itching ears want to hear. They will turn their ears away from the truth and turn aside to myths" (2 Timothy 4:3–4 NIV).

Isn't this a picture of what we see happening in some churches today? People are saying, "Give me a Christianity that caters to me. Don't bore me with Bible doctrine. Keep it lively, interesting, and exciting. Keep it motivating. Don't judge me or tell me to change my lifestyle. That's the kind of faith I want."

What is Paul's antidote to this slipsliding of truth? "Preach the word! Be ready in season and out of season. Convince, rebuke, exhort, with all longsuffering and teaching. For the time will come when they will not endure sound doctrine" (2 Timothy 4:2–3).

Christians in these last days need to be on guard against this move toward a one-world religion or the push to set aside "the things that divide us" in the name of unity. These are foreshocks of the Antichrist.

Jesus asked the question, "When the Son of Man comes, will He really find faith on the earth?" (Luke 18:8). A better translation of that passage would say "*the* faith." When Christ returns for His church, will He find *the* faith on Earth? Will He find true believers with a biblical worldview?

Yes, I think He will find it in places. But in other prominent places where it ought to be, it may very well be missing. That is why we need to teach, preach, and hold on to the Word of God.

So the white horse comes. The rider appears to be a force for good, but in reality he is the embodiment of evil. To some he might seem like the Messiah, but he is the false messiah. He is not Jesus Christ; he is the Antichrist.

THE RED HORSE

> When He opened the second seal, I heard the second living creature saying, "Come and see." Another horse, fiery red, went out. And it was granted to the one who sat on it to take peace from the earth, and that people should kill one another; and there was given to him a great sword. (Revelation 6:3–4)

When we read the words *fiery red*, we are reminded of the description of the Devil in Revelation 12:3, who is represented as a "great, fiery red dragon." Satan himself is the one behind the wars and struggles on this planet, from the beginning of time right up to today's heartbreaking headlines. Jesus said of Satan in John 10:10, "The thief comes only to steal and kill and destroy" (NIV).

Notice the difference between Jesus Christ and the Antichrist. At the coming of Jesus Christ, we have peace on Earth, while at the coming of the Antichrist, we have peace taken from Earth.

The text says that a great sword is given to the rider of the red horse. The Greek word used here for *sword* speaks of the short, stabbing sword that a Roman soldier used in close combat.

Rome, of course, had an amazing army, with many brilliant strategies and tactics they used to subdue their enemies. We have seen them depicted in films like *Gladiator* and others, where soldiers marched into battle holding those big shields the size of a door and carrying their long spears.

They would march in unison, and if there was a barrage of arrows, they would bunch together and put up those shields over and in front of them, creating an almost impenetrable box. As they entered close combat, however, they would cast the large shield aside because it was far too cumbersome to carry. They had a smaller round shield and used a short sword when they were up close and personal with an opponent.

GOOD TO KNOW

At the coming of Jesus Christ, we have peace on Earth, while at the coming of the Antichrist, we have peace taken from Earth.

This is the same sort of sword that might be used by an assassin, perhaps hidden under a robe. That is the sword carried by the rider of the red horse. Is he also the Antichrist? Using such an assassin's sword, it could mean that he will show one face to the world and then suddenly show himself to be something else. He will seem like a friend and then, in a vulnerable moment, will pull out his sword and stab his surprised victim through the heart. And he will do this through war.

Our nation has seen some horrible wars in our history. In World War I, more than ten million people lost their lives. It was so horrific that it was described as "the war to end all wars." But of course it was only twenty years later when another far more terrible war, World War II, shook the world, killing fifty million people. As awful as these wars were, however, they are nothing compared to the scale of war that will be released by Satan during the Great Tribulation.

The destruction could occur in one of two ways—or perhaps even in both ways. The devastation might result from a series of natural disasters, as we have seen in earthquakes, tsunamis, fires, and volcanic eruptions.

On the other hand, it might be a situation in which all the nuclear arsenals of nations all over the world will be released at once.

Although most of us weren't alive to see it, we've all heard about the two atomic bombs dropped on Japan during World War II when they refused to surrender. It is estimated that around 200,000 people died in Nagasaki and Hiroshima as a result.

Yet today, one nuclear submarine carries enough explosive firepower in its warhead equal to forty times the force of every bomb exploded in World War II put together. It has been estimated by some that there are 23,000 nuclear weapons in the world now. But it wouldn't take that many to unleash global destruction. It would only take a few.

For years we lived by what was called the MAD theory—an acronym for mutually assured destruction. In the Cold War with the Soviet Union, no one wanted to risk starting a war that would completely decimate both nations. So neither side used its weapons (though we may have come close to using them a couple of times).

Now, however, we live in a different world. It is not just about the so-called superpowers like Russia, the United States, and China. Now we have rogue nations like North Korea and Pakistan with such weapons. Iran is growing closer by the day to developing its own arsenal of nukes—and their stated goal is to wipe Israel off the map.

Years ago President Ronald Reagan said, "Man has used every weapon he has ever devised. It takes no crystal ball to perceive that a nuclear war is likely, and in a nuclear war, all mankind would lose." [14]

That is true. And it's interesting to note that the red horse of war is immediately followed by the black horse of scarcity and famine, with death close behind.

Death rides a pale horse.

THE BLACK HORSE AND THE PALE HORSE

> When He opened the third seal, I heard the third living creature say, "Come and see." So I looked, and behold, a black horse, and he who sat on it had a pair of scales in his hand. And I heard a voice in the midst of the four living creatures saying, "A quart of wheat for a denarius, and three quarts of barley for a denarius; and do not harm the oil and the wine."
>
> When He opened the fourth seal, I heard the voice of the fourth living creature saying, "Come and see." So I looked, and behold, a pale horse. And the name of him who sat on it was Death, and Hades followed with him. And power was given to them over a fourth of the earth, to kill with sword, with hunger, with death, and by the beasts of the earth. (Revelation 6:5–8)

The Greek word translated "pale" is *chloros*. It's where we get our word *chlorine*. It means this horse was a shade of yellowish green—not an attractive color. It is one associated with sickness and even death. In 2020 we witnessed how quickly a pandemic can devastate the world as COVID-19 claimed more than three million lives and sickened millions of others.

The successive horsemen look like this: the white horse comes, ridden by a so-called good guy who is really a bad guy. He is followed by a red horse bringing war, which is followed by a black horse representing famine and disease and all the terrible aftermath of a worldwide conflict. Inevitably, death, on the pale horse, comes next.

It makes me think of what scientists call a nuclear winter, which follows a nuclear blast. The *Los Angeles Times* published an article that said such a winter would ultimately kill more people than the original atomic explosion. [15]

This scenario, unimaginable to previous generations, could easily unfold in our time. Why would God permit this? Because He is a God of justice, and He has determined to let evil run its course before He establishes His kingdom of righteousness.

Nevertheless, remember this: even during this hellish Tribulation period, the Lord will extend opportunity after opportunity for people to turn from their sins, believe, and be saved.

These chapters in Revelation present a bleak scenario, don't they? It certainly demonstrates what the ultimate result of sin will be on our world and reminds us that sins—even so-called little sins—are nothing to play with or take lightly.

The Antichrist is close. He could be alive today. But the Bible doesn't tell us to watch for the Antichrist; it tells us to watch for Jesus Christ.

GOOD TO KNOW
During the Tribulation period, the Lord will still extend opportunities for people to be saved.

Right now the restraining force in the world is the Holy Spirit working through the church of Jesus Christ. But once the church is removed in the Rapture, the Antichrist will be revealed.

HOW, THEN, SHOULD WE LIVE?

In view of all these devastations, deceptions, and dangers lying just over the horizon of our day, how should we as Christians live our lives as we await our Lord's return?

The apostle Paul writes a beautiful paragraph on how we ought to view and live our lives in these last days before Christ's return at the Rapture:

> For you yourselves know perfectly that the day of the Lord so comes as a thief in the night. For when they say, "Peace and safety!" then sudden destruction comes upon them, as labor pains upon a pregnant woman. And they shall not escape. But you, brethren, are not in darkness, so that this Day should overtake you as a thief. You are all sons of light and sons of the day. We are not of the night nor of darkness. Therefore let us not sleep, as others do, but let us watch and be sober. For those who sleep, sleep at night, and those who get drunk are drunk at night. But let us who are of the

day be sober, putting on the breastplate of faith and love, and as a helmet the hope of salvation. For God did not appoint us to wrath, but to obtain salvation through our Lord Jesus Christ, who died for us, that whether we wake or sleep, we should live together with Him. (1 Thessalonians 5:2–10)

No, we are not "appointed to wrath." We will not be here when God pours out those terrible judgments during the days of the Tribulation. In fact, Christ will remove His bride, His church, before the Antichrist is revealed. So how should we live in light of that?

The apostle Paul gives us three instructions.

1. Wake up.

Let us not sleep, as others do. (verse 6)

There are people in the church today who have gone to sleep—and I don't mean nodding off during a boring sermon. What this means is they are lethargic, passive, even lazy, and don't bother to watch the signs of the times. There seems to be a disconnect between their so-called spiritual lives and their real, walking-around-on-earth lives. Instead of walking in the Spirit as they ought to do, they are sleepwalking.

So the Bible is saying that we need to wake up to the urgency of the time. We need to open our eyes to what is transpiring all around us and give some thought to the nearness of our Lord's return.

2. Sober up.

Let us who are of the day be sober. (verse 8)

I spent the first seventeen years of my life around drunken people, so I feel that I can speak somewhat authoritatively on this. My mother was a raging alcoholic, and I spent a good deal of time in bars, waiting for my mom to get done drinking.

Here was the cycle of my life through pretty much every day of my childhood when I lived with my mom. She would have some cocktails before dinner and then go out. She would come home raging drunk and then scream, yell, and throw things around. Then she would pass out.

Then she would do the same thing the next day and the next.

The Bible is saying, "Sober up."

I think we can interpret this both literally and figuratively. First of all, we know the Scriptures command us not to be drunk. How can you keep from getting drunk? Don't drink alcohol in the first place. If you drink, you could fall under the influence of the alcohol, and you don't want to run the risk.

Jesus said in Luke 21:34, "Be careful, or your hearts will be weighed down with carousing, drunkenness and the anxieties of life, and that day will close on you suddenly like a trap" (NIV). An expanded translation from the Greek says, "But be on guard, so that your hearts are not weighed down with the giddiness of debauchery and the nausea of self-indulgence" (AMP).

As for me, I don't want to be under the influence of anyone or anything but Jesus Christ and His Holy Spirit.

That is the first and obvious interpretation. But we can also be intoxicated with other things—things that aren't the main thing. In other words, I can become preoccupied with stuff. I can become distracted, wrapped up in, and sometimes distressed by what I'm going to eat, where I'm going to live, or what I'm going to wear. I can be diverted from a simple walk with Christ by the pursuit of money, hobbies, vacations, politics, or a thousand other substitutes for God.

Paul was saying, "Don't let yourself become overly preoccupied. Don't make your life about the pursuit of fame or money or material possessions. Stay alert and wide awake, so that you will be ready when the Rapture comes."

3. Suit up.

> Putting on the breastplate of faith and love, and as a helmet the hope of salvation. (verse 8)

Chained as he was to Roman guards during the latter part of his ministry, Paul had a lot of time to research Roman armor. Knowing Paul, I'm guessing that he struck up conversations with those guards: "What's your name? . . . Where are you from? . . . So, tell me about your armor. How do these things work?"

I have some friends who are police officers, and I've asked them to describe the items they carry on their Sam Browne, or utility belt. I will say, "What do you do with this thing? What does that do? Where does that go?"

It's the same with today's soldier going into combat and all the equipment they wear.

In this passage Paul was saying, "Suit up. Put on the armor of God."

Why?

Because, as Bible teacher Warren Wiersbe has said, "The Christian life is not a playground; it's a battleground." [16] If you are a Christian, you're in a battle whether you like it or not.

Someone might say, "Well, I don't like war. I'm a spiritual pacifist."

All right. Then prepare to be defeated—or devoured.

Every believer needs to learn how to strap on his or her armor and learn how to handle the sword of the Spirit, which is the Word of God.

As you wait for the Lord to come for His church, *wake up, sober up,* and *suit up.*

I love the way Paul summed things up in Romans 13, from the J. B. Phillips New Testament:

> Why all this stress on behaviour? Because, as I think you have realised, the present time is of the highest importance—it is time to wake up to reality. Every day brings God's salvation nearer. The night is nearly over, the day has almost dawned. Let us therefore fling away the things that men do in the dark, let us arm ourselves for the fight of the day! Let us live cleanly, as in the daylight, not in the "delights" of getting drunk or playing with sex, nor yet in quarrelling or jealousies. Let us be Christ's men from head to foot, and give no chances to the flesh to have its fling. (verses 11–14 PH)

The night is nearly over, the day has almost dawned! If ever there was a time when we needed to be wide awake, it is now.

THREE TAKEAWAY TRUTHS

- Be on guard against any "peace" or "unity" that compromises biblical truth.
- The Antichrist cannot be revealed until the church is taken away in the Rapture.
- In these last days, all Christians should be awake and alert spiritually.

CHAPTER ELEVEN

What Heaven Knows About Earth

And they cried with a loud voice, saying, "How long, O Lord, holy and true, until You judge and avenge our blood on those who dwell on the earth?"
(Revelation 6:10)

IN THIS CHAPTER

- Those in Heaven may know more than you think.
- What to remember when it seems like God is late
- Understanding the identity and role of the 144,000

I don't like to be late to anything, but I *especially* don't like walking into a movie after it's already started.

Let's face it. If you miss the first part of a movie, you miss a lot. Sometimes it's in those opening frames and initial scenes of a film where you get a handle on the main characters and learn who's who and what's what. If you come in and sit down ten minutes after the movie has already begun, you might never know what's going on.

So that's my priority: get there on time.

My wife, Cathe, has another priority.

She always has to get popcorn first. It's like an unwritten law: *must have popcorn at the movie.* Obtaining that popcorn is even more important to her than being there when the movie starts. (In the interest of full disclosure, I like popcorn, too. But after all, priorities are priorities.)

Here in Revelation, as we reach chapters 6 and 7, the "movie" is well underway. The music is swelling, and the real action of the book has begun. In chapters 1 through 5, the apostle John has set the stage. Now the great conflict has begun and is accelerating.

THE GREAT CONFLICT

It almost looks as though evil will reign on Earth, and the Antichrist will win the day. Thankfully, however, we know how all this will end. (Spoiler alert!) Jesus Christ *will* return, Satan and his cohorts will be defeated, and Jesus will establish His kingdom of righteousness on Earth.

In chapters 6 through 19 of Revelation, we witness twenty-one judgments that will be unleashed in the world during the seven-year period of the Great Tribulation. Within the pages of Revelation, we have three distinct series of future judgments: seven seals, seven trumpets, and seven bowls.

Let me say at the outset that God doesn't enjoy any of it.

Yes, Psalm 2 tells us that the Lord laughs in derision at those who rebel against His Son. But speaking to His own rebellious people in Ezekiel 33:11, the Lord said, "As surely as I live, . . . I take no pleasure in the death of the wicked, but rather that they turn from their ways and live. Turn! Turn from your evil ways!" (NIV).

In both the Old Testament and the New, the Scriptures present a God who is good, loving, and merciful. But at the same time, He is righteous and just. In the book of Revelation, He is looking at a world that has rejected His Son and His sacrifice for sin. And now, having rejected God's mercy and God's love, the world faces His just and righteous wrath.

This is what plays out through the remaining chapters of the book. As I stated earlier, the four horsemen, described in the first eight verses of chapter 6, serve as an overview, or flyover, of the entire book.

It's at this time the Antichrist begins to enforce his agenda on Planet Earth. His pseudo benevolence gives way to bloodthirsty vengeance on all who dare to disagree with him. Following the black horse of famine, we have the pale horse, bringing pestilence, disease, and all the rest.

We also see a group of courageous believers in Christ who have been put to death for their faith. Our story picks up with these believers, now safely in Heaven and out of Satan's reach forever.

"HOW LONG, O LORD?"

> When He opened the fifth seal, I saw under the altar the souls of those who had been slain for the word of God and for the testimony which they held. And they cried with a loud voice, saying, "How long, O Lord, holy and true, until You judge and avenge our blood on those who dwell on the earth?" Then a white robe was given to each of them; and it was said to them that they should rest a little while longer, until both the number of their fellow servants and their brethren, who would be killed as they were, was completed. (Revelation 6:9–11)

Who are these people? These are men and women who have received Jesus Christ as Savior during the Great Tribulation, after the church has been raptured. Included among these may be some of the people you shared the gospel with but who didn't make a decision. After the church is caught up to meet the Lord in the air, however, they will realize what has happened, commit their lives to Christ, and stand up for their faith.

Notice in verse 5 that we are given two reasons why they will be martyred. These people will have been slain . . .

> for the Word of God, and
> for the testimony they have held.

In other words, because they are true followers of Jesus, they will stand up for God's Word, and the Antichrist simply won't tolerate this. They also will be known for the word of their testimony. They will have fearlessly proclaimed their faith in Jesus, even in the face of savage opposition.

Are you standing up for the Word of God in the same way? Do people know where you stand as a follower of Jesus Christ? Do you express your opinion openly?

Secondly, do you have a good testimony? Do people know the story of how you came to faith in Christ?

The truth is that if you are speaking up for the Word of God and have a good testimony, then you also will face something similar to what these people will face.

Why is that? Because, as we have already noted, "the spirit of the antichrist,

GOOD TO KNOW

If you are speaking up for the Word of God and living out your faith, you will face some persecution in this world.

which you have heard is coming *and even now is already in the world*" (1 John 4:3 NIV, emphasis added). I'm not saying that you will be put in prison or put to death for your faith, though in some parts of the world you would be. What I am saying is that you ought to expect some persecution in some way, shape, or form.

The Bible clearly says, "Yes, and all who desire to live godly in Christ Jesus will suffer persecution" (2 Timothy 3:12).

Or as *The Message* renders it, "Anyone who wants to live all out for Christ is in for a lot of trouble; there's no getting around it."

So if you said to me, "Greg, I'm never persecuted or hassled. I get along with everyone. No one ever disagrees with me or challenges me," I would say that something in your life isn't as it should be. Again, the Bible says that if you are living a godly life, then you will face opposition in some form.

Sometimes Christians, however, are persecuted for the wrong reasons. Sometimes Christians are persecuted for being obnoxious or unnecessarily confrontational or just downright rude. Christians face opposition and scorn if they are overly judgmental, petty, or mean-spirited. That's not legitimate persecution; that's just people reacting to an annoying person in their midst. Nevertheless, we should be persecuted for standing up for what is right and for the word of our testimony. This was the case with the believers who waited under the altar in Heaven.

And that brings us to the heart of this chapter.

WHAT DO PEOPLE IN HEAVEN KNOW ABOUT EVENTS ON EARTH?

What do people in Heaven know about what's transpiring here on Earth? Do they know? Do they even care? Could they be watching us even now?

There seem to be two schools of thought on this topic. Some insist that once we are in Heaven, we will be so preoccupied with worshiping God that the last thing on our minds will be events on Earth. Besides, with all the tragedies and sorrow on our poor broken planet, it wouldn't really be Heaven if we had to experience sadness while watching events unfold.

Others imagine the people in Heaven watching our every move, as though we were part of a reality TV show. According to this line of thought, loved ones in Heaven might even intervene in our lives from time to time, directing our steps and helping us know what to do.

You might be surprised to hear that I believe both views are incorrect.

Maybe you would say, "Why should I even care about this, Greg?"

Here's the answer: you *will* care if you have a loved one who now lives in Heaven. That is certainly true in the case of Cathe and me. In 2008 our thirty-three-year-old son Christopher suddenly and unexpectedly entered the presence of God after dying in an automobile accident. Clearly, it was the worst moment of our lives when we heard that news, and we still grieve and miss him every day.

I believe the moment Christopher took his last breath on Earth that he took his first breath in Heaven. The moment he closed his eyes on earth, he opened them in Heaven. I've always been interested in what happens in the afterlife, but now I want to know everything I can know. What is my son doing there right now? What can I expect when I get there? What do people know about all the goings-on back here on Earth?

I've become a student of Heaven, and I've also become a student of *hope*. How can we have hope in the midst of crisis?

I think in time we all will become interested in these topics, because the older we get, the more people we know will die and pass into eternity.

"That's depressing," you might say. "Why should I want to read about that in a book?"

My answer is simple: life is hard.

Maybe you didn't get that memo. Frankly, it's time that you did.

But even though life is hard, it's also true that God is good, and He will give you the strength and hope that you need in life.

MORE THOUGHTS ABOUT HEAVEN

We touched on the subject of Heaven in chapter 8. Here are some additional observations. I must acknowledge the writings of my friend Randy Alcorn here, as his outstanding book *Heaven* really helped me expand my thinking on this topic.

People in eternity are aware that loved ones are not saved.

In Luke 16 Jesus told a story about a nameless rich man and a poor man named Lazarus. Both men died, and Jesus told how Lazarus went to a place of comfort called Abraham's bosom, and the rich man went to a place of torment called Hades.

Prior to the death and resurrection of Jesus, when an unbeliever died, he or she went to a place of comfort, waiting for the day when Jesus would die, be raised again, and open the door to Heaven. If you died as a nonbeliever, you went to Hades, which also was a place of waiting, and you lived in torment and agony.

"But Greg," someone will say, "isn't this just a parable?"

No, because in parables, Jesus would say "a certain man" and not name any individual. In this case Jesus gave a name, indicating these were real people and that this actually happened.

In this rich-man-poor-man story, the virtue was not in being poor, and the sin was not in being rich. The sin was that the rich man was so preoccupied with himself and with his wealth that he had no compassion for anyone else and no interest in God. Lazarus, an apparently disabled beggar, lived off the scraps that fell from the rich man's table.

In the course of time, death knocked on the doors of both men. Death is no respecter of persons. It doesn't matter whether you are wealthy or impoverished, famous or unknown. Everybody dies. Death is the great equalizer.

In the eternal realm, in the divided place of waiting, the rich man was in torment in Hades, and Lazarus was experiencing comfort and rest in Abraham's bosom (or "in the place of the righteous dead," as it says in the Living Bible).

Our Lord's story suggests that people in eternity are fully conscious of what is transpiring back on Earth. The rich man saw Abraham from afar and shouted to him:

> "Please, Father Abraham, at least send him [Lazarus] to my father's home. For I have five brothers, and I want him to warn them so they don't end up in this place of torment."

> But Abraham said, "Moses and the prophets have warned them. Your brothers can read what they wrote."

> The rich man replied, "No, Father Abraham! But if someone is sent to them from the dead, then they will repent of their sins and turn to God."

> But Abraham said, "If they won't listen to Moses and the prophets, they won't be persuaded even if someone rises from the dead." (Luke 16:27–31 NLT)

The rich man in Hades was fully conscious of Abraham on the paradise side of the afterlife. He wanted to warn his brothers about the place of torment. From my reading, this indicates knowledge in eternity about what is happening on Earth.

GOOD TO KNOW
In the afterlife we are the same people and possess the same memories

In the afterlife we are the same people and possess the same memories. In fact, I'm convinced that we will know *more* in Heaven than we know on Earth, not less. We don't all get a collective lobotomy when we move from Earth to glory. This man in Hades remembered things. He recalled his five brothers and was concerned for them.

When people believe in Jesus on Earth, it is public knowledge in Heaven.

In Luke 15, Jesus told a story about three things that were lost and then found again.

Anyone who knows me would agree that I tend to lose things. And the older I get, the more I seem to lose. I lose my car at the mall all the time, coming out to the parking lot with no clue as to where my wheels might be in that vast sea of vehicles. So I have to walk around with my electronic keys, pushing the red button and listening for my car to beep at me. It's a little embarrassing.

In His first account, Jesus told a story about a shepherd with one hundred sheep who loses one. So he leaves the ninety-nine and goes and searches for the sheep. When the shepherd finds the lost animal, he wraps it around his shoulders and returns to the fold, saying to his friends, "Rejoice with me because I have found my lost sheep" (verse 6 NLT). Then Jesus added this amazing application: "In the same way, there is more joy in heaven over one lost sinner who repents and returns to God than over ninety-nine others who are righteous and haven't strayed away!" (verse 7 NLT).

Then Jesus told the story about a woman who lost a coin. It may not seem like a big deal to lose a coin, but back in this day, married women would wear a headband, or wedding band. Within this band they would have coins. To lose a coin from this wedding band, then, would be like losing your wedding ring. Obviously you would search high and low to try and find it. The coin would have both monetary and sentimental value.

So she searched until she found it. Happily calling in her friends and neighbors, she said, "Rejoice with me because I have found my lost coin" (verse 9 NLT).

Then Jesus added these words: "In the same way, there is joy in the presence of God's angels when even one sinner repents" (verse 10 NLT).

Then finally Jesus told the familiar parable of the prodigal son. The father in the story waited and waited for his son to come home, and when he did, he rejoiced and threw a big party.

Two things jump out at me from this trio of stories. First, a wave of joy rolls across Heaven when even one person repents and turns to God. The residents of Heaven break out in applause and cheering. This reminds us of how important evangelism is to God. He cares deeply about lost men and women.

The second thing I note here is Christ's statement that "there is joy in the presence of God's angels" over one sinner who repents. Notice that Jesus didn't say there was joy *among* the angels themselves, though there may be. Rather, He said there was joy *in the presence of* God's angels. I'm not saying that the angels don't rejoice. They probably do. But in this case, I think Jesus might have been speaking of something else. In fact, He may have been speaking of the loved ones who have preceded us to Heaven being aware when someone comes to Christ because of their lives and testimonies.

Imagine that you are up in Heaven, and you get word (or see with your own eyes) that your daughter, your son, your great-grandchild, or the old buddy that you used to work with and shared the gospel with has finally come to Christ. Heaven rejoices, and you celebrate too, knowing that God gave you the privilege of having a part in that person's salvation.

To me, it's just a reminder that your life's impact isn't over just because you leave this planet. If you have lived for Christ and have taken time to sow seeds of the gospel in people's hearts, then God will continue to honor those efforts after you have moved on into eternity. One of the people you have influenced for Christ might have a child who also comes to Christ. Who knows? That young person might become the next Billy Graham,

GOOD TO KNOW

If you have lived for Christ and have taken time to sow seeds of the gospel in people's hearts, then God will continue to honor those efforts after you have moved on into eternity.

leading thousands or millions to the Lord. And all of that eternal fruit will be credited to your account.

I think it is possible that we may be aware of such things in Heaven.

People in Heaven know about the time and place of events on Earth.

> I saw under the altar the souls of those who had been slain for the word of God and for the testimony which they held. And they cried with a loud voice, saying, "How long, O Lord, holy and true, until You judge and avenge our blood on those who dwell on the earth?" (Revelation 6:9–10)

Again, these are people who were martyred for their faith during the Tribulation period and are safely in Heaven. But notice how they're aware of what is happening on Earth. They know they were killed and their blood was shed for following Christ. They also were aware of time passing on Earth.

They're asking, "How long, O Lord, until You avenge us?"

In verse 11, they are told they "should rest a little while longer."

There is a connection between believers in Heaven and believers on Earth.

Verse 11 speaks of the martyrs' "fellow servants and their brethren" back on Earth. The heavenly martyrs are concerned about those who are still in the midst of the battle, in the terrible days of the Great Tribulation, and they seem to be aware of the injustice being done to them.

MEANWHILE, BACK ON EARTH . . .

> I looked when He opened the sixth seal, and behold, there was a great earthquake; and the sun became black as sackcloth of hair, and the moon became like blood. And the stars of heaven fell to the earth, as a fig tree drops its late figs when it is shaken by a mighty wind. Then the sky receded as a scroll when it is

rolled up, and every mountain and island was moved out of its place. And the kings of the earth, the great men, the rich men, the commanders, the mighty men, every slave and every free man, hid themselves in the caves and in the rocks of the mountains, and said to the mountains and rocks, "Fall on us and hide us from the face of Him who sits on the throne and from the wrath of the Lamb! For the great day of His wrath has come, and who is able to stand?" (Revelation 6:12–17)

In the first part of Revelation 6, we read about the four horsemen of the apocalypse—a moment when God apparently allows man to unleash his own fearsome weapons. But now in this latter part of chapter 6, God Himself brings His judgment upon Earth. Verse 13 mentions the very stars of Heaven falling to Earth.

What is the reaction to these terrifying judgments? In verse 16 we read that nonbelievers try to hide from God and from "the face of Him who sits on the throne."

When facing death, people sometimes will come to their senses and turn to the Lord for help. I've heard many stories of people coming to Jesus on their deathbed. Thank God for His mercy! Thank God that He will forgive a person, no matter how wicked of a life he or she has lived, if they will turn to Jesus, even in those last moments of life.

Think of the thief who was crucified next to Jesus at Calvary. The Greek word translated "thief" means more than a shoplifter. It speaks of a criminal who may have even launched an insurrection or committed murder. He was probably a rebel against the Roman occupation. But when he turned to Jesus in the last moments of his life and gasped out, "Lord, remember me when You come into Your kingdom" (Luke 23:42), Jesus forgave him.

The Lord said, "Today you will be with Me in Paradise" (verse 44).

My own mother came to Christ shortly before she passed away.

More often than not, however, people will die as they have lived. The people described here in Revelation 6 are dying with hearts that are still hardened toward God. But instead of crying out to God for mercy, they plead with the mountains and rocks to hide them.

WHO ARE THE 144,000?

In Revelation 7 John introduces us to a mysterious group of people who have a prominent role in those turbulent days:

> After these things I saw four angels standing at the four corners of the earth, holding the four winds of the earth, that the wind should not blow on the earth, on the sea, or on any tree. Then I saw another angel ascending from the east, having the seal of the living God. And he cried with a loud voice to the four angels to whom it was granted to harm the earth and the sea, saying, "Do not harm the earth, the sea, or the trees till we have sealed the servants of our God on their foreheads." And I heard the number of those who were sealed. One hundred and forty-four thousand of all the tribes of the children of Israel were sealed. (verses 1–4)

Who are these 144,000 servants of God? I can assure you, they are *not* Jehovah's Witnesses. I bring this up because for many years this group believed they were the 144,000 identified in the Scriptures. But then, as their numbers began to exceed that total, they had to adapt their theology accordingly. Now they say these are a special, or elite, group of Jehovah's Witnesses.

To even claim to be one of these people is rather curious, because they don't exist yet. They're still in our future. Furthermore, it's clear from the text they are drawn from the twelve tribes of Israel—Jewish people.

Apparently after the church is caught up to Heaven at the Rapture, God will single out this special group of 144,000 Jews who find Jesus as their Messiah. Revelation 14:3 tells us they will have their own song, which only they know. No one can sing their song but them. In the next verse we read that they "follow the Lamb wherever He goes." In other words, they stay very close to God. No one can bring a charge of falsehood against any of these witnesses; they live blameless lives.

In spite of the Antichrist's fierce hatred of this group, he can't harm them. They're like indestructible superheroes, but not because of their own power. It's because they are protected by God. At the end of the book of Revelation, they stand on Mount Zion with Jesus Himself.

What's more, they are *preachers*. They'll be like 144,000 apostle Pauls, unleashed on the world all at once. Or maybe they'll be like 144,000 kosher Billy Grahams, roaming the planet.

Will people on Earth, then, still be given a chance to believe, even in the midst of the Tribulation period? You'd better believe it!

In addition to this, John wrote about an angel who declared the gospel:

> Then I saw another angel flying in the midst of heaven, having the everlasting gospel to preach to those who dwell on the earth—to every nation, tribe, tongue, and people—saying with a loud voice, "Fear God and give glory to Him, for the hour of His judgment has come; and worship Him who made heaven and earth, the sea and springs of water." (Revelation 14:6–7)

You might describe this as an angelic mop-up mission. This is God, in His great mercy, giving everyone on Earth who wants to respond to the gospel a final opportunity before the end. Jesus Himself told His disciples, "And this gospel of the kingdom will be preached in the whole world as a testimony to all nations, and then the end will come" (Matthew 24:14 NIV).

We certainly need to do this before the Rapture as well, knowing that whoever receives the Lord before He returns for His church will be spared the terrors of the Great Tribulation. But this is one more assurance the entire world will hear the gospel and will have an opportunity to respond before Christ returns and the end comes.

I say "end." But it really will be a new beginning.

The result of the preaching of the 144,000—and presumably this angelic presentation of the everlasting gospel—will result in the largest revival in human history. Revelation 7:9 tells us that so many people become believers in the Great Tribulation that their number can't be counted.

Great salvation, great mercy, and great joy will emerge from the greatest horrors this world has ever seen. Heaven's eternal ranks will grow beyond measure as Earth groans under judgment. How frustrating that must be for the Evil One and his generals!

ARE PEOPLE IN HEAVEN WATCHING US RIGHT NOW?

The 2012 Olympics in London were viewed by a global audience of one billion people. Those who watched, however, couldn't help but notice a lot of empty seats at many of these events.

Why was that?

As it turned out, wealthy corporate sponsors bought up many of those seats but somehow didn't get tickets to the people who wanted to go. Foreign governments held many more, some trying to grab a financial windfall by charging exorbitant prices for them. The result was that many of the venues were half empty, even though athletes desperately tried to obtain tickets for their families.

It's more encouraging and inspiring for athletes to perform in the presence of loved ones and friends cheering them on rather than in front of empty seats.

The fact is that you and I are being cheered on right now, at this moment.

Who is cheering us on?

Heaven is cheering us on.

The book of Hebrews tells us, "Therefore we also, since we are surrounded by so great a cloud of witnesses, let us lay aside every weight, and the sin which so easily ensnares us, and let us run with endurance the race that is set before us, looking unto Jesus, the author and finisher of our faith" (12:1–2).

You and I are in the race of life at this very moment, and this passage tells us that we are surrounded by "so great a cloud of witnesses." Who is in that great cloud?

It must have something to do with the magnificent passage right before Hebrews 12, which is Hebrews 11 and its description of the great men and women of faith who have gone on before us. These are people who, though imperfect as we are, served the Lord with courage, faithfulness, and perseverance. These would include Abraham, Sarah, Joseph, Moses, Rahab, Gideon, and the prophets. The list goes on. Some have called this roll call of God's servants in Hebrews 11 the Hall of Faith. I wrote a book about these believers called *World Changers*.

Is the author of Hebrews saying that we are being personally cheered on by Abraham in Heaven? Is he watching us face our daily challenges and saying, "Keep going! Keep running! Keep pressing on"? Or, is the author simply saying that Abraham is an example for us, urging us to follow in his footsteps of faith?

Honestly, I don't know.

It may very well be that Heaven is watching Earth right now and that in some way, shape, or form, our departed loved ones are in the grandstands, cheering us on.

But even if they aren't, I know this much: *Jesus is watching us.* And He is the entire reason for our race, the reason we run with endurance.

Coming back to Hebrews 12, Jesus is "the author and finisher of our faith" (verse 2). The Olympic Games started in Greece and may have been the premiere sporting event in the first century. In the ancient games, there were no corporate sponsorships. Back then, Nike was a god they worshiped, not a shoe they wore.

At the end of the race, an emperor or some high official would give out crowns of laurel leaves to the winner. No, it wasn't a gold or silver medal, but that award was highly desired and coveted by every participant. If you were running a race, you might see the emperor at the end, holding out the reward for the winner. And that certainly would give you added motivation to run well.

In our lives, it isn't the emperor who waits at the end, but the King of kings and Lord of lords, our Creator, Savior, and Friend. We run for an audience of One. We run for Jesus. And the wonderful thing about it is that He not only waits at the end to welcome us across the finish line, but He is also with us every step of the way.

He is saying, "Keep going! You can do this! You're almost home!"

None of us know when our lives will end. It may be years from now. It may be tomorrow or even before the sun sets on today.

The main thing is that we want to be ready.

THREE TAKEAWAY TRUTHS

- If persecuted for the right reasons, Christians have abundant reason to rejoice.
- We may not realize the full impact we had on Earth for the Lord—until we get to Heaven.
- When you seek to live a godly life, all Heaven roots for you.

CHAPTER TWELVE
Apocalypse Now

And I saw the seven angels who stand before God,
and to them were given seven trumpets.
(Revelation 8:2)

IN THIS CHAPTER
- The beginning of the seven trumpet judgments
- Why God's judgment should be a very solemn subject
- What the story of Jonah shows us about the heart of God.
- Three ways in which God answers our prayers

In Revelation, chapter 8, God's judgment falls on Earth in a terrible, frightening way.

Whenever you raise the topic of God's judgment on our world, some people have a knee-jerk answer: "It's about time."

They seem to have no problem with the prospect of God's fiery wrath falling upon a world that has rejected His Son and His Word. In fact, they will tell you that it is long overdue. If they were honest, they might even admit taking a certain amount of pleasure at the thought. They're like "the sons of thunder" who wanted to call down fire from Heaven to vaporize the Samaritans who had turned Jesus away (see Luke 9:51–56).

I can certainly understand this train of thought and have felt that way myself at times.

I just don't think it's pleasing to the Lord. In fact, the Lord rebuked His prophet Jonah for that very same attitude. You may remember that the Lord had commanded Jonah to preach to the people of Nineveh, which was the capital city of the evil Assyrian empire. These Ninevites were a sadistic and wicked people, and Jonah, a patriotic Jew who hated the enemies of Israel, flat-out didn't want to go to them. Besides that, Jonah half suspected that the Assyrians might actually repent, and God would forgive them and spare them.

Jonah didn't want them to be forgiven and spared. He wanted them to be judged and smashed.

Most likely you know the story: God's reluctant prophet took passage on a ship headed in the opposite direction from Nineveh. Did he really think he could run away from God? Probably not, but he was so upset about the task that God had given him that he decided to give it a shot. Then, in the midst of a terrifying storm at sea (sent by God), Jonah went overboard and was swallowed by a great fish (also sent by God). Three days later Jonah repented, and God commanded the fish to vomit up His spokesman on dry land—somewhere near the road to Nineveh.

Jonah followed through this time and preached the message that God had given him: "Forty more days and Nineveh will be overthrown" (Jonah 3:4 NIV).

Yes, he obeyed. But he was the most reluctant, foot-dragging preacher you could imagine, and he hoped with all his heart that no one would listen to him.

Nevertheless, they did listen, because God had prepared their hearts. The whole city responded to Jonah's preaching, humbled themselves, and sought the mercy of Heaven. It probably was the greatest revival in human history. Even so, Jonah held out hope that God would still judge the city and blast them off the map.

But here's a part of that story that's often overlooked.

After he had preached and the people had repented, we read that Jonah "went out of the city to the east and sat down in a sulk. He put together a makeshift shelter of leafy branches and sat there in the shade to see what would happen to the city" (Jonah 4:5 MSG).

It was like going to a movie. Jonah had his popcorn and Milk Duds, and he sat there in his seat somewhere above the city, waiting for God to pour out judgment in Dolby Digital and 3-D on those disgusting Assyrians.

On the other hand, it wasn't much like being at the movies at all, because the prophet was sitting in the blazing Middle Eastern sun instead of an air-conditioned theater.

The Lord caused a large, leafy plant to grow up, bringing welcome shade over Jonah's head, and the prophet was ecstatic about the plant. Now he could watch in comfort as the judgment fell! But judgment didn't come, and in the meantime, God sent a worm to gnaw through the plant stem and wither Jonah's shade.

Already angry, Jonah was beside himself at the loss of his shady plant. In fact, he was so miserable that he didn't want to live anymore and asked God to just kill him.

Here's how the Lord replied: "You have been concerned about this plant, though you did not tend it or make it grow. It sprang up overnight and died overnight. And should I not have concern for the great city of Nineveh, in which there are more than a hundred and twenty thousand people who cannot tell their right hand from their left—and also many animals?" (Jonah 4:10–11 NIV).

Jonah didn't care about the men and women who would die, or even the little ones, who didn't know left from right. God was saying, "You should be rejoicing that I spared all of those people and their animals."

It's just one more reminder that God takes no delight in the death of the wicked (see Ezekiel 33:11), and neither should we. We shouldn't rejoice over anyone being judged by God and cast away from His presence. Frankly, every one of us deserves such judgment, but God has shown mercy to us in Christ and allowed us to experience His forgiveness and salvation. It is His nature to love and to forgive. He doesn't want to judge people, but He must judge people.

Why, you ask? Why must God judge people?

Because God is not only loving, but He is also righteous and holy.

In Revelation 4:8, we read about those mighty angelic beings who did not rest day or night and kept repeating, "Holy, holy, holy, Lord God Almighty, who was and is and is to come!"

Notice they don't say, "Faithful, faithful, faithful" or "Eternal, eternal, eternal," though He is all of those things. They say, "Holy, holy, holy"—and there's a reason for that. Because our God is holy, He cannot look at sin.

Habakkuk 1:13 says of God, "Your eyes are too pure to look on evil; you cannot tolerate wrongdoing" (NIV).

This is why Jesus cried out from the cross, "My God, My God, why have You forsaken Me?" (Matthew 27:46; Mark 15:34). In that moment, bearing all the sin of the world for all time, Jesus absorbed the wrath of God that should have fallen on us. For the first time in eternity, the Father and Son experienced a separation as God had to look away from Jesus.

GOOD TO KNOW

Why must God judge people? Because God is not only loving, but He is also righteous and holy.

As Paul wrote in Romans, "Consider the goodness and severity of God" (Romans 11:22). He is good because He gave His one and only Son to suffer and die for our sins. He is severe because His wrath had to fall on the innocent Lamb of God.

Revelation 8 is all about severity as His judgment falls on a world that has spurned His offer of pardon and rejected His Son, Jesus, who shed His blood for the sins of the world.

A STILLNESS BEFORE THE STORM

When He opened the seventh seal, there was silence in Heaven for about half an hour. And I saw the seven angels who stand before God, and to them were given seven trumpets. Then another angel, having a golden censer, came and stood at the altar. He was given much incense, that he should offer it with the prayers of all the saints upon the golden altar which was before the throne. And the smoke of the incense, with the prayers of the saints, ascended before God from the angel's hand. Then the angel took the censer, filled it with fire from the altar, and threw it to the earth. And there were noises, thunderings, lightnings, and an earthquake.

So the seven angels who had the seven trumpets prepared themselves to sound.

The first angel sounded: And hail and fire followed, mingled with blood, and they were thrown to the earth. And a third of the trees were burned up, and all green grass was burned up.

Then the second angel sounded: And something like a great mountain burning with fire was thrown into the sea, and a third of the sea became blood. And a third of the living creatures in the sea died, and a third of the ships were destroyed.

Then the third angel sounded: And a great star fell from heaven, burning like a torch, and it fell on a third of the rivers and on the springs of water. The name of the star is Wormwood. A third of the waters became wormwood, and many men died from the water, because it was made bitter.

Then the fourth angel sounded: And a third of the sun was struck, a third of the moon, and a third of the stars, so that a third of them were darkened. A third of the day did not shine, and likewise the night.

And I looked, and I heard an angel flying through the midst of heaven, saying with a loud voice, "Woe, woe, woe to the inhabitants of the earth, because of the remaining blasts of the trumpet of the three angels who are about to sound!" (Revelation 8:1–13)

As Revelation 8 begins, John witnesses a vast silence in Heaven that lasts for half an hour. Why does this celestial silence descend? Because all of Heaven is in awe, anticipating the judgments that God is about to release. If there are pins in Heaven, it's quiet enough to hear one drop.

Have you ever been to a really noisy restaurant? Sometimes when we go out to eat, we try to get there early to beat the dinner crowd. Before long, however, the place fills up and the noise level gets so high that you can hardly hear each other speak across the table.

I think some people imagine Heaven to be a hushed, quiet place, where people recline on cloud banks, plucking little harps that sound like wind chimes, and angels walk around on tiptoes. This passage, however, seems to indicate that the silence was truly remarkable. And it only lasted for half an hour.

Personally, I think Heaven is a vibrant, busy, happening place.

The writer of Hebrews says of Heaven,

> You have come to . . . the city of the living God, the heavenly Jerusalem, and to countless thousands of angels in a joyful gathering. You have come to the assembly of God's firstborn children, whose names are written in heaven. You have come to God himself, who is the judge over all things. You have come to the spirits of the righteous ones in heaven who have now been made perfect. (Hebrews 12:22–23 NLT)

Countless thousands of angels in a joyful gathering. Heaven is rocking. Heaven is hopping. Redeemed people and angels are running a thousand different directions, serving the Lord. There is worship, there are announcements being made, and there are victory shouts going up every time someone on Earth gets saved.

And then, for half an hour, there is a complete and utter silence.

Something very, very momentous is about to happen, and all Heaven seems to know about it.

Zephaniah 1:7 says, "Stand in silence in the presence of the sovereign LORD, for the awesome day of the LORD's judgment is near" (NLT).

I'm reminded of the silence in the courtroom after a long trial, as the jury foreman stands and prepares to read the verdict. Everyone in the courtroom holds their breath. What will the verdict be?

"We, the people, find the defendant . . . "

Everyone keeps silence and strains to hear. Why? Because someone's future, or even their very life, will be determined by how that verdict reads.

The fact that the heavenly pause lasts for half an hour reminds us that God is in no hurry to release His wrath. This is no rush to judgment. Rather, it's a final accounting after a long, long, patient wait.

Verse 2 seems to indicate that some high-ranking angels are involved in this operation. John said, "I saw the seven angels who stand before God, and to them were given seven trumpets." These weren't just any seven angels, but *the* seven angels who stand before the throne. To these particular angels, God gives seven silver trumpets.

From what we can discern from the Scriptures, it would seem that angels have distinct rankings, as in the military. Are there private first-class angels all the way up to five-star general angels? Maybe or maybe not, but there is definitely an authority structure and angels with different levels of power.

In Daniel 10, for instance, the prophet shoots a quick prayer up to Heaven, and an angel is immediately dispatched with an answer. Apparently that angel had a lower ranking. In the process of completing his mission, he was held up for twenty-one days by a higher-ranking fallen angel, or demon. Then the Lord dispatched the archangel Michael, who made the fallen angel back down and allowed the first angel to break through to Daniel with the Lord's answer to his prayer. (You can read the account for yourself in Daniel 10.)

> **GOOD TO KNOW**
>
> The fact that the heavenly pause lasts for half an hour reminds us that God is in no hurry to release His wrath.

When God wanted to announce the coming of John the Baptist, the one who would announce the coming of the Messiah, He sent one of Heaven's most renowned angels, Gabriel. This powerful messenger told the aging Zacharias that he would be the father of a boy named John, who would become the forerunner of Christ.

Zacharias, however, was old and couldn't quite believe his ears. Since when do senior citizens like him and his wife produce babies? Instead of receiving God's mighty messenger with awe and submission, Zacharias chose that moment of all moments to be guarded and skeptical:

> And Zacharias said to the angel, "How shall I know this? For I am an old man, and my wife is well advanced in years." (Luke 1:18)

Can you believe it? Zacharias wasn't really sure if Gabriel was legit. He was saying, in effect, "How do I know that you are who you say you are? And why should I believe such an incredible story?"

I love how Gabriel answered him:

> "*I am Gabriel.* I stand in the presence of God, and I have been sent to speak to you and to tell you this good news." (verse 19 NIV, emphasis added)

It's as though he were saying to Zacharias, "You have no idea who is speaking to you. I'm not just any old angel. I am Gabriel, *and I stand in the presence of God.*"

And that is the case with the seven angels in Revelation 8. These are a special class of angels who stay near the throne, and they are the ones entrusted with the seven trumpets that signal God's judgment on the world.

THE SEVEN TRUMPETS

The seven trumpet judgments can be divided into two sections. The first four are directed by God toward the environment and are similar to the plagues that came upon Egypt under Moses and Aaron. The final three are spread on all of humanity.

Due to the COVID-19 pandemic, *plagues* is a word that we're hearing more often. Maybe you're thinking, "Wait, I thought those were from ancient history."

No, we've had plagues throughout history, of course, but the Bible tells us that in the last days there will be an increase of plagues. Here's a 2020 headline from *The Jerusalem Post*: "Why do some Christians believe coronavirus is an apocalyptic prophecy?" [17]

Let me answer that. We believe it could be an apocalyptic prophecy, to use their verbiage, because the Bible says we will see this sort of thing in the last days.

One thing is clear: global warming is coming. I don't mean the kind that allegedly inconveniences a few polar bears in the Arctic, but the kind that will burn up one third of Earth's trees and all the green grass (verse 7). The first trumpet blast targets Earth's vegetation. This will decimate crops and forests, filling the air with smoke and ash. It will also affect the food supply and the global economy.

The second trumpet blast in verse 8 describes a great mountain burning with fire thrown into the sea. Notice that John says it is *like* a great mountain. He isn't saying that it literally is a mountain, but he is using first-century terminology to describe something in the future. What is he talking about? We don't really know. It could be an asteroid or a meteor, which of course would bring devastating results on our planet.

In verse 8, one-third of the seas become blood. Perhaps this refers to the red tides caused by billions of dead microorganisms poisoning the water.

In verse 10, the description of the falling star named Wormwood might be describing a devastating exchange of nuclear weaponry. The scenario we read about here actually parallels what scientists call a nuclear winter, as I mentioned earlier in this book. This follows nuclear warfare with more devastating effects than the battle itself.

These trumpet judgments are so terrible that in the middle of them, God sends an angel with a message:

> And I looked, and I heard an angel flying through the midst of heaven, saying with a loud voice, "Woe, woe, woe to the inhabitants of the earth, because of the remaining blasts of the trumpet of the three angels who are about to sound!" (verse 13)

It's as though the Lord were saying, "I don't want to do this. I have already released My wrath on Earth, and there is more to come—but I don't want to bring the rest of it. I am loving and good, but I am also righteous and just. More wrath is coming, and it is terrible."

Why does He give this warning to Planet Earth? Because—even at this late date—He wants people to repent.

Some might read of these terrifying judgments in Revelation 8 and say, "I don't accept this. I don't agree with what happens here. It doesn't seem right to me."

But it really doesn't matter how you and I might feel about this description of future events. They *will* happen. The prophecies *will* be fulfilled. In Romans 3:4, the text says, "Indeed, let God be true but every man a liar." In other words, these events will take place whether you like it or not and whether you agree or not.

Others might respond, "I'm very excited about this. I can't wait for judgment to fall. I'm looking forward to God's setting things to rights."

That attitude is no better. These judgments break the heart of God, and it should break our hearts as well.

WHAT HAPPENS TO OUR PRAYERS?

Then another angel, having a golden censer, came and stood at the altar. He was given much incense, that he should offer it with the prayers of all the saints upon the golden altar which was before the throne. And the smoke of the incense, with the prayers of the saints, ascended before God from the angel's hand. (8:3–4)

What happens to our prayers when they are offered to God?

It depends . . . because not all prayer is offered to God. I think it is entirely possible to say your prayers but never really pray at all.

We teach our children to say their prayers, and sometimes they are memorized prayers: *Now I lay me down to sleep, I pray the Lord my soul to keep.* Hopefully, they will move beyond that. Maybe it would be better to teach them to pray, to actually talk to God, rather than teach them prayers.

It is possible, however, to pray and yet never be heard by God. Remember the story Jesus told about the two men—a Pharisee and a despised tax collector—who went into the temple to pray? He said,

> "The Pharisee stood and prayed thus with himself, 'God, I thank You that I am not like other men—extortioners, unjust, adulterers, or even as this tax collector. I fast twice a week; I give tithes of all that I possess.' And the tax collector, standing afar off, would not so much as raise his eyes to heaven, but beat his breast, saying, 'God, be merciful to me a sinner!'" (Luke 18:11–13)

Jesus said that God heard the sinner but not the Pharisee. Why? Because this proud religious leader didn't really pray to God; he "prayed thus with himself." The truth is that his prayers had nothing to do with God. They were little more than self-congratulations.

Sometimes we can get so caught up in our flowery words that we don't even think about what we are saying. We're just saying words without really even thinking about God.

The tax collector in the Lord's story, however, cried out to God in his humility and need. His prayer was only seven words long, but it was enough. God heard him, and he "went down to his house justified" (verse 14).

God hears and answers our prayers when they are offered to Him in sincerity and humility. But sometimes when we don't see the results we expected, we will say, "God didn't answer my prayer."

What we really mean is that He didn't answer our prayer in the affirmative. In other words, He didn't say yes to our request. All prayers are answered in three ways: yes, no, or wait. In Revelation 8:3, we find out what happens to those wait prayers. They are duly noted and saved for the right moment.

God is aware of each and every request made for His glory and in His will. But He may not answer those prayers according to our timetable.

GOOD TO KNOW
God answers our prayers three ways: yes, no, or wait.

Let's go back to that story of Zacharias, the father of John the Baptist. The first thing Gabriel said to him was, "Do not be afraid, Zacharias, for your prayer is heard; and your wife Elizabeth will bear you a son" (Luke 1:13).

What prayer was that?

It was the prayer that Zacharias and Elizabeth made as a young couple, hoping that God would bless them with a baby. They had prayed that prayer, and God heard them. *But the answer took at least thirty years.*

It was a really long wait, and this godly husband and wife had given up hope that the desire of their hearts ever would be fulfilled.

It reminds us that God will answer in His way and His time. But we must never forget that He is "able to do immeasurably more than all we ask or imagine, according to his power that is at work within us" (Ephesians 3:20 NIV).

That was the case with Zacharias and Elizabeth. They not only would get a son, but they also would get a boy who would grow into a prophet. In fact, he would be the greatest prophet who ever lived—and a direct forerunner of the Messiah.

Sometimes God says wait to us, and we don't like it. Nevertheless, as time passes, He answers our prayer in His own way and in His own time.

Your prayers are noted in Heaven, and not one prayer is wasted. They're all in God's to-do box. Even if you have forgotten about them, God has not. The answer may not come for thirty years, or it may come in a form that you never imagined or expected. But it will come.

Maybe you've been praying for your child to come to Christ, but he or she hasn't come around yet. Then one day you leave this life, and your son or daughter is still unsaved. Perhaps with your last breath you say, "My prayer wasn't answered."

But wait. There is more to life than just life on Earth; life continues on in eternity. Maybe your child will come to Christ at your funeral service. I believe that when someone believes in Jesus as a result of our testimony on Earth, we will be aware of it in Heaven.

We need to see the bigger picture. As that great theologian Buzz Lightyear has reminded us, it is "to infinity and beyond."

In verse 3, a powerful angel brings a golden censer with much incense and prepares to offer it with "the prayers of all the saints" on the golden altar in Heaven. This angel is saying, "Lord, it is now time for these prayers to be answered." He puts them on God's desk, if you will.

Have you ever felt that if you could just pray with a certain person, that God would hear your prayers more quickly? We tell ourselves, *I need to get that pastor to pray for me, or this godly woman.*

I can think of times when I've had the privilege of praying with Billy Graham, and I thought to myself, *God will hear this prayer for sure, because Billy Graham has His attention.*

It's true that Billy had God's attention. But so do you. You have the same access to the throne of God that he does.

A prayer that the church has been praying for two thousand years is, "Even so, come, Lord Jesus." Because after all of the judgments, plagues, and catastrophes have run their course on our planet, Jesus Himself will return to Earth in glory.

And after the Second Coming, the millennial reign of Christ will arrive. And after that, New Jerusalem will come down from Heaven, flashing like a beautiful gem, and Heaven and Earth will become one.

Jesus has taught His disciples in every nation and in every century to pray, "Your kingdom come. Your will be done on earth as it is in heaven" (Matthew 6:10). The church has prayed that prayer for two thousand years, and it will be answered. God's kingdom will come to Earth, but not until His judgment has fallen.

What do we learn from Revelation 8:3?

NEVER UNDERESTIMATE THE POWER OF PRAYER

When you are praying according to God's will, your prayer is unstoppable.

"That's fine, Greg," you say, "but how do I know what God's will is?"

Answer: by carefully studying the Scriptures. Jesus made this promise in John 15:7: "If you abide in Me, and My words abide in you, you will ask what you desire, and it shall be done for you." Another translation says, "If you maintain a living communion with Me and My Word is at home with you, you can ask at once for yourself whatever your heart desires, and it is yours."

We gravitate immediately toward the latter part of that verse. *Whatever my heart desires . . .* But God is not a genie. The fact is that if you walk in fellowship with God and study the Word of God, you will begin to pray according to the will of God. *Then* you will start seeing your prayers answered.

The apostle John tells us 1 John 5:14–15, "This is the confidence we have in approaching God: that if we ask anything according to his will, he hears us.

And if we know that he hears us—whatever we ask—we know that we have what we asked of him" (NIV).

In view of this, we should never give up or back down. Rather, we should keep on praying. Jesus said, "Ask, and it will be given to you; seek, and you will find; knock, and it will be opened to you" (Matthew 7:7). In the original language, there is an ascending intensity to the terms *ask*, *seek*, and *knock*. It is like starting off politely and then becoming more aggressive, refusing to let go. We become like Jacob, who wrestled with the Lord and said, "I won't let You go unless You bless me!" (Genesis 32:26).

Luke 18:1 tells us that we "should always pray and not give up" (NIV).

GOD'S TIMING IS NOT ALWAYS OUR TIMING

The Bible tells us that "He has made everything beautiful in its time" (Ecclesiastes 3:11).

In Revelation 6 we read about the martyrs in Heaven, men and women who had been put to death for their faith during the Great Tribulation. They were aware of the injustice of their deaths and aware that they had fellow servants on Earth who were still being mistreated. Remember what they prayed?

> "How long, O Lord, holy and true, until You judge and avenge our blood on those who dwell on the earth?" (verse 10)

In other words, "Hey Lord, this isn't right! When are You going to correct it? When will you take action against those who are crushing Your people."

The text tells us that "a white robe was given to each of them; and it was said to them that they should rest a little while longer, until both the number of their fellow servants and their brethren, who would be killed as they were, was completed" (verse 11).

Don't you love that? *A little while longer . . .*

It reminds me of taking a trip with small children in the car. An hour or so goes by, and little voices pipe up from the back seat, "How much longer, Daddy? When are we going to get there, Mommy?"

And what do they say? "We're almost there! It's just a little bit longer."

The Tribulation saints prayed, "When will You avenge us?"

Just a little bit longer.

We pray, "Lord, when will You return for us?"

Just a little bit longer.

"When will You answer my prayer?"

Just a little bit longer. Hang on, now. I am in control, and I am accomplishing everything according to My perfect will.

Know this: God's delays are not necessarily His denials. Keep praying about whatever it is you are praying about, and don't lose heart.

THREE TAKEAWAY TRUTHS

- The story of Jonah reveals to us God's heart for sinners to repent.
- The prospect of judgment should not only break our hearts, but it should motivate us to share the gospel more urgently with our loved ones who do not know the Lord.
- Amazing things happen when you pray according to God's will.

CHAPTER THIRTEEN
When All Hell Breaks Loose

Then the fifth angel sounded: And I saw a star fallen from heaven
to the earth. To him was given the key to the bottomless pit.
(Revelation 9:1)

IN THIS CHAPTER
- Our greatest assurance in tumultuous times
- Continuation of the seven trumpet judgments
- The origin of Satan and his demons

Have you ever been seated in a restaurant where the tables were so close that you could hear the conversation of the people next to you?

You didn't really want to hear their conversation, but it was distracting you. You couldn't help but pick up a sentence here and there. Maybe you were making an honest attempt to tune their voices out and give attention to the person you were with. But then you heard someone say, "I'm about to tell you something extremely confidential. I don't want you to share this with anyone."

Did you tune in to those words and listen?

"Oh Greg, of course not. That would be eavesdropping."

I don't believe it. Of course you listened! Why? Because we all like to hear a secret. We all like to get the inside scoop.

I like to play that game with my grandchildren. I will say, "Do you want to know a secret?"

And they always do.

Sometimes I'll just make up something random and whisper it in their ears. It may not mean much of anything, but they're delighted by the idea of hearing a secret.

When they were quite a bit younger and we'd be leaving to go somewhere, I would say, "We can go out the normal way, or we can go out the *secret* way. Who wants to go out the secret way?"

They all would raise their hands. "I do, I do, Papa!"

And then I would take them out a side door instead of the front door, and they loved that. We all like to know secrets.

In Psalm 25:14 we read, "The secret of the LORD is with those who fear Him." That means He shares His secrets with those who walk close to Him and obey Him day by day.

Speaking of secrets, we would love to understand what's happening in our nation and the world as we glance through the headlines and see all the war, strife, rumors, and chaos. We see the Middle East boiling like a pot on a red-hot stove burner, and we look on in amazement at the unprecedented moral meltdown and violence in our own country. Sometimes it seems so puzzling and perplexing, and we wonder what's happening to our world.

It's really no secret.

God has predicted so many of the things we see happening right now. But here is the secret we all need to know—the secret behind everything.

God is in control.

Nothing that happens in our world, or will happen, surprises Him in any way. Nothing throws Him, perplexes Him, or sends Him back to the drawing board. That's even true—perhaps especially true—in Revelation 9, where we find ourselves smack dab in the middle of the most horrific, mind-boggling times that our world ever will experience.

"GREATER ANGUISH"

Speaking of the Great Tribulation, Jesus said in Mark 13:19–20, "For there will be greater anguish in those days than at any time since God created the world. And it will never be so great again. In fact, unless the Lord shortens that time of calamity, not a single person will survive. But for the sake of his chosen ones he has shortened those days" (NLT).

Where is the church in all this?

I believe the church will be safe in Heaven, following the Rapture, alluded to in Revelation 4. In chapter 5, we see God's people worshiping the Lamb in Heaven.

We don't really appear again on the world scene until chapter 19 when Christ comes back again in the Second Coming, and we return with Him to Earth. Until that time, we will be in Heaven, under the protection of the Lord Himself.

Try to imagine what it will be like when all believers are suddenly removed from the planet, along with that restraining force of the Holy Spirit working through the church. All the godly restraints and standards that now exist in our world will be swept away in an instant, allowing evil to wash across the nations like a dark tsunami.

Do you remember what happened when the levies around New Orleans gave way during Hurricane Katrina? With all restraints removed, the storm surge quickly flooded and overwhelmed that city. And that's the way it will be following the Rapture.

Even now, you can see the people in our own culture pushing against any kind of moral restraints or biblical standards. They will say things like . . .

We don't like the way you Christians think.

We don't appreciate your beliefs.

You Christians are hate-mongers.

You're puritanical, narrow-minded, bigoted people.

We're sick of all your outdated rules and regulations.

With the church out of the picture at last, those outside of Christ will get what they say they've always wanted. God will remove all restraint and let the dark side run wild.

I'm reminded of the plagues that came against Pharaoh and Egypt in the book of Exodus. Moses, you may remember, demanded the release of the Jews, and Pharaoh resisted. As a result, a series of devastating plagues swept the land. As it turned out, those plagues weren't random at all, but each was directed against one of Egypt's gods or idols. One of those gods was a frog-god named Heqet.

So the Lord brought a plague of frogs on the land.

It's as if the Lord said to them, "So, you've got a frog-god? You're into worshiping frogs? Fine. I'll give you all the frogs you can handle. I'll cover the land with frogs. There will be frogs in your beds, frogs in your sandals, frogs in your ovens. Everywhere you walk, they'll be squishing and crunching under your feet. And then when they die, the land will reek of them."

GOOD TO KNOW

The church does not appear again on the world scene until chapter 19 when Christ comes back again in the Second Coming, and we return with Him to Earth.

The same is true in the book of Revelation. God is saying, in effect, "You want sin? You want to indulge in these things? You want all of those annoying, narrow-minded Christians out of the way? Be careful of what you ask for, because I'm going to give you that. Let me know how it works out for you!"

C. S. Lewis once said, "There are only two kinds of people in the end: those who say to God, 'Thy will be done,' and those to whom God says, in the end, 'Thy will be done.' All that are in Hell, choose it. Without that self-choice there could be no Hell." [18]

Following the rapture of the church, God says to humanity, "Okay, *your* will be done. Here you go."

And just as you would expect, all hell breaks loose.

A FALLEN STAR

Then the fifth angel sounded: And I saw a star fallen from heaven to the earth. To him was given the key to the bottomless pit. And he opened the bottomless pit, and smoke arose out of the pit like the smoke of a great furnace. So the sun and the air were darkened because of the smoke of the pit. Then out of the smoke locusts came upon the earth. And to them was given power, as the scorpions of the earth have power. They were commanded not to harm the grass of the earth, or any green thing, or any tree, but only those men who do not have the seal of God on their foreheads. And they were not given authority to kill them, but to torment them for five months. Their torment was like the torment of a scorpion when it strikes a man. In those days men will seek death and will not find it; they will desire to die, and death will flee from them.

The shape of the locusts was like horses prepared for battle. On their heads were crowns of something like gold, and their faces were like the faces of men. They had hair like women's hair, and their teeth were like lions' teeth. And they had breastplates like breastplates of iron, and the sound of their wings was like the sound of chariots with many horses running into battle. They had tails like scorpions, and there were stings in their tails. Their power was to hurt men five months. And they had as king over them the angel of the bottomless pit, whose name in Hebrew is Abaddon, but in Greek he has the name Apollyon. (Revelation 9:1–11)

We've all heard (and grow weary of hearing about) great actors or singers whose personal lives have spiraled out of control because of alcohol or drugs. We call these people fallen stars.

In Revelation 9, we're introduced to another kind of fallen star. Again, it's not a situation as in Revelation 8, where an asteroid or a meteor strikes the earth. The fallen star in Revelation 9 refers to an angelic being—whom I believe to be Lucifer, or Satan.

Satan is a fallen angel. In the prophecy of Isaiah we read these startling words:

"How you are fallen from heaven, O shining star, son of the morning! You have been thrown down to the earth, you who destroyed the nations of the world. For you said to yourself, 'I will ascend to heaven and set my throne above God's stars. I will preside on the mountain of the gods far away in the north. I will climb to the highest heavens and be like the Most High.' Instead, you will be brought down to the place of the dead, down to its lowest depths." (14:12–15 NLT)

In Ezekiel 28 the Devil is described as once being the model of perfection—until wickedness was found in him, and he lost his exalted position.

Here in Revelation 9:1, God gives to Satan the key to the abyss, or the bottomless pit. What is the bottomless pit? It seems to be a prison for fallen angels—apparently the worst of the lot. In Jude 1:6 we read, "And I remind you of the angels who did not stay within the limits of authority God gave them but left the place where they belonged. God has kept them securely chained in prisons of darkness, waiting for the great day of judgment" (NLT).

So even in the ranks of fallen angels, it appears that what some do may be worse than others. As a result, some are imprisoned in the bottomless pit.

In a confrontation with a group of fallen angels in Luke 8:31, the demons "begged Jesus repeatedly not to order them to go into the Abyss" (NIV). Here in Revelation 9, that fearsome pit is being opened up.

Imagine, if you can, that in one day at a certain hour, every prison in the world released all its prisoners. That would be bad enough. But to take it further, imagine that every one of these prisoners—including rapists, murderers, and terrorists—were armed with weapons of mass destruction and encouraged to go out and create havoc in the world. That gives you a sense of what happens as the door to this bottomless pit is thrown open and all of these powerful, malevolent demons come crawling out.

GOOD TO KNOW

Just as God has His high-ranking angels in His army, like Michael and Gabriel, the Devil seems to have the same.

John calls them locusts, but I don't believe this is literal. I believe these beings are demonic creatures, supernatural soldiers in the kingdom of darkness. Something about these creatures reminds John of locusts, but he also speaks of them as having hair like a woman and armor like a soldier. As accurate and amazing as the Greek language might be, I think the old apostle struggles for words here. What he wants to communicate is that these beings are aggressive, ferocious, powerful, intelligent, and utterly cruel.

Their leader is called Apollyon, or Abaddon. We don't know if this is a reference to the Devil here or to a powerful demonic being who works under Satan's authority. Just as God has His high-ranking angels in His army, like Michael and Gabriel, the Devil seems to have the same.

Where did these fallen angels come from? The Scriptures tell us that when Lucifer—who became Satan—left Heaven, he took one-third of the heavenly hosts with him. These became fallen angels, or demons.

Satan, while nowhere near to being the equal of God, is still very powerful. He is not, however, omnipresent, meaning that he can't be in two places at one time. If Satan is in New York, then he can't be in Los Angeles. Instead, he has a vast network of demons doing dirty work in the world, under his direction.

The purpose of demons seems to be twofold. They want to hinder the purposes of God and extend the power of Satan. In 1 Thessalonians 2:18, Paul mentions that he wanted to preach in a certain city, "but Satan blocked our way" (NIV). Sometimes God allows that to happen.

In 2 Corinthians 12, Paul recalls the privilege he had of being caught up into Heaven and seeing glory. It was an incredible experience for him, but it also brought with it some challenging physical effects. He wrote, "Lest I should be exalted above measure by the abundance of the revelations, a thorn in the flesh was given to me, a messenger of Satan to buffet me" (verse 7). The word that Paul used here for *buffet* means to "rap or strike with a fist." So Paul had to face some pretty stiff demonic opposition in the course of his ministry.

It can happen to any of us. As believers we can be hassled, tempted, or oppressed by Satan and his minions, but he certainly can't control us.

Let me add this: If you are not a Christian, you have a big bull's-eye painted on your chest, and there is nothing you can do to stop Satan from gaining a foothold in your life. The only power Satan fears is Christ Himself. That is why a believer has a place of safety and refuge, and a nonbeliever is vulnerable and has no refuge.

What follows are three truths that we all need to remember about the Devil and his army of demons.

TRUTHS WE NEED TO REMEMBER ABOUT THE DEVIL

There are people who claim not to believe in demons. But that's just foolish, because they're certainly out there.

1. Demons are real and aggressive

C. S. Lewis summed it up like this in *The Screwtape Letters*: "There are two equal and opposite errors into which our race can fall about the devils. One is to disbelieve in their existence. The other is to believe, and to feel an excessive and unhealthy interest in them. They themselves are equally pleased by both errors and hail a materialist or a magician with the same delight." [19]

That really sums it up. Some don't believe at all, while others are obsessed with demons and always looking for demonic activity.

The truth is that demons are real, and they're constantly looking for trouble.

In Job 2:1–2 we read about a time when the angels of the Lord appeared before God, and Satan was among them. The Lord asked Satan, "From where do you come?"

Satan replied, "From going to and fro on the earth, and from walking back and forth on it" (NLT). Another translation reads, "I have been patrolling the earth, watching everything that's going on."

The Devil is like a stalker. He keeps looking for an area that he can get into: an unlocked door, an unguarded heart, a vulnerability. The apostle Peter takes it a step further and describes Satan as walking about "like a roaring lion, seeking whom he may devour" (1 Peter 5:8).

In other words, Satan and his demons are a restless evil, constantly looking for ways to destroy lives.

2. Though powerful, demons have clear limitations.

Here is something that Satan doesn't want you to know. His power might be considerable, but it is clearly limited. Coming back to the story of Job, the Lord allowed Satan to inflict calamity on His loyal servant, but *with limitations*. Satan accurately complained that God had put a "hedge" of protection around His servant.

God has put a hedge of protection around you, too.

He never will give you more than you can handle.

In 1 Corinthians 10:13 the Bible says, "No temptation has overtaken you except such as is common to man; but God is faithful, who will not allow you to be tempted beyond what you are able, but with the temptation will also make the way of escape, that you may be able to bear it."

One night when Jesus was sitting around with His disciples, He looked over at Peter and said, "Simon, Simon! Indeed, Satan has asked for you, that he may sift you as wheat. But I have prayed for you, that your faith should not fail" (Luke 22:31–32).

How would you feel if Jesus made that statement to you? Wouldn't that concern you just a little? It certainly would me. I can imagine being with Jesus when He turns to look at me and says, "Hey Greg? Are you listening to Me?"

"Yes, Lord."

"The Devil has been asking for you by name, Greg."

"What?"

"He's been asking that you would be taken out of the care and protection of God."

I would be shaking in my sandals if Satan had singled me out by name and had asked that God would remove His protection from me. What a frightening thought! And you'll notice that this wasn't some demon asking for Peter; it was Satan himself.

But then He added, "I have prayed for you, that your faith would not fail."

GOOD TO KNOW

We are no match for Satan. But on the other hand, he has clear limitations.

It's a good reminder to all of us. When Satan comes knocking at your door, it would be a great idea to say, "Would you mind getting that, Lord?"

You and I are no match for Satan, a mighty spirit being with a great army of fallen angels. But on the other hand, he has clear limitations.

Those nightmare creatures described in Revelation 9 have been given power, but again, also with limitations. In verse 3 we read they are given power, but *power* here means permission. In verse 4, they are told who they can harass and who they're not allowed to harass. In verse 5, they are commanded only to sting, but not to kill, their victims.

In particular they are told they can only touch those "who do not have the seal of God on their foreheads" (verse 4).

Who are these people the demons are commanded not to harm? They are believers. These are people who have come to Christ in the Tribulation period, and God has sealed them. In other words, He has put His own identity tag on them and said, "Hands off! Don't touch them."

As I pointed out, the Lord calls His church to Heaven at the Rapture, but many will come to Christ after that and will be alive in this Great Tribulation.

The demons obey the Lord—not because they want to, but because they must.

Here is the good news. When you believe in Jesus, God places His seal, His mark of ownership, on you as well. When the Devil sees that ID tag and realizes that you are the property of the Lord Jesus Christ, he knows that he is very limited in what he can do in your life.

Why? Because he is afraid of God.

3. Demons flee at the name of Jesus Christ.

In the book of James, we're given this piece of information:

> Are there still some among you who hold that "only believing" is enough? Believing in one God? Well, remember that the demons believe this too—so strongly that they tremble in terror! (2:19 TLB)

In Philippians, Paul declares these powerful words:

> Therefore God exalted him [Jesus] to the highest place and gave him the name that is above every name, that at the name of Jesus every knee should bow, in heaven and on earth and under the earth, and every tongue acknowledge that Jesus Christ is Lord, to the glory of God the Father. (2:9–11 NIV)

Satan's evil army might have certain powers, but compared to the name of Jesus, their power is like comparing a weak flashlight bulb with a lightning bolt.

SATAN'S ENDGAME

Again, in Revelation 9:5–6 we read, "Their torment was like the torment of a scorpion when it strikes a man. In those days men will seek death and will not find it; they will desire to die, and death will flee from them."

There will be many suicide attempts in those days, and none of them will be successful. What a horrible time this will be.

But this is the Devil's bottom line. He knows that he can't really win the ultimate battle, and he knows his time is short. So while he can, he will do what he does so well. He will torment people.

That's his endgame with everyone, but he never will let anyone know that up front. But Jesus summed it up for us in John 10:10. Speaking of Satan He said, "The thief comes only to steal and kill and destroy" (NIV).

The Devil doesn't walk up to you and say, "Good morning. I am the Devil . . . Lucifer . . . Satan . . . the Great Dragon. Maybe you've heard of me. Anyway, I'm here for one purpose, and that is to ruin your life. I hate you, I hate your family, and I hate everything about you. Bottom line, I just want to bring you misery, sorrow, pain, and guilt. Whatever it takes, I want to inflict maximum torment on you."

How many people are going to go for that? Not very many.

So when the Devil approaches someone, he comes with all his enticements, hiding his true purpose behind his back. He says, "What are you into? What gets you excited? Women? Men? Money? Drugs? Alcohol? Pleasure? Religion? Power? I've got it all. Take your pick. Check it out."

He throws out his line with some very attractive bait on the end of it.

But there is also a hidden hook.

And he will use his line to reel you in.

In contrast to Satan's purposes, Jesus said in John 10:10, "I have come that you might have life, and that more abundantly." Satan wants to torment and destroy, and Jesus wants to bring overflowing life. Tragically, given a choice, most people will pick Satan over Jesus. Go figure!

THE SINS OF THE TRIBULATION PERIOD

In verses 20–21 of Revelation 9, we learn the five most prominent sins of the Tribulation period. It is worth noting that these sins are very much with us today:

> But the rest of mankind, who were not killed by these plagues, did not repent of the works of their hands, that they should not worship demons, and idols of gold, silver, brass, stone, and wood, which can neither see nor hear nor walk. And they did not repent of their murders or their sorceries or their sexual immorality or their thefts.

So what are the prominent sins of the Tribulation period?

Idol worship

The first of the Ten Commandments says, "You shall have no other gods before Me" (Exodus 20:3). The second commandment is related to the first: "You shall not make for yourself a carved image" (verse 4).

Someone will say, "That's no problem, Greg. I have no inclination to bow down before some weird-looking idol made of metal or stone."

But what is an idol? *An idol is anyone or anything we put in the place of God.* It might be some kind of image, but it could also be something else.

I remember Pastor Chuck Smith telling the story of a tribe in New Guinea that had a birth defect within their tribe. Because they had intermarried, everyone had the same physical defect: one leg was shorter than the other. These people also worshiped an idol, and, as it happened, the little god they worshiped also had one leg shorter than the other.

In other words, they were essentially worshiping themselves.

The truth is, people in the United States of America worship all kinds of gods instead of the true and living God. We say things like, "Yes, I'm into spirituality. I'm just not in favor of organized religion." Which is code for saying, *I'm making this up as I go along.*

I read an article in *USA Today* about the fastest-growing spiritual group in America. The article said,

> For decades, if not centuries, America's top religious brand has been "Protestant." No more. . . . Where did they go? Nowhere, actually. They didn't switch to a new religious brand; they just let go of any faith affiliation, or label. . . . This group, called "Nones," is now the nation's second-largest category after Catholics, and outnumbers the top Protestant denomination, the Southern Baptists. [20]

What do Nones believe? They don't believe in anything in particular; they are just open to spirituality. That is a slippery slope. It is also idolatry. These people are, in effect, making up their own god.

G. K. Chesterton once said, "When a man stops believing in God, he doesn't then believe in nothing, he believes in anything."

Although they may never admit it, people effectively make a god in their own image. Here's what I mean. You often will hear people say, "Well, *my* god would never judge a person. *My* god would never judge a person for not accepting Jesus Christ."

Guess what? Your god is *you*. You just made him up. Your god is fake, because you can't edit out the parts of the Bible you don't like. If you treat the Word of God like a buffet line and say, "I will take this aspect of God, but I don't like that one," then you will end up with a god of your own making. It won't be the God of the Bible. And that god of yours won't be able to save you in the final day because it isn't real.

Again, this is idolatry. And it is a sin that will be carried over into the Great Tribulation.

Murder

In the last thirty years there has been a 560 percent increase in violent crime—even more in recent months. America seems to be on a killing spree. Mass shootings, where the gunman cuts innocent people down at random, have definitely increased in our time. These heartless, senseless acts of violence will only escalate in the last days. Sad to say, it's only going to get worse.

Sorceries

The word *sorceries* here is from the Greek word *pharmakeia*, from where we get our English words *pharmacy* and *pharmaceutical*. A literal translation would be "druggings."

In both ancient as well as modern times, sorcery and witchcraft are always connected to drug use. It is no coincidence that the counterculture of the sixties that was so into drugs later turned to Eastern mysticism and occultism in the wake of their drug use. In the tribulation period drug use will escalate—and even get worse. People probably will be ingesting drugs by the handfuls in a vain attempt to escape the severe realities of those terrible years.

Sexual immorality

This is from the Greek word *porneia*, where we get our English word *pornography*. With the advent of the Internet, of course, pornography issues in our nation and world have greatly multiplied. What, then, will happen when the restraining influence of the church is suddenly withdrawn from the world? Right will be wrong, and wrong will be right. Unfettered by any constraints, sexual immorality will rule the day.

Someone will call it "freedom." But after a while, it won't feel like freedom at all.

Theft

In the wake of almost any riot or natural disaster, thieves move in like vultures, tearing away anything of value. We saw this during the riots across our nation in the wake of George Floyd Jr.'s death in Minneapolis. People will exploit a tragedy by breaking into damaged businesses or homes to carry away whatever they can. It's a sickening sight, but it will only get worse in the Tribulation.

Wouldn't you think that with all this eruption of wickedness, violence, and sorrow, that people would turn to God?

Some will. But most won't.

Revelation 9:20 says, "But the rest of mankind, who were not killed by these plagues, did not repent of the works of their hands, that they should not worship demons."

Here is a how modern paraphrase renders those verses:

> The remaining men and women who weren't killed by these weapons went on their merry way—didn't change their way of life, didn't quit worshiping demons, didn't quit centering their lives around lumps of gold and silver and brass, hunks of stone and wood that couldn't see or hear or move. There wasn't a sign of a change of heart. They plunged right on in their murderous, occult, promiscuous, and thieving ways. (9:20–21 MSG)

It reminds me of the story of Pharaoh in the book of Exodus, who saw all those miracles but continued to harden his heart. In the end, his heart got so hard that it couldn't be broken.

BITTERSWEET

In Revelation 10, we encounter a mighty angel holding a mysterious little book.

> I saw still another mighty angel coming down from heaven, clothed with a cloud. And a rainbow was on his head, his face was like the sun, and his feet like pillars of fire. He had a little book open in his hand. And he set his right foot on the sea and his left foot on the land, and cried with a loud voice, as when a lion roars.

Then the voice which I heard from heaven spoke to me again and said, "Go, take the little book which is open in the hand of the angel who stands on the sea and on the earth."

So I went to the angel and said to him, "Give me the little book."

And he said to me, "Take and eat it; and it will make your stomach bitter, but it will be as sweet as honey in your mouth."

Then I took the little book out of the angel's hand and ate it, and it was as sweet as honey in my mouth. But when I had eaten it, my stomach became bitter. And he said to me, "You must prophesy again about many peoples, nations, tongues, and kings." (verses 1–3, 8–11)

Have you ever seen a really large man walking a very small dog? You see that miniature thing (resembling a rat) at the end of the leash, and you think to yourself, *No self-respecting, manly male would have a dog like that!*

In this chapter we have an even greater curiosity. We see a mighty, towering angelic being with a tiny little book in his great big hand.

The apostle John ate that little book, as he was instructed, and just like the angel said, it went down sweet but turned bitter in his stomach.

Have you ever eaten something that was sweet going down, but it almost immediately made you feel sick? It reminds me a little of the time I consumed eight hot, fresh, Krispy Kreme doughnuts in one sitting.

I guess I got just a little carried away. Since the sign was illuminated in the window, I knew that the doughnuts were right out of the oven, glistening and throwing out that fragrance that nothing in the world can match. I bought a dozen of them, got some cold milk (mandatory) and before I could even think about it, I had consumed eight of them.

They were wonderful going down. Eight minutes later, however, I was asking myself, "What have I done?"

What is the meaning, then, of this little book delivered by the hand of an angel—a book that seems so sweet but turns so bitter? The message, I believe, is that the Word of God that is so sweet to those of us who love Him is a bitter, hateful thing to those who have rejected Him.

For a Christian, the Word of God is like food. As the patriarch Job said, "I have treasured the words of his mouth more than my daily bread" (Job 23:12 NIV). Jesus said, "Man shall not live by bread alone, but by every word that proceeds from the mouth of God" (Matthew 4:4).

For believers, studying the Bible is a treat; it's like a feast, and we love it. For those outside of Christ, it's just misery and torment. They don't understand it, and they don't like it.

Some hear the gospel and say, "That's what I want. I believe that. I want Jesus right now."

Others hear that same word and say, "I hate that. I don't want anything to do with it. And what's more, I hate you for telling me about it."

That is how people react to the gospel. As the apostle Paul wrote, to some it's the fragrance of life itself; to others, it smells like death warmed over (see 2 Corinthians 2:15–16).

The words of the book of Revelation—even with the realization of God's wrath and judgment finally falling on our rebellious planet—are sweet to us because we understand that the God we know, love, and trust is working out His perfect plan.

The idea of God's righteous judgment is a bitter pill for many to swallow. Until these world-shaking events take place, however, we have the opportunity to declare a message of His forgiveness, grace, and salvation in Christ.

It's a sweet message.

It tastes like life.

GOOD TO KNOW

For believers, studying the Bible is a treat. But for those outside of Christ, it's just misery and torment.

THREE TAKEAWAY TRUTHS

- No matter how bad this world gets, God is in control, and there are no surprises with Him.
- As Christians, we are protected by God from the power of the Devil.
- God's message of forgiveness to a lost world is a "sweet" message.

CHAPTER FOURTEEN

Light in a Very Dark Place

*And I will appoint my two witnesses, and they will
prophesy for 1,260 days, clothed in sackcloth."
(Revelation 11:3 NIV)*

IN THIS CHAPTER

- Why Jerusalem is a focal point of end times prophecy
- The past, present, and future significance of the temple
- What we learn from the two witnesses
- The apostle John receives another glimpse of Heaven.

It's amazing how far a little light will go in deep darkness.

Maybe you've been on one of those guided tours of deep caverns in the earth, like Carlsbad Caverns or the Oregon Caves. Far underground, away from every hint of daylight, the guide will turn out all the lights and let you experience that inky blackness for a moment. It's a darkness so intense, so black, that you can almost feel it. Then maybe the guide will strike one little match, and it looks like a blowtorch! Light from that tiny flame fills that dark place.

In Revelation 11, we see two very bright lights that God will raise up in the darkest time that will ever come upon the face of the earth.

The deep darkness I'm speaking of is the coming Great Tribulation. And the two lights God will raise up are known in the book of Revelation as "the two witnesses."

AT THE HALFWAY MARK

In the very middle of the book of Revelation's twenty-two chapters, there is a sudden shift in the narrative.

Imagine you got caught up in a good movie, where you found yourself identifying with the lead character in the drama. Maybe you think to yourself, "I wish this were happening to me. I wish I could be in this story." And then suddenly, in the blink of an eye, you are! You become one of the main characters in the movie.

In a sense, that is what happens to the apostle John in Revelation 11. Up to this point, not unlike a TV newsperson, he has been reporting on what he has seen, giving us information as the vision transpires before his eyes. Then suddenly he goes from being a reporter to being a character in the story, a participant in the action.

Here is how it unfolds in the Scriptures:

> Then I was given a reed like a measuring rod. And the angel stood, saying, "Rise and measure the temple of God, the altar, and those who worship there. But leave out the court which is outside the temple, and do not measure it, for it has been given to the Gentiles. And they will tread the holy city underfoot for forty-two months. And I will give power to my two witnesses, and they will prophesy one thousand two hundred and sixty days, clothed in sackcloth."

> These are the two olive trees and the two lampstands standing before the God of the earth. And if anyone wants to harm them, fire proceeds from their mouth and devours their enemies. And if anyone wants to harm them, he must be killed in this manner. These have power to shut heaven, so that no rain falls in the days of their prophecy; and they have power over waters to turn them to blood, and to strike the earth with all plagues, as often as they desire.

> When they finish their testimony, the beast that ascends out of the bottomless pit will make war against them, overcome them, and kill them. And their dead bodies will lie in the street of the great city

which spiritually is called Sodom and Egypt, where also our Lord was crucified. (11:1–8)

Revelation 11 opens with a prophetic focus on the last days in the city of Jerusalem. Of course—Jerusalem.

Ironically, Jerusalem means "the city of peace." Yet more wars have been fought at her gates than any other city in the entire world. From the siege of David in 1,000 BC to the Six-Day War in 1967, Jerusalem has experienced forty-six sieges and partial destructions. The city has been burned to the ground five times, and yet it always rises from the ashes. In just the last twenty-five years, it has been the scene of four wars.

GOOD TO KNOW
God says that Jerusalem will be at the heart of the final conflicts of mankind.

Here we are now today, and as usual, the Middle East, Israel, and specifically Jerusalem, are in the news.

Yet according to the Scriptures, the worst is yet to come.

God says that Jerusalem will be at the heart of the final conflicts of mankind. In Zechariah 12:3 we read, "On that day I will make Jerusalem an immovable rock. All the nations will gather against it to try to move it, but they will only hurt themselves" (NLT).

As we open up Revelation 11, we see right away that the temple has been rebuilt. Has this happened yet? No, not yet. For this prophecy to be fulfilled, a couple of things have to happen.

1. Jerusalem would have to be once again in Jewish hands.

Of course, this only happened quite recently, with Israel becoming a nation in 1948, and more specifically with the Six-Day War in 1967. That is when Jerusalem actually fell into Jewish hands again.

2. The temple will have to be rebuilt.

The apostle John wrote the book of Revelation around AD 95. This means that the temple, which was standing in Jesus' day, already had been destroyed by General Titus and the Roman army. Jesus spoke of this destruction in Matthew 24:2, asserting that "not one stone shall be left here upon another, that shall not be thrown down." And that, of course, is exactly what happened.

We can conclude, then, that the temple John speaks of in Revelation 11 is a future temple. In fact, the initiative for building this future temple will come from the Antichrist himself.

It's my belief that this temple will be rebuilt during the first half—the first three-and-a-half years—of the Tribulation period. This is a very significant point, because after the temple is rebuilt and animal sacrifices are restored, the Antichrist will commit an act described by Jesus as "the abomination of desolation."

Here is how the Lord described this future event in Matthew 24:15–21:

> "Therefore when you see the 'abomination of desolation,' spoken of by Daniel the prophet, standing in the holy place . . . then let those who are in Judea flee to the mountains. Let him who is on the housetop not go down to take anything out of his house. And let him who is in the field not go back to get his clothes. But woe to those who are pregnant and to those who are nursing babies in those days! And pray that your flight may not be in winter or on the Sabbath. For then there will be great tribulation, such as has not been since the beginning of the world until this time, no, nor ever shall be."

Note that these words are clearly addressed to Jews; Jesus tells them to pray that this incident doesn't take place on a Sabbath day. This will be the sign that precisely marks the midpoint of the Tribulation period—and warns of the great cataclysmic judgments that will follow.

The apostle Paul gives us more detail about this event in 2 Thessalonians 2:4, 9–10. Speaking of the Antichrist, he wrote,

> He will exalt himself and defy everything that people call god and every object of worship. He will even sit in the temple of God,

claiming that he himself is God. . . . This man will come to do the work of Satan with counterfeit power and signs and miracles. He will use every kind of evil deception to fool those on their way to destruction, because they refuse to love and accept the truth that would save them. (NLT)

We know the temple will be rebuilt. But there's a little problem with that, isn't there? As I mentioned in an earlier chapter, a mosque sits there, a mosque known as the Dome of the Rock. Next to it is another mosque-like building called the Al-Aqsa Mosque. These two buildings are very important to the world of Islam. In fact, Muslims around the world believe the Dome of the Rock to be the place where their prophet Mohammed ascended into Heaven.

It just so happens that these Islamic buildings rest on the Temple Mount, the general area where the first and second Jewish temples once stood. So how does that work out? If you want to rebuild the temple, it would mean removing the Dome of the Rock mosque, which would launch a worldwide jihad like we've never seen before.

So how does this happen? How do the future temple builders overcome this obstacle? Here's another possibility: An article in *Biblical Archaeology Review* revealed that the actual location of Solomon and Herod's temples were twenty-six meters away from the Dome of the Rock. If that study is valid, then it means the temple could be rebuilt without disturbing the Dome of the Rock.

Frankly, I don't know *how* it is going to happen.

I just know that *it is* going to happen—and that the Antichrist will be the one who initiates it. For this reason, *any* movement toward the rebuilding of the temple should be of great interest to the student of Bible prophecy. If you look at the news some morning and see a story about the temple being rebuilt, then "look up and lift up your heads, because your redemption draws near" (Luke 21:28).

After the Antichrist has erected an image of himself in the temple and commands people to worship it, the world grows very, very dark as God's judgment begins to fall. But God always has His representatives, doesn't He? The

Scriptures also tell us that He will have 144,000 Jewish evangelists combing Earth, declaring His name, and living under His protection. It's a reminder that God always has His people behind the scenes. And they tend to emerge in times of darkness and stress.

I think of the book of Esther in the Scriptures. She was a beautiful Jewish girl who was plucked from obscurity, won a beauty contest, and became the queen of the world's mightiest empire. At the same time, a vain and wicked man named Haman had hatched a plot to have all of the Jews in that same empire put to death. Queen Esther's uncle Mordecai, the kindly, godly man who had raised her, came to her and described the plight of her fellow Jews. He told her, "If you remain completely silent at this time, relief and deliverance will arise for the Jews from another place, but you and your father's house will perish. Yet who knows whether you have come to the kingdom for such a time as this?" (Esther 4:14).

GOOD TO KNOW

Any movement toward the rebuilding of the temple should be of great interest to the student of Bible prophecy.

Esther stepped up and risked her position and her very life, using her position as queen to avert the plot and save her countrymen. Then, in perfect, poetic justice, the evil Haman who had hatched the plot ended up hanging on the very gallows he had erected for others.

God had placed Esther behind the scenes in a place of influence. Esther could have said, "I respect you, Uncle Mordecai, but there's no way I'm going to jeopardize my position as queen of the Persian Empire. No one needs to find out that I'm a Jew. If I keep quiet, no one will know. No, I'm going to be careful and play it safe."

But Esther didn't do that. At the critical moment, she put everything on the line and stood up for her fellow Jews.

For such a time as this . . .

Could it be that God has placed you where you are for such a time as this? You may be the only Christian in your family or the only believer in your neighborhood or on the floor of your dorm at college. You may be the only follower of Jesus Christ in your workplace or in your classroom. As our culture plunges into darkness, will you stand up for your faith in Jesus at such a time as this? Will you use your influence where you can, when you can?

There is another story of someone who used his influence in dark times. The Scriptures give us the story of Nehemiah, cupbearer of King Artaxerxes, ruler of the mighty Medo-Persian Empire. To be a cupbearer meant that you were in close proximity to the king at all times, making sure that you drank of the king's beverages before he did. If that drink happened to be poisonous, that would be the end of your job—and your life. The cupbearer, however, was more than someone who simply tasted the king's food and drink. He would also be a close adviser to the king and someone with great influence.

But Nehemiah, like Esther, was a Jew. He had heard that the walls of Jerusalem had been flattened by the Babylonians and lay in ruin. He knew that the few Jews who had returned to that devastated city were living "in great distress and reproach" (Nehemiah 1:3), and he couldn't take it anymore. Risking everything, putting his position and his life on the line, he leveraged his influence and asked this Persian king to allow him to journey to Jerusalem to rebuild the walls.

Just making such a request could have cost Nehemiah his head. But he asked anyway and did what he could, working behind the scenes.

Thinking back to an earlier time, I'm reminded how an obscure Jewish slave girl influenced her pagan master, Naaman, to seek out the prophet Elisha in Israel to find healing for his leprosy. Naaman was a mighty general in Syria, a famous military figure, and a man of great power and influence. Yet God had His representative, a little Jewish maid, behind the scenes. And when General Naaman was in great personal distress, she spoke up and told him about a prophet of the living God.

Naaman believed her, followed through, and was healed.

You may not think you have much influence. And yet it is God Himself who has placed you where you are in this particular season of your life. When the time comes and the opportunity arises, use what influence you have to speak up for Jesus Christ.

Sometimes that influence will be quiet, subtle, and behind the scenes. At other times, it will be seen and felt all over the world. And that is the case of God's two witnesses in Revelation 11.

THE TWO WITNESSES

Who are these powerful, mysterious witnesses who seem to suddenly burst onto the world scene at such a troubled time? Revelation 11:3–6 gives these intriguing details:

> "I will appoint my two witnesses, and they will prophesy for 1,260 days, clothed in sackcloth." They are "the two olive trees" and the two lampstands, and "they stand before the Lord of the earth." If anyone tries to harm them, fire comes from their mouths and devours their enemies. This is how anyone who wants to harm them must die. They have power to shut up the heavens so that it will not rain during the time they are prophesying; and they have power to turn the waters into blood and to strike the earth with every kind of plague as often as they want. (NIV)

Stopping rain? Turning water into blood? Calling down fire from Heaven? Which people from the Scriptures come to mind when you read such things?
  Moses and Elijah.

Witness One: Elijah

I feel certain that one of these witnesses will be Elijah. Why?

Because Malachi, the last book of the Old Testament, says that God would send Elijah before "the great and dreadful day of the LORD" (4:5) will come.

The Scriptures, then, say that Elijah will appear before Christ returns again to Earth. John the Baptist came in the spirit and the power of Elijah, but John was still John. I believe that Elijah is still coming and will be one of the two witnesses described in Revelation 11.

From the book of 1 Kings, we recall that it was Elijah who told King Ahab that it wouldn't rain another drop on Israel until he gave word that it would. And of course, Elijah's signature miracle was calling down fire from Heaven to consume that sacrifice on top of Mount Carmel. (Read the whole exciting story in 1 Kings 17–18.)

Elijah was someone who always spoke the truth and wasn't intimidated by an evil king (Queen Jezebel was a different story). You didn't want to mess with Elijah. And I believe that he will be one of God's two powerful witnesses in the Tribulation period.

Who is the second?

Witness Two: Moses

Some suggest that the second witness could be Enoch, and I can't rule that out. There are only two people mentioned in the Bible who never died but were caught up alive into Heaven: Elijah and Enoch. Elijah was caught up to Heaven in a fiery chariot, and the Bible says that "Enoch walked steadily with God. And then one day he was simply gone: God took him" (Genesis 5:24 MSG).

Because he never tasted death on Earth, perhaps Enoch could be the other witness, standing alongside Elijah. But I still favor Moses. It was through Moses that God brought the plagues upon Pharaoh. It was Moses who turned the Nile River into blood at the touch of his staff.

In addition to these things, there is an interesting postscript regarding the body of Moses, after he died. We read about it in Jude 1:9:

> Yet Michael, one of the mightiest of the angels, when he was arguing with Satan about Moses' body, did not dare to accuse even Satan, or jeer at him, but simply said, "The Lord rebuke you." (TLB)

Maybe the Devil wanted to desecrate the body of this great man of God, but the archangel Michael told him, "You leave that body alone." Was it because God was saving Moses for this special occasion in the future?

Another interesting note is that Moses and Elijah made a joint appearance at the transfiguration of Jesus up on that mountain. The Bible describes that moment like this:

> As [Jesus] was praying, the appearance of his face changed, and his clothes became as bright as a flash of lightning. Two men, Moses and Elijah, appeared in glorious splendor, talking with Jesus. They spoke about his departure, which he was about to bring to fulfillment at Jerusalem. (Luke 9:29–31 NIV)

There was Moses, representing the Law, on one side of Jesus, and Elijah, representing the Prophets, on the other side, giving testimony to what Jesus was about to accomplish.

I believe these will be the two men whom God will raise up at this dark time in the world's history.

What will these witnesses do? Revelation 11:6 speaks of the "days of their prophecy." We need to be aware that the word *prophecy* in the New Testament doesn't necessarily refer to predicting the future, though it could include that. It means "to speak forth," "to proclaim," or "to preach." The primary objective of these two witnesses, then, will be to preach the gospel and call people to Christ during the second half of the Tribulation period.

GOOD TO KNOW

The primary objective of the two witnesses will be to preach the gospel and call people to Christ during the second half of the Tribulation period.

The witnesses will be strongly opposed. But that's nothing new, is it? Everyone who preaches God's truth will be opposed. Persecution of Christians is on the rise, even as I write these words, and it will increase during the Tribulation period. The apostle Paul tells us that "everyone who wants to live a godly life in Christ Jesus will suffer persecution" (2 Timothy 3:12 NLT).

Revelation 11:7–10 describes what happens after the two witnesses complete their testimony:

> When they finish their testimony, the beast that ascends out of the bottomless pit will make war against them, overcome them, and kill them. And their dead bodies will lie in the street of the great city which spiritually is called Sodom and Egypt, where also our Lord was crucified. Then those from the peoples, tribes, tongues, and nations will see their dead bodies three-and-a-half days, and not allow their dead bodies to be put into graves. And those who dwell on the earth will rejoice over them, make merry, and send gifts to one another, because these two prophets tormented those who dwell on the earth.

This is the first reference to the Antichrist as "the beast." Notice that he comes out of the bottomless pit, or abyss, where God had locked away the worst demonic beings. As we noted, they are released on Earth in Revelation 9.

What does the Antichrist do? He makes war against these men who are declaring the Good News on a darkened, destruction-wracked planet. But notice this: Antichrist can't do anything to them until they've finished their testimony.

That's great news. This tells me that as a Christian, *you are indestructible until God is done with you.* There is a day appointed for your death, and you really have nothing to say about when that day will be. Until that day comes, "no weapon formed against you shall prosper" (Isaiah 54:17). God will keep you and protect you until it's time for you to leave this earth.

"Okay, Greg," you say, "does that mean I can eat hamburgers, pizza, and pasta and never exercise?" I would answer that God has given you stewardship over your body and the responsibility to care for it as you would any other gift of God. In view of that important stewardship, I think you should take care of your body. You should eat properly and exercise. I am sure that will improve the *quality* of your life. But ultimately, the *quantity* is up to God.

Even if there is some plot against you, it won't succeed unless it is your time. If it *is* your time, then Heaven will open for you, and the greatest adventure of all will begin.

I think of Paul the apostle when, as a Roman prisoner, he was shipwrecked on an island. As he was gathering wood for the fire, a venomous viper bit him. Paul, however, simply shook it off into the fire and went on his way. Why didn't he die from that deadly bite? Because it wasn't his time. Years later in a Roman dungeon, his time finally came, and he embraced it.

When the two witnesses are finished with their testimony, the Antichrist kills them and leaves their bodies lying in the street for the whole world to see. This is no doubt meant to desecrate and dishonor the deceased prophets of God.

Again, the Scriptures say that "for three and a half days some from every people, tribe, language and nation will gaze on their bodies and refuse them burial" (Revelation 11:9 NIV).

In years gone by, some wondered how this could even happen. I read a commentator from a hundred years ago who actually questioned this statement. He said, "How could all the people in the world possibly look at the bodies of these men lying in Jerusalem?"

Well, we know the answer today, because now we have something known as cell phones, that we carry around. Some 96 percent of Americans have them, and I read that seventeen billion mobile devices will be in use by 2024. So you can pretty safely say that most people either have a cell phone or have access to a cell phone. People will be taking videos of this incident and posting it on social media.

Everyone, all over the world, will be able to see it. In addition, news crews will be there with their satellite trucks. Images of the dead witnesses probably will be projected onto giant video screens in places like Times Square. The camera will zoom in for a tight shot of their dead faces, and millions will take it in and celebrate the event.

Verse 10 says, "The inhabitants of the earth will gloat over them and will celebrate by sending each other gifts, because these two prophets had tormented those who live on the earth" (NIV).

How did these prophets torment people?

They spoke the truth.

It's like that even today. When you speak the truth of Scripture, it will be a torment for some to hear. They will hate you for just saying what is right. You might even speak nicely and kindly with a smile, but hearing the truth will still infuriate some people.

I want to live the way I want to live, so don't you dare quote the Bible to me, you puritanical, narrow-minded, bigoted hate-monger! Who are you to judge me?

What's that all about? Why do they hate you? Why do they become so angry? The fact is that you torment them by just being you, a follower of Jesus. You torment them by believing in the absolute truths of the Scriptures. They can't handle even the idea of someone believing that the Bible is literally true.

King Ahab saw Elijah walking toward him and said, "Is that you, O troubler of Israel?" (1 Kings 18:17).

But Elijah wasn't the troubler of Israel. He simply spoke the Word of God to them, and they hated him for it. The trouble was something that Israel brought on itself by rejecting God's laws and then reaping the consequences.

That still happens. People will break God's laws, reap the terrible consequences, and then turn their anger on Christians because we told them it would happen.

After the death of the witnesses, the world turns it into a twisted holiday, having parties and giving gifts to each other. It's like an upside-down Christmas. Since it comes from the Antichrist, maybe it will be Anti-Christmas.

GOOD TO KNOW

When you speak the truth of Scripture, it will be a torment for some to hear.

We wish you an Anti-Christmas, we wish you an Anti-Christmas . . .

Or maybe they will call it Dead Prophets Day.

George meets Tom in the street and says, "Hey, I got you a little something for Dead Prophets Day. It's a cool little Beast idol."

Someone will write a hit song, and it will be all over the Internet, with people repeating the words and dancing to the tune.

But then the party will be over. Revelation 11 describes the shocking moment:

But after the three and a half days the breath of life from God entered them, and they stood on their feet, and terror struck those who saw them. Then they heard a loud voice from Heaven saying to them, "Come up here." And they went up to heaven in a cloud, while their enemies looked on.

At that very hour there was a severe earthquake and a tenth of the city collapsed. Seven thousand people were killed in the earthquake, and the survivors were terrified and gave glory to the God of heaven. (verses 11–13 NIV)

The great joy of the people turns into great fear. On millions of TV, smartphone, tablet, and computer screens, the two dead men open their eyes and stand to their feet, and then they are lifted up bodily to Heaven. God suddenly crashes the party of those who had been celebrating the death of His faithful witnesses.

I'm reminded of another party that God crashed in the book of Daniel.

King Belshazzar was the grandson of King Nebuchadnezzar, who had come to believe in the true God of Israel. His grandson didn't follow in his footsteps. In fact, Belshazzar went out of his way one day to mock the God of Israel. At a great banquet of notables in Babylon, which devolved into a drunken orgy, he had the bright idea of taking out the special gold and silver vessels that had been used for the worship of God in His temple in Jerusalem. He basically said, "Let's drink wine out of these. Let's praise the gods of gold and silver, bronze and iron, wood and stone."

It was a bad idea.

In fact, it became his last idea.

Here's what happened, as described in Daniel 5: "Suddenly, they saw the fingers of a human hand writing on the plaster wall of the king's palace, near the lampstand. The king himself saw the hand as it wrote, and his face turned pale with fright. His knees knocked together in fear and his legs gave way beneath him" (verses 5–6 NLT).

Turn out the lights. The party was over.

The writing on the wall said, "Mene, Mene, Tekel, Upharsin," which meant, "God has numbered your kingdom, and finished it; you have been weighed in the balances, and found wanting; and your kingdom has been divided, and given to the Medes and Persians" (see verses 25–28).

Normally when we step onto a scale, we want to weigh less than we do. But on God's scales, we want to weigh more. We want more weight. God was saying, "Belshazzar, you are a lightweight. In fact, you are a bantamweight. You have no substance in your life at all."

God's judgment fell that very night, and the Medes and Persians invaded the city, overthrew the Babylonian Empire, and King Belshazzar was slain.

Revelation 11 gives a similar outcome. God's witnesses were resurrected, abruptly terminating the worldwide holiday celebrating their death. And then judgment fell. We read, "In the same hour there was a great earthquake, and a tenth of the city fell. In the earthquake seven thousand people were killed, and the rest were afraid and gave glory to the God of heaven" (verse 13).

I don't know if the people on Earth are really believing at this time or simply acknowledging that God has stepped in to do something big. They had not responded to the message of the two witnesses, and now they faced even more crushing judgments.

Revelation 11 closes with the seventh trumpet—and an amazing glimpse into Heaven:

> And there were loud voices in heaven, saying, "The kingdoms of this world have become the kingdoms of our Lord and of His Christ, and He shall reign forever and ever!" And the twenty-four elders who sat before God on their thrones fell on their faces and worshiped God, saying:
>
> "We give You thanks, O Lord God Almighty, the One who is and who was and who is to come, because You have taken Your great power and reigned. The nations were angry, and Your wrath has

come, and the time of the dead, that they should be judged, and that You should reward Your servants the prophets and the saints, and those who fear Your name, small and great, and should destroy those who destroy the earth."

Then the temple of God was opened in heaven, and the ark of His covenant was seen in His temple. And there were lightnings, noises, thunderings, an earthquake, and great hail. (verses 15–19)

This again reminds us there is a heavenly audience to all that transpires on Earth. As the two prophets are restored to life and ascend into God's presence, it's as though a portal is opened into Heaven, giving us a glimpse of the other side.

In the book of Acts, the first martyr, Stephen, had a similar glimpse into glory. As he was being stoned to death, the curtain parted, and he cried out, "Look! I see the heavens opened and the Son of Man standing at the right hand of God!" (Acts 7:56).

That is what is happening here in Revelation 11. John is describing a brief glimpse into glory. The believers in Heaven, represented by the twenty-four elders, give thanks to God that His kingdom is about to come to Earth, just as it is in Heaven.

The ark of the covenant we read about here is the original. The earthly copy, the one constructed by Moses and the Israelites in the wilderness never has been found, although many have searched for it. (Including Indiana Jones.)

This brings up a very important point. Heaven is the real deal, the eternal dwelling place. Earth is the copy, the temporary dwelling place. The best things you have ever seen or felt on this earth are but glimpses of far greater things to come.

Think about the best moments of your life—perhaps your wedding day, or the day your child was born. Or maybe it was a special moment with someone you love, as the sun was setting. Think of the most beautiful place you've ever been, or an amazing film or photograph you have seen. Heaven is far greater than that.

Certain moments linger in our memory. We say to ourselves, *That was the best. I wish it could have lasted longer. I wish it could always be that way.* But even these wonderful moments that so filled your heart with joy are only a glimpse, a brief taste, of what is to come. Heaven is the original. Earth is the copy. Moses was commanded by God to build a tabernacle, a tent. But it was only a replica of the original one that already exists in Heaven.

GOOD TO KNOW

Heaven is the real deal, the eternal dwelling place. Earth is the copy, the temporary dwelling place.

C. S. Lewis took those thoughts a step further, writing: "The hills and valleys of Heaven will be to those you now experience not as a copy is to an original, nor as a substitute is to the genuine article, but as the flower to the root, or the diamond to the coal." [21]

How should we react to this glimpse of Heaven given to us in Revelation 11? Look at verse 18: "You should reward Your servants the prophets and the saints, and those who fear Your name, small and great."

Most of us aren't prophets, but if you are a Christian, then you are indeed a living saint. It doesn't matter if you have never performed a miracle or have never seen a halo around your head when you looked in a mirror. A saint is simply another term for a true believer. And what will happen to the saints? The Bible says that one day we will be rewarded by God Himself. We will stand at the judgment seat of Christ and receive the rewards that are waiting for us even now.

In Galatians 6:9 we read, "So let's not get tired of doing what is good. At just the right time we will reap a harvest of blessing if we don't give up" (NLT). In 1 Corinthians 3:8 the apostle writes, "The one who plants and the one who waters work together with the same purpose. And both will be rewarded for their own hard work" (NLT).

This should cause us to want to do everything we can for God's glory while we're still living on this broken planet, before the days of God's judgment. As I have often said, you can't take it with you, but you can send it on ahead. Every investment we make in life for God's glory will result in an eternal reward. This includes the use of your time, the use of your gifts and talents, and the investment of your resources in kingdom projects here on Earth.

We really have no concept what these heavenly rewards will be like or what they will mean to us through all the ages of eternity. But you can count on this: the Creator of all beauty, joy, peace, light, and laughter knows how to reward His own sons and daughters.

In the meantime, God has given each of us a calling, and we need to stay faithful to Him to the very end.

THREE TAKEAWAY TRUTHS

- Like the two witnesses that God sends to preach the gospel, we also have an opportunity to influence our world for good.
- If you are a Christian, you are indestructible until God is done with you.
- This world is temporary, but anything we do for the kingdom of God will result in eternal rewards.

CHAPTER FIFTEEN
Overcoming the Devil

And they overcame him by the blood of the Lamb and by the word
of their testimony, and they did not love their lives to the death.
(Revelation 12:11)

IN THIS CHAPTER
- Some things to know about spiritual warfare
- The war in Heaven between Michael and the Dragon
- What the Devil doesn't want you to know
- Three ways to overcome Satan

As followers of Jesus Christ, we are in a battle that will last for the rest of our lives, whether we like it or not. We really don't have a choice in the matter. Ephesians 6:12 tells us clearly that "we are not fighting against flesh-and-blood enemies, but against evil rulers and authorities of the unseen world, against mighty powers in this dark world, and against evil spirits in the heavenly places" (NLT).

Even though we don't have a say about being in the battle, we do have a choice: We can win the battle or lose it. We can gain ground or lose ground. We can advance or retreat. That much, at least, is up to us. He has given us all the power and authority we need to take a stand against our adversary; we just have to make up our minds whether we will use it or not.

HOW TO OVERCOME THE DEVIL

Up until Revelation 12, it has been as though we are looking around at happenings on the earth from a heavenly perspective. Beginning in chapter 12, the scene changes. Instead of being up there looking down, we are up there looking around.

Revelation 12 describes a war in Heaven.

A war in Heaven? Could that be right?

Indeed it is. In fact, it is a war among the angels.

Earlier in Revelation we noted how angels are likened to stars. That being the case, we might refer to Revelation 12:7–12 as "Star Wars."

> And war broke out in heaven: Michael and his angels fought with the dragon; and the dragon and his angels fought, but they did not prevail, nor was a place found for them in heaven any longer. So the great dragon was cast out, that serpent of old, called the Devil and Satan, who deceives the whole world; he was cast to the earth, and his angels were cast out with him.
>
> Then I heard a loud voice saying in heaven, "Now salvation, and strength, and the kingdom of our God, and the power of His Christ have come, for the accuser of our brethren, who accused them before our God day and night, has been cast down. And they overcame him by the blood of the Lamb and by the word of their testimony, and they did not love their lives to the death. Therefore rejoice, O heavens, and you who dwell in them! Woe to the inhabitants of the earth and the sea! For the devil has come down to you, having great wrath, because he knows that he has a short time."

Considering these verses, then, what are some things that Satan, our adversary, doesn't want us to know?

WHAT THE DEVIL *DOESN'T* WANT YOU TO KNOW

Satan is mighty, but God is almighty. Satan is a destroyer, but God ultimately will destroy the destroyer.

Here is what we know about God. He is *omnipotent*, meaning that He has unlimited power. He is *omniscient*, meaning that He has unlimited knowledge. And He is *omnipresent*, meaning that He is present everywhere.

Satan is nowhere near to being the equal of God.

The Devil has none of those qualities. He is strong, but he is not omnipotent. He has great knowledge, but he is not omniscient. He has a vast army of underlings, but he is not omnipresent and can only be in one place at one time. When we say, "The Devil was tempting me," it's more likely that one of his demons from his well-organized network of fallen angels was doing the dirty work.

In the heavenly scene depicted in Revelation 12, we see Michael the archangel and Satan fighting it out. If Satan has an equal in the heavenly realm, it would be Michael, not God.

So here are two powerful angels warring against each other—two angels who once delighted to serve the Lord side by side.

> **GOOD TO KNOW**
>
> If Satan has an equal in the heavenly realm, it would be Michael, not God.

It's not unlike what happened in America's Civil War. General Grant, who led the Union forces, and General Lee, who led the Confederate forces, had attended West Point together and fought side by side in the Mexican-American war. At the outbreak of hostilities in the Civil War, however, they found themselves on opposite sides of the battlefield, trying to destroy one another. Ultimately, General Grant prevailed over General Lee.

In the same way, we find Michael prevailing over Lucifer, who became Satan. Mighty and clever as he may be, the Devil is nowhere near to being the equal of God, his Creator.

The Devil can do nothing in the life of the Christian without God's permission.

This may come as a surprise to some, but the Devil does have some access to Heaven. In Revelation 12:8 we read, "They did not prevail, nor was a place found for them in heaven any longer."

What we are reading about in Revelation 12 has not happened yet; it is yet future. This tells us that at this moment, Satan still has some level of access to Heaven.

How much access? We don't know. Before he fell, however, he had an all-access pass to Heaven. In those days, before man and woman were created and placed on Earth, Lucifer was a high-ranking angel, with some kind of leading responsibility for leading worship. But then he rebelled against God, leading a rebellion that involved up to one-third of the heavenly hosts. After that, it's reasonable to assume that he lost his all-access pass, if you will, but he retains some access to this day.

It won't always be so.

One thing is clear: Satan is on his way down. If you follow him, then you will go down with him.

I find it interesting that Michael and his angels fight with "the dragon," or Satan. The grammatical construction in the Greek indicates that Satan starts the battle. The passage could be translated, "Michael and his angels *had* to fight the dragon."

So the Devil starts this fight with Michael—and something prompts him to do it. We can only speculate what that cause might be. Could the Rapture have something to do with this launching of hostilities? You'll remember that in 1 Thessalonians 4:16 we read, "The Lord Himself will descend from heaven with a shout, with the voice of an archangel." We assume this is Michael, because he is the only angel so identified in the Scriptures. Perhaps the Lord's calling His church home is the flash point, angering Satan and prompting him to attack Michael.

GOOD TO KNOW

When the Devil wants to attack God's servants, he has to first get permission from God.

As to Satan's current access to Heaven, it seems more like a matter of being summoned by God than just wandering wherever he wants to go. It reminds me of being called into the principal's office, an event that happened to me many times during my school years. It was not a happy feeling when it was announced to the entire class that Greg Laurie had been summoned to the principal's office for something he'd done.

In the same way, the Devil is sometimes summoned into the presence of God. The book of Job gives us a behind-the-scenes example of this. In Job 1:6–7 we read,

One day the members of the heavenly court came to present themselves before the LORD, and the Accuser, Satan, came with them. "Where have you come from?" the LORD asked Satan.

Satan answered the LORD, "I have been patrolling the earth, watching everything that's going on." (NLT)

What a perfect description of Satan—just checking everything out, roaming about like a lion looking for prey.

Then the LORD asked Satan, "Have you noticed my servant Job? He is the finest man in all the earth. He is blameless—a man of complete integrity. He fears God and stays away from evil." (Job 1:8 NLT)

In a loose paraphrase, the Devil replied, "Give me a break! Does Job fear you for nothing? He knows who butters his bread! He loves and respects You because You have placed a hedge of protection all around him."

Here's the point: the Devil wanted to attack Job, but he recognized there was a wall of protection around God's servant.

In the same way, when the Devil comes our way, he has to first get permission from God. He can't just run through our lives willy-nilly. Know this: whatever God allows in your life, He allows for a purpose.

This includes tragedies.

He has allowed tragedy in my life, and no doubt He has allowed a certain amount of hardship, or even tragedy, in yours. We wonder why sometimes and can't make any sense of it. What we can know for sure, however, is that God never will give us more than we can handle. And when we are tempted, there is always a way out.

In 1 Corinthians 10:13, Paul wrote, "No temptation has overtaken you except such as is common to man; but God is faithful, who will not allow you to be tempted beyond what you are able, but with the temptation will also make the way of escape, that you may be able to bear it."

Sometimes the way out of that temptation is as simple as using the door and just walking away.

The Devil doesn't want you to know that he is doomed.

In Revelation 12:12 we read: "For the devil has come down to you, having great wrath, because he knows that he has a short time." The phrase that is used here for *great wrath* refers to a violent outburst of rage. The word depicts a turbulent, emotional fury rather than a rational anger.

Commentator John Phillips wrote the following, "Satan is now like a caged lion, enraged beyond words by the limitations now placed upon his freedom. He picks himself up from the dust of the earth, shakes his fist at the sky, and glares around, choking with fury for ways to vent his hatred and his spite upon humankind." [22]

Why is the Devil behaving as a cornered animal, ready to strike? Why is Satan filled with so much venom and hatred? Why does Satan want our destruction? It's because he knows that Jesus Christ is coming back again.

Even if some liberal theologians don't believe it, the Devil believes that Jesus Christ is coming back. As a result, his goal and objective is to wreak as much havoc as he can in that time—and we need to wake up to this reality.

This is why Satan and his demons attack us. Sometimes it seems as though we're getting hit from every side.

I heard a story from the Korean War that illustrates the attitude that we ought to have. As enemy forces were advancing, Baker Company was cut off from the rest of the regiment. For several hours no word was heard, even though headquarters had tried to communicate with this missing unit. Finally a faint signal was received. Straining to hear each word, a soldier asked Baker Company, "Do you read me?"

The reply came through, "This is Baker Company."

"What is your situation?"

The voice on the radio from Baker Company replied, "The enemy is to the east of us. The enemy is to the west of us. The enemy is to the south of us and to the north of us." Then, after a brief pause, the sergeant from Baker Company added, "And we are not going to let them escape this time!"

I like that attitude.

Sometimes it feels as though the Devil is hitting us from north, south, east, and west. Everywhere we turn there is an attack . . . a temptation . . . a hardship . . . a problem . . . an issue. Even so, God will give us the strength to get through things.

The Devil doesn't want you to know that he attacks primarily through accusation.

It is good for us to know how the Devil works. As Paul said, "We are not ignorant of his devices" (2 Corinthians 2:11). It was Victor Hugo, the author of *Les Misérables,* who said, "A good general must penetrate the brain of his enemy."

How does the Devil attack us? It is often through accusation. We read these words in Revelation 12:10: "Then I heard a loud voice saying in heaven, 'Now salvation, and strength, and the kingdom of our God, and the power of His Christ have come, for the accuser of our brethren, who accused them before our God day and night, has been cast down.'"

Satan is "the accuser of the brethren."

It begins when he comes to you with a temptation. And, by the way, it is not a sin to be tempted. It's not the *bait* that constitutes temptation; it's the *bite.* In other words, it is acting on the temptation that passes through your mind.

And let's face it. Temptation can hit us at the worst, most inconvenient times. You may even be in church, listening to a good message, when suddenly the most ungodly, horrible thought is placed in front of you. You think to yourself, *What is this? Where did this come from?*

Again, it is not a sin to be tempted. The thought may have come randomly and was never something you summoned or desired at all.

And then the accuser comes and says, "You are so twisted. What is your problem? Why would you think such a horrible

GOOD TO KNOW

Satan is "the accuser of the brethren."

thought? And you call yourself a Christian? Seriously? You ought to just get up and leave church right now because you don't deserve to be here."

That is your adversary speaking to you, the voice of the accuser, and you need to pull the plug on him. It isn't a sin to have a tempting thought pass through your mind; it is a sin to entertain that thought or give in to the temptation.

And what if you do give in? He tempts you, and you take the bait. Almost immediately the enemy comes to you and says, "What a hypocrite. Don't even think about going to God in prayer and asking for His forgiveness! You're not worthy to even approach God."

What is your response to the accusations of the Devil? You turn to Jesus to intercede on your behalf. Jesus is standing in the gap for you. Just before His arrest, Jesus said to Peter, in a literal translation of the verse, "Simon, Simon, Satan has been asking excessively that you would be taken directly out of the care and protection of God" (see Luke 22:31).

But then He went on to say, "But I have prayed for you, that your faith should not fail; and when you have returned to Me, strengthen your brethren" (verse 32). Jesus was saying, "Peter, the Devil has been asking for you by name. But I have prayed for you. I am interceding for you."

The Bible tells us that Christ intercedes for us in Heaven. In Romans 8:33–34 we read, "Who will bring any charge against those whom God has chosen? It is God who justifies. Who then is the one who condemns? No one. Christ Jesus who died—more than that, who was raised to life—is at the right hand of God and is also interceding for us" (NIV).

THREE POTENT WAYS TO OVERCOME SATAN

In Revelation 12:11, we are introduced to a group of believers who are able to overcome Satan, even in the time of his great wrath. Remember, this takes place within the tribulation period. The Rapture has already taken place. One group of believers, who were saved during the Great Tribulation, already have been martyred. We read about them in Revelation 6:10, as they cry out, "How long,

Sovereign Lord, holy and true, until you judge the inhabitants of the earth and avenge our blood?" (NIV).

But what about these believers in Revelation 12:11? How do they overcome the Evil One? Here is the clear answer: "They triumphed over him by the blood of the Lamb and by the word of their testimony; they did not love their lives so much as to shrink from death" (NIV).

How do you overcome Satan?

1. You overcome Satan by the blood of the Lamb.

The next time the enemy comes to you and says that you aren't worthy to approach God, do you know what I would advise?

Agree with him!

Say to the enemy, "You're right! I'm not worthy to approach God, and I never have been. What's more, I never will be worthy to approach God. *My access to God's presence isn't based on my worthiness. It is based on what Christ did for me on the cross.*"

Sometimes we slip into a works-righteousness mentality as Christians. Here is how we think. We say to ourselves, "I did really well today. I got up in the morning and read four chapters from my Bible. I said grace over my meal at lunch—even as others were watching. I even shared my faith with someone at work. I'm doing pretty well, spiritually. I know I can approach God with confidence."

But maybe the next week you slept in and didn't read your Bible. You forgot to say grace over your meal, and you didn't share Jesus with anyone. So you say to yourself, "I'm not doing as well as I should. I'm not worthy to approach God—let alone ask Him for help."

Yes, all of these things that I just mentioned are important, but let's not get sidetracked. Your access to God through Christ is already there. It already has been purchased for you and paid in full by Jesus on the cross. If you have done well, that's good. Approach God with thanksgiving. If you have sinned, approach God and say, "Father, I have sinned. This is why I need the blood of the Lamb."

The Devil always will try to keep you away from the cross.

The Holy Spirit always will bring you to the cross.

The Devil will accuse and condemn you and say that you can't go to God. But the Holy Spirit will convict you and convince you and say that you *must* come to God. If you are feeling bad about some wrong that you have done, that's a good thing. It means that your conscience is functional and working.

We have a smoke alarm in our house that seems to go off all the time. If my wife cooks an egg, the smoke alarm goes off, even though there is no fire or even discernible smoke. The thing is hypersensitive and annoying. But I would rather have a hypersensitive smoke alarm, which might save my life someday, than a nonfunctional smoke alarm that will let me sleep while my house burns down.

If your conscience is sensitive, that is a positive thing. The Bible says that it is possible to sear your conscience, as with a hot iron, so that it no longer even functions (see 1 Timothy 4:2).

You want your conscience to be sensitive and open to the work of the Spirit. But it isn't your conscience that wins you access to God; it is the blood of the Lamb. My access to God is a result of what Jesus has done for me. *Period.* Hebrews 10:19–20 says, "And so, dear brothers and sisters, we can boldly enter heaven's Most Holy Place because of the blood of Jesus. By his death, Jesus opened a new and life-giving way through the curtain into the Most Holy Place" (NLT).

In Ephesians 2:13 the apostle Paul wrote, "Once you were far away from God, but now you have been brought near to him through the blood of Christ" (NLT).

The apostle John tells us that "if we walk in the light as He is in the light, we have fellowship with one another, and the blood of Jesus Christ His Son cleanses us from all sin" (1 John 1:7).

Like the old hymn says, there is power in the blood. The Devil doesn't want us to talk about the blood—and he certainly doesn't want us to appropriate the blood.

I asked Billy Graham years ago if an older Billy could speak to a younger Billy who was just starting out in ministry, what would he say that the younger Billy should emphasize more? He answered, "I would preach more on the cross of Christ and the blood, because that is where the power is!"

I have never forgotten those words and have tried to implement them through the years.

Why all the emphasis on blood? For one reason: It's because Jesus died on the cross and met the righteous demands of a holy God. Because of this sacrifice, because He willingly shed His blood, I can approach the Lord anytime, no matter what I have done, if I will confess my sin and ask for His forgiveness.

Early in the book of Exodus, we read how God instituted a holy day called Passover. The Israelites were to slay a lamb and then apply the blood over their doorway, on the top and on the right and the left. When God's judgment came upon the land, the angel of death passed over all the houses where the blood had been applied.

GOOD TO KNOW

The only thing that gives us access to God is the blood of the Lamb.

So we apply the blood of Jesus on our lives by faith. And we overcome the Evil One by the blood of the Lamb.

2. You overcome Satan by the word of your testimony.

When a believer is cleansed and walking in fellowship with God, it's just natural that he or she will want to tell others. When it comes to promoting our faith in Christ, I'm reminded of an old football cliché: the best defense is a good offense. In other words, instead of trying to just hold our ground, we should make it our aim to gain ground and move forward. Identifying yourself as a Christian is a good way to make yourself accountable—even to nonbelievers.

At your workplace, you look for opportunities to say, "I'm a Christian. I believe in Jesus Christ. He changed my life, and He can change yours!" You don't have to be overbearing or obnoxious about it; you simply state who you are and what is important to you. With your family or in your neighborhood, you simply tell people, "I'm a follower of Jesus."

The moment you put that stake in the ground, things will change. Your fellow workers and students, your neighbors, and your family will be watching you. Count on it! They will be evaluating you and the way you respond to life situations. Though they may never say it out loud, they're thinking things like,

So that's how a Christian acts under pressure. . . . That's how a believer treats his wife. . . . That's how a Christian wife treats her husband. . . . That's how Christians raise their children.

They are watching you, taking note of every time your foot slips—or your tongue slips. There's nothing worse than being called to account by nonbelievers, especially when they are right.

Has that ever happened to you? You did something inconsistent, and your non-Christian friend said, "Hey, I thought you were a Christian. Why did you do that? Why did you respond that way?"

This group in Revelation 12 overcame Satan by the blood of the Lamb and *by the word of their testimony.* In other words, they spoke up about their faith in Christ. They told their personal stories of coming to faith in Jesus—even in a world under the shadow of Antichrist. The fact is that everyone has a testimony. What is your testimony? It's basically just telling your story.

Someone will say, "But I don't have much of a story. Nothing very dramatic has happened in my life, and I've never gone through any great adversity."

You don't have to go through adversity to have a testimony. Just tell your story. Just express what the Lord means to you and what He has done for you.

3. You overcome Satan by not loving your life so much as to shrink from death.

These believers understood that their lives belonged to God. They had already seen others martyred, as we read about earlier in Revelation. They knew their situation. They were followers of Jesus in the Tribulation period with the Antichrist in control, and they could lose their lives at any time. But as far as they were concerned, that was up to God. They knew their times were in His hands. Bearing these things in mind, they spoke up for their faith in Christ, in spite of the probable consequences.

This is such an important mindset.

When push comes to shove, our lives aren't our own anyway. Our lives belong to God. He decides the day of our birth, and He determines the day of our death. God decides the beginning, and God decides the end. On every tombstone you will see a date of birth followed by a date of death, with a dash in between. That thin line between birth and death is your part. That is where you have your testimony and seek to live for Him.

As long as you are alive, you may as well live boldly, not fearing persecution and not fearing death. Your life, your very existence, is in the hand of God.

The story is told of a believer who was brought before one of the Roman emperors and told to renounce his faith, giving glory to Caesar. But he wouldn't do it.

The emperor said, "Give up Christ, or I will banish you."

"But you can't banish me from Christ," the believer replied, "for He has said, 'I will never leave you nor forsake you.'"

The emperor said, "I will confiscate your property."

"My treasures are laid up in Heaven," the Christian said, "and you can't touch them."

The emperor said, "I will kill you."

The Christian replied, "I have been dead to this world in Christ for forty years. My life is hid with Christ in God. You can't touch it."

The emperor turned to some of the members of his court and said in complete disgust, "What you can do with such a fanatic?"

This was a man who did not love his life so much as to shrink from death, and he overcame Caesar and Satan.

May God give us more people like this.

THREE TAKEAWAY TRUTHS

- There is no opt-out measure; all Christians are locked in a spiritual battle whether they like it or not.
- Although Satan is powerful, he is not God's equal, and God gives us power to overcome him.
- Because God holds our lives in His hand, we do not have to fear persecution.

CHAPTER SIXTEEN

Christmas in the Book of Revelation

And the dragon was enraged with the woman,
and he went to make war with the rest of her
offspring, who keep the commandments of God
and have the testimony of Jesus Christ.
(Revelation 12:17)

> **IN THIS CHAPTER**
> - An unusual account of the Incarnation of Jesus
> - Identifying the woman and the dragon
> - How Satan has tried to stop God's work throughout history
> - What an ancient, spiritual conflict has to do with believers today

Sometimes we might think we've heard it all when it comes to Christmas.

We've read the accounts in Matthew and Luke umpteen times, heard countless sermons, and conclude that we have the biblical account of the birth of Jesus pretty much wired.

But there is more. More, perhaps, than we have ever imagined.

In Revelation 12, we see a view of Christmas from the heavenly perspective, and it isn't exactly Currier and Ives. In fact, there isn't a yule log, holly berry, snowflake, or sleigh bell to be found.

Instead of Mary and Joseph, angels and shepherds, wise men and innkeepers, we have a different cast altogether. We have a pregnant woman being pursued by a powerful dragon who seeks her death. As she prepares to give birth, he hovers over her, waiting to destroy her baby.

Christmas?

Yes, but probably from an angle we've never seen before. It surely shows one thing. That the original Christmas, two thousand years ago, was a time of great conflict in the heavens and on Earth.

To this day, Christmas is a time of conflict. The pressure in our culture to shop, buy, and pursue all-out materialism grows more insane every year. And the madness starts earlier and earlier on the calendar. Thanksgiving used to be the one day when all the malls were shut down. Not anymore. Now the retailers have decided to open their doors on Thanksgiving, starting the Christmas buying rush before Black Friday. This retailing on steroids has created and maintained a culture of chaos around the holiday season. As someone recently said, retailers have basically ruined every holiday that we have.

GOOD TO KNOW

Satan did everything in his power to stop the first Christmas from happening.

Did you read any accounts of Black Friday sales in recent years? News reports told of crowds shattering windows, beating each other up in the aisles, and threatening one another's lives. Two people were shot outside a Wal-Mart in Florida. One man took his girlfriend's three-year-old son to Kmart for a midnight sale. He left with a fifty-one-inch flat-screen television—but forgot the kid.

We read about Christmas traffic jams, families coming unraveled, domestic violence, and counseling offices filled with depressed, even suicidal, clients. Christmas is supposed to be a happy time, a peaceful time. But in many homes, it hasn't been that for years. If ever.

The idea of a traditional family gathering for the holidays seems to be something of the past, with so many broken homes resulting from divorce. Family gatherings can be problematic. We have to go visit dad and his new wife, then spend time with mom and her new live-in boyfriend. Then we have to figure out how to respond to all the stepbrothers, stepsisters, and step in-laws.

It's awkward, uncomfortable, and seems to lend itself to all kinds of disappointments and interpersonal conflicts.

But no matter how much conflict we experience today, it can't compare to the conflict that preceded the very first Christmas, when God became man.

Revelation 12 shows us that Satan didn't want there to be a Christmas at all and did everything in his power to stop the birth of Jesus on Earth. His efforts to thwart the Incarnation might have succeeded . . . but God intervened.

Thankfully, God always has the last word.

THE DRAGON AND WONDER WOMAN

Now a great sign appeared in heaven: a woman clothed with the sun, with the moon under her feet, and on her head a garland of twelve stars. Then being with child, she cried out in labor and in pain to give birth.

And another sign appeared in heaven: behold, a great, fiery red dragon having seven heads and ten horns, and seven diadems on his heads. His tail drew a third of the stars of heaven and threw them to the earth. And the dragon stood before the woman who was ready to give birth, to devour her Child as soon as it was born. She bore a male Child who was to rule all nations with a rod of iron. And her Child was caught up to God and His throne. (12:1–5)

Who is this wonder woman of Revelation 12:1? First, let me tell you who she *isn't*. She isn't Mary, the mother of Jesus. In fact, I believe the woman in this incredible vision is actually the nation Israel, and the child that she bears is Jesus Christ.

Verse 1 speaks of a "garland of twelve stars." You may remember that in the dream God gave to young Joseph in Genesis 37, Israel was symbolized by a sun, a moon, and eleven stars, with Joseph being the twelfth star. That is the first instance of the imagery of twelve stars, so when it is repeated again in the book of Revelation, we make the connection that God intends us to make: both instances refer to the nation Israel. This is called "the rule of first mention."

The Messiah came from Israel, and He will one day rule over the whole Earth. In verse 5 we read that "she bore a male Child who was to rule all nations with a rod of iron." Where have we heard that expression before? Again, going back to its first mention in the Scriptures, we find those words in Psalm 2. In this messianic psalm, God the Father says to the Messiah:

"You are My Son,
Today I have begotten You.
Ask of Me, and I will give You
The nations for Your inheritance,
And the ends of the earth for Your possession.
You shall break them with a rod of iron;
You shall dash them to pieces like a potter's vessel." (verses 7–9)

There is that same picture again. The image refers to a time on Earth known as the Millennium, after the battle of Armageddon and the Second Coming of Christ.

The word *millennium* means "thousand" and refers to the future thousand-year reign of Christ on Earth. At this point as believers, we will have been raptured into Heaven already and will return with Christ when He comes again in great glory. At this time, Satan will be chained and out of the way, and we will be in our glorified bodies, ruling and reigning with Jesus.

But why would Jesus need to rule Earth with "a rod of iron"?

Because during this thousand-year period, not everyone will *want* to be ruled by Christ—as difficult as that might be to believe. The survivors of the Tribulation period still will be on Earth, as well as their descendants. And even though Christ's ten-century rule will be perfect in every way, there will be short-lived rebellion at the end of the thousand years, led by the newly released Satan. After that rebellion is quickly squashed, the New Jerusalem will come down to Earth out of Heaven, and we will experience the new heavens and the new Earth.

Not only does Christ rule with a rod of iron during the Millennium, but we also will have the privilege to rule *with* Him. In the story we refer to as the parable of the talents, the master speaks these words to a faithful servant who has wisely invested his life and resources: "Well done, good and faithful servant; you were faithful over a few things, I will make you ruler over many things. Enter into the joy of your lord" (Matthew 25:21).

Have you ever wondered what that meant? It means that as a wise steward of your life and as a faithful follower of Jesus, you will have delegated authority under the King of kings to rule and reign with Him.

THE IDENTITY OF THE DRAGON

> Behold, a great, fiery red dragon having seven heads and ten horns, and seven diadems on his heads. His tail drew a third of the stars of heaven and threw them to the earth. (12:3–4)

This dragon is none other than Satan, the fallen angel who was once named Lucifer, "son of the morning." Seven heads and ten horns? It sounds like something out of one of those old Godzilla movies, doesn't it?

The heads and horns on this dragon are symbols. The word *head* comes from the word *diadem*, which also could be translated "crown." This symbolizes power, authority, and intelligence, and Satan possesses all of these things. Our adversary has vast intelligence and has had thousands of years to perfect his craft of attacking men and women and wreaking chaos, pain, sorrow, and havoc on Earth.

In 2 Corinthians 4:3–4 Paul wrote, "If the Good News we preach is hidden to anyone, it is hidden from the one who is on the road to eternal death. Satan, who is the god of this evil world, has made him blind, unable to see the glorious light of the Gospel that is shining upon him or to understand the amazing message we preach about the glory of Christ, who is God" (TLB).

Satan, whom Paul labeled as "the god of this evil world," is so clever that he has fooled many people into thinking that he doesn't even exist—while in reality he controls their very lives.

The "ten horns" spoken of in this passage refer to ten confederated nations who will be working with the Antichrist at this time. Later we will read that it's

REVELATION: A BOOK OF PROMISES

the dragon who gives the Antichrist his authority. In other words, Satan energizes this charismatic coming world leader, who will have ten nations working together with him. (More about this later.)

GOOD TO KNOW

Two things to remember about Satan: he is anti-Semitic, and he is anti-Christ.

In verse 4 we read that this dragon "drew a third of the stars of heaven and threw them to the earth." This refers to the circumstances of Satan's fall, when he took one-third of the angels of Heaven with him. These fallen angels, or demons, now do his dirty work in our world. They are Satan's storm troopers, if you will.

Notice the fierce anger and aggression of this dragon in verse 4: "The dragon stood before the woman who was ready to give birth, to devour her Child as soon as it was born."

Here are two things you need to bear in mind about Satan: he is anti-Semitic, and he is anti-Christ. He hates Israel, and he hates Jesus Christ and all who belong to Him. He has nurtured a special hatred for the Jewish people from the days of Pharaoh to Haman to Hitler to Stalin to Iran and to Hamas.

He would devour Israel in a moment—if he could.

So far, he hasn't been able to. But he will keep trying.

SATAN HATES CHRISTMAS

These graphic images in Revelation 12 give us the big picture of what Christmas is really all about—and why Satan hates it with everything in him. I believe we are witnessing this hatred in our own culture as we see left-leaning groups hell-bent on killing Christmas in the Western world. They don't want manger scenes on public property. They don't want Christmas carols in our public schools. In some cities, officials have even banned innocuous Christmas trees.

I don't even know if these anti-Christmas activists fully understand what they're doing. In fact, I very much doubt that they do. I am reminded of the Lord's statement from the cross when He prayed for those who had crucified Him, saying, "Father, forgive them, for they do not know what they do" (Luke 23:34).

The banning of manger scenes in public places, the banning of Christmas carols from public schools and public events, and all hostility toward Jesus Christ is directly linked to the dragon in Revelation 12, waiting with bared fangs to devour the Child about to be born.

The Devil, who hates both Jewish people and their Messiah, knows exactly what he is doing. It's a cosmic feud that goes all the way back to the first book of the Bible. In fact, it goes back to the very first Christmas passage—the first Messianic passage—in the Bible. God speaks these words in Genesis 3:15, after Adam and Eve sinned against Him and ate the forbidden fruit. The Lord said to the Devil, "And I will put enmity between you and the woman, and between your offspring and hers; he will crush your head, and you will strike his heel" (NIV).

The Lord was putting Satan on notice. A Coming One would crush his head, while Satan would only manage to bruise His heel. This is speaking of Jesus, who doomed and crushed the head of Satan on the cross. But the Devil did bruise the Lord's heel. Speaking of the coming Messiah in Isaiah 53, the prophet told us, "He was wounded for our transgressions, He was bruised for our iniquities; the chastisement for our peace was upon Him, and by His stripes we are healed" (verse 5).

At the cross Satan was crushed and Jesus was bruised.

By the way, that is precisely how to kill a snake. You crush his head. Don't ever pick up a snake by the tail, because he can rear around and bite you. No, you have to smash your heel down on his head, which is exactly what Christ did.

From this announcement in Genesis, then, Satan knew there would be a Coming One from the woman's seed who would crush his head. In time, he would understand that this future Savior would come from the Jewish race.

In Exodus, Satan worked through Pharaoh, seeking to kill all the Jewish boys at birth. In the book of Judges, we can see Satan using Israel's neighbors, seeking to destroy the nation. In 1 Samuel, we see Saul trying to murder David, thus stopping the Messianic line. In Esther, we have the plot of the anti-Semitic Haman to wipe out Jews all over the world.

All of these murderous plots failed, but Satan wasn't done yet. Not by a long shot. Having failed to wipe out the people of God in the messianic line, he attempted to murder the Messiah Himself before He could do His saving work. Remember when those mysterious wise men blew into town, having seen a star in the east? These magi wanted to locate, honor, and worship the newborn King of the Jews. That was the last thing you wanted to say to a paranoid, powder-keg tyrant like King Herod. The fact of the matter is that Caesar had given *him* the title of King of the Jews.

This announcement from the wise men seemed like a direct threat to his throne. After checking out the matter with his scholars, he determined that this royal baby would be born in Bethlehem. So what did Herod do? He sent his soldiers to Bethlehem to put to death all the baby boys under the age of two, in a nightmare attempt to put an end to this newborn Messiah.

But God had warned Joseph in a dream to flee to Egypt, frustrating Herod's (and Satan's) murderous plan.

Christ was born and grew into manhood. But the attacks continued. At the very outset of His ministry, Satan tempted Him in the wilderness. At one point, the Devil showed Jesus all the kingdoms of the world in a moment of time. The Evil One said to Jesus, "All these things I will give You if You will fall down and worship me" (Matthew 4:9).

Jesus never challenged or refuted Satan's statement. If it had been a lie, Jesus would have confronted that lie. But what Satan said in that moment was technically true. At this time, Satan is the "god of this world" and has control of the kingdoms of the world. The Devil was saying to Jesus, in effect, "Look, Jesus, we both know why You are here. You are here to purchase back that which was lost in the Garden of Eden. But there's no need to battle for it. I will give You that title deed to the world on a silver platter. There doesn't have to be a cross or suffering or bearing the sins of the world. I'll give all that to You in this moment if You will only give me the satisfaction of bowing down and worshiping me."

Jesus of course resisted and refuted Satan, saying, "Away with you, Satan! For it is written, 'You shall worship the Lord your God, and Him only you shall serve'" (Matthew 4:10).

Satan wanted to divert Jesus from His course.

But Jesus refused to be diverted.

The attacks continued after Jesus began His ministry. They even tried to put him to death in His hometown of Nazareth. A mob actually took Christ to the edge of a cliff and were preparing to push Him off, but the Bible tells us in Luke 4 that He calmly passed through their midst and went His way.

Why was He able to walk away from a murderous mob that was hell-bent on killing Him? Because it wasn't His time. His hour had not yet come.

This is a reminder that as a Christian, you are indestructible until God is done with you. But when your hour comes, when your date with destiny arrives, when your moment to enter eternity is here, there is nothing you can do to change it. That is why you want to live your life well and for the glory of God in the interim.

And then His hour finally came. What was that hour?

It was the hour when He would suffer and die for the sins of the world. As Jesus told His captors in the Garden of Gethsemane, "Every day I was with you in the temple courts, and you did not lay a hand on me. But this is your hour—when darkness reigns" (Luke 22:53 NIV).

In a way, it could look as though the Devil prevailed. Jesus was betrayed by Judas Iscariot, tried by a phony, kangaroo court, sentenced to death by Pilate, crucified on a cross, and then buried in a borrowed tomb.

But then God raised Him from the dead, fulfilling prophecy and completing His mission.

The whole purpose of Christmas was so that Jesus would be born in that manger in Bethlehem, live a perfect life, and one day die for our sins. The birth of Jesus happened to make possible the death of Jesus. That is why, to this day, Satan, the dragon, wants to kill the real meaning of Christmas. Frankly, the Devil doesn't care if you shop 'til you drop, cover your house with a million light bulbs, decorate a Christmas tree, or even make your yearly pilgrimage to church. But if you take the time to contemplate what Christmas is really all about and worship the newborn King, he will be angry. If he can't stop Christmas altogether, then he will settle for hiding its meaning.

TOO BEAUTIFUL?

Maybe the problem with our Christmas celebrations is that we have made them all too beautiful. We love all the images of sleighs and snow, delight in the fragrance of Christmas candles and freshly baked goodies, take pleasure in all the brightly wrapped packages under the tree, and lose ourselves in the lovely music of the holiday.

The celebration can be beautiful.

But the story itself is wrapped in tragedy: A little Baby was born to spill His blood and die on a cross in the prime of a perfect life. That is why red is the color of Christmas. It is not because Santa wears red, because holly berries are red, or because we like red wrapping paper. Christmas is red because that's the color of the blood of Jesus, shed from the cross. He was born to die that we might live.

Sometimes in our attempts to beautify and sanitize Christmas, we might miss the essential message.

That's why this vision in the book of Revelation, portraying the heavenly perspective of Christmas, is so startling. Instead of the soft, fragrant, gentle elements to which we're accustomed in our celebrations, we see a pregnant woman crying out in pain, a fearsome, fiery red dragon, and a Child snatched from the jaws of destruction.

GOOD TO KNOW

Sometimes in our attempts to beautify and sanitize Christmas, we might miss the essential message.

Yes, the dragon's plan to stop Christmas—or, more specifically, the birth of Jesus Christ—was thwarted, and his whole plan backfired (for him) in the worst way possible. But he still hates every reminder of the Child who came to die. Why? Because that Child became a Man who sealed his doom.

THE BATTLE GOES ON

Again, what did God say when He announced the Messiah was coming in Genesis 3:15? He said to the Devil, "I will put enmity between you and the woman, and between your offspring and hers; he will crush your head, and you will strike his heel" (NIV).

In other words, this isn't just a battle between God and Satan; it is between Satan's *seed* and God's *seed*.

Who is God's seed? We are—all the true followers of Jesus around the world. By contrast, Satan's seed are those who follow the Devil. There is no middle ground, and there are no neutral countries in this ceaseless warfare. In reality, you are either following God right now, or you are following Satan.

Someone might say, "I don't agree. I don't even *believe* in God or Satan."

That really changes nothing. If you don't believe and follow God's Son, the Bible says that you have been blinded by the god of this world, who is controlling your life.

This is the battle between God's seed and Satan's seed. Like it or not, as a follower of Jesus, you will face hostility because of that fact. Jesus said very clearly, "If the world hates you, you know that it hated Me before it hated you. If you were of the world, the world would love its own. Yet because you are not of the world, but I chose you out of the world, therefore the world hates you" (John 15:18–19).

"That's not very nice," someone may say. "I don't like all this talk about hate."

I don't either, but that is the reality of the world we live in, a world wrapped in an ancient war. The truth is that if you dare to speak up for Jesus Christ, publicly acknowledging that you love Him and belong to Him, then you will be treated differently. You will begin to be treated as He was treated.

Our choice as believers, then, is to either fight in the spiritual battle or be overcome and overtaken by the enemy. We can choose victory or defeat, winning or losing, advancing or retreating.

Simply put, Satan doesn't want you to follow Christ, and he will do everything in his power to keep you from doing that.

Remember the dragon in Revelation 12. He wanted to devour the Son being born two thousand years ago, and to this day he wants to devour all who belong to Him. It's a conflict between God's seed and Satan's seed that will rage until the very end.

In the end, those who belong to Jesus Christ will overcome.
That's the real story of Christmas.

THREE TAKEAWAY TRUTHS

- The "war on Christmas" is not new but part of an ancient conflict between good and evil.
- Let us never be distracted from the true meaning of Christmas: that Christ came to die on a cross for our sins.
- No matter how much Satan tries to thwart the plans of God, he will never succeed. Christ's victory on the cross was Satan's defeat.

CHAPTER SEVENTEEN
Who Is the Antichrist?

All who dwell on the earth will worship him, whose
names have not been written in the Book of Life of the
Lamb slain from the foundation of the world.
(Revelation 13:8)

> **IN THIS CHAPTER**
> * Why we should care about what the Bible says about the Antichrist
> * The Antichrist's identity and agenda
> * Warnings for today about apostasy
> * Where the church will be when the Antichrist emerges

I recently was at the market and as I was checking out, I saw the most beautiful tulips. I decided to buy them and surprise my wife, Cathe.

I remember marveling at how they were so perfect they almost looked artificial, but they were clearly the real thing as I bought them in the fresh flower section of the market.

After I got home, I put them in a vase and could hardly wait to see Cathe's delight. She was very happy with them and went to cut the stems to put them in water, but she couldn't cut through the stems. Then it dawned on her: I had unknowingly bought her fake flowers!

It was hard to believe because they looked so much like the original.

Antichrist will be a very realistic imitation of Jesus Christ, and some will even think he is the Messiah they have been waiting for. Type the word *Antichrist* into Google and you will find thirteen million options to choose from.

Whenever something is popular or successful, you can be sure there soon will be a proliferation of imitations and knockoffs.

Satan, the one the Bible refers to as "the god of this world," is the ultimate imitator and offers cheap copycat reproductions and facsimiles of authentic and eternal truths.

There are real Christians who believe in Jesus, but there are also fake believers—pretenders, posers—who infiltrate the church.

There are genuine miracles in our world, performed by the hand of God, and there are imitations of God's supernatural works. God has His Son, Jesus, and one day Satan will have his "son." We have Jesus Christ, and Satan will have his Antichrist.

This man will be history's vilest embodiment of sin and rebellion.

But don't expect him to look like it. I'm guessing that his eyes won't glow red, he won't be dressed head-to-toe in black, with 666 tattooed on his forehead and steam rising from his body as he walks by.

He will be suave, intelligent, engaging, magnetic, and charismatic. What's more, he will do what no other man has ever been able to do before. He will bring global peace. He will solve the Middle East peace puzzle. He will rid the world of terrorism. He will be so successful that he will be hailed as the greatest peacemaker who has ever lived. No doubt he will win the Nobel Peace Prize. Teachers will have little school children singing his praises. He will even persuade the Jewish nation and Arab nations to sign a peace treaty, paving the way for the construction of the long-awaited third temple on the Temple Mount in Jerusalem.

He will be a satanic superman. But behind the cordial, pleasant persona will be the evilest man who has ever walked Planet Earth—and that is saying something.

WHY SHOULD WE EVEN CARE ABOUT THE ANTICHRIST?

There's not much doubt that conditions are ripe for Antichrist to emerge on the world scene. Some years ago, historian Arnold Toynbee wrote, "By forcing on mankind more and more lethal weapons, and at the same time making the world more and more interdependent economically, technology has brought mankind to such a degree of distress that we are ripe for the deifying of any new Caesar who might succeeded in giving the world unity and peace." [23]

That statement fits the biblical scenario to a T.

Some might ask, "Why should I care about the emergence of the Antichrist? Why even give a passing thought to him?"

Here's one reason: the Bible pays a great deal of attention to him.

There are over one hundred passages in the Scriptures that detail the origin, nationality, career, character, kingdom, accomplishments, treachery, and final doom of the Antichrist. He is discussed in-depth in the book of Revelation as well as the book of Daniel. He is also referenced in 2 Thessalonians and in the book of 1 John. The sheer volume of information about the Antichrist in the Scriptures is enough for us to want to understand who he is and what he will do.

GOOD TO KNOW

The sheer volume of information about the Antichrist in the Scriptures is enough for us to want to understand who he is and what he will do.

But I can think of one additional reason. In the biblical account of the Antichrist, we see evil on our world accelerate and become predominant. But its victory is short-lived. The Antichrist is defeated, Satan is vanquished, evil is overcome, and Jesus conquers all.

In other words, we win in the end, and we need to keep that in perspective.

In the pages of this chapter, we'll take a brief look at the man described as "the beast," "the son of perdition," "the little horn," and "the prince to come."

This is Antichrist, and if Satan ever had a son, it would be him. Is he on the earth right now, getting ready to emerge? No one knows for sure. But we can be certain of this: every passing day brings his emergence closer.

> Then I stood on the sand of the sea. And I saw a beast rising up out of the sea, having seven heads and ten horns, and on his horns ten crowns, and on his heads a blasphemous name. Now the beast which I saw was like a leopard, his feet were like the feet of

a bear, and his mouth like the mouth of a lion. The dragon gave him his power, his throne, and great authority. And I saw one of his heads as if it had been mortally wounded, and his deadly wound was healed. And all the world marveled and followed the beast. So they worshiped the dragon who gave authority to the beast; and they worshiped the beast, saying, "Who is like the beast? Who is able to make war with him?"

And he was given a mouth speaking great things and blasphemies, and he was given authority to continue for forty-two months. Then he opened his mouth in blasphemy against God, to blaspheme His name, His tabernacle, and those who dwell in heaven. It was granted to him to make war with the saints and to overcome them. And authority was given him over every tribe, tongue, and nation. All who dwell on the earth will worship him, whose names have not been written in the Book of Life of the Lamb slain from the foundation of the world.

If anyone has an ear, let him hear. (Revelation 13:1–9)

This first description of the Antichrist sounds like something out of a science fiction movie: *Godzilla Meets the Creature from the Black Lagoon.* Don't let the depictions throw you. John is using figures of speech to describe a fantastic vision that God has given him. Daniel uses similar expressions in his descriptions.

Beyond all the wild imagery, let me simply say this: To understand the beast, you have to first understand his father. To understand Antichrist, you need to know more about Satan himself.

In Revelation 12:3, we already read about seven heads and ten horns: "Another sign appeared in heaven: behold, a great, fiery red dragon having seven heads and ten horns, and seven diadems on his heads."

This latter description of the dragon is a depiction of Satan. So this coming world leader, the Antichrist, is empowered by the Devil himself. In

2 Thessalonians 2:9, the apostle writes that "the coming of the lawless one is according to the working of Satan, with all power, signs, and lying wonders." You might say like father, like son.

But here in Revelation 13:2 we also read about a lion, a bear, and a leopard. What does that mean? To answer that, I would refer you to the book of Daniel, the companion book to Revelation. In the seventh chapter of that book, Daniel was given a vision of four animals, representing four world kingdoms. When Daniel beheld that vision and wrote those words, these kingdoms were mostly future. But now as we look back on what Daniel wrote with twenty-twenty hindsight, we can see how this vision was historically fulfilled exactly.

The lion was a symbol of the kingdom of Babylon.

First, Daniel had the vision of a lion. That was the symbol of the kingdom of Babylon, the great world empire that had taken Daniel captive as a young man, and with which he was now employed as an adviser to the king.

As many Old Testament readers already know, Babylon conquered the nation of Judah and held many of her people captive for seventy years. The great leader of that powerful empire, King Nebuchadnezzar, was influenced by the testimony and ministry of Daniel. This mighty king was replaced by a foolish, heedless grandchild named Belshazzar, who became the last king of Babylon.

Babylon was the lion. Archaeologists who have unearthed ruins dating back to Babylon have uncovered the symbol of a winged lion.

The lion, however, was overcome by a bear with massive strength.

The bear symbolizes the Medo-Persians.

We know that the Medo-Persians conquered Babylon (which was predicted elsewhere in the Scriptures). While the wicked boy-king Belshazzar was reigning, the Medo-Persians were closing in. In fact, it all came down one night when the invading army, led by Darius, swept into the city, put Belshazzar to the sword, and absorbed Babylon into their own vast empire.

The Medo-Persians, in their turn, were overtaken by the Greek army, led by the brilliant military tactician Alexander the Great.

The leopard represents Alexander the Great.

This third successive world power is symbolized by the leopard, known for its great speed. Alexander led the charge, conquered much of the world, and reportedly wept because there were no more kingdoms to conquer.

The fourth beast describes Rome.

Following the leopard, we read in Daniel 7:7 of "a fourth beast, dreadful and terrible, exceedingly strong. It had huge iron teeth; it was devouring, breaking in pieces, and trampling the residue with its feet. It was different from all the beasts that were before it, and it had ten horns."

This is a description of the mighty and unstoppable military machine of Rome. As you study Daniel 7, it's interesting to note there is no fifth world power that eventually conquers Rome. Historically, no one ever did. Rome effectively collapsed under her own weight and was eventually overrun. But there was no army that could have stood against the army of Rome.

From the ashes of Rome, the Antichrist rises. Daniel 7:8 says, "As I was looking at the horns, suddenly another small horn appeared among them. Three of the first horns were torn out by the roots to make room for it. This little horn had eyes like human eyes and a mouth that was boasting arrogantly" (NLT).

GOOD TO KNOW

The Antichrist will embody the splendor of Babylon, the cruelty of the Medo-Persians, the speed of Greece, and the might of Rome.

So from the beast that was Rome, from the remnants of that mighty military machine, the Antichrist emerges.

Looking back a couple of generations, it's easy to see why some people thought Adolf Hitler might be the Antichrist, because he had a powerful military and desired to revive the dreams of the Roman empire. That is exactly what Antichrist is doing as he springs from those roots.

All these creatures, or empires, referenced here in Revelation 13 are embodied in the Antichrist: the splendor of Babylon, the cruelty of the Medo-Persians, the speed of Greece, the might of Rome. Looking back on past world rulers—the pharaohs, Nebuchadnezzar, Alexander the Great, the Caesars, Napoleon, and Hitler—all were forerunners of the coming prince. Drawing on the raw power of Satan himself, he will harness the economic and technological power of the world, bringing about a one-world economy, a one-world government, and a one-world religion. He will lead the mother of all evil empires.

Let's identify some important things about the beast, or the Antichrist.

CHARACTERISTICS OF THE ANTICHRIST

He is energized and empowered by Satan himself.

Sometimes Judas Iscariot is portrayed as a man who was simply misdirected, as someone who wanted the best and wanted to help Jesus but just took a wrong fork in the road and ended up in a bad place.

No.

Judas was a wicked man, and there was a point when Satan himself actually entered his heart (see John 13:27).

Satan will enter the Antichrist, too. In Revelation 13:2 we read that "the dragon gave him his power, his throne, and great authority."

We need to understand, however, that this term *the beast* describes the Antichrist's character, not his appearance. He won't look like some ugly, beast-like creature. I would imagine that he will be very handsome, intelligent, and telegenic. The major TV networks will be falling all over themselves to get him on the air. As they say, the Devil wears Prada. This guy looks good.

GOOD TO KNOW

In effect the beast, or the Antichrist, comes as a fake Christ. Some even will think he is Christ.

As I mentioned before, when we say *Antichrist*, the prefix *anti* not only means "against," but it also means "instead of." The Antichrist will be the archenemy and ultimate opponent of Jesus Christ, and he also will try to replace Him in the esteem and affection of the world's population.

Dwight Pentecost wrote, "Satan is seeking to give the world a ruler in the place of Christ who will be in opposition to Christ so that he can rule over the world instead of Christ." [24] In effect the beast, or the Antichrist, comes as a fake Christ. Some even will think he is Christ.

I have a Facebook page . . . and apparently I have a fake Facebook page. Someone out there has a Greg Laurie Facebook page, where they are impersonating me. It's all a clever ploy to trick people into sending money for non-existent ministry projects.

I don't like having a fake me out there fooling people and misrepresenting me. It's irritating and can cause a great deal of misunderstanding and trouble.

This is what it will be like with the Antichrist. If Jesus Christ ever had a Facebook page, the Antichrist would rip it off, and many would "like" his phony page and seek to be his "friend."

The Antichrist is really a fake Christ whose ultimate purpose will be to deify Satan:

> So they worshiped the dragon who gave authority to the beast;
> and they worshiped the beast, saying, "Who is like the beast? Who
> is able to make war with him?" (Revelation 13:4)

That is what Satan has always wanted: to be deified, to be worshiped. This is the very reason Lucifer was thrown out of Heaven. He wanted to be worshiped like God. In Isaiah 14 he said, "I will ascend to the heavens; I will raise my throne above the stars of God; . . . I will ascend above the tops of the clouds; . . . I will make myself like the Most High" (verses 13, 14 NIV).

So, if anything can be sweet to the Devil, being worshiped will be sweet to him. But it won't last long.

He will occupy himself with killing Christians.

> It was granted to him to make war with the saints and to over-
> come them. And authority was given him over every tribe, tongue,
> and nation. (Revelation 13:7)

During the Tribulation period that is still to come, many believers will be martyred for their faith. But this is nothing new, is it? Already we are seeing an anti-Christian mentality become more popular and more widely accepted. It's one thing when this takes place in an Islamic country, where Christians are imprisoned or even put to death for simply believing in Jesus. But it's another thing when this sort of bias and persecution begins to invade a nation that was founded on Judeo-Christian principles.

Here is something to consider. Though we don't know if the Antichrist himself is alive on Earth today, there are *antichrists*, plural.

The term *Antichrist* isn't actually used in the book of Revelation, though the text refers to the same person under different names. The word *Antichrist* comes from the first epistle of John:

> Little children, it is the last hour; and as you have heard that the Antichrist is coming, even now many antichrists have come, by which we know that it is the last hour. They went out from us, but they were not of us; for if they had been of us, they would have continued with us; but they went out that they might be made manifest, that none of them were of us. (1 John 2:18–19)

Who is the Antichrist? He is an individual who at some point will appear on the world scene. But according to John, it is also a person who once made a profession of faith but has turned his or her back on God. That is antichrist behavior.

We might get caught up in contemporary events and politics and seek to identify the Antichrist to come. That's why it's so crazy when people get hung up thinking that if they take, for instance, the vaccine for COVID-19, that is the mark of the Beast. No, it isn't. Because when the Antichrist is revealed, people will know it. They will know that he is the coming world leader. (By the way, if you're a Christian, you shouldn't be around to know it anyway.) So this is not something we have to be worried about.

But perhaps the bigger question is this: "Am I tolerating antichrist behavior and attitudes in my own life—today?"

Have you put something or someone in the place of Christ? Are you opposing Him in some way? Have you cut yourself off from other believers and effectively turned your back on God? If so, then you yourself could be antichrist.

The author of Revelation, the apostle John, also wrote some epistles. In 1 John 2:22 He wrote, "Who is a liar? Anyone who says that Jesus is not the Christ. Anyone who denies the Father and the Son is an antichrist" (NLT).

The Antichrist is coming to dominate the globe.

Verse 7 says that "authority was given him over every tribe, tongue, and nation." What a coup! How will he pull that off?

Not in the way you might expect.

The Antichrist isn't going to come blasting onto the world scene and brutally bludgeon everyone into submission. At least, not at first. No, again, he will emerge as a peacemaker. He will seem personable and reasonable. He will come in economically difficult times, with recriminations and wars raging in different parts of the world. Through some brilliant political moves, combined with his incredible charisma, he will do what no one has ever been able to do before: he will bring solidity to the economy and usher in world peace. He won't start violently; he will start peacefully. He will even help the Jews rebuild their long-desired temple again.

> **GOOD TO KNOW**
>
> The Antichrist isn't going to come blasting onto the world scene and brutally bludgeon everyone into submission. At least, not at first.

Think about the constant conflict that has gone on and on between Israel and the Arab nations. They sign a peace treaty in the morning and break it before lunch. Think of all the US presidents who have brokered peace agreements between Israel and the Palestinians or other Arab nations. The Antichrist, however, will succeed where all others have failed. Israel and the Arabs will honor *this* peace agreement. The shelling, the rockets, the terrorism, and the border skirmishes will cease. The amazing politician who pulls this off will be so successful that some people will hail him as a messiah . . . or *the* messiah.

And that is the very point of his whole masquerade.

THE FALSE PROPHET

The Antichrist won't be alone in this political *tour de force*. He will have a powerful accomplice at his side:

> Then I saw another beast coming up out of the earth, and he had two horns like a lamb and spoke like a dragon. And he exercises all the authority of the first beast in his presence, and causes the earth and those who dwell in it to worship the first beast, whose deadly wound was healed. He performs great signs, so that he even makes fire come down from heaven on the earth in the sight of men. And he deceives those who dwell on the earth by those signs which he was granted to do in the sight of the beast, telling those who dwell on the earth to make an image to the beast who was wounded by the sword and lived. (Revelation 13:11–14)

You've heard of the dynamic duo of Batman and Robin. This is the demonic duo of the Antichrist and his false prophet, or religious guru. If you added Satan (or the dragon) to the mix, you would have an unholy trinity. Our God exists in three Persons: God the Father, God the Son, and God the Holy Spirit. Satan, the imitator, wants a trinity too. So you have Satan in the place of God, the Antichrist in the place of Jesus Christ, and the false prophet in the place of the Holy Spirit. These three evil ones will work together to accomplish their goals.

A new religion will come on the scene that everyone can embrace. It probably will be comprised of a mixture of the world's main religions, intertwined with occultism. Bear this in mind: any time you hear about the move toward a one-world religion, you are experiencing a foreshock—a tremor—of the coming Antichrist.

One of the things I appreciate the most about America is our freedom to worship. I appreciate the freedom I have to preach in our church, declaring what I believe without fear of reprisal. I appreciate the freedom we enjoy to send that same message out through media outlets like TV, radio, and the Internet. I appreciate the freedom that others have to hold views that are different from my own. Though I may not agree with them, I am grateful that we can say what we believe in our culture today.

Even if I were able to, I would never impose the Christian faith on anyone. I would never want Christianity forced on people who didn't want to believe. We have a reasonable faith, and our desire is to bring people to Christ as we share that faith with them. God Himself says, "Come now, and let us reason together" (Isaiah 1:18). I would never want to force anyone to believe what I believe.

In our culture today, we see things moving toward an embracing of all faiths. In other words, we are told, "All faiths are equal. We're all praying to the same god; we're just following different roads.

I worship the God of Abraham, Isaac, and Jacob. I worship the God of the Bible who sent Jesus Christ. *There is no other God.* As time goes on, there will be more and more "tolerance" for any faith except the "intolerant" faith of Bible-believing Christians. There will be less and less tolerance for that.

This is why we have to be very careful, remembering that the Devil, that ancient dragon, is very smart. We might even find ourselves fighting him on one side and setting up house for him on the other. We might be fighting all the evil and depraved things that Satan is throwing at us from one side and not be aware that he has slipped in our backdoor as an "angel of light" (see 2 Corinthians 11:14), wearing the cloak of religion and respectability.

When he wants to, he can slip into the disguise of a magnificent angel. That is why Paul was being so careful in the book of Galatians, declaring that "even if we or an angel from heaven should preach a gospel other than the one we preached to you, let them be under God's curse!" (1:8 NIV).

Why did Paul say that? Because Satan is a fallen angel.

If the Devil were to appear to you today, God forbid, I guarantee that he would not have red skin, horns, hooves, a pitchfork, and a pointed tail. In a recent TV commercial, he is portrayed as slick-looking dude with gelled hair, a black silk shirt, and a gold chain. He wouldn't appear in that way either. No, he would be a stunning angel. And if you didn't know better, you would be awestruck at his appearance.

He will have no problem setting up a false religion that will attract millions of adherents. In fact, he has a lot of experience in that department.

One of the signs of the end times will be people turning away from the faith. The Bible speaks of an apostasy, a major departure from the faith. In 2 Thessalonians 2:3, Paul speaks of "a great rebellion against God" (NLT), with even professed believers turning away from Him. 1 Timothy 4:1 declares that "in the last times some will turn away from the true faith; they will follow deceptive spirits and teachings that come from demons" (NLT).

In 2 Timothy 4:3–4 we are warned that "the time will come when they will not endure sound doctrine, but according to their own desires, because they have itching ears, they will heap up for themselves teachers; and they will turn their ears away from the truth, and be turned aside to fables."

That term *itching ears* means that in the last days there will be an itch for novelty. In fact, you can hear such things today. There are people out there who say that we need to reimagine the church.

No, we don't. What we need to rediscover is how Jesus set up the church in the first place and return to that template. You go to some churches today and people don't even bring their Bibles with them. The sermons are short and are more like pep talks than messages from God's Word. But here's the problem: these "sermonettes" will end up producing "Christianettes."

Ultimately what we want to hear and *need* to hear is the Word of God. That is all that matters, and that is the antidote to the deceptions and diabolical imitations we will see more and more of in the last days.

GOOD TO KNOW
The Word of God is our antidote to the Devil's deceptions and imitations.

Paul said it clearly, to his young protégé, Timothy: "Preach the Word of God urgently at all times, whenever you get the chance, in season and out, when it is convenient and when it is not. Correct and rebuke your people when they need it, encourage them to do right, and all the time be feeding them patiently with God's Word" (2 Timothy 4:2 TLB).

We have to beware of any movement toward a mindset of "all faiths are equal with our faith." We have to have eyes wide open to any move away from the Word of God as the source of our authority, away from any teaching that detracts from the uniqueness of Christ.

The coming false prophet, Antichrist's loyal sidekick, will be able to perform signs and wonders. Some people say, "I want to see miracles in church." I do, too. But it is God who decides when and where to do miracles. And we have to be careful. In Revelation 13:13–14 we read that this false prophet "performs great signs, so that he even makes fire come down from heaven on the earth in the sight of men. And he deceives those who dwell on the earth by those signs which he was granted to do."

Can the Devil do miracles?

In one sense he can. But not any miracle. In the book of Exodus, God's spokesman Moses went into Pharaoh's court and demanded the release of the Jewish people. He did a series of miracles to convince the Pharaoh. As you might remember, Pharaoh's magicians were able to duplicate or imitate a number of the miracles—not all of them, but several of them. That just reaffirms that the Devil is a master of imitation and is able to duplicate—or approximate—certain legitimate miracles.

The Devil even will go so far as to stage a fake resurrection of Antichrist. In verse 3 John wrote, "I saw one of his heads as if it had been mortally wounded, and his deadly wound was healed. And all the world marveled and followed the beast."

It sounds as though there will be an assassination attempt against Antichrist—possibly after he has become very successful and popular on the world scene. Someone tries to kill him, and everyone thinks he is dead. But then he recovers from what looked like a mortal wound. This will be Satan's version of the death and resurrection of Jesus. After this, many will flat-out worship the Antichrist.

WHO IS THE ANTICHRIST?

I have no idea who the Antichrist might be. Neither do you. Neither does anyone else, and it is a waste of time to speculate.

Over the years people have come up with all kinds of crazy theories. But why spend time and effort trying to determine the identity of the Antichrist when the Scriptures tell us that he won't even emerge until after we are caught up to meet the Lord in the air in the Rapture? The fact is that we won't be around to find out who he is. Our job isn't to be looking for Antichrist, our job is to be looking for Jesus Christ. That is the emphasis of the Scriptures.

Jesus said, "When these things begin to happen, look up and lift up your heads, because your redemption draws near" (Luke 21:28).

Jesus didn't say, "When these things *are* happening, look up." He said, "When these things *begin to happen*, look up." The Antichrist has not emerged yet. The Tribulation has not begun yet. But we can see the foreshocks of those days—like the foreshocks before an earthquake, reminding us that the big one is coming.

It's time to look up. It's time to focus on that blink-of-an-eye moment when we will suddenly find ourselves in His presence.

And it's time to make sure we are ready for that day of days.

THREE TAKEAWAY TRUTHS

- The Devil will always try to deceive with cheap imitations, including counterfeit religions.
- Although the church will be raptured before the Antichrist is revealed, it's possible for someone to be "antichrist"—that is, against Christ.
- It's no use speculating about the actual identity of the Antichrist. We should be looking for Jesus Christ.

CHAPTER EIGHTEEN
The Mark of the Beast

He causes all, both small and great, rich and poor, free and slave,
to receive a mark on their right hand or on their foreheads, and
that no one may buy or sell except one who has the mark or the
name of the beast, or the number of his name.
(Revelation 13:16–17)

IN THIS CHAPTER
- Clearing up the mystery of the mark of the Beast
- The future economic system of the Antichrist
- What happens to those who take the mark of the Beast
- The false prophet's role in this society
- How the Antichrist will rebuild the temple
- Five things to know about the 144,000

I heard the story about two Christians who were standing by the side of a road, holding up a large sign. On it they had written this message in bold letters:

THE END IS NEAR. TURN AROUND BEFORE IT'S TOO LATE.

The first driver that went by rolled down his window and yelled, "Leave us alone, you religious nuts!"

There was a screeching of tires, followed by a big splash. One of the Christians turned to the other and said, "Maybe we should have written BRIDGE OUT instead."

The end of the world. We have heard of this before. Didn't Chicken Little have something to say on that topic? Are Bible-believing Christians the only ones who talk about the end times?

As it turns out, we aren't the only ones.

There is a group of atomic scientists who get together periodically and update what they call the Doomsday Clock. The Doomsday Clock was established back in 1947 as a way for atomic scientists to warn the world about the danger of nuclear weapons.

The idea was that when the clock struck twelve, that meant it was the end. Man would be poised to detonate this weaponry, bringing on the end of all things on the planet. Sometimes they move the minute hand back one minute, and sometimes they move it forward one minute, depending on the world conditions. When it was established initially in 1947, they set the clock at six minutes to midnight. Back in 2010, it was moved back to seven minutes before midnight because they thought some progress had been made.

In the next update, in 2015, they set the clock at five minutes to midnight, followed by a move to two-and-a-half minutes to midnight in 2017 and another reset to two minutes in 2018.

But then on January 27, 2021, the clock jumped to 100 seconds to midnight. [25] Now they're not even counting it in minutes.

In other words, the end has drawn nearer.

But we know that anyway, don't we? We have never been closer to the end of the world than we are right now.

The end is near, certainly. *But so is the new beginning.* The Bible also speaks of a new start on our world, a time when righteousness will reign supreme. There will be no perversion, no murder, no terrorism, no war, no starvation, no heartbreaking problems of any kind. Why? Because Isaiah 11:9 says the knowledge of the Lord will fill the earth. That's the good news. The bad news is that it will get worse—much worse—before it gets better.

GOOGLE 666

Revelation 13 describes some very dark times during what the Bible describes as the tribulation period. Satan's son, if you will, has emerged on the scene.

Best known as Antichrist, he will be the evilest man who has ever lived—history's vilest embodiment of sin and rebellion.

As we noted in the last chapter, he will not work alone. He will have his devilish worship leader and spiritual guru, the false prophet, at his side.

> Then I saw another beast coming up out of the earth, and he had two horns like a lamb and spoke like a dragon. And he exercises all the authority of the first beast in his presence, and causes the earth and those who dwell in it to worship the first beast, whose deadly wound was healed. He performs great signs, so that he even makes fire come down from heaven on the earth in the sight of men. And he deceives those who dwell on the earth by those signs which he was granted to do in the sight of the beast, telling those who dwell on the earth to make an image to the beast who was wounded by the sword and lived. He was granted power to give breath to the image of the beast, that the image of the beast should both speak and cause as many as would not worship the image of the beast to be killed. He causes all, both small and great, rich and poor, free and slave, to receive a mark on their right hand or on their foreheads, and that no one may buy or sell except one who has the mark or the name of the beast, or the number of his name.
>
> Here is wisdom. Let him who has understanding calculate the number of the beast, for it is the number of a man: His number is 666. (Revelation 13:11–18)

If you were to do a Google search on the number 666, you would find 584 million results (as of this writing). You might also find 584 million different ideas about what it actually means. I don't think anyone can answer this "mark of the Beast" question with any certainty. But this much we do know: Antichrist will introduce a cashless society. He will require people to receive a mark on their bodies—and no one will be able to buy or sell in the world without that mark. The endgame of this is to cause people to engage in devil worship.

Could we imagine such a scenario unfolding in our time?

Yes, we can easily see how it could quickly fall into place and become a reality. In fact, the technology needed to accomplish such a system is already here. Forty years ago this would have seemed implausible, if not impossible. But now we can see how quickly such a system could be put into place.

GOOD TO KNOW

This much we do know: Antichrist will introduce a cashless society.

As my friend Mark Hitchcock has said, "The fact that the words of Revelation 13 were penned in the age of wood, stones, swords, and spears makes this prophecy one of the most powerful proofs of the inspired nature and reliability of God's Word that one could have imagined. Who could have predicted a one-world economic system that controls all commerce but God?" [26]

God has no more difficulty speaking about the future than He does about the past. He sees it all in the present tense because He is eternal. Sometimes we don't even know the recent past all that well and forget many of the details.

Or at least I do. I will have some adventure or experience and tell my wife about it, trying to explain what happened. She always interrupts me in the middle of the story and asks some obscure question like, "What color shirt was he wearing?"

Seriously? Who cares about his shirt? I just want to finish the story, but she always wants details. Then maybe a month later I will be telling the story to someone else, and she will say, "You left out part of it. The part about what so-and-so said."

"You weren't even there!" I will protest.

"No," she will reply, "but I remember how you told the story." The frustrating thing is that she's usually right. She remembers my own experience better than I do because I don't bother myself with recalling details.

But God does. Not even one detail escapes Him. He not only has perfect recall of every detail of the past, but He also knows the future with complete accuracy. In other words, He isn't going out on a limb when He speaks about what will happen. In Isaiah 46:9–10, the Lord says, "Don't forget the many times I clearly told you what was going to happen in the future. For I am God—I only—and there is no other like me who can tell you what is going to happen. All I say will come to pass, for I do whatever I wish" (TLB).

THE MARK OF THE BEAST

The changing global economy right now is fascinating to follow. It is so fluid that no one knows where it will end up.

But we know, don't we?

I saw a discussion recently on one of the news channels where the host was interviewing a financial expert. "The real reform," this expert said, "is some kind of a banking union where everyone signs onboard. There will be some kind of banking overlord, a banking union that everyone will have to bow down to."

Can this actually happen?

Yes, it can.

There will be a banking union. It will be global. And there will be an overlord with a solution that people literally will bow down to. The leader behind it all will be the Antichrist, and it will feature his distinctive mark. The Antichrist's economic policy will be very simple. "Take my mark and worship me, or starve to death. No mark, no merchandise. No seal, no sale."

I read an article in the *New York Daily News* with the headline "'Human barcode' could make society more organized, but invades privacy, civil liberties." The article said,

> Microchip implants have become standard practice for our pets, but have been a tougher sell when it comes to putting them in people. . . . There are already, and increasingly, ways to track people. Since 2006 new US passports include radio frequency identification tags (RFID) that store all the information in the passport, plus a digital picture of the owner.

In 2002 an implantable ID chip called VeriChip was approved by the US Food and Drug Administration. The chip could be implanted in a person's arm, and when scanned, could pull up a 16 digit ID number containing information about the user. [27]

A science fiction author was quoted in the article, saying, "I would insist on every individual having a unique ID permanently attached—a barcode if you will—an implanted chip to provide an easy, fast, inexpensive way to identify individuals."

It's easy to see the logic in this. You no longer have to carry a wallet around. It doesn't matter if you lose your credit card—you have your ID on you at all times. All they have to do is scan it.

Now am I saying that this particular technology will be the mark of the Beast? No, I'm not. The mark may be something totally different than this. I'm just saying that the ability to pull off the scenario described for us in Revelation 13 already exists.

GOOD TO KNOW

The ability to pull off the scenario described for us in Revelation 13 already exists.

I don't know when the Tribulation period will begin. It could be five years from now or fifty years from now or longer. But no one has to wonder about the technology to make such a worldwide system plausible. It could begin tomorrow.

At the same time, however, it would also be foolish to overreact and get silly about the whole thing. In other words, don't panic when Disneyland puts a stamp on the back of your hand as you enter the park. Nor is getting the COVID-19 vaccine equivalent to taking the Mark of the Beast. And don't lose any sleep if you go to an office building with an address that happens to be 666. The Scriptures urge us to be aware and alert, but not anxious or fidgety.

What we do know is that someday soon, a great delusion will come upon the world. Speaking of the Antichrist, 2 Thessalonians 2:9–12 says, "This man will come to do the work of Satan with counterfeit power and signs and miracles. He will use every kind of evil deception to fool those on their way to destruction, because they refuse to love and accept the truth that would save them. So God will cause them to be greatly deceived, and they will believe these lies. Then they will be condemned for enjoying evil rather than believing the truth" (NLT).

What I find interesting about this passage is that it says that these people will refuse to believe the truth that could save them.

I have found that many people will reject Christ out of hand without even investigating what He says. They will reject the Bible without even reading it or claim that it is full of "contradictions."

But when pressed, they can never identify these so-called contradictions because they haven't read the Bible and refuse to read the Bible. They choose rather to believe a lie.

What is the lie? When it is fully realized in the Tribulation period, the lie is that Antichrist is God. And people will buy into this because God will send them a delusion. What does that mean? Simply this: Those who turn from the truth of God to the Antichrist and refuse God's answer of salvation will be turned over to their own self-willed choice. God will confirm their choice and send a deluding influence upon them.

The best illustration I can think of is what happened to Pharaoh, the king of Egypt, in the book of Exodus. Moses and Aaron performed miracles by the hand of God before Pharaoh's eyes to confirm that they were speaking the word of God. But what happened? The Scriptures say that Pharaoh "hardened his heart." He hardened his own heart again and again, until we suddenly read that *God* hardened Pharaoh's heart.

A better translation might say that God strengthened Pharaoh's heart.

God has given you a free will, and He will not force you to believe something that you don't want to believe. He will come to you and seek to convince you of the truth of the Scriptures, and the Holy Spirit will nudge your heart and seek to draw you to the Lord. But God has given you the ability to resist Him. And if you persist in hardening your heart against Him, time after time, a day will come when God will strengthen you in your own resolve and your own unbelief.

But what about the person who responds to the Holy Spirit, believes the Good News, and places trust in Jesus? God will strengthen that resolve as well.

He will help that person to believe in Him, strengthening them in the decision they have made.

A VOICE LIKE A DRAGON

In Revelation 13:11, we read this interesting description about the false prophet: "he had two horns like a lamb and spoke like a dragon."

The first beast of Revelation 13, the Antichrist himself, is ominous and powerful with seven heads, ten horns, and ten crowns, speaking of vast political authority. In contrast, the second beast is more like a docile lamb, reminding us that he is a spiritual leader. In contrast to the Antichrist having horns that represent power, this beast seems comparatively harmless. Yet verse 11 tells us he "spoke like a dragon."

He looks like a lamb but speaks like a dragon.

When you think of a lamb, you think of a gentle, nonaggressive creature. But he speaks with the voice of Satan himself and is as lethal as the Antichrist—but in a very different way.

I'm reminded of a baby rattlesnake. If you have ever seen an adult rattler coiled up, using its rattle, you know what that means. *Back away! Don't come near!* We know that. A baby rattler, however, is almost cute. They're like a toy miniature of an adult, with a little head, tiny fangs, and an itty-bitty rattle. You may be tempted to pick it up. But you'd better not. Their venom is potent, just like an adult's.

> **GOOD TO KNOW**
>
> The false prophet is more like a docile lamb, reminding us that he is a spiritual leader.

And by the way, the false prophet won't be called "the false prophet." He probably will have an ingratiating personality and an impressive title that will draw people to him like a magnet. This spiritual guru will lead many people down the path of destruction.

Having a voice "like a dragon" means you can make anything sound plausible and reasonable. Today we talk about tolerance of acts that the Bible clearly condemns. But who could be against tolerance? How could any reasonable, rational individual be against "women's reproductive rights," "death with dignity," or "religious tolerance"? But what do these things really mean? Women's reproductive rights mean they have the right to murder their unborn baby. Death with dignity means euthanasia of the elderly. Religious tolerance means that you tolerate every religion except the one that dares to say that Jesus Christ is the only way to God the Father. It is new verbiage for a new time, and it reminds us that a new world order is coming.

Former Soviet Union President Mikhail Gorbachev spoke about that in a news conference after 9/11 when he said, "If we act as we did [after September 11], uniting efforts of fighting against terrorism, if we maintain the coalition, we will not only prevent a new Cold War, but we could get a new world order that is so desirable for all of us." [28]

Sorry, Mr. Gorbachev, I am not interested.

But many will be.

This Antichrist will inaugurate this new world order.

REBUILDING THE TEMPLE

There is no Jewish temple in Jerusalem today. The first one was envisioned by King David, built by King Solomon, and destroyed by Nebuchadnezzar and his Babylonian army. The second was rebuilt after the seventy-year Jewish exile in Babylon, was enhanced by King Herod, and was destroyed by Titus and the Roman army in AD 70.

Why is the destruction of this second temple so significant? Because Jesus predicted it in Matthew 24, stating clearly that not one stone will be left upon another. This is key because Matthew 24 is largely about events that have still not happened. But Jesus began with an event that we can now look back on with twenty-twenty hindsight and see that it happened exactly as He said it would. The magnificent temple that stood in Jesus' earthly lifetime was completely—stone by stone—destroyed and dismantled by the Romans.

Back in those days they didn't have explosives. Today you can watch a building being blown up to make room for another building. You've probably seen some of those videos. They put all the explosives in the right places, someone pushes a button, and the building seems to shudder and then just fall in on itself.

The Romans, however, didn't have such technology. Yet Jesus said the building would be completely taken down. How would that happen? For that matter, *why* would that happen?

One version is that when Roman legions set fire to the temple in Jerusalem, the gold in the temple melted into the cracks and crevices of the stones. Titus gave the command to dismantle the temple stone by stone in order to retrieve that gold—and the words of Jesus literally were fulfilled.

But the Scriptures also say that the temple will be rebuilt. In a fairly recent poll in Israel, two-thirds of Israelis indicated that they want to see that happen—they want to see the temple rebuilt. This couldn't have even happened until the Jews were back in their homeland again. Why would anyone else want to rebuild the Jewish temple? Also, it couldn't happen until Jerusalem was under Jewish control again—which didn't take place until 1967. So, everything is in place for that to happen.

Why does it matter whether the temple will be rebuilt?

Because the Bible *says* that it will be rebuilt.

The Antichrist eventually will erect an image of himself in that temple and will command people to worship him. This is a key moment in the Tribulation period that Jesus described as "the abomination of desolation."

Jesus warned, "When you see the 'abomination of desolation,' spoken of by Daniel the prophet, standing in the holy place [the temple], . . . then let those who are in Judea flee to the mountains. . . . And pray that your flight may not be in winter or on the Sabbath. For then there will be great tribulation, such as has not been since the beginning of the world until this time, no, nor ever shall be" (Matthew 24:15–16, 20–21).

GOOD TO KNOW

The Bible is clear that the temple will be rebuilt.

Paul gave us more detail in 2 Thessalonians 2:4. Speaking of Antichrist he wrote, "He will oppose and will exalt himself over everything that is called God or is worshiped, so that he sets himself up in God's temple, proclaiming himself to be God" (NIV).

Shifting for a moment out of this deep darkness, let's move now from Revelation 13 to Revelation 14, into the celestial light of Heaven. As we do, we will see a change in emphasis from the world's future to our future as believers. We will also encounter another kind of "mark." Only this is a mark that every believer should desire.

FROM DARKNESS TO LIGHT

> Then I looked, and behold, a Lamb standing on Mount Zion, and with Him one hundred and forty-four thousand, having His Father's name written on their foreheads. And I heard a voice from heaven, like the voice of many waters, and like the voice of loud thunder. And I heard the sound of harpists playing their harps. They sang as it were a new song before the throne, before the four living creatures, and the elders; and no one could learn that song except the hundred and forty-four thousand who were redeemed from the earth. These are the ones who were not defiled with women, for they are virgins. These are the ones who follow the Lamb wherever He goes. These were redeemed from among men, being firstfruits to God and to the Lamb. And in their mouth was found no deceit, for they are without fault before the throne of God. (Revelation 14:1–5)

So who are these people? We learned about them earlier in this book. They are 144,000 messianic believers—Jews who have found Jesus as their Messiah. God will send them out to proclaim the gospel during the Tribulation period, and they will be protected by God. The Antichrist can't take them out—not even one of them.

The last time we read about them, they were on Earth, preaching the gospel. Now in Revelation 14, we read about their being in Heaven. What I love is there are still 144,000, not 143,999. Not one of them was lost. Jesus said in John 18:9, "Of those whom You gave me I have lost none."

God does not lose us. He will get us safely to Heaven. He never takes His eyes off of us.

What is true of these believers in Heaven should also be true of believers on Earth. There are five takeaway truths about these believers that we need to be aware of.

FIVE TRUTHS ABOUT THE 144,000 IN HEAVEN

1. They have the mark of God the Father, not the Antichrist.

Verse 1 of Revelation 14 speaks of their "having His [the Lamb's] Father's name written on their foreheads." They have the heavenly Father's name on their foreheads.

Since my own mother was married and divorced seven times, I had a lot of last names that I could choose from. I chose the last name of Oscar Felix Laurie, one of the men my mom had married. Of all of her husbands, Oscar was the only one whom I ever loved and respected. He was the only "father" who treated me like a father ought to treat a son. Though he wasn't my biological father, in every way he behaved as a father toward me. I'd had plenty of names to choose from, but I chose his for my last name. For me, it was the name above all names.

In the same way, you can choose whom your father will be. Everyone has two choices: You can be of your father the Devil, or you can be a worshiper of your heavenly Father. It's like that question you hear thrown around these days: *Who's your daddy?* If you are wise, you will use the name above all names, the Lord Jesus Christ.

It's interesting that these believers have God's name, or mark, on their foreheads.

If you travel very much, you've experienced a TSA agent in the security line, asking for your identification. And then the agent will pull out a mysterious little blue light and go over your ID with it. What is that thing?

It's like a miniature black light, and the agent is looking for a hologram that will authenticate it. It's just a tiny little light, but with the aid of that light, the official can find a mark of your identity that you cannot see with your naked eye.

Likewise, there is a mark on you that only God can see. He knows those who belong to Him. Many people during the Tribulation period will receive Antichrist's mark, but we want *God's* mark. We want His ID tag attached to us. We want to proudly say that we belong to Him. The Bible tells us, "Do not grieve the Holy Spirit of God, with whom you were sealed for the day of redemption" (Ephesians 4:30 NIV).

We are sealed with God's Holy Spirit.

This word picture springs from biblical times, when a king would send a document. He would seal up the scroll or letter with wax and then imprint the wax with his own signet ring. That would tell anyone who saw or handled the document, "This is royal business. This belongs to the king. Don't mess with it . . . or else!"

> **GOOD TO KNOW**
>
> If you are a believer in Christ, then you belong to the King. He has marked you, He has sealed you, and you have His ID tag on you.

It's the same with God's mark. If you are a believer in Christ, then you belong to the King. He has marked you, He has sealed you, and you have His ID tag on you. You are His property.

I read a story about an old gentleman who was known for his godly life. Someone asked him one day, "What do you do when you are tempted, old man?"

He replied, "I just look up to Heaven and say, 'Lord, your property is in danger.'"

2. They sing a new song.

Verses 2–3 say, "I heard a voice from heaven, like the voice of many waters, and like the voice of loud thunder. And I heard the sound of harpists playing their harps. They sang as it were a new song before the throne, before the four living creatures."

So, will there really be harps in Heaven?

Actually, John was simply describing some kind of stringed instrument. Maybe they were like traditional harps, or maybe they were more like electric guitars. John could only use his first-century frame of reference. Whatever instruments they were, this will be beyond the most awesome worship moment you could ever imagine. It will echo across the heavens like thunder. And they won't be singing some tired old chorus or hymn number 232 from a dusty hymnal.

No, this will be a *new* song.

Every believer should have a new song.

Psalm 40 gives us these words: "He lifted me out of the pit of despair, out from the bog and the mire, and set my feet on a hard, firm path, and steadied me as I walked along. He has given me a new song to sing, of praises to our God. Now many will hear of the glorious things he did for me, and stand in awe before the Lord, and put their trust in him" (verses 2–3 TLB).

If you have trusted in Christ, if you have been lifted from a pit of despair, you have a new song. Did you know that? I don't mean that literally it has to be a song with musical notes and lyrics. It's the idea that you have a new *message*, something new to talk about that comes bubbling up from within you. Don't keep singing the same old song. Sing the new song! Let other people know what Christ has done for you. That is what these believers in Heaven are doing, and that is what we ought to do right here on Earth.

3. They lived pure lives.

In verse 4 we read, "These are the ones who were not defiled with women, for they are virgins." This may be literal or symbolic or both. To be undefiled means they are not immoral. Here is a simple truth to remember. It almost seems ridiculous to put this in a book, but I will do it anyway. *If you are single, then you are not supposed to have sex.* Are we clear?

Here's another statement. *If you are married, then you are only to have sex with your spouse.* (Who is a member of the opposite sex, I might add.)

That is the plan God has set forth in His Word.

Anything else, however you may characterize it, is sin.

If you have an argument with this, your argument is with God. The Bible says in 1 Corinthians 6:9–10, "Don't you realize that those who do wrong will not inherit the Kingdom of God? Don't fool yourselves. Those who indulge in sexual sin, or who worship idols, or commit adultery, or are male prostitutes, or practice homosexuality, or are thieves, or greedy people, or drunkards, or are abusive, or cheat people—none of these will inherit the Kingdom of God" (NLT).

The purity of the 144,000, however, probably speaks of a spiritual commitment. On more than one occasion, the Bible compares following after other gods to adultery. In James 4:4 the apostle says, "You adulterers and adulteresses! Do you not know that friendship with the world is enmity with God? Whoever therefore wants to be a friend of the world makes himself an enemy of God."

To love this world means that you are committing spiritual adultery. So you have a choice. You can be the world's friend and God's enemy, or you can be God's friend and the world's enemy. You have to be in one camp or the other; you can't be in both.

4. They are sincere in their faith.

Verse 5 tells us, "And in their mouth was found no deceit, for they are without fault before the throne of God."

There is no deceit or hypocrisy of any kind in their lives.

Sometimes people put on an act and try to appear to be Christians. We need to understand what a hypocrite is, because I think we frequently misuse this word. Let's say that you are building something and your nonbelieving friend is there with you. Swinging your hammer, you miss the nail and hit your thumb. You scream and maybe even say a few words you shouldn't have said.

And your nonbelieving friend says, "Hypocrite."

But are you really being a hypocrite? I don't think so. I think you are being a *human*.

So when I mess up (not if but when), I may say the wrong thing or do the wrong thing. In some way, shape, or form, I will fall short. It is only a matter of time. When that happens, I will say, "I'm so sorry for saying that or acting that way. It's not the way I should respond as a Christian."

Am I being a hypocrite?

No, I'm just being a flawed person like everyone else on the planet who said or did the wrong thing.

A hypocrite, however, is different. Today we use the word as a criticism or even an insult. But back in the first century, the word simply meant "actor." The words *hypocrite* and *actor* were used interchangeably.

It was Greece that really introduced drama to the world. In ancient Greece, if you were portraying a character in a play, you would hold a little mask in front of your face. The audience would understand that it meant you were portraying a particular character. So when you had the mask in front of your face, you were the *hypocrite,* or actor.

What does it mean when the Bible says we are hypocrites? It simply means that we are playing a part. We're not being our genuine selves.

Judas was a hypocrite, pretending to be something and someone that he was not. Pretending to be a follower of Jesus, he was in reality an enemy of Jesus. So it is when we act as though we are Christians when we are not. Maybe we even fool a few people for a few years. But here's the bottom line: you will fool some of the people all of the time, you will fool all of the people some of the time, but you never will fool God any of the time.

5. They follow the Lamb wherever He goes.

In Luke 9:23, Jesus said, "If anyone desires to come after Me, let him deny himself, and take up his cross daily, and follow Me."

I think sometimes that Jesus has a lot of people today who are more like Twitter followers. If you have a Twitter account, you have "followers." And if you spend any time on that platform, you know it is a place for a lot of conflict, disagreement, and general unpleasantness. Some so-called "followers" of Jesus are that way.

They say they are following Him, but they spend more time arguing with Him.

True following is a lot more than that. When Jesus first encountered Matthew sitting at a tax collection booth, He said to him, "Follow Me."

Matthew wasn't a believer at the time. In fact, he was regarded as a traitor in his own nation because he was a Jew working for the hated Romans. Even so, Jesus walked right up to him, looked at him, and said, "Follow Me" (Matthew 9:9).

And that's exactly what Matthew did. He immediately stood up, left everything behind just as it was, and followed Jesus from that day forward.

What did Jesus really mean when He said, "Follow Me"? In the original language, the term could be translated "follow *with* Me," rather than "follow behind Me." In other words, "Let's take a walk together. Let's walk side by side."

The other day I took a walk with my wife. It didn't start well because I just bolted out the door and started walking briskly.

Cathe said, "Greg! Slow down and wait for me!"

She was right. The way to walk with your wife is not to stride out ahead of her. It's not the way to walk with the Lord, either—racing ahead of Him or lagging behind Him. To be a follower of Jesus means that we are never alone. *He walks with us.*

Sometimes Cathe will take a walk with her girlfriends. She will say, "I'm going on a walk, Greg."

"Who are you going with?" I will ask.

Then she identifies the women, and I will say, "You're going on a *talk*, not a *walk*." And those talks can take a couple of hours—maybe even more. When I go for a walk, I'm more about the walking than the talking. It only takes me about forty-five minutes, and I'm done.

The Lord would like to go on a "talk" with you—not just a walk. It's not about how fast you move or how much ground you cover.

He will say to you, "So what's going on? What's happening in your life? What are you dealing with? What are your questions? What are your concerns? What are you passionate about?"

That's a walk *and* a talk. It is fellowship. It is companionship.

But there is another interesting facet to the Lord's command in Greek, "Follow Me." It also

GOOD TO KNOW

To be a follower of Jesus means that we are never alone. *He walks with us.*

could be translated, "Walk the same road with Me." A command is implied here, with the idea of doing this continuously. A paraphrase might sound something like this: "I, Jesus, command you to follow Me, walking with Me along the same road each and every day, not just on Sunday."

He doesn't want to be your Sunday Jesus. He wants to be your Monday Jesus. And your every-day-of-the-week Jesus.

Notice that the text in Revelation 14 says they "follow the Lamb wherever He goes" (verse 4). In other words, He wants you to follow Him where He leads. Sometimes He may lead us on a path of difficulty or suffering, and we will say, "But Lord, I don't want to go that way." No, you follow Him wherever He goes. You travel with Him on the road of His choosing. Jesus said, "You are My friends if you do whatever I command you" (John 15:14).

It's not for us to pick and choose what we like in the Bible and what we don't like. This is a package deal. We walk with Him each and every day and follow Him when it's easy and pleasant and when it is not so easy and pleasant.

These 144,000 in the book of Revelation were walking with God one day on Earth, and the next day they were walking with Him in Heaven. That is how it will be with us, if we belong to Jesus Christ. One day we start our journey on this planet, and before the day is over, we will walk right into Heaven.

If you walk with the Lord on Earth, you also will walk with Him in Heaven.

If you walk away from the Lord on Earth, you will walk away from Him, right into eternity.

THREE TAKEAWAY TRUTHS

- Even as things get darker than ever before, we can always remember that God will ultimately prevail.
- Believers do not have to worry about the mark of the Beast. All who trust in Christ have God's seal on them.
- God longs for us to walk with Him—every day of our lives.

CHAPTER NINETEEN

Things to Do Before the End of the World

"Be dressed for service and
keep your lamps burning."
(Luke 12:35 NLT).

IN THIS CHAPTER

• How we ought to live in expectation of the Christ's return
• Making the most of studying Bible prophecy
• Biblical principles on living a godly life
• Avoiding spiritual lethargy

Let's imagine for a moment that we knew the day and hour when Jesus was coming back again.

We don't, of course.

Jesus said that no one would know that day or hour.

But let's pretend for a moment, for the sake of a point, that we did know. Let's say we had a sure word that Jesus Christ would come for us at 3:00 sharp, tomorrow afternoon.

What would we be doing at 2:45?

I'm guessing that we would be pretty saintly during those final fifteen minutes of waiting. We would be wearing our Sunday morning smiles and our Jesus-come-quickly attitudes. We would make sure that we were right in our relationships with family and friends and that there would be no unconfessed sin in our lives.

The thing is, we *don't* know when He will come. It might very well be tomorrow afternoon at 3:00. But it might not be too. There is no way of knowing. But shouldn't we have that same smile and attitude and live every day as though it were the day that Christ could come?

The Bible has a great deal to say about the imminent (any moment) return of Jesus. There are 250 chapters in the New Testament, and Christ's return is mentioned no less than 318 times in those chapters. Statistically, one in every twenty-five verses mentions the return of Jesus Christ.

Our Lord spoke of this often. In Mark 8:38, He said, "Whoever is ashamed of Me and My words in this adulterous and sinful generation, of him the Son of Man also will be ashamed when He comes in the glory of His Father with the holy angels."

In John 14:2–3, Jesus said, "I go to prepare a place for you. And if I go and prepare a place for you, I will come again and receive you to Myself; that where I am, there you may be also."

I became a Christian in 1970, when a genuine revival known as the Jesus Movement was in full swing and many young people were coming to Christ. Back then, there was a lot of talk about the "soon return of Jesus." It was very popular to see bumper stickers on cars with slogans like, "In case of Rapture, this car will be unmanned." There were many other bumper stickers that essentially said that Jesus is coming.

But here it is, almost fifty years later, and He still hasn't come.

There are those who say, "You guys were all wrong. He hasn't come and probably won't."

But here is what the Bible says in response to that, in 2 Peter 3:9:

> The Lord isn't really being slow about his promise, as some people think. No, he is being patient for your sake. He does not want anyone to be destroyed, but wants everyone to repent. (NLT)

Back in 1970 I was praying that Jesus Christ would come back. Aren't you glad that God didn't answer my prayer?

Maybe you or some of your loved ones have come to Christ since 1970. The fact is the Lord is waiting for that one last person to be saved before He returns.

I believe that man or woman—the last person to be redeemed from sin—is walking somewhere on Earth right now. The moment he or she turns to Christ and believes, we will all be caught up to meet the Lord in the air.

Peter continues on and says this:

> But the day of the Lord will come as unexpectedly as a thief. Then the heavens will pass away with a terrible noise, and the very elements themselves will disappear in fire, and the earth and everything on it will be found to deserve judgment.

> Since everything around us is going to be destroyed like this, what holy and godly lives you should live, looking forward to the day of God and hurrying it along. (2 Peter 3:10–12 NLT)

If you really believe that Jesus is coming, Peter says, it should impact the way you live. If it doesn't impact the way you live, then you are completely missing the point.

Whenever a pastor starts a sermon series or writes a book about the last days, some people get very excited. They want to learn about Armageddon, the Antichrist, the Second Coming, the Rapture, and all the rest of it.

It's good to be interested. It's useful to study these things.

But the whole point of studying Bible prophecy is to seek to be ready for His return, prompting us to live godly lives. If all we are interested in is names and dates and places and world events, then as I have said, we've missed the point.

GOOD TO KNOW

If all we are interested in is names and dates and places and world events, we've missed the point of Bible prophecy.

As Jesus once told some of his critics, in effect, "You guys have strained out a gnat and swallowed a camel" (see Matthew 23:24). In other words, "You were so focused on the minutia that you missed the big picture" or "You didn't see the forest for the trees."

WHEN THE THIEF COMES...

In Luke 12, Jesus spoke words that I believe are directly addressed to us, because we are living in the last days before His return:

> "Let your waist be girded and your lamps burning; and you your-selves be like men who wait for their master, when he will return from the wedding, that when he comes and knocks they may open to him immediately. Blessed are those servants whom the master, when he comes, will find watching. Assuredly, I say to you that he will gird himself and have them sit down to eat, and will come and serve them. And if he should come in the second watch, or come in the third watch, and find them so, blessed are those servants. But know this, that if the master of the house had known what hour the thief would come, he would have watched and not allowed his house to be broken into. Therefore you also be ready, for the Son of Man is coming at an hour you do not expect." (verses 35–40)

Do you see *therefore* in verse 40? Whenever you see the word *therefore*, find out what it is there for. Jesus made a series of statements, and at the conclusion He said, "Therefore . . . *be ready*" (emphasis added). That's His whole point.

Peter, however, still felt a little fuzzy about the Lord's point. In verse 41 he said, "Lord, do You speak this parable only to us, or to all people?"

At that question, the Lord launched into another illustration, or parable.

> "Who then is that faithful and wise steward, whom his master will make ruler over his household, to give them their portion of food in due season? Blessed is that servant whom his master will find so doing when he comes. Truly, I say to you that he will make him ruler over all that he has. But if that servant says in his heart, 'My master is delaying his coming,' and begins to beat the male and female servants, and to eat and drink and be drunk, the master of that

servant will come on a day when he is not looking for him, and at an hour when he is not aware, and will cut him in two and appoint him his portion with the unbelievers. And that servant who knew his master's will, and did not prepare himself or do according to his will, shall be beaten with many stripes. But he who did not know, yet committed things deserving of stripes, shall be beaten with few. For everyone to whom much is given, from him much will be required; and to whom much has been committed, of him they will ask the more." (verses 42–48)

The idea that Jesus was communicating was simply this: These servants did not know when their master was returning. Because of this, they were to be on the watch for him, alert and ready for his return.

Applying this parable to our lives, how should Christians live in these last days?

HOW SHOULD WE LIVE AS BELIEVERS IN THE LAST DAYS?

We should be shining lights in a dark place.

Luke 12:35 says, "Let your waist be girded and your lamps burning."

What does that mean? Back in those days they wore long, flowing robes with a belt that you would cinch around your waist. When you wanted freedom of movement, you could pull your robe up above your knees and retighten your belt, giving you more mobility. You could answer the door quickly. You could move quickly.

To have "your lamps burning" meant that you would have sufficient oil in them. In those days they carried a saucer-like device, with a floating wick in it that they would light. Think of it as a first-century equivalent of a flashlight. If we would update this verse for today, it would be like saying, "Have fresh batteries in your flashlight," or "Keep your cell phone charged."

I always charge my phone every night so I will be ready for the day with all its demands and activities and all that is coming. It's become a valuable piece of equipment to me. I wouldn't want to be in a situation where I needed to communicate with someone and my phone was redlining. That's the idea here. Be mobile. Be prepared. Be alert. Be ready for whatever. That is how the Lord wants us to live, even if He doesn't return as quickly as we had hoped.

We should be watching for His appearance.

Look at Luke 12:37: "Blessed are those servants whom the master when he comes, will find watching."

Jesus said, "When you see these things begin to happen, look up" (Luke 21:28).

As we look at what is happening in our world today, we can have our Bible in one hand and our tablet or phone in the other, watching Bible prophecy being fulfilled right before our eyes. The Middle East is a powder keg with a short fuse, lying next to a lit match. It could blow up at any time. So many things happening in our contemporary world point toward New Testament passages that describe the end times. This would include the nightmare outbreak of excessive acts of violence in our culture—more than we have seen before or even imagined.

We need to be ready to go.

When I go on a trip, I always pack my bags the day before. This is especially true if it's an early morning flight, as so many of my flights seem to be. I always will have everything ready to go because I want to be at the gate for my flight in time. In fact, I like to get there ahead of time. My wife often says that I leave for the airport way too early. But the peace of mind is worth it to me, knowing that I won't miss my flight.

That's the idea behind Jesus' words to gird up your loins and have your lamps bright and shining. In other words, cinch up your belt, have all your stuff together, and make sure that you have some extra batteries for your flashlight.

Here's another way to put it: Have your bags packed, and have your comfortable shoes by the door and ready. Be ready to bolt out of there at a moment's notice.

To be ready for the return of Jesus is to be engaged in activities that you would not be ashamed of if Jesus were to come. It's a good thing to ask yourself periodically, "This place that I'm about to go to . . . this thing I'm about to do, . . . would I be embarrassed or ashamed to be doing that thing if Jesus were to come back?"

If the answer is yes, or even "well . . . maybe," then don't do it.

If you can't pray over your plans for the evening and ask God to bless them, then change your plans. If you can't write "Hallowed be Thy name" over your activity, then find another activity.

As I said earlier, if we really believe that Jesus is coming, then it should cause us to live godly lives. In 1 John 3:2–3, the apostle writes: "Yes, dear friends, we are already God's children, right now, and we can't even imagine what it is going to be like later on. But we do know this, that when he comes we will be like him, as a result of seeing him as he really is. And everyone who really believes this will try to stay pure because Christ is pure" (TLB).

> **GOOD TO KNOW**
> To be ready for the return of Jesus is to be engaged in activities that you would not be ashamed of if Jesus were to come.

We should not only be ready, but we should be anxiously awaiting His return.

Notice Luke 12:36: "You yourselves be like men who wait for their master, when he will return from the wedding, that when he comes and knocks they may open to him immediately."

I used to have a dog that would sleep by the door to our bedroom. We didn't let him sleep in the room with us. One of the reasons for that was that he would sometimes have nightmares and start whimpering in his sleep. What in the world could he have been dreaming about? Cats chasing him? I don't know what his problem might have been, but his whines in the middle of the night would wake me up, so we made him sleep outside the room.

Since he couldn't be inside with us, he would lean up against the door all night long. Sometimes I would think someone was knocking on the door because he was scratching. I know that he leaned against the door because when I woke up in the morning and opened the door, he pretty much rolled into the room. The moment he saw me, he was so excited. He would jump to his feet and start going around in circles. In his mind he was saying, *Happy days are here again. The skies are blue. We're going for a walk! I know we are!*

I read a prayer somewhere that said, "Lord, make me the person my dog thinks I am."

Bottom line? Be anxiously awaiting His return. We should have an eagerness in our heart whenever we think about it.

Have you ever been waiting for some close friends to come visit you? Maybe they're from out of town, and you haven't seen them for a long time. Then you get a text that says they just landed. Then you get another text that says they're driving over and should arrive in fifteen minutes. As the time gets close, you start looking out your window, watching for the car. Then when it pulls up in the driveway, you're so excited. And then—there they are, walking up the stairs to your front door! You open the door and throw your arms around them because you're so happy to see their familiar faces. You hug them tight because you've missed them.

That is how we should be waiting for the return of the Lord—not hiding in a corner, dreading it, but looking forward to it with real anticipation. That is the idea being communicated here.

We are to be working.

Luke 12:43 says, "Blessed is that servant whom his master will find so doing when he comes."

He is *doing* something. He doesn't just talk a good game, he gets up out of his chair and goes to work. He's willing to get his hands dirty. James 2:20 tells us that "Faith without works is dead." If watching is the evidence of faith, then working is the evidence of faith in action. Watching for the Lord's return will help us prepare our own lives, but getting involved in the Lord's work will ensure that we bring others with us.

Jesus is saying there is a *blessedness* in living this way. Luke 12:37 says, "Blessed [happy] are those servants whom the master, when he comes, will find watching." *Happy.* We're not talking about a miserable, repressive, confining way to live when we speak about waiting for the return of the Lord. It is a happy, joyful, purposeful way to live.

C. H. Spurgeon said, "It is a very blessed thing to be on the watch for Christ, it is a blessing for us now. How it detaches us from this world! You can be poor without murmuring; you can be rich without worldliness; you can be sick without sorrowing; you can be healthy without presumption. If you are always waiting for Christ's coming, untold blessings are wrapped up in that glorious hope." [29]

In contrast to the believer who is watching and waiting, we have this portrait of an unprepared servant in Luke 12:45–46: "If that servant says in his heart, 'My master is delaying his coming,' and begins to beat the male and female servants, and to eat and drink and be drunk, the master of that servant will come on a day when he is not looking for him."

This would be a picture of a person who thinks that he or she is a believer, but in reality is not because of the way he or she lives.

The apostle Paul adds some very specific instruction about how we ought to be living in light of our Lord's soon return:

> And do this, knowing the time, that now it is high time to awake out of sleep; for now our salvation is nearer than when we first believed. The night is far spent, the day is at hand. Therefore let us cast off the works of darkness, and let us put on the armor of light. Let us walk properly, as in the day, not in revelry and drunkenness, not in lewdness and lust, not in strife and envy. But put on the Lord Jesus Christ, and make no provision for the flesh, to fulfill its lusts. (Romans 13:11–14)

Verse 11 is interesting. Paul wrote, "Knowing the time . . ." The J. B. Phillips translation states it this way: "Why all this stress on behaviour? Because, as I think you have realised, the present time is of the highest importance—it is time to wake up to reality. Every day brings God's salvation nearer" (PH).

We need to wake up. This phrase is used often in Scripture. In Ephesians 5:14, we read, "Wake up, sleeper, rise from the dead, and Christ will shine on you" (NIV).

Paul isn't writing to nonbelievers here; these words are for Christians. He is addressing his remarks to genuine believers whose spiritual lethargy and laziness made them appear and act as though they had no life flowing in their spiritual veins.

Have you ever had someone call you very late at night or very early in the morning? It's never a good thing to get a call at 2:00 in the morning.

You answer the phone, "Hello."

The person says, "Hi. Did I wake you?"

At this point we usually lie and say, "No. I was already up." (Why do we lie about that?)

Whatever the case, we're really only about half-awake. The fog of sleep still clouds our thoughts and blurs our speech.

In the Romans 13 passage, Paul was saying, "Wake up. Open your eyes. Splash some cold water on your face if you need to, but come awake!"

These words have more relevance to an older believer than a younger one. Many young Christians—not unlike young people—are full of energy. New believers are excited and want to win people to Christ and change their world. When you get older, you look forward to taking a nap.

Napping to a young person is like punishment. But when you mention it to people with a few years under their belt, they will think it sounds pretty good. I don't know about you, but I get really sleepy after eating a big meal. After Thanksgiving, it's like I slip into a coma.

Those of us who have known the Lord for many years may be in more danger of falling asleep spiritually than those who are younger in the faith.

Those who are young in the faith may recognize how vulnerable they are to the attacks of the enemy. They may say, "I have to be careful. I don't know that much. I have to keep my guard up. I want to do things for the Lord."

The person who is older in the faith may smile indulgently and say, "Yes, yes, I've heard all that years ago. I know, I know. Been there, done that."

Mature believers are in danger of becoming lazy and lethargic. Maybe we have been feasting on the Word of God for years, hearing message after message, reading book after book, without any real outlet for what God has taught us in our lives.

We are actually in danger of falling asleep in the light—resting on our laurels, living in our past.

Paul would say, "Come awake! Come up out of the mist and fog. Get your eyes open and get yourself ready, because the coming of the Lord is much nearer than you imagine!"

Paul continues on and tells us that there are things we must get rid of in our lives and things we must be engaged in. He gives us something we must put off and something we must put on. "Cast off the works of darkness," he said, and "put on the armor of light" (Romans 13:12).

Have you ever fallen into a septic tank? Let's imagine for a moment (gross as that thought might be) that you actually did. May I offer a word of advice about those clothes you were wearing? They're over with! Don't wash them. It would only ruin your washing machine. *Just throw them out.* Those clothes are done.

Paul was saying, "Cast off the works of darkness as though you fell into a septic tank. Strip 'em off. Cast them from you. Get rid of them. And then in their place, put on the armor of light. Trade in the old for the new. Suit up."

In the next verse, the apostle is very specific about the deeds of darkness—the septic tank articles of clothing—we are to discard: "not in revelry and drunkenness, not in lewdness and lust, not in strife and envy" (Romans 13:13).

GOOD TO KNOW

Mature believers are in danger of becoming lazy and lethargic.

We are to avoid drunkenness.

Here is a word for last days believers. It is so simple, it's a no-brainer. But surprisingly, some people are missing this: don't party and drink. That is revelry and drunkenness. These words, used together, picture drunken individuals walking—staggering—through the streets, making a lot of noise. We might call them "party animals" today.

It almost seems ridiculous to bring something like this up. Why do I have to say that Christians ought not to get drunk? Because there are some Christians out there today who say, "I have the liberty to drink, and I know when to stop." Even so, they will come *under the influence of* alcohol, and it will make them behave in ways and say things they would normally never do or say.

As believers, we want to be under the influence of our God. That is how we are to live as last days believers, not being filled with spirits but filled with the Holy Spirit.

We are to stay away from immorality.

Romans 13:13 says, "Not in lewdness and lust . . ."

Lewdness is a Greek word that could simply be translated "bed." It has the same connotation that it does today when someone says, "They went to bed together." We all know what that means; it's another way of saying they had sexual relations.

The word *lust* used here is one of the ugliest words in the Greek language. It describes someone who is not only given over to immorality but is incapable of feeling shame. It speaks of shameless excess and the complete absence of restraint. This isn't just a person who has been immoral. This is a person who is not only living immorally, but they are shameless about it. They proclaim it. They're proud of sleeping around. It is the very thing that Hollywood promotes so aggressively today. They want to make bad things look good, and they want to make good things look bad.

Here's what scares me. I speak to people who profess to be believers and yet admit to having affairs or living with their boyfriend or girlfriend before marriage. And somehow they have managed to rationalize this and say they "have grace for it" or that "God is okay with it."

But God is not okay with it. This is a sin against Him.

These are the things we want to be aware of or steer clear of.

In some parts of the country, you'll sometimes see a sign along the road warning of a deer or elk crossing. If you're driving along one of those highways about twilight, you really need to keep your eyes open and use your peripheral vision. A deer could dart across the road in the blink of an eye and be right in front of you. In the same way, we need to stay alert and not be sleepy or careless as we move along the highways of our lives.

The moment you become spiritually lethargic is the moment you become vulnerable to these sins. Think of King David, a good and brave king of Israel who loved the Lord. He was a wonderful, powerful, and godly man. But after years of walking with the Lord, David allowed his spiritual life to slip into cruise control. Instead of leading his troops into battle, he sent his general instead and stayed home to relax.

In the book of 2 Samuel we read, "One late afternoon, David got up from taking his nap and was strolling on the roof of the palace. From his vantage point on the roof he saw a woman bathing. The woman was stunningly beautiful. David sent to ask about her, and was told, 'Isn't this Bathsheba, daughter of Eliam and wife of Uriah the Hittite?' David sent his agents to get her. After she arrived, he went to bed with her" (11:2–4 MSG).

GOOD TO KNOW

The moment you back off in the battle with Satan and his demons is the moment you become vulnerable.

David, the warrior-king, should have been leading his troops as he always did. Instead he thought to himself, *I'm going to kick back for a while. I've worked so hard, led so many battles. I'm just going to take some time off.*

He had no idea that this decision would make him more vulnerable to danger than if he had been on the front lines, fighting with the enemies of Israel. It reminds me of a young man I met years ago when I was speaking over in Hawaii. I ran into him in a mall, and we started talking. I asked him where he went to church.

"I used to go to church," he said.

"Why don't you go anymore?" I asked him.

"I am on a spiritual vacation," he told me.

"What exactly is that?"

"Well," he explained, "I'm just sort of taking some time off from my Christian life."

"That is no vacation, buddy. You can't take a vacation from God."

We had a long talk there in that mall, and he ended up recommitting his life to the Lord. He is still serving the Lord today, I'm happy to say.

The truth is that the moment you back off in the battle with Satan and his demons is the moment you become vulnerable. The moment you let yourself become sleepy and drowsy in your spirit is the moment you become spiritually weak, and the vultures begin circling.

That is why Paul told his young friend Timothy, "Flee the evil desires of youth and pursue righteousness, faith, love and peace, along with those who call on the Lord out of a pure heart" (2 Timothy 2:22 NIV).

Those words aren't merely directed to young people. It says to "flee the evil desires of youth." You can be an older man or woman chasing after those desires—a dirty old man or a "cougar," as they are sometimes called. You haven't gotten the memo that you are old. You should act mature and be an example instead of acting like some crazed teenager.

Another thing, don't feed those lusts by looking at pornography or reading trashy novels. It's like throwing gasoline on a fire. Starve your lust rather than feeding it. Stay away from anything that encourages immoral living.

Some of you may be thinking, *I don't live this way, Greg. I don't get drunk, and I'm not immoral.* That is wonderful. God bless you. But here is one additional danger that may hit a little closer to home.

We should not compete or argue with one another.

In Romans 13:13, Paul said, "Not in strife and envy."

What does this mean? Strife refers to persistent contention, bickering, petty disagreement, and enmity. This reflects a spirit of antagonistic competitiveness that fights to have its own way, regardless of the cost or the effect on others.

It is really the desire to prevail over other people. This is a person who wants the highest prestige, the greatest prominence, the most recognition. They want to be top dog, and they can't tolerate losing or coming in second.

Have you ever played a game with someone who became unreasonably upset or angry over losing?

You say, "Hey, it's just a game. Relax."

"I don't care. I'm going home."

Some people live their lives that way. They always have to be the number-one person and can't tolerate losing. They know how to direct conversations toward themselves and seem to crave the attention. They always have to be the star and be better than everyone else.

But this isn't right. We're not competing with one another in the body of Christ. Our competition is not with fellow Christians. It is with the world, the flesh, and the Devil. Those are our enemies.

And then Paul speaks of envy. This term describes someone who can't stand being surpassed and begrudges others' success and position. Have you ever felt that way?

I remember a Christmas from years ago. I was a little boy, living in an apartment complex in Costa Mesa. I had a friend that I grew up with, and we were showing each other our presents. I was happy with what I got for Christmas until I saw what *he* got. I can remember it to this day. It was a little plastic scuba diver. Basically, you wound it up, and it sank to the bottom of the pool, with little bubbles coming out. This was 1960s technology, and it was pretty lame by today's standards. But I'd never seen anything like it. I thought it was the coolest toy ever. Was it really better than the toy I had? No. But he had it, and I didn't. As a result, I wasn't happy with what I had anymore.

It sounds childish, I know. But do we really outgrow that attitude?

My neighbors are doing a room addition.

My friend got a raise.

That couple I see on Facebook is always going somewhere wonderful.

My fellow pastor's ministry is booming. His church is growing by leaps and bounds.

It's been said that envy shoots at another and wounds itself. The only person you hurt when you allow envy into your heart is yourself. I hate to break it to you, but the person you are envying probably has no idea how you feel and most likely could care less. It's really all about your suffering because of a bad attitude.

I heard about a crab fisherman who would carry the crabs he had caught in an open bucket. Someone said, "Why don't you put a lid on that bucket? Aren't you afraid that your crabs will get out?"

"No," he replied. "The moment one of them climbs out, the other ones reach up and pull him back down."

Don't we do that sometimes? *How dare you succeed! How dare you do well! You come back down here with the rest of us where you belong!*

Focus your energies on becoming like Jesus.

After a number of negatives—beware of this, take care with that—Paul gives us something extremely positive to focus on. In Romans 13:14 it says, "But put on the Lord Jesus Christ, and make no provision for the flesh, to fulfill its lusts."

This refers to a practical, day-by-day choice to "put on" Jesus Christ, embracing Him again and again. It's just like in the morning when you put on your clothes and get ready for the day. Most of us pay at least some attention to how we look when we step out the door in the morning. Even the people who look like they don't care probably care more than many people do. (It's a cultivated careless look.)

You care about the way you look, and there's nothing wrong with that. We put our clothes on and expect them to do what we do and go where we go. Most of us like practical clothing that breathes, moves with us, and feels comfortable.

This is the idea of "putting on" the Lord Jesus Christ. It's inviting Him into every area of your life on a daily basis, asking Him to be a part of all that you say and do and think. He goes with you where you go and becomes part of your decision-making process.

He is Lord of every day of your life. He is Lord when you go to church, when you go to the beach, when you go to the movies, when you go out to dinner, and when you head off for work in the morning. He is Lord of *all*. And if He is not Lord of all, then He is not Lord at all.

I like the Phillips translation of Romans 13:14: "Let us be Christ's men from head to foot, and give no chances to the flesh to have its fling" (PH).

Someone might say, "But what if Jesus doesn't come in your lifetime, Greg? Isn't this chapter about how to live in the last days just so much wasted ink?

Let's just say, for the sake of an illustration, that Jesus doesn't come in my lifetime—or in yours. Does that mean we were wrong to believe that He could come back at any moment? Is that a bad thing to live in readiness to meet God? To serve God? To refuse to get drunk? To avoid arguments? To try to walk as close as you possibly can with Jesus Christ?

Are those negative things?

No, they are very positive things.

I want to be ready to meet God. I want to remember that whether Jesus comes for me today or not, I could very easily leave this planet and go to Him. If you are ready to meet God at a moment's notice, then you don't have to walk around in doubt and fear. As Paul said, "to live is Christ, and to die is gain" (Philippians 1:21). It doesn't mean that a Christian has a death wish. It doesn't mean that a Christian gets up in the morning and says, "I hope I die today." What it does mean is that if we do die today or tomorrow, we will meet God and don't have to be afraid.

If He comes for us, we will be ready.

If we go to Him, we will be ready.

Ready is a very happy way to live.

THREE TAKEAWAY TRUTHS

- Christ's imminent return should motivate spiritual activity, not lethargy.
- There's no such thing as a "spiritual vacation" in the Christian life.
- The Bible has clear instructions for what Christians should do while they await Christ's return.

CHAPTER TWENTY
America and Armageddon

Then I heard a loud voice from the temple saying to the seven angels, "Go and pour out the bowls of the wrath of God on the earth."
(Revelation 16:1)

IN THIS CHAPTER
- The bowls of wrath of the Tribulation period
- How to endure persecution and tribulation
- When the Battle of Armageddon will take place
- Where America is in Bible prophecy

I heard about an airplane that was having severe engine trouble. The conversation with the nearest control tower went something like this.

"Pilot to tower. Pilot to tower. We are four hundred miles from land. We are eight hundred feet above water. All our engines are out. Please advise. Please advise."

There was a momentary pause and then the reply came back: "Tower to pilot. Tower to pilot. Repeat these words after me: 'Our Father which art in heaven, hallowed be thy name. . . .'"

Sometimes there isn't much left but the end.

That is where we find ourselves now in Revelation 15 and 16. We have arrived at what we could describe as the grand finale, with the final blows that are about to hit Planet Earth. We will be reading about seven plagues of judgment that will fall upon this world. It is time to say, "Our Father which art in heaven. . . ."

Sadly, most of the people in the world at that time won't be willing to say that at all. As a result, they will die as they have lived: bitter in spirit and hardened against God. And that, by the way, is why this judgment has to come. At that point, God understands there is nothing left to say.

As difficult as it may be for us to accept, there are people that we know who have steeled themselves against God and against the convicting power of His Holy Spirit and will probably never turn. But here is an all-important point: *we don't necessarily know who those people are.* That is why we should never give up on praying for people and sharing the gospel with people. Life is full of surprises. There are people you never thought would come to Christ in a million years who will pray and ask Jesus to come into their hearts, possibly after some great crisis. So don't give up! God knows who these people are, and you don't.

How many people in the first century would have predicted that Saul of Tarsus, the world's number one Christian hater, would turn to Christ? Probably not even one.

This would be like hearing that Bill Maher became a Christian and that he was leading a Bible study over at Howard Stern's house, with atheists Richard Dawkins and Ricky Gervais in attendance, and Lady Gaga leading worship.

Implausible? Yes.

Impossible? No.

No one is beyond the reach of God. Think of the most hardened nonbeliever you know—a person you can't imagine, not in your wildest dreams, carrying a Bible and following Christ. Now . . . let me encourage you to pray for that person.

The conversion of Saul of Tarsus was like that, and if God reached him, then He can surely reach the person you are thinking of right now.

Nevertheless, there can come a point of no return for a man or woman who continually rejects Christ.

In Revelation 15 and 16, it seems that most people on Earth already have made up their minds to resist God to the end. I am referring here to the final half—the last three-and-a-half years—of the Tribulation period. By this time, people have either made the decision to follow Jesus Christ and have been sealed by the Holy Spirit, or they have taken the mark of the Beast, the signature of the Antichrist, and are eternally separated from God.

Once a person has taken this mark, there is no turning back.

So now judgment arrives in full force.

"CLOSING TIME"

In 1869 the French chemist Marcellin Berthelot wrote these prophetic words: "Within a hundred years of physical and chemical science, men will know what the atom is. It is my belief when science reaches this stage, God will come down to earth with His big ring of keys and will say to humanity, 'Gentlemen it is closing time.'" [30]

Closing time. Effectively, that is what God is saying here.

In these chapters, Antichrist has already emerged on the scene and has set into place his new global economy. He has his military, his numbering system, and his one-world religion. Those who have longed for globalism finally will have their desire fulfilled. God's judgment, however, soon will be unleashed against this one-world government and its evil ruler.

God's judgments are never haphazard or random. God is always very specific in the way He judges and when He judges. He takes no pleasure in judging people. In fact, the Lord Himself says, "As surely as I live, declares the Sovereign LORD, I take no pleasure in the death of the wicked, but rather that they turn from their ways and live. Turn! Turn from your evil ways! Why will you die?" (Ezekiel 33:11 NIV).

Nevertheless, while God is loving, He is also just.

While God is forgiving, He is also righteous.

In the end, if people reject His offer of forgiveness and grace, there must be repercussions. Otherwise, there could be no justice in this world.

> **GOOD TO KNOW**
> God is always very specific in the way He judges and when He judges.

SUPER BOWLS OF JUDGMENT

We have all heard of the Super Bowl. In these chapters of Revelation, we see seven massive bowls of God's wrath being poured out on Planet Earth.

The residents of Earth, however, won't be able to say they weren't warned. God has given ample warning of this impending doom. In fact, He is doing so again in the pages of this book you are holding in your hands. During the

Tribulation period itself, He will raise up 144,000 fervent Jewish evangelists who will cover the planet with the gospel, and many will come to faith as the result of their ministry.

Then God raises up two witnesses, possibly Moses and Elijah, brought back to Earth from their place in Heaven. They, too, will have a powerful testimony that will be heard and seen by people all around the globe, probably utilizing modern technology. They will be killed by the Antichrist, and their bodies will lie where they have fallen in the streets of Jerusalem. But they will rise from the dead and ascend to Heaven while everyone watches.

If these supernatural marvels aren't enough, God will send out an angel who will fly through the heavens, declaring the everlasting gospel in what might be described as a mop-up operation.

People will hear the gospel.

And just as it is today, some will respond and some won't.

THE FINAL CHORD

The great composer Johann Sebastian Bach was known to love his naps. According to one story, his children had developed a surefire way of waking him up. They would go over to his piano and play a composition. (You can do that when you are one of the children of Bach.) Then they would get to the last note and they would stop, neglecting to play the last note. That would always wake up the composer. Bach couldn't stand leaving the composition up in the air. He would get up out of his bed, walk over to the piano, and play the final chord.

In Revelation 15–16, we find God playing the final chord. He will not leave His final judgment up in the air or unresolved.

Concerning God's judgment, in Romans 1:18–22 we read,

> But God shows his anger from Heaven against all sinful, evil men who push away the truth from them. For the truth about God is known to them instinctively; God has put this knowledge in their hearts. Since earliest times men have seen the earth and sky and

all God made, and have known of his existence and great eternal power. So they will have no excuse [when they stand before God at Judgment Day].

Yes, they knew about him all right, but they wouldn't admit it or worship him or even thank him for all his daily care. And after a while they began to think up silly ideas of what God was like and what he wanted them to do. The result was that their foolish minds became dark and confused. Claiming themselves to be wise without God, they became utter fools instead. (TLB)

This process will only intensify in the Tribulation period.

But perhaps as you have studied these prophetic passages, you've noticed something missing—someone you think would be there, who doesn't seem to be there at all.

I am talking about the United States of America.

WHERE IS THE UNITED STATES OF AMERICA?

One of the most striking things about Bible prophecy is not only who is mentioned, but also who is *not* mentioned. It is clear there will be a number of radical global shifts in those days. A new superpower will emerge—a ten-nation confederacy—with a satanic superman, the Antichrist, at the helm.

We don't know which countries will form the ten-nation superpower, although we can guess. Other nations are easily identified, including Israel and Iran-Persia. Many believe that Russia and China can be tagged as major players in the end times scenario.

GOOD TO KNOW

The United States is *conspicuously* absent from the prophetic scheme.

But what about the United States? How could a nation of our size and stature not be mentioned in the prophetic scheme? Our very absence is noteworthy. We are *conspicuously* absent. Why is that?

Let's begin our consideration by reading the text itself:

> Then I saw another sign in heaven, great and marvelous: seven angels having the seven last plagues, for in them the wrath of God is complete.
>
> And I saw something like a sea of glass mingled with fire, and those who have the victory over the beast, over his image and over his mark and over the number of his name, standing on the sea of glass, having harps of God. They sing the song of Moses, the servant of God, and the song of the Lamb, saying:
>
> > "Great and marvelous are Your works,
> > Lord God Almighty!
> > Just and true are Your ways,
> > O King of the saints!
> > Who shall not fear You, O Lord, and glorify Your name?
> > For You alone are holy.
> > For all nations shall come and worship before You,
> > For Your judgments have been manifested." (15:1–4)

Who are these people singing these praises in Heaven? These are what we would describe as Tribulation saints. In other words, these are people who have come to Christ during the terrors of the Tribulation period, possibly as a result of the preaching of the 144,000 or the two witnesses or the angel in the heavens. These are people who have believed in Jesus and, refusing the mark of the Beast, have been put to death.

Notice that these martyrs are standing before a sea of glass mingled with fire. Why? Many of us remember Johnny Cash's hit record, "Ring of Fire," but what is this? The image of glass and fire may symbolize the fiery trials these saints have just endured as they gave their lives as martyrs. Then again, it might also symbolize the judgment of God that is about to fall. Or perhaps both realities are represented here. God's judgment is certainly connected to the way His adversaries have treated His people.

God takes it personally when His people come under attack—just as you would take it personally if someone attacked your child or your grandchild.

Remember when Saul of Tarsus, the notorious Christian killer I already mentioned, met Jesus on the Damascus Road? He had just presided over the death of the first martyr of the church, Stephen, and he was on his way to another city to kill even more Christians.

Whom did he meet on the way? Jesus Himself. What did Jesus say to Saul? "Saul, Saul, why are you persecuting Me?" (Acts 9:4).

Notice that Jesus didn't say, "Saul, Saul why are you persecuting My people?" No, Jesus made it personal. He said, "You're persecuting *Me*."

When God's people come under persecution, it is personal to the Lord. But now this judgment is about to fall.

There's something else about the image of a *sea* of glass, mingled with fire. Water is often a picture in the Scriptures of both trials and judgment. For instance, when God sent the global flood in the days of Noah, those floodwaters protected Noah and his family in their ark, but those same waters were judgment upon the nonbelieving people. The waters of the Red Sea were opened up for the Israelites to cross over on dry land, but those same waters came back down on the pursuing Egyptian army. Water, then, is a symbol of both deliverance and judgment.

GOOD TO KNOW
Water is a symbol of both deliverance and judgment.

Even when we are baptized as Christians, the water symbolizes both death to the old nature and a new life. The Bible says, "Do you not know that as many of us as were baptized into Christ Jesus were baptized into His death? Therefore we were buried with Him through baptism into death, that just as Christ was raised from the dead by the glory of the Father, even so we also should walk in newness of life" (Romans 6:3–4).

When you go into that water, it's like having a funeral service for your old life.

I recently baptized a man who told me that he had lived a very sinful life and that I might need to hold him under the water a bit longer than normal.

Years ago I remember baptizing someone down at Newport Beach, California, in a little spot there known as Pirate's Cove. We were about waist high in the water, and I was standing there talking to this individual about what baptism means. As we spoke, I suddenly noticed bubbles coming up. Looking down, I saw a scuba diver, evidently looking at our ankles.

It was just a bit distracting! So I knocked on his tank, he came up out of the water, and I asked him if he would mind diving somewhere else.

In the imagery from Revelation 15, we see water and fire, images that the Scriptures use to portray both judgment and deliverance.

Verse 2 tells us that these martyrs "have the victory over the beast, over his image and over his mark and over the number of his name."

How did they do it? By refusing his mark and turning away from his image. This would have been an incredibly courageous decision, because they would have done so realizing it would cost them their lives. Although you and I as believers will not go through the Tribulation period per se, we can all count on going through *tribulations* as Christians—personal tribulations. John 16:33 and 2 Timothy 3:12 assure us that we will face tribulation and persecution in our lives.

These experiences are never easy, but if you are being harassed, criticized, excluded, mocked, or persecuted for your faith in Jesus, then you have reason to be encouraged. Jesus Himself told us, "Blessed are those who are persecuted for righteousness' sake, for theirs is the kingdom of Heaven. Blessed are you when they revile and persecute you, and say all kinds of evil against you falsely for My sake. Rejoice and be exceedingly glad, for great is your reward in heaven" (Matthew 5:10–12).

Jesus used the word *blessed* twice in this passage. In other words, He was saying, "Those who are persecuted for My sake will be doubly blessed." Since we know that the word *blessed* also could be translated "happy," it's as though He were saying, "Happy, happy are the persecuted for My sake."

Now, it doesn't feel so happy when it's actually happening. But you can wear such attacks as a badge of honor, knowing that you are being hated or slighted or hurt because you so faithfully represent Jesus Christ.

Notice that the passage doesn't say you will be blessed for being obnoxious, overly judgmental, or for simply being a mean person. No, if you are being singled out for persecution, then you'll want to make sure that you're being attacked for the right reason—for being a humble, gracious, loving follower of Christ.

KEEPING YOUR SONG WHEN TIMES ARE TOUGH

Even though Revelation 15 focuses mostly on God's judgment, there is one detail in this account that I really love.

Notice that the martyrs mentioned here, those who have come through the searing fires of persecution, *have not lost their song.*

In verses 3–4, the Bible says they sang "the song of Moses." How this speaks to me! The fact is that you and I cannot control our circumstances. (Trust me. I have tried. It doesn't work.) But we can control our *reaction* to the circumstances. To state it another way, you can't control what happens to you, but you can control *how* you react to what has happened to you.

The story of Paul and Silas in Philippi in Acts 16 is a case in point. The two apostles had been brutally beaten by the city magistrates for simply preaching the good news of Jesus. With their backs ripped open and bleeding, they were thrown into a dungeon and placed in cruelly uncomfortable stocks and chains.

But then in verse 25 we read, "But at midnight Paul and Silas were praying and singing hymns to God, and the prisoners were listening to them." When believers can praise God in the midst of their crises, tragedies, or trials, the world outside of Christ takes notice. When you are enduring some painful hardships and can still praise God, nonbelievers will pay attention.

GOOD TO KNOW
The martyred believers sing "the song of Moses," a song the Israelites sang after they had been delivered from Pharaoh and his army.

The believers in Revelation 15 had come through the worst fire imaginable, actually being put to death for their faith. Yet on the other side in Heaven, they are singing songs of praise.

My friend Marty Goetz talks about being a young Jewish boy who envied Christians as they celebrated Christmas. While Marty's family was celebrating Hanukkah, he would hear believers singing songs like "Hark! The Herald Angels Sing," "Silent Night," and "Joy to the World." He so admired the beauty and joy of those Christmas carols. In time, Marty became a believer in Jesus as his Messiah.

In my opinion, Christians have the best music of any religion. We sing a lot because we have something to sing about. And we had best get ourselves in practice now, because we certainly will be singing in Heaven.

These martyred believers sing "the song of Moses." That's a song the Israelites sang after they had been delivered from Pharaoh and his army. You can find this song in Exodus 15 and also in Deuteronomy 32.

Here are a few points to consider:

- The song of Moses was sung at the Red Sea. The song of the Lamb is sung at the crystal sea.

- The song of Moses is a song of triumph over the Pharaoh. The song of the Lamb is a song of triumph over the Antichrist.

- The song of Moses is how God brought His people out. The song of the Lamb is about how God brought His people in.

- The song of Moses is the first song in the Scriptures. The song of the Lamb is the last song in the Scriptures.

Remember, these people have suffered and died for their faith. Yet we read of no grumblings or criticisms of God. Instead, their mouths are full of praise. In their song, they declare that the Lord is just and true in His ways.

In other words, they had faith that He knew what He was doing.

WHEN LIFE DOESN'T MAKE SENSE

Every one of us has encountered times in life that just don't make sense. We experience tragedies, injustices, slander, and unfair treatment. Our emotions want to scream out, *This isn't right! This isn't fair!* It's at these times—these very moments—that we need to trust God and just worship Him as best we know how. We need to give Him praise, not because of our circumstances, but simply because He is good.

As the psalmist said, "Oh, give thanks to the LORD, for He is good! For His mercy endures forever" (Psalm 106:1).

Notice this verse *doesn't* say, "Give thanks to the Lord when you *feel* good." Rather, we are to give thanks because He *is* good.

What calamity are you facing? What trial is before you? Here is your response: *worship God*—not because of your hardship but because of the sovereignty and glory of your God.

When you get to Heaven, it will all be explained, but until that day we live on promises, not on explanations.

"THEY DID NOT REPENT"

In Revelation 16 we learn more about the divine judgments that will one day—and perhaps soon—fall on our world.

> Then I heard a loud voice from the temple saying to the seven angels,
>
> "Go and pour out the bowls of the wrath of God on the earth."
>
> So the first went and poured out his bowl upon the earth, and a foul and loathsome sore came upon the men who had the mark of the beast and those who worshiped his image.
>
> Then the second angel poured out his bowl on the sea, and it became blood as of a dead man; and every living creature in the sea died.

Then the third angel poured out his bowl on the rivers and springs of water, and they became blood. And I heard the angel of the waters saying:

> "You are righteous, O Lord, the One who is and who was and who is to be, because You have judged these things. For they have shed the blood of saints and prophets, and You have given them blood to drink. For it is their just due."

And I heard another from the altar saying, "Even so, Lord God Almighty, true and righteous are Your judgments."

Then the fourth angel poured out his bowl on the sun, and power was given to him to scorch men with fire. And men were scorched with great heat, and they blasphemed the name of God who has power over these plagues; and they did not repent and give Him glory.

Then the fifth angel poured out his bowl on the throne of the beast, and his kingdom became full of darkness; and they gnawed their tongues because of the pain. They blasphemed the God of heaven because of their pains and their sores, and did not repent of their deeds. (Revelation 16:1–11)

The people on Earth are "scorched with great heat" but still refuse to change their ways or to seek God during their calamity. In fact, they do the very opposite: they blaspheme God.

Here is a hard reality: *If the love of God doesn't bring you to repentance, then the judgment of God won't bring you to repentance.* The Bible says it is the goodness of God that leads us to repentance (see Romans 2:4). If an individual continues to resist His goodness, kindness, and grace, then in the end they will receive judgment—and they have chosen it for themselves.

From where does this all judgment emanate? We read in verse 1 that it comes from the temple. What temple? The temple in Heaven. It's important to remember that Heaven is a real place. In fact, it is *the* real place.

What do we enjoy about life on Earth? We like the beauty, the moments of fun and relaxation, the love and companionship of family and friends. There are so many things that we enjoy, and we ought to, because God has given us these things in His generosity and kindness. But here is what we need to realize: Heaven isn't some dim, wispy copy of Earth. No, Heaven is the original, and Earth is the copy.

GOOD TO KNOW

If the love of God doesn't bring you to repentance, then the judgment of God won't bring you to repentance.

The earthly Jewish temple in Jerusalem was a copy, a Xerox, of the real temple in Heaven. In Hebrews 8:5 we read, "[The priests] serve at a sanctuary that is a copy and shadow of what is in heaven. This is why Moses was warned when he was about to build the tabernacle: 'See to it that you make everything according to the pattern shown you on the mountain'" (NIV).

Here is my point: the things that you enjoy most on Earth will be waiting for you in Heaven, but in a perfected state. You won't miss out on anything.

As C. S. Lewis wrote, "All the things that have ever deeply possessed your soul have been but hints of [Heaven]—tantalizing glimpses, promises never quite fulfilled, echoes that died away just as they caught your ear." [31]

Lewis also said, "If I find in myself a desire which no experience in this world can satisfy, the most probable explanation is that I was made for another world. If none of my earthly pleasures satisfy it, that does not prove that the universe is a fraud. Probably earthly pleasures were never meant to satisfy it, but only to arouse it, to suggest the real thing." [32]

The real thing is Heaven.

In Revelation 16, however, we read that the seven angels bearing the seven bowls of God's wrath emanated from the temple in Heaven. And with the sixth bowl comes Armageddon:

Then the sixth angel poured out his bowl on the great river Euphrates, and its water was dried up, so that the way of the kings from the east might be prepared. And I saw three unclean spirits like frogs coming out of the mouth of the dragon, out of the mouth of the beast, and out of the mouth of the false prophet. For they are spirits of demons, performing signs, which go out to the kings of the earth and of the whole world, to gather them to the battle of that great day of God Almighty.

"Behold, I am coming as a thief. Blessed is he who watches, and keeps his garments, lest he walk naked and they see his shame."

And they gathered them together to the place called in Hebrew, Armageddon. (verses 12–16)

There is that word: *Armageddon.*

Have you ever heard that word tossed around? It sounds so ominous. Even frightening. People usually use it to describe a worst-case scenario or the ultimate conflict. It has come into our language as a metaphor, but it is more than a figure of speech. In fact, it is a reality that will actually happen.

In his book *What in the World Is Going On?* my friend David Jeremiah writes of the time when General Douglas MacArthur stood on the deck of the USS Missouri in Tokyo Harbor, signing a peace agreement with Japan and effectively bringing World War II to a close. MacArthur made this statement: "We have had our last chance. If we do not now devise some greater and more equitable system, Armageddon will be at our door." [33]

Soon after he was inaugurated as our fortieth president, Ronald Reagan was astounded by the complexities of the Middle East. On May 15, 1981, President Reagan wrote these words in his diary: "Sometimes I wonder if we are destined to witness Armageddon." [34]

A little bit later in 1981, after Israel bombed the Iraqi nuclear reactor, President Reagan went back to his diary and wrote these words: "Got word of Israeli bombing of Iraq—nuclear reactor. I swear I believe Armageddon is near." [35]

I wonder what General MacArthur and President Reagan would think of the events happening in our world today?

Armageddon is, first of all, the name of an actual place. The Bible says that the final battle of humanity will be fought in a specific geographical spot known as the Valley of Megiddo, within the borders of Israel.

Down through history, many battles have been waged in this place. It is where Gideon defeated the Midianites. It is where Deborah and Barak defeated the Canaanites. King Saul was killed in the Valley of Megiddo in a battle with the Philistines.

But why here? Why would one of the final conflicts on Earth be fought in such a place?

Napoleon himself ventured an opinion on that subject. In 1799 the great French general stood looking out across Megiddo and made this statement: "All the armies of the world could maneuver their forces on this vast plain. . . . There is no place in the whole world more suited for war than this. . . . [It is] the most natural battleground on the whole earth." [36]

And it is in this place where the superpowers of the last days will come head-to-head. It will be the forces of the Antichrist, ten confederated nations, going against the kings of the East.

But there are no "good guys" in this conflict. The kings of the East will be motivated by Satan as much as the ten-nation army that will oppose them.

The bottom line here is that Satan loves bloodshed.

Jesus said of him, "The thief comes only to steal and kill and destroy" (John 10:10 NIV). The Devil loves chaos, carnage, and conflict, and his own demon armies will be behind this vast battle.

The kings of the East will march across the Euphrates River to reach the battle site in Israel. This river is the dividing line between what we call the Near East and the Far East. It is 1,800 miles

GOOD TO KNOW

There are no "good guys" in this conflict. The kings of the East will be motivated by Satan as much as the ten-nation army that will oppose them.

long and 3,600 feet wide, with an average depth of thirty feet. But it will be dried up when the eastern kings make their march.

Who are these kings of the East?

No one can say with certainty. Revelation 9:16 says that this great army will number 200 million people. The intriguing thing is that there weren't 200 million people in the whole world when John wrote the book of Revelation. This clearly shows that Armageddon will be a future event, not something that happened in John's lifetime, as some have suggested.

Who on the planet could field an army of 200 million?

China could.

At this writing, the population of China is estimated at about 1.4 *billion* people. To put that in perspective, the population of the United States is around 335 million. [37] China has almost a billion more people than we have in the United States. In 1997, China announced that they could raise an army of 352 million soldiers. That means they could send 200 million to invade the Middle East and still have 152 million soldiers in reserve to defend China. In the last decade or so, China has emerged as both a military and economic superpower.

Does "kings of the East" refer to China or to some combination of China, India, and Japan? No one really knows.

COMING BACK TO THE QUESTION, WHERE IS AMERICA?

Coming back to a question I raised earlier, where is the undisputed present-day superpower—the United States of America? How could a nation of our size and stature not be mentioned in the prophetic scheme? The absence is significant. Let me offer some possible options.

The United States may have been decimated by a nuclear attack.

Terrible as it may be to contemplate, this could certainly happen. There are possibly as many as 22,000 nuclear weapons on the planet today, held mostly by the world's superpowers. Then there are rogue nations like North Korea and Iran that are developing them or already have them.

North Korea has threatened on numerous occasions to destroy the United States with nuclear weapons—as has Iran. It could happen. I pray that it doesn't, hope it doesn't, and don't necessarily think that it will happen.

But it could.

The United States might simply decline as a world power.

Nations have a shelf life. Nations come and go historically, some more quickly than others. As Mark Hitchcock pointed out in his book *Is America in Bible Prophecy?* the might of the Babylonian Empire lasted only 86 years. The powerful Persian Empire did better, lasting for 208 years. The glory of Greece was eclipsed after 268 years. Mighty Rome ruled for almost nine centuries. [38] As of this writing, the United States is 245 years old and counting. Every nation will have a beginning, middle, and end. As the prophet Isaiah wrote, "All the nations of the world are but a drop in the bucket. They are nothing more than dust on the scales" (Isaiah 40:15 NLT).

As the dollar gets weaker, other currencies become stronger. As China emerges as an economic power, things could change, and we could just simply diminish as a world power—fade like a shadow in the noonday sun. It has happened to countless other nations and could very possibly happen to us. If it did, we might simply fall into line as one of the nations supporting the Antichrist.

America may experience a great revival.

This is by far my favorite option. This is not to suggest that a revival would eliminate us as a world power, but if a revival were to sweep our land, we could have a great and godly influence on our planet in the time that we have left. Such a massive turn toward God would change the climate of our country.

I believe the only hope for America is for us to have a spiritual awakening. This is what I am praying for and what we all need to be praying for.

Why would this change things?

Let's play this scenario out for a moment or two. Let's imagine that we had a great awakening in the United States, with thousands or even millions of Americans coming to faith in Christ. We're due for such a revival, don't you think? There have been several great spiritual awakenings in the history of our country. What if we had another?

As stated earlier, our nation's population now is somewhere around 335 million. How many people in our country have a saving relationship with Jesus Christ? I don't know. Let's be conservative and say that one-third of Americans become Christians because of this great revival. That means when the Rapture comes, more than 111 million Americans would disappear from the planet.

Would that change our country?

Absolutely. It would hardly be recognizable!

Literally overnight, such an event would drastically affect industry, government, the military, business, agriculture, education, and medicine. We simply would collapse as a superpower overnight. And in the vacuum we would leave behind, other superpower players would step to the forefront.

Yes, the United States is powerful and influential today, but that situation is always temporary. It was once said that the sun never set on the British Empire. England was once a superpower, but it isn't anymore. I saw one listing of the top ten most powerful nations in the world, and it listed the United Kingdom as sixth. Their influence and might ebbed away in a relatively few years, and it could certainly happen to the United States as well.

> **GOOD TO KNOW**
> The United States is powerful and influential today, but that situation is always temporary.

I am praying that the United States will have at least one more mighty spiritual awakening before these events in Revelation begin to unfold. When we sing "God Bless America," it is a prayer. The lyrics say, "God bless America, land that I love. Stand beside her and guide her through the night with a light from above."

That is what we need. We need the light from above to guide us out of our confusion and self-destructive behavior. The song speaks of the God that our founding fathers believed in, the God of the Bible. This is the God we need to return to, not the god or goddess of your choice or some foggy, wispy notion of spirituality. We need to return to the true and living God, and I believe that need is critical. I believe that if we would turn to Him and repent of our sins as a nation, then we could witness a great revival in our time.

Sodom was once a great power in her day, a city-state with an army and economic clout. But God judged her, essentially wiping both Sodom and Gomorrah off the map.

You might be surprised at how the Bible identifies the specific sins of these two cities. In Jeremiah 23:14 we read, "I see that the prophets of Jerusalem are even worse! They commit adultery and love dishonesty. They encourage those who are doing evil so that no one turns away from their sins. These prophets are as wicked as the people of Sodom and Gomorrah once were" (NLT).

What were their specific sins? "They commit adultery and love dishonesty. They encourage those who are doing evil." Isn't that a clear picture of what our contemporary culture glorifies and how so many Americans live today? We live in a time in our nation when right is wrong and wrong is right. Truly, much of what our nation once believed in and valued has been turned upside down within the last few generations.

Here is another assessment of the sins of Sodom. Ezekiel 16:49–50 tells us that "Sodom's sins were pride, gluttony, and laziness, while the poor and needy suffered outside her door. She was proud and committed detestable sins, so I wiped her out, as you have seen" (NLT).

"Pride, gluttony, and laziness." Think of our country and our sense of entitlement. Everyone expects to be entertained. Everyone expects everything to be given to them on a silver platter.

I am reminded of a statement made by a Roman satirist named Juvenal in AD 100. Speaking of Rome and her decline, he said, "There's only two things that concern them: bread and circuses." [39]

Rome had fallen into such a state of decline that they just wanted to be entertained. The Roman leaders knew they could pacify the masses with increasingly more graphic and violent entertainment and loaves of bread.

It seems to me that is what America is like today. *Who cares about what is right and wrong? Entertain us.* But in the process, we are entertaining ourselves to death. Nations as mighty as we once were are again rising on our world. The Bible says that people in the last days will be "lovers of pleasure rather than lovers of God" (2 Timothy 3:4).

But it isn't too late for us.

We can still turn to the Lord and still see a great awakening in our land. I believe that the United States of America, right here and right now, has two choices before her. One is revival and the other is judgment.

We know from Revelation 15–16 that judgment is on its way.

Let's be praying that revival will come first.

THREE TAKEAWAY TRUTHS

- When He executes judgment, God is not haphazard, but deliberate and particular.
- Believers today have a "song to sing"—even when persecuted, we can rejoice and be a powerful witness to a watching world.
- The best hope for America is a great spiritual revival.

CHAPTER TWENTY-ONE
Beauty and the Beast

*Then one of the seven angels who had the seven bowls came
and talked with me, saying to me, "Come, I will show you the
judgment of the great harlot who sits on many waters."*
(Revelation 17:1)

IN THIS CHAPTER
- What we discover from the fall of Babylon
- Babylon is both a religious and economic system.
- Why the church can celebrate in the end
- The choice we are given today

I heard the story of a little boy who liked to visit his grandparents. One of his favorite things about his grandparents' house was a beautiful antique grandfather clock. He loved to hear it chime on the hour. In fact, his favorite time of day was noon, when the clock would chime and chime and chime.

One day he was in the living room, playing on the floor with his toys, when noon arrived. The little guy stopped playing to listen to the clock and count its chimes.

One, two, three, four, five, six . . . the boy counted each chime.

Seven, eight, nine, ten, eleven, twelve . . .

But then, the clock kept on chiming.

Thirteen, fourteen, fifteen, sixteen.

The clock chimed sixteen times. Evidently something had gone wrong with the old clock's inner mechanism, but the little boy didn't understand that.

He ran into the kitchen where his grandmother was making lunch and said, "Grandma! It's later than it has ever been before!"

That's a pretty good description of the time in which we are living.

In previous chapters, I've written about the danger of rogue nations developing nuclear weapons—and the frightening possibility of such weapons falling into the hands of terrorists.

Some time ago I read about a ten-ton meteor that streaked across the sky and exploded over Russia's Ural Mountains, with the power of an atomic bomb blast. One person described it like a scene from an Armageddon movie. Its sonic blast shattered countless windows and injured over a thousand people.

In the same week, astronomers reported that a huge asteroid came within seventeen million miles of hitting Earth (which is pretty close, in space terms). The asteroid was 147 feet across. Asteroid impact expert Jay Melosh said, "Something that size would have hit the Earth with the energy of a thermonuclear bomb." [40]

Are these signs of the times? I believe they are. Jesus warned of "signs in the sun, in the moon, and in the stars; and on the earth distress of nations, with perplexity, the sea and the waves roaring; men's hearts failing them from fear and the expectation of those things which are coming on the earth, for the powers of the heavens will be shaken" (Luke 21:25–26).

In his book on Revelation, the late Adrian Rogers wrote, "I believe that the shadows of the end of the age are lengthening, the sands of time are running low, and we are standing on the threshold of the second coming of Jesus Christ and the rapture of the church." [41]

FROM BAD TO WORSE

In Revelation 17 the unprecedented turmoil and terrible bloodshed of the Great Tribulation continues to rage on our planet. I do not believe that we believers will be on Earth at this time; we already will have been caught up to meet the Lord in the air at the rapture of the church. You might say that we will be sitting this one out.

I have called this chapter "Beauty and the Beast." Remember the Disney movie and the song sung by the teapot, Mrs. Potts, to the little cup named Chip? *Tale as old as time, song as old as rhyme, beauty and the beast.* That little snippet of the song came to me as I studied Revelation 17.

Tale as old as time, song as old as rhyme. Who is the Beast? That is the Antichrist, wreaking havoc on Planet Earth. Who is the beauty? That would be the church, waiting safely in Heaven for the moment when we will return to Earth in triumph behind the Lord Jesus Christ.

Meanwhile, on Earth, things go from bad to worse:

> Then one of the seven angels who had the seven bowls came and talked with me, saying to me, "Come, I will show you the judgment of the great harlot who sits on many waters, with whom the kings of the earth committed fornication, and the inhabitants of the earth were made drunk with the wine of her fornication."
>
> So he carried me away in the Spirit into the wilderness. And I saw a woman sitting on a scarlet beast which was full of names of blasphemy, having seven heads and ten horns. The woman was arrayed in purple and scarlet, and adorned with gold and precious stones and pearls, having in her hand a golden cup full of abominations and the filthiness of her fornication. And on her forehead a name was written:
>
> MYSTERY, BABYLON THE GREAT, THE MOTHER OF HARLOTS AND OF THE ABOMINATIONS OF THE EARTH.
>
> I saw the woman, drunk with the blood of the saints and with the blood of the martyrs of Jesus. And when I saw her, I marveled with great amazement.
>
> But the angel said to me, "Why did you marvel? I will tell you the mystery of the woman and of the beast that carries her, which has the seven heads and the ten horns. The beast that you saw was, and is not, and will ascend out of the bottomless pit and go to perdition. And those who dwell on the earth will marvel, whose

names are not written in the Book of Life from the foundation of the world, when they see the beast that was, and is not, and yet is. (17:1–8)

What in the world is happening here? The Bible describes this vision as "Mystery Babylon." Most of us love a really good mystery—a whodunnit that keeps us turning pages or glued to our seat in front of the TV.

This, too, is a mystery . . . but it is also explained.

As we noted early on in this book, the purpose of the book of Revelation is not to conceal; it is to *reveal*. In fact, the very word *revelation* means *the unveiling*. God wants to unveil and make understandable to us the images that are before us in this final book of the Bible.

In this passage, "Mystery Babylon" is introduced, pictured as a prostitute, dressed in red, and riding on a beast. A scarlet harlot.

Babylon is a picture of man's kingdom on earth. In many ways Babylon is what we might call a code word in the Bible, representing something more than its name. For instance, when we say "Madison Avenue," we are not talking so much about a particular street in New York City. We're speaking more about advertising executives or publicity or promotion. When we use the word "Hollywood," we aren't necessarily talking about the actual city of Hollywood. We're speaking about the movie industry as a whole. It's the same when we say "Wall Street." There really is an actual Wall Street in New York City, but for the most part we're speaking of commerce or the stock market.

It's the same with the term *Babylon*. It was once the name of a great city and nation on Earth that became an empire. But in this context, it means something more than the name of a point on the map.

When Peter wrote to scattered believers who had suffered persecution, he spoke of the church in Rome, saying, "She who is in Babylon, chosen together with you, sends you her greetings" (1 Peter 5:13 NIV). His readers would have understood Peter to mean Rome when he said "Babylon." Rome was like the Babylon of its day.

GOOD TO KNOW

Babylon is a picture of man's kingdom on Earth.

In this context in Revelation, Babylon refers to the worldwide political, economic, and religious kingdom of the Antichrist.

THE ORIGINS OF BABYLON

To understand Babylon, we need to go back to her origins. Ancient Babylon first appeared on the plains of Shinar, in the book of Genesis. That is where the world's first dictator, Nimrod, established the world's first religious center. Nimrod is described as a mighty hunter of men's souls, in defiance of the Lord.

This is after the Flood, after Noah and his family came out of the ark to a world that had been washed clean of evil. God had specifically told humanity to spread out across the planet.

Nimrod, however, had other ideas.

In defiance of God's clear directions, this dictator instructed the people to build a mighty tower that became known as the Tower of Babel. In one sense, it was the forerunner of the modern skyscraper. The actual height of the tower, however, wasn't as important as the objective, or purpose, of the structure. The tower was built to look to the stars, to see one's destiny. In that sense, Babylon became ground zero for astrology and man-centered religion. All the religions of the world relate back to what happened at Babel. The Tower of Babel is a classic example of man trying to reach God rather than acknowledging that God has reached down to man.

The Tower of Babel was a monument to themselves.

> The people who lived there began to talk about building a great city, with a temple-tower reaching to the skies—a proud, eternal monument to themselves. (Genesis 11:3 TLB)

This is a picture of manmade religion. People want God, but they want Him on their own terms.

They want forgiveness, but they don't want repentance.

They want Heaven, but they certainly don't want Hell.

Babylon was the beginning of humanism. Though the Lord told the people to spread out, instead they pulled together to worship—not God, but themselves. They wanted to be unified in a global community.

And they were so proud of the tower they had built! In a sense, they were saying, "Watch out, God. There's a new kid in town. Check out this thing we've erected by working together."

I love how the text in Genesis says that God "came down" to see the city (see Genesis 11:5). He came down. It's as though He had to stoop very low to even see it. It's like when a little child speaks to you, and you squat down or bend over to look him or her in the eyes and listen.

A better analogy might be a bunch of ants laboring away at an inch-high ant hill. That's how that so-called mighty tower appeared in Heaven's perspective. It was as though God said, "I'm going to have to go down there to the plain of Shinar, get on My hands and knees, and take out my magnifying glass, so I can check out this thing you guys have been working on!"

God scattered the global community.

God checked it out. Then He sent a great confusion among the people so they could no longer communicate, and they scattered (finally) across the world. Babel ultimately morphed into the great world empire of Babylon under the rulership of Nebuchadnezzar and, later, Belshazzar. Belshazzar was in charge when Babylon was overtaken by the Medo-Persian forces.

GOOD TO KNOW

The color scarlet, or red, reminds us of the fiery red dragon mentioned in Revelation 13—a picture of Satan himself.

With that in mind, let's come back to our text before us in Revelation 17. Here we have Babylon revisited, or reborn.

In verse 3, we have the strange image of the scarlet harlot riding the beast. (You might call it the rodeo from Hell.) The color scarlet, or red, reminds us of the fiery red dragon mentioned in Revelation 13—a picture of Satan himself.

The Devil, of course, is behind all of this, including the Antichrist and his false religious system.

We speak frequently about the separation of church and state in the United States of America. This, however, is the ultimate merging of church of state. People are given a choice: either believe in this religion, follow the Antichrist, and accept his mark, or die.

Back at the Tower of Babel, the people of Earth were saying, "Hey, let's come together. Let's be unified." Yet God deliberately divided and scattered them because they were coming together for the wrong reason.

People still do this today. We hear people say, "Let's set aside our religious differences and all come together as one. Don't all religions teach essentially the same thing?" It was Mahatma Gandhi who said, "I consider myself a Hindu, Christian, Muslim, Jew, Buddhist, and Confucian."

What he really should have said is, "I consider myself a *confusion*."

If you embrace all religions, then you have no religion at all. I read an interview in which Paul McCartney gave his views on God. He was quoted to say, "I believe in a spirit. That's the best I can put it. I think there is something greater than us, and I love it, and I am grateful to it, but just like everyone else on the planet, I can't pin it down. I am happy not pinning it down. I pick bits out of all the religions—so I like many things that Buddhists say, I like a lot of things that Jesus said, that Mohammed said." [42]

Maybe Sir Paul ought to just "let it be."

What McCartney is advocating is nothing new at all. In fact, it is almost as old as humanity. It is the religion of Babylon.

Paul said he liked a lot of things that Jesus said, but one of the things Jesus did say is: "I am the way, the truth, and the life. No one comes to the Father except through Me" (John 14:6).

This false religion might be very appealing to a wide swath of people, but it is also deadly. In the Tribulation period, this one-world religion takes the form of a great prostitute draped in red.

Verse 4 says that this scarlet harlot Babylon has in her hand a golden cup full of abominations and the filthiness of her fornication. A golden cup, of course, speaks of something expensive and valuable; the abominations speak of moral and spiritual filth. In other words, she is sipping on a luxurious, deadly cocktail.

You may have read about the cruise ship that was adrift off the coast of Mexico a few years ago. A fire broke out in the engine room, and the ship lost all power, plunging it into darkness. There was no food. The toilets were overflowing. The hallways were full of excrement and urine.

But that's not how the cruise started out. Everyone had been excited to launch out on this luxurious voyage where the guests would be pampered with food, entertainment, and marvelous scenery. A cruise! How exciting! How wonderful! What a fun prospect!

No one anticipated that a luxury boat would morph into a dung boat. It was a horrifying nightmare of a voyage.

That's a picture of the Tribulation period. What people don't understand is that it all starts out so promising and hopeful. The world recovers from the shock of losing millions of people at the Rapture, and here comes this vision of a new era of global peace and prosperity.

A robust economy returns to the world, and people are making money hand over fist. There's a new religion that, at long last, everyone can agree on. Best of all, you have a clever, charismatic leader whom everyone seems to like and trust.

But then this "man of peace" shows his true colors. After helping the Jews rebuild their temple, he erects an image of himself in that temple and commands people to worship it. That is called the abomination of desolation.

And that's where the luxury voyage takes a bad turn. Just like that cruise ship floating dead in the water off of Mexico, the religion of Antichrist becomes an abomination that stinks to high heaven. It might be served up in a golden cup, but it smells like the brimstone of Hell.

The apostle John, who was naturally baffled by what he was seeing in this vision, had an angel standing by to explain things to him:

> "Why did you marvel? I will tell you the mystery of the woman and of the beast that carries her, which has the seven heads and the ten horns. The beast that you saw was, and is not, and will ascend out of the bottomless pit and go to perdition. And those who dwell on the earth will marvel, whose names are not written in the Book

of Life from the foundation of the world, when they see the beast that was, and is not, and yet is." (17:7–8)

In another translation, verse 8 reads, "The beast you saw was once alive but isn't now. And yet he will soon come up out of the bottomless pit and go to eternal destruction" (NLT).

The beast ascends from the bottomless pit, only to sink back again into eternal destruction. Remember who this beast, or the Antichrist, really is. He is the Devil's cheap imitation of the Messiah. As we have noted already, the prefix *anti* not only means "against," it also means "instead of." Satan has his unholy trinity: he takes the place of God, Antichrist is in the place of Jesus Christ, and the false prophet is in the place of the Holy Spirit.

Apparently at some point, there is a successful assassination attempt against the Antichrist, and he somehow survives it. Everyone thinks he is dead, but he is alive again. That, we presume, is the Devil's version of the death and resurrection of Christ. After the Antichrist is seemingly wounded beyond recovery and his fatal wound is healed, everyone marvels at this miracle and follows the Beast in awe and worship. We are told that the dragon, or Satan, gives the beast his power. People worship the beast and say, "Who is like the beast?" Full-tilt devil worship breaks out after this so-called resurrection from the dead (see Revelation 13:1–4).

Babylon is not only a religious system, but it is also an economic entity in the last days. Revelation 17 focuses on the religious aspects of Babylon, while Revelation 18 focuses on the city's political and economic characteristics. One thing is clear: Babylon is not only a mentality; it also will become a supercity:

> After these things I saw another angel coming down from heaven, having great authority, and the earth was illuminated with his glory. And he cried mightily with a loud voice, saying, "Babylon the great is fallen, is fallen, and has become a dwelling place of demons, a prison for every foul spirit, and a cage for every unclean and hated bird! For all the nations have drunk of the wine of the wrath of her fornication, the kings of the earth have committed fornication with

her, and the merchants of the earth have become rich through the abundance of her luxury." (Revelation 18:1–3)

"Babylon the great" isn't so great at all. Bigger isn't always better. Notice that this supercity, this mega-religious and economic power, is also the dwelling place of demons.

This whole empire, as powerful as it becomes, will come down quickly. Satan's ship is a sinking ship. In the long run, sin cannot win and faith cannot fail. If you become a lover of Babylon, in any of its forms, then you are following a lost cause.

As we read about the destruction of Babylon and how quickly it falls, it makes us wonder if it has been smashed by an asteroid or a nuclear weapon:

"The kings of the earth who committed fornication and lived luxuriously with her will weep and lament for her, when they see the smoke of her burning, standing at a distance for fear of her torment, saying, 'Alas, alas, that great city Babylon, that mighty city! For in one hour your judgment has come.'" (Revelation 18:9–10)

Standing at a distance for fear of her torment? Could that be a fear of radio-active fallout? At this point, nobody knows. But I know this much: at the appointed hour, Babylon and everything that's a part of it will go down. At a time of His choosing, God will say, "That's it. The party's over."

GOOD TO KNOW

Satan's ship is a sinking ship. In the long run, sin cannot win and faith cannot fail.

What is true of Babylon can be true of an individual life as well. The Bible tells us that we can be sure our sins will find us out (see Numbers 32:23). Sometimes when we sin and nothing bad happens—we don't get caught or found out—we may tell ourselves that God has given us a pass.

Trust me, He hasn't. Don't confuse God's grace with leniency. He hasn't turned a blind eye to your sin, and He still will deal with it. But He may also give you an opportunity to repent so that you won't have to face the full ramifications of it. Ecclesiastes 8:11 says, "When a crime is not punished quickly, people feel it is safe to do wrong" (NLT). Nevertheless, the punishment will come.

And it comes to Babylon as well.

What are "beauty and the beast" doing at this point?

The beauty—we who form Christ's beautiful bride—will be in Heaven singing the "Hallelujah Chorus"—literally:

> After these things I heard a loud voice of a great multitude in heaven, saying, "Alleluia! Salvation and glory and honor and power belong to the Lord our God! For true and righteous are His judgments, because He has judged the great harlot who corrupted the earth with her fornication; and He has avenged on her the blood of His servants shed by her." (Revelation 19:1–2)

WHY WILL WE BE CELEBRATING IN HEAVEN?

We will celebrate because the power of God has vanquished evil.

When Christians speak of the end of "the world," we are really speaking of the unrighteous world system driven by Satan and steered by wicked people whom he has blinded and deceived. Let's face it. We get weary of seeing evil, cruelty, and injustice prevail time after time in our world. On this occasion, however, we finally will see righteousness prevail—and it will fill our hearts with gladness.

We will celebrate and rejoice because our Lord reigns.

"Alleluia! For the Lord God Omnipotent reigns!" (19:6)

Until that day when Christ sets foot on the Earth, mankind will continue to sin. God will allow man the freedom to make his own stupid choices, right up until the very end. But when the Lord says, "That's it," then that's it!

We will celebrate because the marriage of the Lamb has come.

"Let us be glad and rejoice and give Him glory, for the marriage of the Lamb has come, and His wife has made herself ready." And to her it was granted to be arrayed in fine linen, clean and bright, for the fine linen is the righteous acts of the saints." (Revelation 19:7–8)

On more than one occasion, the church is compared to a bride—the bride of Christ. Some men don't like that metaphor. They will say, "I don't want to be a bride." Get over it! You *are* a bride, and Jesus is the groom. One day there will be that heavenly wedding, and we will be presented to Him.

Just as a husband and wife need to be faithful to one another and keep their vows, we need to be faithful to the Lord. If you break your vows to your spouse and are sexually involved with someone else, you commit adultery. But we can commit spiritual adultery as well. Did you know that? How? By loving this world system. By loving Babylon. James 4:4 says, "You adulterous people, don't you know that friendship with the world means enmity against God? Therefore, anyone who chooses to be a friend of the world becomes an enemy of God" (NIV).

What exactly do the Scriptures mean by "the world"? After all, there's nothing wrong with appreciating what God has made on Earth, with all its beauty and wonder. No, we're not supposed to hate the planet that God has given us to live on. As the Scriptures say, "The earth is the LORD's, and all its fullness" (Psalm 24:1). Frankly, I think Christians can appreciate nature more than anyone else alive because we see in it the handiwork of our heavenly Father. When the New Testament speaks of "the world," however, it is speaking of a system of thought or a mentality. It is a way of thinking embraced by people outside of Christ. In fact, it mirrors the thinking of those people who built the Tower of Babel in the years after the Flood.

Even though we may sing, "It's All About You, Jesus," it really isn't sometimes. In fact, sometimes it's all about me . . . what I want . . . what pleases me . . . what makes me look good in the eyes of others.

I like this contemporary version of the familiar "love not the world" passage in 1 John 2:15–17:

Don't love the world's ways. Don't love the world's goods. Love of the world squeezes out love for the Father. Practically everything that goes on in the world—wanting your own way, wanting everything for yourself, wanting to appear important—has nothing to do with the Father. It just isolates you from him. The world and all its wanting, wanting, wanting is on the way out—but whoever does what God wants is set for eternity. (MSG)

No, we do not want to be spiritual adulterers or adulteresses. God has called us to be faithful to Him.

Does this mean that we somehow isolate ourselves from the world, withdrawing into some kind of sanitized safe zone where we never rub shoulders with those outside of Christ? Of course not. We would have to leave the planet to avoid contact with the world and the world system.

The apostle Paul dealt with this issue in his first letter to the church in Corinth. Corinth was known for its immorality and corruption. He said, "When I wrote to you before, I told you not to associate with people who indulge in sexual sin. But I wasn't talking about unbelievers who indulge in sexual sin, or are greedy, or cheat people, or worship idols. You would have to leave this world to avoid people like that" (1 Corinthians 5:9–10 NLT).

> **GOOD TO KNOW**
>
> On more than one occasion, the church is compared to a bride— the bride of Christ.

Paul went on to explain himself with these words: "But I am saying that you shouldn't act as if everything is just fine when one of your Christian companions is promiscuous or crooked, is flip with God or rude to friends, gets drunk or becomes greedy and predatory. You can't just go along with this, treating it as acceptable behavior" (verse 11 MSG).

We want to influence people and win them to Christ. And we can't do that if we cut ourselves off from contact with the unsaved world. Vance Havner said, "We are not to be isolated but insulated, moving in the midst of evil but untouched by it." I would add the thought that we are to infiltrate our world, permeating our contemporary culture with the gospel.

We will celebrate in Heaven because the marriage supper of the Lamb begins.

I've always liked that word *supper*. They use that term a lot in the South. Most of us say *dinner*, but there's something warm and homey and comfortable about the word *supper*, don't you think? (Well, let's face it, I just like to eat, whatever you call the meal.)

I wonder what this wedding supper will be like. A formal sit-down affair? I hope not. More like a buffet, maybe? A little more casual, perhaps, with foods from every nation in the world? If you're looking for me, you'll probably find me over in the Mexican or Italian section of the buffet. When we stopped in Italy on the way to Israel a few years ago, we had some pizza in Rome. You've never had pizza until you've had it in Italy!

GOOD TO KNOW

You and I have two cities from which to choose. We can choose the city of man or the city of God. Babylon or the New Jerusalem. The Antichrist or Jesus Christ.

Can you imagine sitting down with all your loved ones and the great heroes of the Bible and having a meal? The Bible says that will really happen. In Matthew 8:11 Jesus said, "And I tell you this, that many Gentiles will come from all over the world—from east and west—and sit down with Abraham, Isaac, and Jacob at the feast in the Kingdom of Heaven" (NLT).

I try to picture in my mind what this might be like.

"Hey Moses, could you pass the manna?"

"Excuse me, Elijah, but my meat needs a little more fire. Could you call down a little more?"

"Lot, would you please pass the salt?"

Imagine having a cup of coffee (after dessert) and asking David what it was like to fight Goliath, getting Moses to talk about what it was like up there on Mount Sinai, or maybe asking Mary what it was like to carry the Son of God in her womb. Imagine having breakfast with Spurgeon or tea with C. S. Lewis. And imagine, of course, being reunited with loved ones who have gone on before you.

This isn't fantasy land. These things are all promised to the child of God.

But they are not the hope of the child of Babylon.

You and I have two cities from which to choose. We can choose the city of man or the city of God. Babylon or the New Jerusalem. The Antichrist or Jesus Christ.

This world is our present location, but it is not our home. One day we will go home—to our *real* home. As David said in 1 Chronicles 29:15, "We are here for only a moment, visitors and strangers in the land as our ancestors were before us. Our days on earth are like a passing shadow, gone so soon without a trace" (NLT). When you become a Christian, you become a citizen of Heaven, your authentic and forever home, where our Lord Jesus Christ lives.

Cathe and I have four granddaughters, Stella, Lucy, Rylie, and Allie—and a grandson named Christopher.

Our home is filled with all kinds of toys for the grandkids. As grandparents we want to make our home as accessible and fun for them as we can. When little Allie was three, she loved to come over and be with us and play with all the toys.

And then suddenly, out of the blue, she would look up and say, "Home."

With that, she would walk right over to the front door.

"Allie, where are you going?"

"Home."

When she wanted to go, she wanted to go!

Have you ever felt that way? You look at life here on Earth, and suddenly you realize, "This is nice, but it isn't home. I want to go home."

There are some great moments in this life, and hopefully we all have some sweet memories. But there are also some very sad, hurtful, and difficult moments. There are times when life just leaves us cold, and we say, "Home."

Paul, sitting in a prison cell, spoke of his desire to "depart and be with Christ, which is far better" (Philippians 1:23).

He was effectively saying, "Home!"

And for the believer, Heaven is the home that should fill our hearts with longing. E. M. Bounds wrote,

Heaven ought to draw and engage us. Heaven ought to so fill our hearts and hands, our manner and our conversation, our character and our features, that all would see we are foreigners, strangers to this world, natives of a nobler clime, fairer than this. . . . The very atmosphere of the world should be chilling to us and noxious, its suns eclipsed and its companionship dull and insipid. Heaven is our native land and home to us, and death to us is not the dying hour, but the birth hour. [43]

For the believer in Christ, life on Earth—with all its bumps, disappointments, and bruises—is as bad as it will get for the Christian. Following this life, we will enter Heaven.

For the nonbeliever, this life is as *good* as it gets. It's all downhill from here, with the terrifying prospect of God's judgment and an eternity separated from Him in Hell.

The choice for each one of us is about as fundamental as it gets. Will it be Babylon or the New Jerusalem, Hell or Heaven?

For this brief moment in time, the decision is still up to you.

THREE TAKEAWAY TRUTHS

- Babylon is a picture of the world system—and its fall a warning to those who love this world system over God.
- The church celebrates the judgment of Babylon because it means that Christ rules and reigns.
- Everyone has a choice between what "city" they will choose to live in: Babylon or the New Jerusalem?

CHAPTER TWENTY-TWO

The Second Coming of Jesus Christ

I saw heaven standing open and there before me was a white horse, whose rider is called Faithful and True. With justice he judges and wages war.
(Revelation 19:11 NIV)

IN THIS CHAPTER

- Jesus comes to Earth in the Second Coming.
- The significance of the marriage supper of the Lamb
- Why Christians can look forward to the judgment seat of Christ
- What will happen when Jesus comes again

I heard about a traveling salesman who was out on the road. After a long day of work, he got back to his hotel room late, exhausted. Getting ready to turn in, he sat on the edge of his bed and took off one of his big, heavy boots. It dropped on the floor with a loud thud.

Then it dawned on the man that there were people in the room below him, and he probably just woke them up. So he took more care with the second boot, pulling it off and gently setting it down on the floor. Then he got into his pajamas and went to bed.

Just as he began to drift off, there was a knock at the door. When he opened the door, he saw another man in his pajamas, standing there with dark circles under his eyes.

The man said, "Would you just let the other shoe drop so I can get some sleep?"

In Revelation 19, the other shoe is about to drop.

The most significant event in all of human history—apart from the birth, death, and resurrection of the Lord Jesus Christ—is about to take place.

Jesus Christ is coming again.

"AT THE SOUND OF HIS APPROACH"

It is not only Christians who believe in the return of Jesus Christ. Not long ago, a Gallup poll revealed that 66 percent of the American public believes that Jesus will return to Earth in the near future. That is 25 percent more than those who claim to be born again. So there is a sense in the air, even among nonbelievers, that Christ is coming back again to the planet.

Why is He returning?

Christ is coming to judge His enemies, to set up His kingdom, and to rule over Earth for one thousand years, while Satan will be bound and unable to work his evil in the world.

From Genesis to Revelation, the Bible refers to the Second Coming many times. It is mentioned 1,800 times in the Old Testament and three hundred times in the New Testament. Statistically, one verse in every twenty-five refers to the Second Coming of Christ. It is spoken of in twenty-seven Old Testament books and twenty-three New Testament books. For every prophecy in the Bible about the first coming of Jesus, there are eight prophecies about the Second Coming of Jesus.

GOOD TO KNOW

For every prophecy in the Bible about the first coming of Jesus, there are eight prophecies about the Second Coming of Jesus.

One message is clear in the Bible: Christ will come back again to Earth. It was Spurgeon who said, "The sound of His approach should be as music to our ears." In fact, I think our very reaction to the Lord's return is a good barometer of where we are spiritually. If you are right with God, you will look forward to the return of Jesus. If you are not right with God, you will dread His return.

It's like the little boy waiting for his dad to get home from work. Usually he was excited, watching through the window for his father's car to pull up in the driveway so he could run out to meet him. But on a day when the boy had been in trouble, he wasn't looking forward to his father's appearance at all. In fact, his mother's ominous words still rang in his ears: "Just wait until your father gets home!" Why had he lost his joy? Because he knew there was something between him and his dad and that he probably would be facing punishment.

I love it when my grandkids see me and run to greet me. They're always so excited. Why? Because I never discipline them. That is not my job. I'm there to be a "grand" parent! To encourage them, and be amazed by them.

I was in a restaurant with my grandson Christopher, his parents, and my wife the other night. "Keefer" (a nickname his sister Allie gave him because she couldn't pronounce *Christopher*) was making quite a mess, at my encouragement. I told my son Jonathan, Christopher's dad, that my job as a grandparent was to encourage creativity and self-expression.

He told me that I sounded like a hippie parent. In other words, I will let the parents deal with the difficult stuff. I just want the grandkids to look forward to my arrival.

That is how we should feel when we think of the return of Jesus to Earth. John wrote in Revelation 22:20, "He who testifies to these things says, 'Surely I am coming quickly.'" And John responds, "Amen. Even so, come, Lord Jesus!" That is what every believer ought to say when they hear that Christ is returning: "Amen. Come, Lord Jesus!"

JUST BEFORE HIS COMING

We've read about what is happening on Earth just prior to the Lord's return—with the devastating bowl judgments and the massive forces in the Battle of Armageddon coming against one another.

But what is happening in Heaven at this time?

Here's the answer: Some indescribably wonderful and awesome things will take place. After the rapture of the church and before the Second Coming of Jesus Christ, the residents of Heaven will experience the judgment seat of Christ and the wedding supper of the Lamb.

Let's follow along with the apostle John as he seeks to put words to these events as best as he can:

> And I heard, as it were, the voice of a great multitude, as the sound of many waters and as the sound of mighty thunderings, saying, "Alleluia! For the Lord God Omnipotent reigns! Let us be glad and rejoice and give Him glory, for the marriage of the Lamb has come, and His wife has made herself ready." And to her it was granted to be arrayed in fine linen, clean and bright, for the fine linen is the righteous acts of the saints.
>
> Then he said to me, "Write: 'Blessed are those who are called to the marriage supper of the Lamb!'" And he said to me, "These are the true sayings of God." And I fell at his feet to worship him. But he said to me, "See that you do not do that! I am your fellow servant, and of your brethren who have the testimony of Jesus. Worship God! For the testimony of Jesus is the spirit of prophecy." (Revelation 19:6–10)

Jesus liked to speak about the marriage supper of the Lamb and referred to it in many of His parables. It's clear in all this imagery that Christ is the bridegroom, and the church is the bride. In 2 Corinthians 11:2, the apostle Paul wrote, "I am jealous for you with a godly jealousy. I promised you to one husband, to Christ, so that I might present you as a pure virgin to him" (NIV). In his letter to the Ephesians, Paul gave this directive: "For husbands, this means love your wives, just as Christ loved the church. He gave up his life for her to make her holy and clean, washed by the cleansing of God's word. He did this to present her to himself as a glorious church without a spot or wrinkle or any other blemish. Instead, she will be holy and without fault" (Ephesians 5:25–27 NLT).

On your wedding day you want to look your best. So if you're a man and you're not married yet, this is not the day to wear your favorite T-shirt with holes in it. You need to buy, borrow, or rent a tux. Ladies, you will want to wear a beautiful bridal gown, and you probably don't want to drive to church in it, stopping off to have a burrito on the way. You don't want to spill any salsa on the gorgeous gown. The big moment comes when those doors open up, and the bride steps forward, probably hanging on to her dad. The bridal march begins, and everyone stands up and turns their attention to her.

At the marriage supper of the Lamb, things will be a little different. It won't be the bride who is the center of attention; it will be the Bridegroom. We will be presented to Him, and we will want to be wearing our best clothing, without spot or wrinkle.

What does this refer to? Verse 8 tells us that she is dressed in fine linen, or the righteous acts of the saints.

When you become a Christian, you are forgiven of all your sins, and the righteousness of Jesus Christ Himself is placed (so to speak) in your spiritual bank account. That is the process we call justification, when we are all made righteous *positionally*.

I, Greg Laurie, right now, am a righteous man.

"Really, Greg?" you might say. "I don't know about that. Are you sure you can say you're all that righteous?"

But wait a minute. I didn't say that I always *act* righteously. I just said that positionally, I am a righteous man. In fact, I'll even take it a step further. This very moment you are reading a book written by a living saint.

I am a saint (you don't have to call me Saint Gregory) just as all who have a relationship with Jesus Christ are saints. *Saint* is another word for a true believer. So when you become a Christian, you not only are forgiven of your sins, but the righteousness of Christ is deposited into your account.

But what about those clean, white-linen, "righteous acts of the saints" with which the bride of Christ adorns herself? This isn't talking about positional righteousness. This is talking about *practical* righteousness, or the righteousness that comes as a result of positional righteousness. This is speaking about what we have actually done with our lives.

The Scriptures declare that "by grace you have been saved through faith, and that not of yourselves; it is the gift of God, not of works, lest anyone should boast" (Ephesians 2:8–9).

However, once you *are* saved, there should be evidence of that salvation; there should be good works in your life. It comes down to this: you can have works without faith, but you cannot have real faith without works. The only way others can tell whether you are a Christian is by watching you. At the end of each day, at the end of each year, and at the end of your life on Earth, you should have something to present to the Lord—a life that (by His enabling) has been lived righteously.

GOOD TO KNOW

Saint is another word for a true believer.

It isn't enough to pray a salvation prayer or walk down an aisle in an evangelistic crusade or church service. There needs to be change in your life and spiritual fruit.

Is there spiritual fruit in your life? Is there evidence in your life that you are a true follower of Jesus? If you were arrested for being a Christian, would there be enough evidence to convict you? By that I don't mean how many Bibles you own or whether you have a fish sticker on your car's back window or bumper.

No, it's more like this. What if we interviewed your spouse, your family, your neighbors, or your friends and asked them, "What evidence do you see in this person's life that he or she is a true believer in Jesus Christ?"

This is what the Bible refers to when it speaks of "the righteous acts of the saints."

THE JUDGMENT SEAT OF CHRIST

After the Rapture and before the Second Coming, there will be an event in Heaven that we all will be a part of. Attendance will be mandatory. It's called the judgment seat of Christ.

Judgment?

Now, this isn't a judgment about whether or not you will get into Heaven. At this point, you already will be there. We might better describe this event as an awards ceremony.

At the Academy Awards ceremony, Hollywood gives out Oscars for people who do the best job of pretending to be someone else. At the heavenly awards ceremony, however, it won't be about pretending; it will be about authenticity. It will be about genuine Christian lives lived out for the glory of God.

It will be about being faithful in the little things.

In Matthew 10:42 Jesus told us that "if anyone gives even a cup of cold water to one of these little ones who is my disciple, truly I tell you, that person will certainly not lose their reward" (NIV). In other passages, Jesus tells us to be faithful in the little things, the secret things, because one day our Father who sees in secret will reward us openly.

What will we be judged for at the judgment seat of Christ? The apostle Paul gave us the answer in 2 Corinthians 5:10: "For we must all appear before the judgment seat of Christ, that each one may receive the things done in the body, according to what he has done, whether good or bad."

You might say, "Wait a second . . . I'm a little confused here. I thought only nonbelievers were going to face judgment."

The Scriptures, however, speak of *two* judgments.

And they are as different as they can be.

There is the Great White Throne judgment spoken of in Revelation 20. That is for nonbelievers only, and it will be terrible beyond imagination. At that judgment, it will be plainly declared to nonbelievers that their names have never been written in the Book of Life, they are not going to Heaven, and they are bound for the lake of fire.

The judgment seat of Christ, however, is for believers. And it won't be about punishment but about rewards. As Jesus said in Revelation 22:12, "Behold, I am coming quickly, and My reward is with Me."

What will be judged at that time? Going back to 2 Corinthians 5:10, you will be judged for what you have done with your life, whether it was good or bad. The word translated *bad* in that passage doesn't speak of something morally or ethically evil. It could be better translated "worthless," or perhaps "empty." One commentator wrote, "He [Jesus] will reveal whether our works have been good or bad ('worthless'). The character of our service will be revealed . . . as well as the motives that impelled us." [44]

The "bad" spoken of here refers to a Christian whose life on Earth has largely been wasted. They still will enter Heaven because they are saved by the grace of God and have put their faith in Jesus. But it will come out at that time that they didn't take advantage of the opportunities God gave them, and they didn't do very much with their lives.

GOOD TO KNOW

The judgment seat of Christ is for believers, and it won't be about punishment but about rewards.

Another way we might say it is that what they have built through the years of their lives won't pass inspection. Paul explained it in those terms in 1 Corinthians 3, beginning with the reminder that Jesus Christ Himself is the only true foundation in life:

> Let each carpenter who comes on the job take care to build on the foundation! Remember, there is only one foundation, the one already laid: Jesus Christ. Take particular care in picking out your building materials. Eventually there is going to be an inspection. If you use cheap or inferior materials, you'll be found out. The inspection will be thorough and rigorous. You won't get by with a thing. If your work passes inspection, fine; if it doesn't, your part of the building will be torn out and started over. But *you* won't be torn out; you'll survive—but just barely. (verses 10–15 msg)

Is that passage encouraging? Well yes, it is. But in another sense, it is very sobering.

One day I will stand before Jesus Christ, and He will look carefully at the building materials I used through the days and years of my life on Earth.

Some of us will pass inspection. The Lord will say, "Well done, good and faithful servant. Enter into the joy of your Lord." Others will hear the Lord say, "You enter in, too, because I love you and bought You with My own blood. But the building of your life really doesn't pass inspection. You could have done so much more."

We are told in 1 Corinthians 9 that we should discipline ourselves in this life so that we won't be disqualified from our race. You don't want to lose your testimony and end up "good for nothing." That's what Jesus meant when He said that if salt loses its saltiness, it isn't good for anything (see Matthew 5:13). What good is unsalted salt? What good is an uncarbonated Coke? (Or for that matter, a nonfat, decaf latte?)

At the Oscars, sometimes a particular movie will wow all the critics and sweep the awards at the ceremony. Will it be that way in Heaven? Will Billy Graham sweep all the awards? Will all the big names in the Bible and church history make a big haul?

Maybe. In fact, I hope they do.

But this intimate time with Jesus won't be about how much you did. It will be about how faithful you were with the tasks and opportunities that God placed in front of you. In that moment, it won't matter what God has called Joe or Jane to do. It will be about *your* life and what the Lord has called *you* to do. If you have been faithful to your task, no matter how small it seems in your own eyes or in the eyes of others, God will reward you.

THE HONEYMOON

The great wedding takes place, and we are presented to the Lord. Now it is time for our honeymoon. Where are we going? To some celestial resort in a distant galaxy? No, we are coming back to Earth with the Lord, and we will witness Him restoring it the way it was meant to be from the very beginning.

Our honeymoon will be the Second Coming of Jesus Christ:

> Now I saw heaven opened, and behold, a white horse. And He who sat on him was called Faithful and True, and in righteousness He judges and makes war. His eyes were like a flame of fire, and on His head were many crowns. He had a name written that no

one knew except Himself. He was clothed with a robe dipped in blood, and His name is called The Word of God. And the armies in heaven, clothed in fine linen, white and clean, followed Him on white horses. Now out of His mouth goes a sharp sword, that with it He should strike the nations. And He Himself will rule them with a rod of iron. He Himself treads the winepress of the fierceness and wrath of Almighty God. And He has on His robe and on His thigh a name written: KING OF KINGS AND LORD OF LORDS. (Revelation 19:11–16)

Verse 11 says that our heavenly Bridegroom is called Faithful and True. This is in contrast to the Devil, who is unfaithful and a liar.

In the eyes of so many in the world, God is never fair in what He does. When people suffer the natural consequences of flaunting God's grace or breaking His commandments, they blame God and call Him unjust.

But He isn't unjust. He is completely just. He is the very definition of justice. He is also faithful and true.

There is one thing we learn about the Lord after we have walked with Him for a while, and it is this: God keeps His promises. *All* His promises. What has He promised us? He has promised to never leave us or forsake us (see Hebrews 13:5). He has promised to bring His peace into our lives (see John 14:27).

> **GOOD TO KNOW**
>
> Our heavenly Bridegroom is called Faithful and True. This is in contrast to the Devil, who is unfaithful and a liar.

And He has promised to come again. In John 14:2–3 Jesus said, "I go to prepare a place for you. And if I go and prepare a place for you, I will come again and receive you to Myself; that where I am, there you may be also."

As Jesus comes back in fulfillment of His promise, He will judge Planet Earth. Whatever judgments fall will be fully deserved and completely just. There will be nothing arbitrary or capricious about this judgment.

Some will say, "How could a God of love bring judgment?"

And I would reply, "How could a God of love *not* bring judgment?" God has clearly declared there are penalties for sin, yet He has offered so many opportunities for people to turn from their sins and receive His offer of full pardon.

The people left on Earth in the Tribulation period who are engaged in the Battle of Armageddon are beyond redemption. Otherwise they would have turned to the Lord and been redeemed. When all is said and done, everyone on the planet will have heard the message and have the opportunity to respond. If they simply refuse to believe, it is their own deliberate decision.

Here are some basic facts about the second coming of Jesus Christ.

When Christ comes back again, it will be public and seen by all.

No one will miss it. Jesus declared, "For the Son of Man in his day will be like the lightning, which flashes and lights up the sky from one end to the other" (Luke 17:24 NIV).

His return will be accompanied by sadness and weeping.

It will be a happy day for Heaven but a sad day for those on Earth. Israel will mourn as they finally realize that Jesus is indeed their Messiah—and always has been. Zechariah 12:10 describes it like this: "Then I will pour out a spirit of grace and prayer on the family of David and on the people of Jerusalem. They will look on me whom they have pierced and mourn for him as for an only son. They will grieve bitterly for him as for a firstborn son who has died" (NLT).

He is coming to bring judgment to Earth.

Some would say that God is too good to punish sin. No, the fact is that God is too good *not* to punish sin. He says in Romans 12:19, "Vengeance is Mine, I will repay."

This, then, is that day.

The day Jesus returns to Earth in glory will be the day of God's righteous vengeance. And He *will* repay. This is the day when righteousness will fill the planet. This day—and this day only—will bring an end to the senseless wars of humanity. No matter how we try, no matter how many human minds labor to find a solution, our world never will wipe out terrorism and violence with military or political solutions. It only will happen when Christ comes back and establishes His kingdom.

Sometimes people get a little confused because we sometimes refer to the return of the Lord as something unexpected and stealthy, like a thief in the night. At other times we speak about it being open and unmistakable, when every eye shall see Him.

So which is it?

The stealthy references refer to the Rapture, when Jesus comes back for His church before the Tribulation. At that time, His people will be transformed in the blink of an eye, and He will gather us together in the clouds and take us to Heaven.

GOOD TO KNOW

Some would say that God is too good to punish sin. No, the fact is that God is too good *not* to punish sin.

At the Second Coming, however, the whole world will see Him.

Revelation 19:11 tells us that He will be riding on a white horse. Back in His triumphal entry to Jerusalem on that first Palm Sunday, Jesus rode a lowly donkey (borrowed, at that). The people cried "Hosanna!" and laid palm branches at His feet. Mere days later, they would turn on Him and cry out, "Crucify Him!"

First they were yelling, "Hail Him, hail Him!"

Not long after that, they were screaming, "Nail Him, nail Him!"

Why did they initially cry "Hosanna!"? The word *hosanna* means "save now." They were essentially saying, "Lord, establish Your kingdom now. Rule and reign now. Get these oppressive Romans out of our country. Give us an independent Israel again. We're ready!"

But He wasn't coming to wear a crown of gold. Not then. He was coming to wear a crown of thorns. He was headed for a Roman cross to die for the sins of the world.

Contrast the coming King of kings on His white horse in Revelation 19:11–16 with the rider of the white horse in Revelation 6:1–2. The latter rider is one of the four horsemen of the apocalypse that we read about earlier—who also sits astride a white horse.

But that is not Jesus Christ; that is the Antichrist.

The Antichrist is an imitator, a knockoff, a deceiver, a great pretender.

The Lord Jesus Christ is the genuine article, riding Air Horse One!

Sometimes people wonder about what Jesus looked like. Even though there are four Gospels, not one of the writers gave us a physical description. Would that have been too much trouble? Couldn't Matthew, Mark, Luke, or John have given us some little hint about His height, His facial features, His eye color, or His hair color? But no, there is nothing.

In Revelation 19, however, there is a description:

> His eyes were like a flame of fire, and on His head were many crowns. He had a name written that no one knew except Himself. He was clothed with a robe dipped in blood, and His name is called The Word of God. (verses 12–13)

His eyes were like a flame of fire.

Have you ever seen fire in someone's eyes? In the eyes of your boss? Your spouse? Your parent? You know that look. It speaks of anger. In this case it is righteous anger, and Jesus is on the cusp of righteous retribution. The Lord is about to bring ultimate judgment on a rebel planet, so His eyes are like flames.

On His head were many crowns.

He has many crowns because He rules over many kingdoms. He is Lord of all. He is sovereign, all-powerful, and all-knowing. He is also our loving, compassionate, forgiving Savior.

His robe is dipped in blood.

Another translation would be "spattered in blood." This may be a reference to the fact that He is coming to bring judgment at the Battle of Armageddon. Then again, it may be a reference to His death on the cross, or perhaps both.

In His first coming He was wrapped in swaddling clothes. In His second coming He will be clothed royally, in a robe spattered with blood.

In His first coming He was surrounded by animals and shepherds. In His second coming He will be surrounded by angels and saints.

In His first coming the door of the inn was closed to Him. In His second coming the door of the Heavens will be open to Him.

In His first coming He was the Lamb of God, sent to die for the sins of the world. In His second coming He is the ferocious Lion of the Tribe of Judah, bringing judgment.

On this day, the day of His second coming, Jesus will be vindicated before everyone. The Bible says that every eye will see Him (see Revelation 1:7). Every knee will bow. Every tongue will confess that Jesus Christ is Lord (see Philippians 2:10–11).

This is *that* day.

OH, BY THE WAY . . .

I have some exciting news for you.

Are you ready for this?

When the King of kings rides out of Heaven on a white horse, *He won't be alone.* Revelation 19 says, "And the armies in heaven, clothed in fine linen, white and clean, followed Him on white horses" (verse 14).

Who are these armies? We know that the Lord will appear with His holy angels, so I think we can assume they will be part of His army (see Matthew 16:27). But Enoch, quoted in the book of Jude, tells us something more. He prophesied, "Behold, the Lord comes with ten thousands of His saints, to execute judgment on all" (Jude 1:14–15).

As one commentator put it, "At the Rapture, He will come for the saints; at the Second Coming, He will come with the saints." [45]

Saints, remember, are all true believers in Jesus Christ. If you have received Jesus as your Savior, that includes you! In Colossians 3:4, Paul tells us that "when Christ who is our life appears, then you also will appear with Him in glory."

When Jesus returns at His second coming, you will return, too.

When Jesus rides through the skies on His white horse, you will ride, too.

You won't be watching from the grandstands; you will be there, with Him.

Notice this army isn't armed. There are no weapons—no swords or spears. In fact, it is interesting how Jesus brings judgment on humanity with just a word: "Now out of His mouth goes a sharp sword, that with it He should strike the nations" (Revelation 19:15).

Our King will do the fighting, and we will stand back and watch in awe.

Just think of the power of God's words. In the beginning God spoke our world and the universe into existence. God said, "Let there be light," and there was light. When Jesus was out on the Sea of Galilee in a violent storm, He said, "Peace, be still!" and stopped the storm in its tracks. That same voice speaks here, bringing final judgment on Earth.

You would think that in the midst of all this, people would be repenting. Right? Here is Jesus Christ, breaking through the clouds, followed by a heavenly army. But what happens? The people of Earth take what little strength they have left and use it to attack Him. In verse 19 we read, "And I saw the beast, the kings of the earth, and their armies, gathered together to make war against Him who sat on the horse and against His army."

GOOD TO KNOW

There are no weapons— no swords or spears. Jesus brings judgment on humanity with just a word.

Are you kidding me? It just shows how wicked and how thoroughly deceived these people really are.

The battle, however, is over before it begins. Verses 20–21 say,

> Then the beast was captured, and with him the false prophet who worked signs in his presence, by which he deceived those who received the mark of the beast and those who worshiped his image. These two were cast alive into the lake of fire burning with brimstone. And the rest were killed with the sword which proceeded from the mouth of Him who sat on the horse.

Notice that the beast and the false prophet are sent to the pit straightaway. They have the dubious honor, or distinction, of being the first ones cast into the lake of fire. Everyone else has to wait for the Great White Throne judgment.

"THE SPIRIT OF PROPHECY"

There was John, an old man, exiled on the barren island of Patmos, receiving all this revelation from an angel.

Can you imagine how overwhelming this must have been?

In Revelation 19:10 John admits that he got a little turned around with this angel, saying, "At this I fell at his feet to worship him" (NIV).

The angel, however, quickly put a stop to that, saying, "Don't do that! I am a fellow servant with you and with your brothers and sisters who hold to the testimony of Jesus. Worship God!" The angel was saying, "Stop that! Do you want to get us both in trouble? Worship God!" Then the angel concluded with this important statement: "For it is the Spirit of prophecy who bears testimony to Jesus" (verse 10 NIV).

What does that mean? It means that if you read the book of Revelation but don't grow in your love for Jesus, then you have missed the point. Remember, Revelation isn't just about the unveiling of our future; it is also an unveiling of Jesus.

He is the centerpiece and the star and the focus of Revelation.

And He should be the centerpiece and the star and the focus of our lives as well. It is all about Jesus.

Prophecy is not given to inflate our brains. It is given to enlarge our hearts and draw us closer to God.

THREE TAKEAWAY TRUTHS
- How we feel about Christ's return is a test of our spiritual health.
- We can look forward to the judgment seat of Christ, knowing we will be rewarded for the things we have done for Him on Earth.
- Jesus will not be alone when He returns; we will return with Him, in triumph!

CHAPTER TWENTY-THREE

Turning the World Right–Side Up

Blessed and holy is he who has part in the first resurrection. Over such the second death has no power, but they shall be priests of God and of Christ, and shall reign with Him a thousand years.
(Revelation 20:6)

IN THIS CHAPTER

- God does not abandon but restores His creation.
- When Heaven and Earth become one
- The Millennial reign of Christ
- Satan will be bound.
- How we can ultimately experience world peace

Years ago I had a dog named Irlo. I didn't name him. He came pre-named. He was a German shepherd, and without question he was the best dog I have ever had.

One night after Cathe had gone to bed, I took Irlo out for his last walk of the evening. As we were walking along, Irlo suddenly saw a cat. He took off like a shot after the cat while I watched, and then he suddenly stopped.

I thought to myself, *That's a pretty bold cat to just stop like that, with eighty-five pounds of German shepherd bearing down on him.* Then I heard some kind of a hissing sound and watched in amazement as Irlo did a quick 180 and came galloping back toward me.

The cat began to trot away again, unharmed and unconcerned. Only it wasn't a cat. It had a white stripe down its back.

Irlo had taken a direct skunk hit to the face, and he was running back to me, his guardian, in real distress. But I didn't want him near me, and I certainly didn't want him in the house. I had left our front door open and knew, in an instant, that he would run for the house. I tried to outrun him and get that front door closed, but he was too fast. Irlo bolted right by me and raced into the living room. Arriving breathless at the house, I opened the back door and immediately exiled him to the back yard, where he began rolling around on the grass.

My wife, who was upstairs in our bedroom asleep with the door closed, and who has a supersonic nose at the best of times, woke up and smelled the stench. "What is that?" she said. "What is that smell?" It was the smell of a dog covered in skunk stench running through our house.

In fact, it took a long time to get that smell out. And it took more time than you might imagine to make Irlo acceptable in our house again.

That is what sin is like. To this very day, our whole world is infected with the stench of sin. Frankly, it smells so bad that it's hard to breathe sometimes. It started in the Garden of Eden and continues unabated down to the twenty-first century.

Since the beginning of time when our first parents chose to go their own way, Satan has been allowed to have his way. The Bible calls him "the god of this world" and "the prince of the power of the air." It seems that our whole world is infected with the stench of sin, with no cure in sight. You can try to escape it, just as my dog tried to roll around in the grass to free himself from the stench of the skunk, but it doesn't work.

But one day God will get rid of that smell forever. When Jesus returns, He will put the world to rights, restoring it to the beauty of ancient Eden.

HEAVEN ON EARTH?

After He returns in glory, riding a white horse and crowned with many crowns, Jesus will rule and reign over this planet for a thousand years.

This will be the period known as the Millennium. Some have pointed out that the word *millennium* never appears in the Bible. That may be true, but the Scriptures do speak of Christ's reigning for a thousand years—which is the same thing. It's what the word *millennium* means.

Have you ever heard someone say, "It was like Heaven on Earth"? You usually say that when you have encountered or experienced something unusually pleasant, beautiful, or poignant.

A friend of mine finally got around to trying a burger at my favorite burger place in the entire world. When I eagerly asked him how he enjoyed the experience, his answer didn't disappoint me. He smiled and said, "It was a taste of Heaven."

We use Heaven as a point of reference when we're trying to describe something way beyond our usual experience or expectations.

Someday, however, Heaven really will come to Earth.

A new world is coming—not just up in some distant heavenly realm, but when Heaven and Earth actually become one. Sometimes Christians will say, "When we die or when we are raptured, we'll be in Heaven with the Lord forever."

But that's not technically true.

As a believer in Christ, you will be in Heaven until the Second Coming, and then you will return to Earth with Him, and Heaven and Earth will become one.

God will not abandon His original creation. No, He will restore it.

One my day my wife Cathe was driving along with our son Jonathan, who was probably around three at the time. She was talking to him about the end times, the rapture of the church, and how we would be caught up to meet the Lord in the air.

Jonathan was listening, trying to take it in and process this information. Cathe told me later that the more she talked about these things, the quieter Jonathan became.

Finally he said, "Mom, I don't *want* to go to Heaven! I don't want to leave this beautiful world that God has made."

It's an understandable response, isn't it? Jonathan's whole point of reference was this world. And, for the most part, so is ours. But we need to grow in our understanding that we will not only leave this place, but we will come back again to a world far better than the one we left.

GOOD TO KNOW

God will not abandon His original creation. He will restore it.

In his excellent book *Heaven*, my friend Randy Alcorn writes these words: "We won't go to Heaven and leave Earth behind. Rather, God will bring Heaven and Earth together into the same dimension, with no wall of separation, no armed angels to guard Heaven's perfection from sinful mankind." [46]

Have you ever seen a totally restored classic car cruise down the street? Maybe a '57 Chevy or '67 Mustang that looked like it just rolled off the showroom floor? It catches your eye, doesn't it? You say, "Beautiful! That's incredible." Most of us love to see something restored to its original condition.

Our God is into restoration. He restores broken lives. He restores lost hopes. He will even restore our aging bodies one day, making them brand-new and better than ever. He's even into restoring our planet, this imperfect world that we call home. According to Ephesians 1:10, God's perfect plan is to bring all things in Heaven and on Earth together under one head, Jesus Christ. Peter preached in Acts 3:21 that Christ must remain in Heaven until the time comes for God to restore everything, as He promised long ago through His holy prophets.

In *Heaven*, Randy Alcorn also points out that God's ultimate plan is to make Earth into Heaven and Heaven into Earth. Just as He removed the wall that divided God from man when Jesus died on the cross, so He also will demolish the wall that separates Earth from Heaven.

Global peace? Yes, it will finally come when the Prince of Peace Himself sits on the throne. The pseudo peace of the Antichrist will only last for three-and-a-half years. Then there will be war like we have never seen on this planet before.

When Christ returns, however, He will bring lasting peace.

As Hal Lindsey pointed out, from the beginning of time humanity has searched for peace. We have written about peace, preached about peace, joined peace movements, marched for peace, given prizes for peace, gone on hunger strikes for peace, and have even gone to war for peace. (World War I was called the "war to end all wars." But it didn't work out very well because World War II followed after about twenty years.) When you hear of someone who was arrested for disturbing the peace, you wonder if there really was any peace to be disturbed.

There are people today who have bumper stickers on their cars that say, "Visualize world peace." And then they cut you off on the freeway.

One day, however, there will be authentic peace. It won't be brought about by a United Nations mandate or by any action of any government anywhere. God Himself will bring it. It will happen when the Creator returns, repossesses what is rightfully His, and hangs a sign over this war-weary planet that says UNDER NEW MANAGEMENT.

Jesus is coming again. And when He comes, we will come with Him.

THE MILLENNIUM

Just as the massive forces engage each other in the Valley of Megiddo in that great conflict we know as the Battle of Armageddon, Christ Himself returns, riding on a white horse and followed by the armies of Heaven (including you and me).

In His first order of business, the Lord removes the Antichrist and the false prophet from the planet and throws them into the lake of fire. Even Satan himself doesn't get thrown into the pit that fast.

With His return to Earth, the one-thousand-year reign of Jesus Christ begins:

Then I saw an angel coming down from heaven, having the key to the bottomless pit and a great chain in his hand. He laid hold of the dragon, that serpent of old, who is the Devil and Satan, and bound him for a thousand years; and he cast him into the bottomless pit, and shut him up, and set a seal on him, so that he should deceive the nations no more till the thousand years were finished. But after these things he must be released for a little while.

And I saw thrones, and they sat on them, and judgment was committed to them. Then I saw the souls of those who had been beheaded for their witness to Jesus and for the word of God, who had not worshiped the beast or his image, and had not received his mark on their foreheads or on their hands. And they lived and reigned with Christ for a thousand years. (Revelation 20:1–4)

What the church has been praying for, for two thousand years, finally will be fulfilled: "Your kingdom come. Your will be done on earth as it is in heaven" (Matthew 6:10).

The first priority? Chaining up Satan and throwing him into the bottomless pit. This is the day of the Devil's humbling. Though he commanded a vast network of demonic powers and ruled over principalities and spiritual might in high places, he will be bound by a simple angel and cast down.

Satan won't go into the lake of fire at this time. In essence, he will be placed in a holding area until God finally settles his case forever.

Lucifer, the son of the morning, the high-ranking angel who once wanted God's throne, who wanted to be worshiped instead of being a worshiper, will be bound and imprisoned. The prophet Isaiah describes this future scene with these words:

> "How you are fallen from heaven,
> O Lucifer, son of the morning!
> How you are cut down to the ground,
> You who weakened the nations!
> For you have said in your heart:
> 'I will ascend into heaven,
> I will exalt my throne above the stars of God;
> I will also sit on the mount of the congregation
> On the farthest sides of the north;
> I will ascend above the heights of the clouds,
> I will be like the Most High.'
> Yet you shall be brought down to Sheol,
> To the lowest depths of the Pit." (Isaiah 14:12–15)

The passage goes on to say, "Everyone there will stare at you and ask, 'Can this be the one who shook the earth and made the kingdoms of the world tremble? Is this the one who destroyed the world and made it into a wasteland?" (verses 16–17 NLT).

Those last two verses make me wonder if we will have some way of viewing the vanquished Satan in his imprisonment during the Millennium. Maybe we will look at him and say something like, "Is that the creature who caused so much trouble ever since the Garden of Eden? He's in the pit now, and he'll be there for a thousand years."

Up to this point, the Devil may have imagined that he was on some kind of a roll, as events seemed to turn in his favor. All the hosts of fallen angels, the Antichrist, the false prophet, and a world full of nonbelieving people were under his dominion. His deceptions had seemingly won over everyone on Earth, as we read in Revelation 13:3–4: "The whole earth was amazed and followed after the beast; they worshiped the dragon because he gave his authority to the beast; and they worshiped the beast" (NASB).

Everything is going Satan's way. The great deceiver may even momentarily deceive himself into believing that his long rebellion against God finally would succeed.

But then Christ comes again, and all Satan's plans come crashing down in a moment. The Lord effectively says, "Enough. Your party is over. You're going down."

Satan's temporary holding place is the bottomless pit, or the abyss. Earlier in Revelation we read of demonic powers coming out of the pit. But they will be locked away again, along with their commander in chief.

Some people imagine that the Devil is ruling in Hell right now, just as God is ruling from His throne in Heaven. But that is not true. Satan is not ruling in Hell. Hell will be his final destination, along with all those who have followed him.

We might refer to this thousand-year period when we rule and reign with Christ as phase one of God's kingdom rule on Earth. Let's look at Revelation 20:4 again: "I saw thrones, and they sat on them, and judgment was committed to them. . . . And they lived and reigned with Christ for a thousand years."

Jesus told us this was going to happen. In Matthew 19:28 He said, "I assure you that when the world is made new and the Son of Man sits upon his glorious throne, you who have been my followers will also sit on twelve thrones, judging the twelve tribes of Israel" (NLT).

Earlier, in Revelation 2:26–27, Jesus said, "And he who overcomes, and keeps My works until the end, to him I will give power over the nations—'He shall rule them with a rod of iron; they shall be dashed to pieces like the potter's vessels.'" In other words, we will rule with the Lord over the Earth.

You might ask, "But who will we be ruling?"

During this thousand-year period, when Christ reigns and the world is filled with the knowledge of the Lord, there still will be unbelievers in the world.

GOOD TO KNOW

Satan is not ruling in Hell. Hell will be his final destination, along with all those who have followed him.

At that time, however, we will be in our glorified bodies, and we will be temptation-proof and sin-proof. (I love that!)

Not everyone will be wiped out in the Battle of Armageddon; the world still will be populated with survivors of the Tribulation period. At that time, everyone will come under the rule of King Jesus.

These survivors will have children and grandchildren and great-grandchildren as the thousand years pass. In the end, after Satan is released from his captivity, he will gather the descendants of the Tribulation's survivors in one, final rebellion against God. This just goes to show that even in a perfect environment, people with sinful hearts still will make wrong choices.

I bring this up because sometimes you will hear people say that if we could just change the culture and the environment, then we could change people's hearts. But that sort of outside-in approach will never, ever work. As the prophet Jeremiah said, "The heart is deceitful above all things, and desperately wicked; who can know it?" (Jeremiah 17:9).

Even after ten centuries of the magnificent reign of Jesus Christ in a restored world, humanity still will rebel against God.

A KING AND HIS INVESTORS

Jesus told a parable in Luke 19 that speaks to this matter of Christians ruling with Christ during those millennium years. What determines what you and

I will do during this amazing thousand-year reign? Is there any connection between what we do in this life and what we will do then?

The answer is yes, and here is the parable that speaks to this question:

"A nobleman was called away to a distant empire to be crowned king and then return. Before he left, he called together ten of his servants and divided among them ten pounds of silver, saying, 'Invest this for me while I am gone.' But his people hated him and sent a delegation after him to say, 'We do not want him to be our king.'

"After he was crowned king, he returned and called in the servants to whom he had given the money. He wanted to find out what their profits were. The first servant reported, 'Master, I invested your money and made ten times the original amount!'

"'Well done!' the king exclaimed. 'You are a good servant. You have been faithful with the little I entrusted to you, so you will be governor of ten cities as your reward.'

"The next servant reported, 'Master, I invested your money and made five times the original amount.'

"'Well done!' the king said. 'You will be governor over five cities.'

"But the third servant brought back only the original amount of money and said, 'Master, I hid your money and kept it safe. I was afraid because you are a hard man to deal with, taking what isn't yours and harvesting crops you didn't plant.'

"'You wicked servant!' the king roared. 'Your own words condemn you. If you knew that I'm a hard man who takes what isn't mine and harvests crops I didn't plant, why didn't you deposit my money in the bank? At least I could have gotten some interest on it.'

"Then, turning to the others standing nearby, the king ordered, 'Take the money from this servant, and give it to the one who has ten pounds.'

"'But, master,' they said, 'he already has ten pounds!'

"'Yes,' the king replied, 'and to those who use well what they are given, even more will be given. But from those who do nothing, even what little they have will be taken away.'" (Luke 19:12–26 NLT)

I guess that Jesus didn't believe in the currently popular concepts of redistribution of wealth and that everyone who participates gets a trophy. The rewards in this story were proportionate to the faithfulness of the stewards.

Clearly, the nobleman who is crowned king is a picture of the Lord Himself. You and I, followers of Jesus, are the servants to whom He gave the resources and responsibilities. What these servants did with their silver determined their future reward and responsibilities. The first servant was appointed to govern ten cities, and the second servant was made responsible for five cities.

GOOD TO KNOW

Our faithfulness to Christ *now* will be somehow connected to what we will be privileged to do *then*.

Someone might ask me, "Greg, do you think we're intended to take this literally—that one day we might have the opportunity to rule over cities on the restored Earth?"

Why not? That certainly could be the case. But one thing is obvious: our faithfulness to Christ *now* will be somehow connected to what we will be privileged to do *then*.

There are three kinds of people in this passage: the super faithful, the less faithful, and the unfaithful. Which category do you think best describes you? If you are a Christian, you fit into one.

Both the super faithful and less faithful received a measure of money called a pound, which was equal to one hundred days' wages for a laborer. Essentially it was three months' wages. So how was one servant able to make ten times as much as the guy who made nothing? The story doesn't say, but he seemed to have no limitations whatsoever. He dove in to his tasks whole hog and ended up being very productive.

The second guy was a bit more on the conservative side. Even so, he was still commended and rewarded. Though he might not have been as effective as the first servant, he accomplished something, and the king was pleased.

There are people who just go for it as Christians. They want to do great things for God, takes risks, and give it their all. The young missionary Jim Elliot was one of those people. He once said, "Wherever you are, *be all there*. Live to the hilt every situation you believe to be the will of God." [47]

Then there are other people who love the Lord and want to serve Him, but they are more cautious, careful, and conservative. While some people are setting the world on fire, these folks are still looking for a match. Even so, the Lord is pleased to use them, and they accomplish some wonderful things in His strength.

The third servant in the parable is not only unproductive, but he has the audacity to impugn his master. Look again at verses 20–21:

> "But the third servant brought back only the original amount of money and said, 'Master, I hid your money and kept it safe. I was afraid because you are a hard man to deal with.'"

Even when the day of reckoning arrived, there was no sense of regret on his part, no sorrow over his lack of productivity. Instead, he actually blamed his boss for his shortcomings. Sounds familiar, doesn't it? He sounds like a lot of people in our day. *It's not my fault. I know that I was fired from my last ten jobs, but it couldn't be helped. All my bosses were unfair and prejudiced against me. . . . My teachers in school were no good and didn't make it interesting for me. . . . I had a tough family life. . . .* And so it goes. These are people who always will blame others and never take the responsibility for their own failures.

In the same way, there are people today who blame God for their troubles, believing Him to be harsh, unjust, or difficult to follow. The problem lies with their faulty view of God; they don't really know Him, and they reject a warped caricature of Him. Some people's view of God goes back to the relationship they had with their earthly father. Maybe your dad was distant and aloof, harsh and angry, or mean and abusive. Or maybe he just wasn't there. Without intending to, you may let that relationship color your view of your Father in Heaven.

GOOD TO KNOW

Our view of God affects everything we do in life.

I never had a dad growing up. But I will tell you this: I've known my heavenly Father for many years now, and He has always been faithful to me. He has never been inconsistent with me. He has always dealt with me in love. No, I don't always understand or even necessarily agree with what He does in my life, but I have submitted to Him because I know that He is looking out for my best interests. I believe that our view of God affects everything we do in life.

It was A. W. Tozer who said, "Nothing twists and deforms a soul more than a low or unworthy conception of God."

The proper motivation for serving the Lord should be a love for God. As the apostle Paul wrote, "For Christ's love compels us" (2 Corinthians 5:14 NIV).

A CONTEMPORARY SETTING

Let's try to put this parable from Luke 19 into a more contemporary setting. Let's imagine that you have ten identical cars that you want to sell. So you get ten people together and give them each one of the cars. Again, everything in the cars is the same: same model, same mileage, same features, same everything.

So you say to these ten people, "You each have a car to sell. I'm going on a trip, and I want all of you to sell these cars and be as productive as you possibly can. I will check in with you in one month when I return."

When you get back, however, you find out that the first guy hasn't tried to sell your car at all. He has simply driven it, racking up substantial miles on it and even getting into a couple of fender benders. You can see right away that there has been body work done on it—and not of the best quality. Looking at the car, you realize that it is worth less than it was when you left a month before. Not only did this individual fail to sell your car, but he also devalued it.

The second guy did a little better. He took your car, sold it, made a tidy profit, bought a couple more cars, and sold them as well. He ended up making you a nice profit.

The accomplishments of the third guy, however, made your jaw drop. He sold your car, bought two more cars, and sold them. With the profits, he bought five more cars, sold them, and purchased ten more, selling them as well. With all the money he made, he bought a Ferrari dealership with your name on it, with a line of people going around the block.

Now, whom do you want to promote in your company? These three employees all had the same opportunity with the same car. One excelled, one didn't excel as much, and one did nothing.

What does this mean to us? Everyone is given the same thing in this parable, and that is how we have to consider its application. What do we have that everyone else has?

We have our lives.

We all have this time span on Earth, graciously given to us by God, who is the Lord of life. But here's the question: What am I supposed to do with my life? According to the Scriptures, I am placed here on this planet to glorify and honor God and to bring forth spiritual fruit. In fact, in Heaven one of the songs we will sing is, "Thou art worthy, O Lord, to receive glory and honour and power: for thou hast created all things, and for thy pleasure they are and were created" (Revelation 4:11 KJV).

I exist for the pleasure of God. I was created to bring glory to Him and to produce spiritual fruit. Jesus said, "You did not choose me, but I chose you and appointed you so that you might go and bear fruit—fruit that will last. . . . This is to my Father's glory, that you bear much fruit, showing yourselves to be my disciples" (John 15:16, 8 NIV).

So here's the deal: I don't get to determine how long I will live on this earth. Yes, I might try. I might eat kale and tofu and take handfuls of vitamins and do all the right things.

But those things won't extend my life. They might increase the quality of my life, and I might feel better, but the length of my life is up to God. God decides when a person is born, and God decides when that person will die. I have nothing to say about those things. The Bible says there is "a time to be born, and a time to die" (Ecclesiastes 3:2).

So what do I do with the brief life in the sun that God has given me? The Bible says that we are here to glorify God. Anything less is a waste of our lives and our potential. Let's not fritter away our years on Earth in trivial pursuits, running after empty preoccupations. Let's invest our lives in the pursuit of God.

We have our money.

The way we view and handle our money is a direct reflection of the priorities of our lives. Jesus said, "For where your treasure is, there your heart will be also" (Matthew 6:21).

You will invest in your passions. If you want to find out what an individual really cares about, take a tour of his or her checkbook or expense account. See where a person is spending money, and you'll know where his or her interests and passions lie.

We have all been given money. Yes, some make more money than others, and some are more financially skilled or successful than others, but here is the one thing we all need to keep in mind: we need to be wise stewards over what God has entrusted to us and invest generously into the work of the kingdom of God.

God will bless generosity. In 2 Corinthians 9:7–8, the apostle Paul writes, "You must each decide in your heart how much to give. And don't give reluctantly or in response to pressure. 'For God loves a person who gives cheerfully.' And God will generously provide all you need. Then you will always have everything you need and plenty left over to share with others" (NLT).

Some say, "I can't afford to give." Really? I can't afford *not* to give. Giving isn't just for rich people; it's for all people. Everyone should invest in the kingdom of Christ.

Here is something to consider: perhaps one of the reasons you are having financial struggles is because you haven't honored the Lord in your giving.

"So what are you saying, Greg? That if I give money to God's work, He will make me rich?"

No, I'm not saying that. But there are certainly Scripture passages that connect the two. Above, you read the 2 Corinthians passage where Paul said that if you give cheerfully, God will generously provide all you need, with plenty left over to share with others.

In Malachi, the last book of the Old Testament, God tells His people, "Bring the whole tithe into the storehouse, that there may be food in my house. Test me in this . . . and see if I will not throw open the floodgates of heaven and pour out so much blessing that there will not be room enough to store it" (Malachi 3:10 NIV).

We all have this ability to give; we all have resources. And God watches very carefully how we invest those resources.

We have the sacred trust of the gospel message.

Jesus has given us the command to go into all the world and preach the gospel. Everyone is called to do that. Everyone should get the gospel out. In his letter to his young associate, Timothy, the apostle Paul spoke of "the glorious gospel of the blessed God which was committed to my trust" (1 Timothy 1:11). Again, in 1 Thessalonians 2:4 he wrote, "But as we have been approved by God to be entrusted with the gospel, even so we speak, not as pleasing men, but God who tests our hearts."

God has given you your life.

God has given you your money.

God has given you the gospel.

We all have those things as Christians. Some don't have more gospel than others; we all have the same amount. Am I getting that gospel out? Are you?

That is my call as a follower of Jesus. Every day of our lives, we need to think about our family, friends, neighbors, and coworkers. Whatever our sphere of influence might be, we need to be doing what we can to spread the Good News about salvation and new life in Jesus Christ.

Just like the nobleman in Jesus' story, Jesus will hold us accountable one day for how we have invested the resources He has placed in our hands. And though we may not understand all the implications of those moments when He evaluates our lives, we can know this: it will have an impact on our eternity.

THREE TAKEAWAY TRUTHS

- True peace will only come to this Earth when Christ establishes His reign.
- Love should be the motivation in everything we do for Jesus.
- All believers are stewards with what God has entrusted them and will be rewarded for what they did with what they received.

CHAPTER TWENTY-FOUR
The Final Judgment of Humanity

And I saw the dead, great and small, standing before the throne, and books were opened. Another book was opened, which is the book of life. The dead were judged according to what they had done as recorded in the books.
(Revelation 20:12 NIV)

IN THIS CHAPTER
- What life will be like during the Millennium
- Satan's final rebellion and defeat
- Understanding what the Bible says about the "second death"
- The purpose of the Great White Throne judgment

Our youngest granddaughter, Allie, had a little rabbit named Fuzzie (who was actually named by Allie's sister, Rylie).

Fuzzie lived in a fairly large cage. Yes, I know, it might seem unfair to put a rabbit in a cage, but it was a pretty nice cage as cages go.

I actually think Fuzzie liked this cage, and I'll tell you why.

Early on we had to teach little Allie the proper protocol for holding a rabbit, because when she took her bunny out of the cage, she sometimes grabbed him by the head. So we would say, "No, Allie, you need to support his bottom, like this."

Allie loved Fuzzie and had lots of fun with him, squealing with delight every time he came out of his cage. And by the time she was done with him, Fuzzie was more than ready to go home. How do I know this? Because as I was carrying him back to his cage one day, he suddenly leaped out of my arms and ran for the open door of his little sanctuary, which was about three feet away. I closed the cage door, and Fuzzie seemed to sigh with relief.

Some people might have thought Fuzzie's cage kept him confined, but the truth is that the cage kept Allie out!

In some ways, this reminds me of how some people view the Bible, with all its absolutes and commandments. They will say, "The Bible tries to keep us from having fun. The Bible keeps us from living life to the fullest."

But the exact opposite is true.

A wise person knows that when the Word of God warns us against something, it's for our *good*. Some people, however, never quite get that and end up having to learn the hard way.

The Bible says, "No good thing will He withhold from those who walk uprightly" (Psalm 84:11). If the Lord holds it back from you, it's because He loves you.

In Revelation 20, the account of the millennial reign of Christ, people on Earth have to learn the hard way.

WORLD PEACE ... FINALLY

In the previous chapter we spoke about how the Devil will be chained up and locked in the pit through the entire thousand years of Christ's reign. During that time, he won't be able to tempt anyone, deceive anyone, harass anyone, or accuse anyone. So things couldn't be better, right?

Yes, but even so, there will be a huge rebellion against God.

How is that even possible?

First of all, it won't involve you or me or anyone who returns to Earth with Jesus. We will be in our glorified, resurrection bodies at this point, and sin or temptation won't be able to touch us. At the same time, however, there will be people in normal, earthly bodies who have survived the Tribulation and come under the rule of King Jesus. These people will have children, and their children will have children. It will be the descendants of these people, a thousand years later, who will participate in a final rebellion of humanity against God.

But let's back up a little before we discuss that rebellion and consider what life will be like in the Millennium. What will our world be like when Jesus comes back to rule and reign over the Earth?

There finally will be world peace.

There will be no more war, no more conflicts, no more threats, no more rockets fired across borders, no more terrorism, and no more nukes.

When Christ comes back again, all wars will cease. Isaiah 2:4 tells us that "the Lord will settle international disputes; all the nations will convert their weapons of war into implements of peace. Then at the last all wars will stop and all military training will end" (TLB).

> **GOOD TO KNOW**
> When Christ comes back again, all wars will cease.

There will be joy, happiness, and no more disabilities.

There will be no more depression or mental illness. There won't be any wheelchairs, walkers, or crutches. No one will be blind or deaf. Isaiah 35:5–6 says, "When he comes, he will open the eyes of the blind and unplug the ears of the deaf. The lame will leap like a deer, and those who cannot speak will sing for joy!" (NLT).

Mortal human beings on Earth will live long lives.

Those of us who return to Earth from Heaven with Christ will live forever. But the mortal men and women who live on Earth will have extended human life. Isaiah 65:20 says, "No longer will babies die when only a few days old. No longer will adults die before they have lived a full life. No longer will people be considered old at one hundred!" (NLT).

It may be that life expectancies will be extended into the hundreds of years as they were in early biblical times.

The animal kingdom will be subdued.

Those of us who are animal lovers will especially enjoy this. All the animals of Earth will be completely tame and docile:

In that day the wolf and the lamb will live together;
the leopard will lie down with the baby goat.
The calf and the yearling will be safe with the lion,
and a little child will lead them all.
The cow will graze near the bear.
The cub and the calf will lie down together.
The lion will eat hay like a cow.
The baby will play safely near the hole of a cobra.
Yes, a little child will put its hand in a nest of deadly snakes without
harm. (Isaiah 11:6–8 NLT)

There won't be any zoos or wild animal parks, and we will have no fear of encountering bears or mountain lions on some path through the forest.

I have always loved animals. I was over in Africa a number of years ago and went on a little safari to see the animals in the wild. We rode in a truck with an open top, and on one occasion our guide drove right up to a pride of lions. They were only yards away from us, and they looked magnificent. There was a male, a female, and some little cubs.

The lions didn't seem bothered by us at all. If they had wanted to, they could have jumped into the back of our open truck and shredded us. I asked the guide, "Why don't the lions attack?"

"They don't see you as a threat," he replied. "But you have to stay in the truck, or they might change their minds."

"No problem," I said. "I'll stay in the truck!"

Unfortunately, there was a drunk guy on the tour who kept saying he wanted to "get out and pet the lions." He was literally trying to climb out of the back of the truck while the guide was saying, "Sir, no . . . you can't." It occurred to me that if one of the lions happened to eat this guy, the lion would have been drunk for a week.

In the Millennium, however, we will be able to pet the lions.

There will be universal justice and righteousness.

There won't be any more corrupt lawyers, activist judges, unjust legal actions, or frivolous lawsuits. In Psalm 72:2–3, 4 we read: "He will judge Your people with righteousness, and Your poor with justice. The mountains will bring peace to the people. . . . He will bring justice to the poor of the people; He will save the children of the needy, and will break in pieces the oppressor."

The curse that has been on humanity because of sin will be lifted. Romans 8:19–21 says, "For all creation is waiting eagerly for that future day when God will reveal who his children really are. Against its will, all creation was subjected to God's curse. But with eager hope, the creation looks forward to the day when it will join God's children in glorious freedom from death and decay" (NLT).

Holiness will prevail.

The whole world will be filled with the knowledge of the Lord. Isaiah 35:8 says, "A great road will go through that once deserted land. It will be named the Highway of Holiness. Evil-minded people will never travel on it. It will be only for those who walk in God's ways" (NLT).

We have hundreds of freeways and highways going in many different directions here in our part of the world, but there aren't any roads like *that* one. I'm looking forward to walking the length of that great highway, surrounded on all sides by people who love and fear the great King over all of Earth.

Trouble in Paradise

A thousand years seems like a long time, but in comparison to eternity, it's just the blink of an eye. And as difficult as it may be for us to comprehend it, trouble and conspiracies will ripple across the world as the Millennium draws to a close.

> Now when the thousand years have expired, Satan will be released from his prison and will go out to deceive the nations which are in the four corners of the earth, Gog and Magog, to gather them

together to battle, whose number is as the sand of the sea. They went up on the breadth of the earth and surrounded the camp of the saints and the beloved city [Jerusalem]. And fire came down from God out of heaven and devoured them. The devil, who deceived them, was cast into the lake of fire and brimstone where the beast and the false prophet are. And they will be tormented day and night forever and ever. (Revelation 20:7–10)

Satan will deceive the descendants of the original survivors of the Tribulation period. These individuals will still have sinful natures, and at the end of time, in Satan's last deception, they will be drawn into a final, futile rebellion against God.

This just reminds us how dark the human heart really is.

Sometimes people will insist that if we could just change a person's environment, we would change the person. They will say, "The reason this person exhibits these behaviors is because of their poverty, their surroundings, or their deprived upbringing."

But that isn't true, and this final rebellion in Revelation 20 proves it. The Millennium will be the best time that the world has seen since the Garden of Eden. Our restored Earth will be as close as you can get to Heaven itself.

GOOD TO KNOW

In Satan's last deception, people will be drawn into a final, futile rebellion against God.

Christ Himself will be running the show, along with Christians who will be in their resurrection bodies. Righteousness, joy, justice, and abundance will fill the planet.

And after a thousand years, there still will be a rebellion. Seriously? Why? How could this be?

The answer is twofold: Satan will still be Satan, the great deceiver and the father of lies. When he is released, he will revert to form and find a way to deceive multitudes of people. Second, people will allow themselves to be deceived because their hearts are wicked.

Ecclesiastes 9:3 says, "The hearts of the sons of men are full of evil and insanity is in their hearts throughout their lives" (NASB). We, too, have that potential for madness and evil, if we allow ourselves to be controlled by our sinful natures instead of the Holy Spirit.

How could such a massive rebellion against God occur in such an environment?

It won't be the first time.

The first rebellion against God happened in Heaven, of all places, among the angels. Lucifer, a high-ranking angel, rebelled against the Lord, even though he was in the very presence of God in all His glory. Lucifer must have been one persuasive angel, because a third of the angels followed him in his rebellion.

The next great rebellion happened in the Garden of Eden. Adam and Eve were in paradise, enjoying daily conversations with God in an environment that was completely free from sin. And yet . . . they listened to the smooth voice of the tempter, ate the forbidden fruit, and changed the whole destiny of mankind.

It happens in our homes too. We raise our children to the best of our wisdom and ability, in the way of the Lord. We teach them the Bible from the time they take their first steps and say their first words. But then, when they come of age, they may rebel against all they have been taught and leave us feeling like failures as parents. (But if we think having a prodigal means that we are failures as parents, then that makes our heavenly Father a failure because He has lots of prodigals, doesn't He?) Even when we raise our kids in a godly environment, teaching them the right way from the beginning, they can still exercise their free wills and go their own way.

It's obvious that Satan does not change, nor does he learn anything in his thousand years of incarceration. He's just like a hardened criminal who spends several years in prison and then picks up his life of crime again immediately upon release. The Devil picks up where he last left off, deceiving human beings and raising hell—quite literally.

In effect, God says to him, "Since you like to raise hell so much, Satan, I am going to send you to Hell." As we read in verse 10, "The devil, who deceived them, was cast into the lake of fire and brimstone where the beast and the false prophet are. And they will be tormented day and night forever and ever."

THE GREAT WHITE THRONE

The Bible teaches there are two deaths, one physical and the other spiritual. Jesus warned that we are to fear the second death more than the first. In Revelation 20:14 we read, "Then Death and Hades were cast into the lake of fire. This is the second death." It is also mentioned in Revelation 21:8: "But the cowardly, unbelieving, abominable, murderers, sexually immoral, sorcerers, idolaters, and all liars shall have their part in the lake which burns with fire and brimstone, which is the second death."

So what is this second death?

It is eternal separation from God.

It is Hell.

Jesus indicated that the death of your body is nothing compared to the conscious, everlasting banishment of a soul from God. One commentator wrote, "The second death is the continuance of spiritual death in another and timeless existence." [48]

Even another said, "Eternity to the godly is a day that has no sunset; eternity to the wicked is a night that has no sunrise." [49]

I have heard some people say, "I don't believe in hellfire."

Perhaps you don't. But you will—one minute after you arrive in Hell.

The fact is that if you are born once, you will die twice. If you are born twice, you will die once. When I say born once, I mean that those who have been born physically, but never have been born spiritually, will suffer two deaths. The first will be physical death, and the second will be spiritual death, when they enter Hell and are separated from God forever.

When I speak of someone being born twice, I mean they are born physically, and then at some point in their lives they receive Jesus as Savior, and they are born spiritually. Those people will die only once, in physical death, but then they will live on in Heaven forever. They never will have to face the second death.

Revelation 20:11–15 describes the truly terrifying scene at the Great White Throne judgment:

Then I saw a great white throne and Him who sat on it, from whose face the earth and the heaven fled away. And there was found no place for them. And I saw the dead, small and great, standing before God, and books were opened. And another book was opened, which is the Book of Life. And the dead were judged according to their works, by the things which were written in the books. The sea gave up the dead who were in it, and Death and Hades delivered up the dead who were in them. And they were judged, each one according to his works. Then Death and Hades were cast into the lake of fire. This is the second death. And anyone not found written in the Book of Life was cast into the lake of fire.

This is an ominous scene, serious and sobering. It is perhaps the most tragic passage in the entire Bible. I'm reminded of the words that Dante imagined on a sign above the gates of Hell: "Abandon hope, all you who enter here."

The apostle John sees a "Great White Throne." *Great* because its purpose is judgment, and it is full of awesome power, and *white* because it is pure. The judgments that emanate from it are righteous.

At this place of judgment, there will be no debate over a person's guilt or innocence. There will be a prosecutor but no defender or advocate. There will be an indictment but no defense mounted by the accused. The convicting evidence will be presented with no rebuttal or cross-examination. There will be no jury but only a judge, whose holy judgment is final and binding for all eternity.

GOOD TO KNOW

The Great White Throne judgment is perhaps the most tragic passage in the entire Bible.

What happens to nonbelievers when they die in the present day? According to the Scriptures, they go to a place called Hades. Our Lord's story in Luke 16 gives us a brief look behind the scenes of this place. Some maintain that the account of the rich man and Lazarus is a parable, but the fact that Jesus used a name in this story indicates that it was an actual event.

Jesus spoke about the death of a rich man, who was a sinner and didn't know God, and the death of a sick, impoverished man named Lazarus. (Not the same Lazarus whom Jesus raised from the dead in Bethany.) Here we have two people placed side by side who died on the same day. One man had believed, and the other had not. Death, of course, is no respecter of persons. Believers die from heart attacks, cancer, and auto accidents just like nonbelievers. Everyone dies and experiences that first, physical death.

What happens to a believer when that moment takes place? They go straight into the presence of God. In Luke 16:22, we read that "the beggar died, and was carried by the angels to Abraham's bosom."

My son Christopher left this world thirteen years ago. It comforts me to think that he was carried by angels into God's presence. I believe that with all my heart, and I believe this is true of every Christian. You leave this world and are carried by angels into the presence of God Himself. If we could only—just for a minute—get an idea of how glorious this will be, it would change the way we view death.

When young Stephen was being martyred for his faith, he was given a brief glimpse of glory. In Acts 7:55–56 we read, "But he, being full of the Holy Spirit, gazed into heaven and saw the glory of God, and Jesus standing at the right hand of God, and said, 'Look! I see the heavens opened and the Son of Man standing at the right hand of God!'" Stephen was seeing over to the other side. He radiated God's glory.

The great evangelist D. L. Moody spoke these words from his deathbed: "Is this dying? Why this is bliss. There is no valley. I have been within the gates. Earth is receding; Heaven is opening; God is calling; I must go." [50]

When a believer dies, he or she goes immediately into the presence of God.

There is no more compartment in Hades known as "Abraham's bosom." When Jesus rose from the dead, that all changed. Now, the Bible tells us, to be absent from the body is to be present with the Lord, in Heaven (see 2 Corinthians 5:8). Paul understood this when he spoke of his "desire to depart and be with Christ, which is far better" (Philippians 1:23).

But the place of torment in Hades that we read about in Luke 16 is still there. It is a place, we read, where people are conscious and suffering pain.

That is where the rich man went when he died, and that is where nonbelievers go until they have to stand before God at the Great White Throne judgment.

There is no such thing as reincarnation.

There is no such thing as purgatory.

There are no second chances beyond the grave—thousands before, but none after.

Physical death is a separation of the soul from the body and a transition from the visible world to the invisible. For the believer, it marks his or her entrance into the presence of God. For the nonbeliever, it is his or her entrance to Hades.

At the Great White Throne judgment, Hades will be emptied of its occupants. It's as though they have been in jail and now must appear before the judge to receive final sentencing. After sentence is pronounced, they will end up in the lake of fire. In that moment, it will be too late for any change of heart, change of mind, last-minute pardon, or a second chance. There are no other chances.

Everyone who has rejected God's offer of forgiveness through Jesus Christ will have to stand before God at the Great White Throne. Yes, it's true that all of us—every one of us—are sinners. However, only those sinners who have refused to open their hearts to Jesus Christ will have to face judgment.

Who will be there in that final day? As Adrian Rogers points out in his book *Unveiling the End Times in Our Time*, there will be "out-and-out sinners," righteous people, procrastinators, and unsaved church members. [51]

Again, who will be there?

There will be out-and-out sinners at this judgment.

These are the people who live apart from God, shake their fist in His face, and are proud of it.

There also will be "religious" people at the Great White Throne.

These might be kind and considerate men and women who volunteer in their community and are always doing benevolent things. We all know people like this. It's not wrong to say there are moral people in this world, because there are, and the Bible doesn't dispute that. What the Bible says is that no one is good enough to get into Heaven on their own merits.

I've met non-Christians who are nicer, more considerate, and more generous than some Christians that I know. But we don't get to Heaven on the basis of niceness. Heaven is not for perfect people; it's for forgiven people.

Sometimes self-righteous people don't think they need forgiveness. They don't see why they need Jesus. They will tell you, "You go preach that gospel in the prisons and on the streets and to criminals, but don't bother me with it. I'm an educated, intelligent, and moral person, so I will be fine."

No, you won't be fine.

The Bible says in Titus 3:5, "Not by works of righteousness which we have done, but according to His mercy He saved us." Everyone needs Jesus: the moral person and the immoral person, the model citizen and the convicted felon.

GOOD TO KNOW

Heaven is not for perfect people; it's for forgiven people.

The apostle John gives us a classic example of this in chapters 3 and 4 of his Gospel. In John 3, we are introduced to Nicodemus, a religious, moral, respectable man and a leader in his community. If we were going to elect a representative for humanity to stand before God and speak for us, we couldn't find a better representative than Nicodemus. Then in John 4, we meet the Samaritan woman at the well in Sychar. This was an immoral woman who had been married and divorced multiple times and was currently living with a guy.

What do both of these people have in common? They both encountered Jesus, they both desperately needed Jesus, and finally, they both believed in Jesus. It's just a reminder that everyone needs Him: the moral and the immoral, the down and outer and the up and outer. We all need the Way, the Truth, and the Life, and no one comes to God except through Him.

Procrastinators will be there too.

Next to the out-and-out sinners and the self-righteous, the procrastinators will be at the Great White Throne as well.

Procrastinators, by definition, are those who put off making a decision about Christ. They're like the Governor Felix, in the book of Acts, who didn't want to face his need for Jesus and told the apostle Paul, "That's enough for now! You may leave. When I find it convenient, I will send for you" (Acts 24:25 NIV).

These are people who might say, "I accept in premise what you say. I believe that the Bible is true. I believe Jesus Christ is the way to God. And one of these days, I'll get things right with Him. One of these days I'll go to church. One of these days I'll make some changes."

But somehow, those days never come.

And then . . . it is too late.

Unsaved church members will be at the same judgment.

These are people who may go to church every week. They may carry a Bible and clap with the worship songs. When there is prayer, they bow their heads and close their eyes.

They know all about God.

But they don't know God.

Jesus spoke of people like these in Matthew 7:21–23:

> "Not everyone who says to me, 'Lord, Lord,' will enter the kingdom of heaven, but only the one who does the will of my Father who is in Heaven. Many will say to me on that day, 'Lord, Lord, did we not prophesy in your name and in your name drive out demons and in your name perform many miracles?' Then I will tell them plainly, 'I never knew you. Away from me, you evildoers!'" (NIV)

Evildoers? Really?

Didn't these guys prophesy in Jesus' name? Didn't they actually cast out demons in His name? Didn't they perform miracles? Aren't those good things? Interestingly, He calls them "evildoers." The fact is that if you are trusting in a "good thing" to get you to Heaven, then a good thing can become a bad thing.

You need to trust in Christ, and Christ alone, to get you to Heaven.

Yes, if you are a Christian there should be good works in your life. As Jesus said, speaking of distinguishing between false prophets and true ones, "You will know them by their fruits" (Matthew 7:16). But those works, no matter how good and how many, won't save you! Maybe someday some will say, "Lord, Lord, didn't we receive communion in Your name? Didn't we get baptized in Your name? Didn't we give a confession in Your name?"

But sadly, if they never actually trusted Christ for salvation, depending on His finished work at the cross, then He will have to say to them, "Away from Me."

THE JUDGMENT BEGINS

And I saw the dead, small and great, standing before God, and books were opened. And another book was opened, which is the Book of Life. And the dead were judged according to their works, by the things which were written in the books." (Revelation 20:12)

God is no respecter of persons. He doesn't care if the world regarded these people as small or great. He won't care if an individual were a king, queen, prime minister, president, billionaire, rock star, or actor. Everyone outside of Christ will stand at the Great White Throne of judgment.

John 3:18 says, "He who believes in Him is not condemned; but he who does not believe is condemned already, because he has not believed in the name of the only begotten Son of God."

So here's the question: If the nonbeliever is already condemned, as this verse states, what's the purpose of the last judgment? Answer: the purpose of this final confrontation between God and man is to clearly demonstrate to the nonbeliever why he or she is already condemned.

The text says that books—plural—are opened and also the Book of Life—singular. What is in these books? The Bible doesn't say, but we could speculate. Perhaps one of these books is the book of God's Law, the commandments. Why did God give us the commandments in the first place? To make us righteous? Not at all. The commandments were given to show us that we are *not* righteous enough—and never will be in our own effort. In Romans 3:19 we are told that the commandments were given "that every mouth may be stopped, and all the world may become guilty before God." The law opens our eyes and closes our mouths. I look at God's holy and righteous standards, and I have nothing to say for myself! I don't have a leg to stand on. It's plain to me and to everyone else that I fall short.

I love it when people say, "I live by the Ten Commandments. That's all the religion I need."

"So," I will reply, "you always live by the Ten Commandments?"

"Yes, I do."

"So what exactly are the Ten Commandments? Can you name them?"

They never can. The truth is that no one lives by the Ten Commandments. There is only one person who has ever kept all of them and that was Christ Himself. No mere mortal can keep these commandments.

But what if you did?

Let's just imagine that somehow, through all the years of your life, you kept all ten of the commandments, but near the very end, you broke one of them.

You would be lost.

The Bible says, "For whoever shall keep the whole law, and yet stumble in one point, he is guilty of all" (James 2:10). Maybe one of the books at the Great White Throne will be the record of the law and how we have broken that law.

Another book might be a record of everything that you have ever said or done. The book of Ecclesiastes tells us that "God will bring every deed into judgment, including every hidden thing, whether it is good or evil" (12:14 NIV). That's just a little bit scary, isn't it? There in that one book would be everything you have ever said or done. Every conversation. Every email. Every text. Every word you've ever muttered under your breath. Every website you've ever opened. Everything you've ever done that you hoped no one would ever see or know.

It is all recorded.

Someone might say, "Greg, this is starting to alarm me!"

But let me remind you that if you are a Christian, you won't be at this judgment. You won't have to face this moment because Jesus has already paid the price for your sin. I love the way Paul expresses it in the book of Colossians: "God made you alive with Christ, for he forgave all our sins. He canceled the record of the charges against us and took it away by nailing it to the cross" (Colossians 2:13–14 NLT).

While the Great White Throne judgment is taking place, you will be on the restored Earth with Christ, savoring those wonderful, thousand years of His rule.

You know, it doesn't really matter where I am as long as I am with Jesus.

Yet there are people who will say, "I never knew about Jesus Christ."

And God will reply, "Yes, you did."

"But I never heard the gospel message!"

"Yes, you did."

Perhaps one of those books that are opened will be a record of every time you've heard the gospel, going back to your earliest days. You heard about Him in that Sunday School when you were nine or that camp you went to as a young teenager. You heard the gospel on a radio broadcast, before you changed the station. Someone handed you a gospel tract on the street, and you read the first paragraph before crumpling it up and throwing it on the sidewalk. Someone spoke to you about Jesus—a friend, a roommate, a neighbor, a coworker, or maybe even one of your grandchildren. Even on your deathbed, someone approached you and shared the gospel.

Some people will say, "How could a God of love send people to Hell?"

The Bible says that God created Hell for the Devil and his angels (see Matthew 25:41). Does the Devil deserve to go to Hell? Of course he does—and so do the demons who have followed him.

If a person ends up in Hell, however, it will be because they have rejected God's offer of forgiveness through Jesus Christ that required the death of the Son of God on the cross. They rejected it again and again and, in effect, followed the Devil.

J. I. Packer wrote, "Scripture sees hell as self-chosen. . . . Hell appears as God's gesture of respect for human choice. All receive what they actually chose, either to be with God forever, worshiping Him, or without God forever, worshiping themselves."

C. S. Lewis wrote, "There are only two kinds of people in the end: those who say to God, 'Thy will be done,' and those to whom God says, in the end, '*Thy* will be done.' All that are in Hell choose it. Without that self-choice there would be no Hell." [52]

If your name is not written in the Book of Life, then you will face eternal separation from God.

There was a show on television called *Inside the Actor's Studio,* where interviewer James Lipton asked various actors a series of questions. One of those questions was, "If Heaven exists, what you would you like to hear God say when you arrive at the Pearly Gates?"

> **GOOD TO KNOW**
>
> If a person ends up in Hell, it will be because they have rejected God's offer of forgiveness through Jesus Christ that required the death of the Son of God on the cross.

Here's how some of the Hollywood stars have replied.

Ben Affleck: "Your friends are in back. They're expecting you."

Ellen Barkin: "Come in. Have a drink. Sit down. Smoke a cigarette."

Angelina Jolie: "You are allowed in."

Johnny Depp: "Wow."

Richard Dreyfuss: "Come in. It's not as boring as you might have thought."

Anthony Hopkins: "What were you doing down there?"

Will Smith: "Good work, dawg."

Robert Redford: "You are too early."

Tom Cruise: "Come on in. You did a good job."

Susan Sarandon: "Let's party."

Robert De Niro replied like this: "If Heaven exists, God has a lot of explaining to do."

But God won't have to explain anything. And neither will we, if we have placed our trust in Jesus Christ for our salvation. If you are a believer entering Heaven, God will say to you, "Well done, good and faithful servant. Enter into the joy of your Lord."

No one will escape meeting Jesus Christ. We can either meet Him as Savior, Lord, and Friend, or we can meet Him as Judge. We can meet him with overflowing joy and inexpressible gratitude, or we can meet Him in terror, dread, and regret.

It truly is the most awesome choice we could ever make.

THREE TAKEAWAY TRUTHS

- The Bible tells us a lot about what to expect during Christ's perfect, millennial reign.
- Satan's rebellion against God shows us the darkness and evil inherent in the human heart.
- We may be surprised by those who will appear before Jesus in the Great White Throne judgment.

CHAPTER TWENTY-FIVE
Heaven on Earth

I heard a loud shout from the throne, saying,
"Look, God's home is now among his people!
He will live with them, and they will be his people.
God himself will be with them."
(Revelation 21:3 NLT)

IN THIS CHAPTER
- God's ultimate plan for Earth is fulfilled.
- What happens after the Millennium
- What will not be in Heaven
- John gets a first sight of the New Jerusalem
- How the hope of Heaven changes and encourages us

A new world is coming. And it will be . . . Heaven.

Heaven will come down to Earth, and they will be one.

Sometimes it's difficult to wrap our minds around this place that we call Heaven. It feels faraway, misty, foggy, or unreal to us, and it's hard to grasp. But it is real. It is as real and solid as the chair in which you are sitting.

I used to carry my granddaughter Lucy on the stairs tucked under my arm, walking in an exaggerated way that shook her up and down.

She loved that.

And I always gave her a choice: "Do you want to go down the stairs the regular way, or the *fun* way?"

Of course she always picked the fun way.

One day when I set her down at the bottom of the stairs, she looked up at me and said, "Papa, will there be stairs in Heaven?"

"Well," I said, "I don't know. Why do you ask?"

"Because," she replied, "I want you to carry me down the steps of Heaven the fun way."

Will I be carrying Lucy up and down heavenly stairs someday? Will she be carrying me? I don't know. But I do know that we'll be having fun together as Lucy grows up and as we both look forward to Heaven.

God's ultimate plan is to bring Heaven and Earth together. He will not abandon His creation; He will restore it. In Acts 3:19–21, in the midst of an impromptu evangelistic sermon in the temple courtyard, Peter declared, "Repent, then, and turn to God, so that your sins may be wiped out, that times of refreshing may come from the Lord, and that he may send the Messiah, who has been appointed for you—even Jesus. *Heaven must receive him until the time comes for God to restore everything,* as he promised long ago through his holy prophets" (NIV, emphasis added).

He will restore the lives of His sons and daughters. He will restore our bodies. He will restore our very planet. He will bring all things in Heaven and Earth together under one head, even Christ, according to Ephesians 1:10.

Randy Alcorn wrote, "We won't go to Heaven and leave Earth behind. Rather, God will bring Heaven and Earth together into the same dimension, with no wall of separation, no armed angels to guard Heaven's perfection from sinful mankind." [53]

Jesus will make Earth into Heaven and Heaven into Earth. By the way, in movie terms, this won't be a sequel but a remake. Many old films these days are being remastered and released again. But the restoration of Earth won't be a remastering; it will be a complete remake. Nevertheless, there will be a connection between the old and the new.

Here is how John captures it in Revelation 21:

> Now I saw a new heaven and a new earth, for the first heaven and the first earth had passed away. Also there was no more sea. Then I, John, saw the holy city, New Jerusalem, coming down out of heaven from God, prepared as a bride adorned for her husband. And I heard a loud voice from heaven saying, "Behold,

the tabernacle of God is with men, and He will dwell with them, and they shall be His people. God Himself will be with them and be their God. And God will wipe away every tear from their eyes; there shall be no more death, nor sorrow, nor crying. There shall be no more pain, for the former things have passed away."

Then He who sat on the throne said, "Behold, I make all things new." And He said to me, "Write, for these words are true and faithful."

And He said to me, "It is done! I am the Alpha and the Omega, the Beginning and the End. I will give of the fountain of the water of life freely to him who thirsts." (verses 1–6)

"Behold, I make all things new."

Yes, a new world is coming.

As someone wrote, "It will be out with the old and in with the new. No more terminal diseases. No more hospitals. No more wheelchairs, walkers, or funerals. No more suffering. No more separations. No more accidents. No more courts. No more prisons. No more lawyers. No more divorces. No more breakdowns or breakups. No more heart attacks. No more strokes. No more Alzheimer's. No more cancer. No more famines. No more disasters."

We all like to get the newest version of something, whether it's a smartphone, a tablet, or a laptop. We love new things, whether it's a new shirt, a new car, a new book, or a new pair of shoes.

Guess what? God loves new things too. And He tells us that one day soon, He will make everything new again.

This won't be like the claim that advertisers make when they promote some product that is supposedly "new and improved." Sometimes the only thing new is a new label. But when God speaks of the new and improved, it isn't hype or salesmanship. It is real, it is accurate, and it will happen exactly as He has said it would.

GOOD TO KNOW

God loves new things, and one day He will make all things new again.

In his commentary on the book of Revelation, Charles Swindoll lists a number of things that are missing from the new Heaven and Earth. Here are some of them:

- No more sea—because chaos and calamity will be eradicated.

- No more tears—because hurtful memories will be replaced.

- No more death—because mortality will be swallowed up by life.

- No more mourning—because sorrow will be completely comforted.

- No more pain—because all human suffering will be cured.

- No more thirst—because God will graciously quench all desires.

- No more wickedness—because all evil will be banished.

- No more night—because God's glory will give eternal light.

- No more closed gates—because God's doors will always be open.

- No more curse—because Christ's blood has forever lifted that curse. [54]

This is because Jesus is making all things new.

By the way, this is already a done deal. No, it hasn't happened yet, according to our timeline. But in another sense, in the *eternal* sense, it's already done. In verse 6 God says, "It is done!" Another version says, "It's happened" (MSG).

This is an interesting term in the original language, speaking of absolute finality. A literal translation would be, "They have become!" The text is in what is called the perfect indicative tense in Greek, which means that this is secure. In other words, God is speaking of the future as though it were already in the past.

The fact is that God doesn't see things the way we see them. We have a past that we can recall, a present where we live in the moment, and an unknown future out in front of us. But God lives in a continuum of time. For Him, the future is the same as the past or even the present. When He talks about the future, He speaks of it with the same accuracy as He could speak of the past. Why? Because He sees *all* things and knows *all* things.

There is a fascinating passage in the book of Ecclesiastes that says, "What is happening now has happened before, and what will happen in the future has happened before, because God makes the same things happen over and over again" (3:15 NLT).

In other words, when God says something will be done, *it will be done* exactly as He has said. There will be a new Earth one day, and it's perhaps nearer than we have imagined. It will happen, and you can take that to the bank.

BEYOND THE MILLENNIUM

Some people look into the Scriptures and can't seem to see anything beyond the millennial reign of Christ. But even the Millennium—a thousand rich, full, wonderful years—will be only a heartbeat alongside the glorious eternity to come.

At the end of the Millennium, as we have already noted, Satan will be released from the abyss and will be allowed to lead a short-lived rebellion, which will be quickly quashed.

That, in essence, is the end of the Millennium.

And it is also the beginning of eternity, as the New Jerusalem comes down from Heaven to Earth, flashing like an exquisite jewel, filling every heart with wonder.

At some point in that process, the old Earth will be destroyed. In Isaiah, God said, "See, I will create new heavens and a new earth. The former things will not be remembered, nor will they come to mind" (Isaiah 65:17 NIV). This parallels Revelation 21:1, where John wrote, "Now I saw a new heaven and a new earth, for the first heaven and the first earth had passed away."

The apostle Peter addressed this as well, writing,

> The heavens will pass away with a terrible noise, and the very elements themselves will disappear in fire, and the earth and everything on it will be found to deserve judgment.... On that day, he will set the heavens on fire, and the elements will melt away in the flames. But we are looking forward to the new heavens and new earth he has promised, a world filled with God's righteousness. (2 Peter 3:10, 12–13 NLT)

I will admit it: in some ways I can't wait for this moment.

This is the culmination of all things. The grand finale. The tour de force. The magnum opus. The masterwork. The *pièce de résistance*! This is when the new Heaven and the new Earth become one glorious reality, and we enter into an eternal timelessness that we will live in forever.

GOD DOESN'T WEAR A WATCH

God sees time differently than we see it. Psalm 90:4 says that a thousand years to God are as yesterday. The apostle Peter reminded readers that to God, a thousand years are as one day, and one day is as a thousand years (see 2 Peter 3:8).

Sometimes it seems to us that God is late. No doubt many in Israel felt that way before Jesus came the first time. They wondered, *When is the Messiah coming? When will He deliver us from the tyranny of Rome? It's been four hundred years since we've heard from a prophet or have seen an angel or witnessed a miracle.* The book of Galatians, however, says that "when the right time came, God sent his Son, born of a woman, subject to the law" (Galatians 4:4 NLT).

At just the right moment, the Messiah was born in the manger in Bethlehem.

In our era, we hear people say, "Why hasn't Jesus come back yet? Isn't He a little late?" In 2 Peter 3:9, however, we read that "the Lord isn't really being slow about his promise, as some people think. No, he is being patient for your sake. He does not want anyone to be destroyed, but wants everyone to repent" (NLT). He's giving people time to repent, before it's too late.

Revelation 21:1 says there will be no more seas on the new Earth. Some surfers and sailors reading these words might feel a pang of disappointment. I can only suggest to you that what God will give you in its place will be far better and that you won't even miss the old pastime. I like to surf, too, but only when the conditions are ideal. Maybe an outside temperature of 88 degrees, a water temperature of 74, two- to three-foot waves, no people sharing the waves with me, and no sharks within one hundred miles. (I'm just a little bit particular about these things.)

Why no more sea? At present, two-thirds of the Earth's surface is covered with water. The remaining one-third includes large areas rendered worthless and uninhabitable because of mountains and deserts. But God, in His new Earth, eliminates the barriers that once separated races and nations as we come together under His lordship.

All people who have trusted Christ in human history will be together. Just think of that! Isaiah will be there, along with Jeremiah, Elijah, Elisha, and all the prophets. Also Eve, Sarah, Ruth, Mary, David, Noah, Jonah, Peter, James, and John will be there too. There also will be contemporary names, like William Wilberforce, Susanna Wesley, Martin Luther King, C. H. Spurgeon, D. L. Moody, Rosa Parks, and the list goes on and on.

GOOD TO KNOW

In His new Earth, God eliminates the barriers that once separated races and nations as we come together under His lordship.

And in your own family tree, all your loved ones who have preceded you to Heaven will be there too. I will see my grandfather and grandmother, my mother, and the father who adopted me. And I will see my son Christopher.

Best of all, God Himself will be there.

I think that when we speak sometimes about longing for Heaven, what we're really talking about, deep down inside, is a longing for God Himself. The

Bible says that He has placed eternity in our hearts (see Ecclesiastes 3:11). Jesus said, "Blessed are the pure in heart, for they shall see God" (Matthew 5:8).

Randy Alcorn wrote, "Seeing God will be like seeing everything else for the first time. Why? Because not only will we see God, he will be the lens through which we see everything else—people, ourselves, and the events of this life." [55]

God speaks with a loud voice in Revelation 21:3, with news He wants all of us to hear: "I heard a loud voice from heaven saying, 'Behold, the tabernacle of God is with men, and He will dwell with them, and they shall be His people. God Himself will be with them and be their God.'"

The tabernacle of God? What is that? In the Old Testament, God would meet His people in the tabernacle, which simply refers to the Tent of Meeting. The priests could only enter the most holy part of that tent, the part where the presence of God resided, once a year, on the Day of Atonement. Later, the tabernacle was replaced by the temple, but the way to approach God was essentially the same. God was distant and separated from the people, and very few people had a close relationship with Him.

GOOD TO KNOW

In the new Heaven and new Earth, we all will have open access to the Father any time we want it, with no appointment required.

But the cross of Jesus changed all that. Because of what Jesus accomplished in His death and resurrection, the tabernacle of God—the dwelling place of God—is with men. This means that in the new Heaven and new Earth, we all will have open access to the Father any time we want it, with no appointment required.

If I could have lived in any era of history, I would have chosen the first century so that I could have been on Earth when Jesus walked this planet. I would have loved to have been one of His disciples—or at least to have been in the multitudes when He spoke and taught. I would love to have heard His voice with my own ears, perhaps even witnessing Him performing a miracle. Most of us would love to have been near to Him during those years, but we weren't given that privilege.

On the new Earth, however, we will have it.

We can approach the Lord Jesus at any time. We can walk and talk with God.

THE NEW CITY

Then I, John, saw the holy city, New Jerusalem, coming down out of heaven from God, prepared as a bride adorned for her husband. (Revelation 21:2)

The word *prepared* is important. Back in John 14:2–3 Jesus said, "I go to prepare a place for you. And if I go and prepare a place for you, I will come again and receive you to Myself; that where I am, there you may be also." Paul used that same word *prepared* in 1 Corinthians 2:9, writing, "Eye has not seen, nor ear heard, nor have entered into the heart of man the things which God has prepared for those who love Him."

The New Jerusalem is a prepared city. John has seen it. John has been catapulted into the future and has seen eternity. He has seen Heaven. He has seen Hell. He has seen the Tribulation period, the Antichrist, and angels. So it is a *real* city.

And because this city comes down out of Heaven, it's reasonable to assume that you and I will have been spending time there while we are in Heaven. And now in Revelation 21:2, that magnificent city of God descends to Earth, as Earth and Heaven become one.

So it's a real city? What are cities like? Cities have buildings. Cities have main streets and side streets. Cities have things to do. Cities have activities and restaurants (I like that part). There are places to go for entertainment. There are parks and cafés.

Will Heaven have those things? Why not? The Bible certainly tells us that we will eat and drink in Heaven. It tells us that we will know one another and speak to each other.

It may be easier to wrap our minds around the heavenly city, knowing that it rests on the new Earth. Somehow, that's easier to picture and imagine. So I will be going up and down the stairs with Lucy "the fun way," and we all will have lots of things to do.

But it won't all be leisure. We will be serving the Lord in this new city in the new world. We will be about our Father's business. Revelation 22:3 says that "His servants shall serve Him." We won't be lying around on clouds and plucking harps; we will have assignments and activities.

Revelation 7:15 speaks of those who are "before the throne of God and serve him day and night in his temple" (NIV).

What does the Lord have in store for us in the future?

We don't know for sure. But I have wondered about some things. Sometimes dreams that we have cherished in this life get shattered or cut short. One child dies, while another has to somehow get through life with devastating disabilities. We feel so sad for them because we imagine they never will be able to do what others do or accomplish what others accomplish.

We say such things because we think in a limited, earthly way. Who knows what God has in store for us in the endless, golden millennia to come? Maybe some of the dreams that went unfulfilled in this life will be gloriously fulfilled in the next. Yes, we need to maximize our opportunities and live as well as we can on Earth, in the years allotted to us. *But we also need to remember that life goes on beyond Earth.* Death for the believer is not the end of life, but the continuation of it in another place.

Maybe unfulfilled dreams here will be fulfilled *there.*

Maybe crushed potential here will be realized *there.*

Maybe godly desires shattered here will be mended *there.*

Revelation 21:4 gives us one of the most beautiful promises in all of Scripture: "And God will wipe away every tear from their eyes; there shall be no more death, nor sorrow, nor crying. There shall be no more pain, for the former things have passed away."

GOOD TO KNOW

Death for the believer is not the end of life, but the continuation of it in another place.

There is great pain in life, isn't there? There are some hurts that are so deep that no words we can say will make them better. I remember speaking on the phone with a pastor friend who had just lost his son. I said to him, "There are no words, there is just the Word. There is no manual, there is just Immanuel. There is God." I shared with him things that I have learned—and am still learning—about dealing with grief. You can't really control it as much as you may try. It's just a process that you have to go through.

But one day all pain will be gone. God said so.

One day all sorrow will vanish like darkness at sunrise. God said so.

One day all mourning will be a thing of the past, either dimly recalled or not remembered at all. There will be no more physical or emotional pain. No pain from a broken body or a broken heart. No more broken bones. No more broken marriages. No more broken lives. Why? Because God will make all things new.

A FINAL WARNING

For all its beautiful images and promises, however, Revelation 21 solemnly reminds us that the new Heaven and new Earth will not be the default destination of every person—but only for those who have believed in Jesus Christ:

> But the cowardly, unbelieving, abominable, murderers, sexually immoral, sorcerers, idolaters, and all liars shall have their part in the lake which burns with fire and brimstone, which is the second death. (verse 8)

I believe there are people inside the church today who will be outside the gates of Heaven then. Attending a church does not give you entrance to Heaven. Being an American does not give you entrance to Heaven. You have to, as an individual, put your faith in Jesus Christ for salvation.

Who is on the outside?

First of all, *the cowardly*. These are people who are afraid to follow Jesus. It takes courage to be a Christian and make your stand for Christ. People may very well harass you, make fun of you, ridicule you, mock you, or ostracize you. In many countries of the world today, you may be physically harmed, lose your livelihood, or even lose your life for following Jesus. Frankly, as our culture changes and grows darker by the day, the situation is getting worse.

Some people are constantly afraid of what other people think of them, which I have always found so amazing. Really? Is it so important to you for people to always think well of you? Would you actually make an eternal decision based on the possibility of someone making fun of you? One day you will stand before God all by yourself. If you have been cowardly, refusing to trust Jesus because of what people might say, then you won't make it into Heaven. You will be shut away from God's presence forever.

Second, the Scriptures mention the *abominable*. You might think, *Abominable? I've heard of the Abominable Snowman, but what does the word really mean?*

It basically means "really bad," comes from the word *abomination*, and signifies a person who is wholly caught up in wickedness and evil. This is a person who has pulled out all the stops and removed all restraints. They have given themselves completely over to evil, and they no longer care who knows about it.

Third, the verse speaks of the *sexually immoral*. The term comes from the Greek word *porneia,* from which we get our English terms *pornographic* or *pornography,* and it speaks of illicit sex. What is illicit sex? It is any sexual activity besides the sexual union of a man and woman within a marriage relationship. That includes premarital sex and extramarital sex.

Next, it speaks of *sorcerers*. When we hear the word, we immediately think of people into magic or the occult who are attempting to cast spells. But it is interesting that the word *sorcery* comes from the Greek word *pharmakeia,* from which we get our English word *pharmacy*. It speaks of the illicit use of drugs. In the pagan religions of John's day, practitioners would use hallucinogenic drugs in the so-called worship of their false gods. This drug use often involved immorality with temple prostitutes and all kinds of vile things.

The next word the verse uses is *idolaters*. An idol isn't restricted to some grotesque image carved out of wood or stone. In fact, it is anyone or anything that takes the place of God in your life.

The idea being communicated in this list is that if you are pursuing these sinful activities in your life, then you will find no place in the kingdom of God.

It is God who makes the rules, and we can either follow them or reject them. Someone might say, "I don't agree with that. *My* god would never condemn people to Hell over things like this."

But who is your god? I really don't know. But it certainly isn't the God of the Bible.

HOW SHOULD THE HOPE OF HEAVEN AFFECT US RIGHT NOW?

The hope of Heaven helps us keep perspective in times of trial.

Life on Earth is full of trials, hardships, sadness, disappointments, and pain—and the older you become, the more you will see of these things. The apostle Paul, however, helps us to keep these troubling realities of life in their proper perspective. In Romans 8:18 he wrote, "For I consider that the sufferings of this present time are not worthy to be compared with the glory which shall be revealed in us."

Paul was essentially saying, "Yes, I understand that life involves significant suffering. But when you lay it alongside the glory that will one day be ours in eternity, it doesn't even register on the scale."

In fact, God will use these difficult situations and experiences in our lives for our good, and one day (not so very long from now) every wrong in our lives will be righted. Pains will be healed, sorrow will be eradicated, and God will make up for all that we have lost here on Earth. Again, Paul gives us a perspective that will help us walk through our troubles and heartaches:

> These troubles and sufferings of ours are, after all, quite small and won't last very long. Yet this short time of distress will result in God's richest blessing upon us forever and ever! So we do not look at what we can see right now, the troubles all around us, but we look forward to the joys in heaven which we have not yet seen. The troubles will soon be over, but the joys to come will last forever. (2 Corinthians 4:17–18 TLB)

Some time ago I had the opportunity of spending time with a couple who had lost a child. As we were talking together, they told me, "We don't want to waste our pain."

What did they mean? Simply this: Pain will come anyway. No matter how you try, you can't control events and circumstances. Pain and sorrow will come knocking on your door in some way, shape, or form, whether you want it to or not and whether you like it or not. So how are you going to deal with it? Will you allow it to embitter you, sidetrack you, or put you under a permanent cloud, or will you use it for God's glory?

How do you use pain for God's glory?

Two names come to mind: Joni Eareckson Tada and Nick Vujicic. Joni was a young, attractive, athletic girl who enjoyed riding horses, hiking, playing tennis, and swimming. As a young teenage girl, however, she misjudged the shallowness of the water and dove into Chesapeake Bay. This resulted in her breaking her neck and becoming a quadriplegic. But even though Joni has spent more than fifty years in a wheelchair, she has brought inspiration, hope, and encouragement to literally millions of people around the world. Had she lived out her life without this disability, I feel confident that God would have used her. But would she have been used in the same way? It doesn't seem likely. God took this tragedy and pain, using it (and continuing to use it) for His glory.

GOOD TO KNOW

God can use the pain we experience in this life for His glory.

Nick Vujicic was born without arms or legs. As a young man, he was very despondent and even suicidal. In recent years, however, through the power of his story and his testimony for Christ, he also has brought encouragement to countless people around the world.

Both Joni and Nick have turned a disability into an ability. They have not wasted their pain.

No one wants pain or disappointment or tragedy in their lives. But our heavenly Father who loves us is powerful, good, and sovereign and can use the pain in our lives for our good and His glory. And again, the Bible says that it doesn't begin to compare with the wonders God has waiting for us just around the corner, in Heaven.

The hope of Heaven helps us to become heavenly minded.

In Colossians 3:1–2 Paul writes, "Since, then, you have been raised with Christ, set your hearts on things above, where Christ is, seated at the right hand of God. Set your minds on things above, not on earthly things" (NIV).

The phrase "set your minds" means "be engaged in a diligent, active investigation." In other words, think about these things. Think about Heaven. Don't be in love with this world. In one of the apostle John's letters, we read, "Do not love the world or the things in the world. If anyone loves the world, the love of the Father is not in him. For all that is in the world—the lust of the flesh, the lust of the eyes, and the pride of life—is not of the Father but is of the world" (1 John 2:15–16).

This command doesn't mean that as followers of Jesus, we can't appreciate the beauties of our planet or the pleasures in life. I think Christians should value beauty and joy and appreciate life more than anyone. "Loving the world," however, speaks of a mentality, an adherence to a culture under the sway of Satan, the god of this world. Don't be caught up in *that*. Don't love *that*. Be heavenly minded instead.

Sometimes you hear a person say, "He's so heavenly minded that he's no earthly good." Really, that is such a stupid statement. I'd rather be someone like that than to be so earthly minded that I'm no heavenly good.

Think Heaven.

And here's the bottom line for every believer today: if we truly believe our Bibles, if we believe in the reality of a new Heaven and a new Earth, then it should motivate us to take as many people with us as possible.

Is this a burden? A heavy obligation? Maybe. But it is also an unspeakable privilege:

> God has given us the privilege of urging everyone to come into his favor and be reconciled to him. For God was in Christ, restoring

the world to himself, no longer counting men's sins against them but blotting them out. This is the wonderful message he has given us to tell others. We are Christ's ambassadors. God is using us to speak to you: we beg you, as though Christ himself were here pleading with you, receive the love he offers you—be reconciled to God. (2 Corinthians 5:18–20 TLB)

THREE TAKEAWAY TRUTHS

- God loves to make things new—Heaven, Earth, and even us.
- Jesus keeps all His promises, and when He says He's remaking Heaven and Earth, you can consider it done.
- Our expectation of Heaven gives us perspective in our pain.

CHAPTER TWENTY-SIX
The Best Is Yet to Come

And he carried me away in the Spirit
to a mountain great and high,
and showed me the Holy City, Jerusalem,
coming down out of heaven from God.
(Revelation 21:10 NIV)

IN THIS CHAPTER

- All believers have a longing for Heaven.
- What we find in the New Jerusalem
- The main attraction of Heaven
- Benefits of the Tree of Life
- How to be admitted into God's eternal city

I heard the story of a man who was near death. He had worked very hard for his money and didn't like the idea that he was about to leave it all behind. In his distress, he prayed and asked God if he could be the exception to the rule and take one suitcase with him to Heaven.

The Lord went along with it and said, "I will make an exception in your case. You can take one suitcase." With that, the man loaded up his suitcase with gold bars. Then he died, arrived at the Pearly Gates, and was met by Peter.

"Welcome to Heaven," Peter said. "I already know about your suitcase arrangement with the Lord, but just out of curiosity, may I see what's in it?"

The man opened up his suitcase and showed Peter what he had brought to Heaven.

"Hmm," said Peter.

Later someone asked Peter about it. "What's with the guy carrying a suitcase? What was in it?"

"It's the funniest thing," Peter replied. "He went to all that effort, pleading with God, and then he shows up with a suitcase full of . . . *asphalt!*"

Now, in case you don't get the punch line, remember that the streets of Heaven are paved with gold.

The fact is that Heaven is a real place for real people, where we will do real things. It isn't some mysterious, atmospheric realm of smoke and mirrors. It isn't some misty, cartoon world of people lounging on clouds or plucking harps.

This is the very real place that the Bible says Abraham was searching for. Like Abraham, you and I are foreigners too. We're passing through this world. We're like someone in a different country.

I remember when Cathe and I were in Italy, and I thought it would be fun to rent a Vespa. A lot of people ride Vespas and other scooters in Italy. At first it was kind of terrifying, but after about twenty minutes I kind of liked it. But then, inexplicably, I managed to get a ticket. I found out later it was because I had accidentally pulled into the bus lane.

I was a foreigner who did not understand what was going on around me, and we're that way in this world. There are things in this world that don't make sense to us. But we're longing for, we're looking forward to, another world. That is the hope of Heaven.

In truth, it is the place that we all have been searching for, all our lives.

Writing about Abraham's lifelong search, the book of Hebrews puts it like this: "By an act of faith, Abraham said yes to God's call to travel to an unknown place that would become his home. When he left he had no idea where he was going. By an act of faith he lived in the country promised him, lived as a stranger camping in tents. Isaac and Jacob did the same, living under the same promise. Abraham did it by keeping his eye on an unseen city with real, eternal foundations—the City designed and built by God" (Hebrews 11:8–10 MSG).

The land of Canaan must have been a beautiful, lush place in those days, but Abraham recognized all along that this world was really not his home. By faith, he understood that his real home was an eternal one, designed and built by God. Deep down inside, I hope we realize that too. The Bible says God has placed eternity in our hearts (see Ecclesiastes 3:11). Our real home is Heaven and the new Earth that is to come.

Randy Alcorn wrote that at present, "we live between Eden and the New Earth, pulled toward what we once were and what we yet will be." [56]

In the final two chapters of Revelation, John used the word *city* eleven times in referring to Heaven, again reminding us that this is a real place. We need to remember that Heaven is being prepared for us and that we are being prepared for Heaven. Everything we go through in life is preparing us for our future— here on Earth in this life and in Heaven in the life to come.

Paul puts it all in context in 2 Corinthians 4:17–18:

> For our present troubles are small and won't last very long. Yet they produce for us a glory that vastly outweighs them and will last forever! So we don't look at the troubles we can see now; rather, we fix our gaze on things that cannot be seen. For the things we see now will soon be gone, but the things we cannot see will last forever. (NLT)

Yes, Jesus has gone to prepare a place for us. By the way, He gave that assurance to His disciples on a night like no other night. He was very heavy-hearted, and in the hours to come, His heart would come near to breaking in the Garden of Gethsemane. He had already dropped the bombshell in revealing that one of them would betray Him. After He identified Judas, and the betrayer went off into the night, Jesus said these words:

> "The time has come for the Son of Man to enter into his glory, and God will be glorified because of him. And since God receives glory because of the Son, he will soon give glory to the Son. Dear

GOOD TO KNOW

In the final two chapters of Revelation, John used the word *city* eleven times in referring to Heaven.

children, I will be with you only a little longer. And as I told the Jewish leaders, you will search for me, but you can't come where I am going." (John 13:31–33 NLT)

Peter protested, telling the Lord that he would follow Him anywhere and even lay down his life for Him. Jesus replied that before the rooster crowed in the morning, Peter would deny Him three times.

Can you imagine the stunned silence that followed?

For these disciples, the world was caving in. *Jesus was going away? One of them would betray Him? Peter would deny Him? How could it be?*

Then Jesus broke the silence with these words:

> "Let not your heart be troubled; you believe in God, believe also in Me. In My Father's house are many mansions; if it were not so, I would have told you. I go to prepare a place for you. And if I go and prepare a place for you, I will come again and receive you to Myself; that where I am, there you may be also." (John 14:1–3)

John the apostle was there that night among the Eleven after Judas had left, reclining right next to Jesus so as to not miss a single word.

Years later as an exile on the lonely island of Patmos where he had been banished, presumably alone, John no doubt thought back to those words: *"I go to prepare a place for you."* And in that stark, desolate place of exile, Jesus gave John a glimpse of that prepared place, that city which was to come:

> And he carried me away in the Spirit to a great and high mountain, and showed me the great city, the holy Jerusalem, descending out of heaven from God, having the glory of God. Her light was like a most precious stone, like a jasper stone, clear as crystal. Also she had a great and high wall with twelve gates, and twelve angels at the gates, and names written on them, which are the names of the twelve tribes of the children of Israel: three gates on the

east, three gates on the north, three gates on the south, and three gates on the west.

Now the wall of the city had twelve foundations, and on them were the names of the twelve apostles of the Lamb. And he who talked with me had a gold reed to measure the city, its gates, and its wall. The city is laid out as a square; its length is as great as its breadth. And he measured the city with the reed: twelve thousand furlongs. Its length, breadth, and height are equal. Then he measured its wall: one hundred and forty-four cubits, according to the measure of a man, that is, of an angel. The construction of its wall was of jasper; and the city was pure gold, like clear glass. The foundations of the wall of the city were adorned with all kinds of precious stones: the first foundation was jasper, the second sapphire, the third chalcedony, the fourth emerald, the fifth sardonyx, the sixth sardius, the seventh chrysolite, the eighth beryl, the ninth topaz, the tenth chrysoprase, the eleventh jacinth, and the twelfth amethyst. The twelve gates were twelve pearls: each individual gate was of one pearl. And the street of the city was pure gold, like transparent glass.

But I saw no temple in it, for the Lord God Almighty and the Lamb are its temple. The city had no need of the sun or of the moon to shine in it, for the glory of God illuminated it. The Lamb is its light. And the nations of those who are saved shall walk in its light, and the kings of the earth bring their glory and honor into it. Its gates shall not be shut at all by day (there shall be no night there). (21:10–25)

Without question, it is difficult to wrap our minds around the description we have just read. Yet this is a very graphic and vivid portrait of Heaven and the new Earth. John is very specific, doing his best with first-century language to describe what is before him.

John used concrete terms. He used specific gems to describe the glory and colors of Heaven. However, it is still a little bit beyond our complete comprehension. But certainly it excites our hope.

Let's identify some key principles here.

THE CITY THAT IS TO COME

There is no need for the sun, moon, or stars in this heavenly city, because it shines with the glory of God Himself. It radiates with vibrant green, sky blue, crimson red, shining gold, deep violet, and more. The gold is so pure that it is translucent.

The city has twelve gates, but not to keep us in. They are always open. There are also walls, but again, not to keep people out or in. They are more like monumental walls, engraved with the names of the twelve tribes of Israel and the twelve apostles. (By the way, the name of Judas won't be on that wall. My guess for the twelfth apostle would be Paul. If I'm wrong, then you can take it up with me when we get there.)

What will we do when we get there? I don't think we will be snapping pictures with our cell phones and posting them on Instagram. I think we will be utterly awestruck. Beyond everything else, however—the glory, the wonders, and the majesties of that place—we will want to see Jesus Himself.

The main event of Heaven is Jesus.

In John 14:3, Jesus said, "I will come again and receive you to Myself; that where I am, there you may be also." It's all about being with Him. Paul spoke about being "absent from the body . . . to be present with the Lord" (2 Corinthians 5:8). In his letter to the Philippians, he flatly stated that he had "a desire to depart and be with Christ, which is far better" (Philippians 1:23).

Yes, certainly we will be in awe and revel over the sights and sounds of the heavenly city and the new Earth. But it all pales in comparison with simply being with Jesus. D. L. Moody said that it is not the jeweled walls or pearly gates that will make Heaven attractive. It is being with God.

Revelation 22:4 says that we will see God's face and that His name will be on our foreheads. Christ promised us this in the Sermon on the Mount when He said, "Blessed are the pure in heart, for they shall see God" (Matthew 5:8). The patriarch Job, in a flash of insight into the eternal, declared, "And after my skin has been destroyed, yet in my flesh I will see God; I myself will see him with my own eyes—I, and not another" (Job 19:26–27 NIV).

In our glorified, made-for-eternity bodies, you and I will be able to see God in all His glory. What an awesome prospect! Vance Havner said, "The New Testament writers did not speak of going to heaven so much as going to be with the Lord. It is not the other shore that charms us so much as it is Jesus on the shore."[57]

Then there is the size of the city. Most commentators agree that the New Jerusalem will be in the shape of a cube, with one thousand five hundred miles in length, height, and width. So how big would that be? If you laid it over the United States, it would cover an area from Canada to Mexico and from Los Angeles to Saint Louis. In other words, its foundation would cover about three-quarters of the United States. But it also soars upward too. (There may be a lot of steps to run "the fun way" with Lucy.)

GOOD TO KNOW

In our glorified bodies, we will see God in all His glory.

In his book *Heaven* Randy Alcorn writes, "We don't need to worry that Heaven will be crowded. The ground level of the city will be nearly two million square miles. This is forty times bigger than England and fifteen thousand times bigger than London. It's ten times as big as France or Germany, and far larger than India. But remember, that's just the ground level."[58]

Anyway, we won't all live in the New Jerusalem. We will live on the new Earth with Christ and go in and out of the city.

What will we see there? Revelation 21:11 mentions "a jasper stone, clear as crystal." Most commentators believe this is a perfectly clear diamond. That would mean that the foundation of the new city would be made up of diamonds and emeralds and other precious stones. No wonder gold is the asphalt of Heaven.

We place great value on diamonds in this world. The Heart of Eternity diamond, all 27.64 carats of it, is blue in color and worth $16 million. Then there is the Steinmetz Pink diamond, or Pink Star, which is worth $83.2 million.

The famous Hope diamond at the Smithsonian is worth $200 to $250 million. The most valuable diamond in the entire world is the Koh-i-Noor diamond. Koh-i-Noor means "mountain of light" in Persian. The diamond is priceless.

The New Jerusalem, the real mountain of light, rests on a foundation of diamond and other precious stones.

The gate leading into the city is made of pearl—not a bunch of pearls, but one solid pearl. (Wow, can you imagine the oyster this must have come from?) As you are no doubt aware, a pearl begins as a foreign substance, such as a grain of sand, which gets inside an oyster shell and irritates the creature inside. The oyster then secretes a substance to cover up the irritant, and that substance hardens into a pearl.

GOOD TO KNOW

Jerusalem is a part of our past, present, and future.

A pearl, then, is the result of pain.

Perhaps the gate of pearl will remind us throughout all eternity that our very entrance to Heaven came about by the pain and suffering of Jesus on our behalf.

In verse 2 of chapter 21, we read that the New Jerusalem comes down out of Heaven "prepared as a bride adorned for her husband." I will never forget the moment my wife, Cathe, walked down the aisle on our wedding day. She looked so beautiful . . . and still does. I, however, looked like something the cat dragged in. I was in a tuxedo, with platform shoes, and I had shoulder-length hair and a red, full beard. (It was the era. What can I say?)

But my bride was a vision of beauty.

And so it is with New Jerusalem, descending majestically out of Heaven and flashing every color of the spectrum and perhaps beyond.

I'm amazed at how many times the Bible speaks of Jerusalem. In fact, there are two cities mentioned in the Scriptures more than any others: Jerusalem and Babylon. Babylon, essentially, is the city of man, and New Jerusalem is the city of God.

Jerusalem is a part of our past, present, and future. In the past it was the capital of Israel, ruled over by David and his descendants. This is where the first temple was erected, built by David's son, Solomon. As we know, Israel rebelled against God and ended up going into captivity in Babylon for seventy years.

After that, they returned to Jerusalem, rebuilding the walls and the temple. This was the city where Christ had a great part of His ministry, and it was outside the walls of Jerusalem where Jesus was crucified.

Jerusalem is a city of the present because God brought her back, in fulfillment of prophecy. On May 14, 1948, Israel became a nation again—effectively starting the prophetic clock ticking.

Jerusalem is also the city of the future. According to the Bible, world history as we know it will end around Jerusalem. Jerusalem will be the center of the final conflict as the Battle of Armageddon rages. When Christ returns to Earth, He will set foot on the Mount of Olives and will enter into the east gate of Jerusalem, establishing His millennial kingdom. Jerusalem will be the focal point of the world in the end times.

And in the future, beyond the thousand-year reign of Christ, New Jerusalem descends from Heaven to rest on the new Earth forever.

Does New Jerusalem exist right now? I believe it does, in Heaven. I also believe that our loved ones who have preceded us are probably there right now. When we get there, our loved ones who have been in Heaven already can show us around. (I love that thought!)

Whenever I'm visiting a city for the first time, I love to talk to the locals and ask a few questions. I will say, "Where's the best place to eat?" Or maybe, "What should I see while I'm here?"

Maybe it will be that way when I first enter New Jerusalem. Maybe a local will show me around for a few centuries. It might be an angel. It might be my son. It might even be Peter, Paul, or Mary. Who knows?

INSIDE THE CITY

What else does the Bible tell us about our heavenly future? Revelation 22 reveals wonders upon wonders:

> And he showed me a pure river of water of life, clear as crystal, proceeding from the throne of God and of the Lamb. In the middle

of its street, and on either side of the river, was the tree of life, which bore twelve fruits, each tree yielding its fruit every month. The leaves of the tree were for the healing of the nations. And there shall be no more curse, but the throne of God and of the Lamb shall be in it, and His servants shall serve Him. They shall see His face, and His name shall be on their foreheads. There shall be no night there: They need no lamp nor light of the sun, for the Lord God gives them light. And they shall reign forever and ever. (verses 1–5)

In Revelation 21 we are given a glimpse of the outside of New Jerusalem as it descends to Earth. In chapter 22 we are privileged to walk through the gates. When that time comes for you and me, we won't need to purchase an admission ticket to get in the door. The gates always will be open to us because Jesus paid the full price of our admission forever, with His own blood, freely given for us.

The Bible's description of Heaven keeps getting more intimate. First it was described as a kingdom, then a city, and now a garden. In the first book of the Bible we see paradise lost; here in the last book of the Bible, paradise is found. The first two chapters of the Bible describe the paradise that God created for man on Earth; the final two chapters of the Bible describe the paradise that God has created for us in Heaven, as Heaven and Earth now become one.

A place of satisfaction

One of the things that strikes us about this new Heaven and new Earth is that it is a place of satisfaction. Even Mick Jagger, famous for his rock number "I Can't Get No Satisfaction" would find satisfaction here. (And I very much hope he has that opportunity.) We are told in verse 17, "Let him who thirsts come. Whoever desires, let him take the water of life freely."

A place of sufficiency

In verse 2, we read, "In the middle of its street, and on either side of the river, was the tree of life, which bore twelve fruits, each tree yielding its fruit every month. The leaves of the tree were for the healing of the nations."

I love the fact that we will have access to the Tree of Life. The book of Genesis tells us the same tree was back in the Garden of Eden at the beginning of human history. But because our first parents ate the forbidden fruit of the Tree of Knowledge of Good and Evil, they were banned from the Tree of Life. Why? Because if they ate from it, they would live forever. God did not want Adam and Eve to live forever in a sinful state, so they were not allowed access to that tree. In fact, God set an angelic guard before it, to make sure that Adam and Eve would have no further access to it.

GOOD TO KNOW

God did not allow Adam and Eve access to the Tree of Life because if they ate from it, they would have lived forever in a sinful state.

But in the new Heaven and Earth, that access will be wide open. Everything that went wrong for our first parents will be made right.

I wonder if, when we get there, we will find Adam and Eve hanging around the Tree of Life. They had been barred from that tree during all their life on the old Earth. But in New Jerusalem, the life-giving tree with healing leaves will be theirs—and ours.

When the Bible speaks of the leaves of the tree being for "the healing of the nations," it uses the Greek word *therapia*, from which we get our English word *therapy*. It's not that anyone ever will be sick in Heaven, because we all will be in our glorified bodies. But it appears that there is health in these leaves, as well as in the fruit. They will taste good and be good for you, which never seems to be the way (for me, at least) with foods on Earth. All the foods that I like best aren't the foods that I ought to be eating. I've got a feeling it will be very different in Heaven.

A place where there is no more curse

Verse 3 tells us, "There shall be no more curse." What is the curse? This is what came to Adam and Eve—and all the human family since—as a result of sin. If it weren't for sin, we never would be sick, never age, and never die. (And I would have a full head of hair.) Death is a direct result of the curse, but in the life to come, that curse will be lifted.

People in our world die every day, every hour, every minute, every second. To be precise, 1.90 people die every second, 114 die every minute, and 6,829 die every hour. On any given day, 163,898 people will die and enter eternity. [59] We've never lived in a world where it was any different. But we will!

A place of service

Again in verse 3 we read, "His servants shall serve Him." Heaven and the new Earth are a place of service. Yes it is a place of rest, but I can only rest for so long, and then I'm ready to go back to work. I like to be busy and active. After I recharge my batteries a little, I want to be productive again. In the new Heaven and Earth, we will serve the Lord. We will have specific tasks to undertake and accomplish for His pleasure and His glory.

In Jeremiah 29:11 the Lord says, "I know the plans I have for you. . . . They are plans for good" (NLT). Will we accomplish *all* those plans here in this brief life on Earth? Of course not! In my opinion, those plans and purposes in God's heart will stretch into eternity. Perhaps the dreams that we did not or could not fulfill here will be fulfilled in the next life.

A place of restoration

Heaven will be a place where tragedy turns to triumph, sadness turns to joy, disability turns to ability, and frustration turns to fulfillment.

In the last chapter I spoke about carrying my granddaughter down the stairs "the fun way" and how we might continue that in New Jerusalem, which happens to be 1,500 miles high. I once posted a question on my Facebook page: What are you looking forward to most in Heaven? I received thousands of responses—some heartwarming and others heartbreaking.

A girl named Liz wrote and said, "What am I looking for in Heaven? I am looking forward to seeing my babies I aborted. Getting them into my arms and loving them as I should have here on Earth. Thank God for His Son and His life shed for a sinner like me so we can look forward to that day. Maybe I will take them down some stairs the fun way too." (In fact, a number of women wrote to me about wanting to see the babies they had aborted.)

Christina wrote, "My sister is handicapped. She cannot walk or talk. But we have this special bond, and I pray one day in Heaven we will have a long conversation full of happiness and joy and walk together hand in hand and maybe even dance a little."

Peter wrote about what he looked forward to most in Heaven: "To see my wife and son again. My son was only twenty-six when he went to be with the Lord in June of 2006. My wife was only forty-nine when she went to be with the Lord in February of this year. I miss them both so much. I look forward to being with them in the presence of the Lord."

Jennifer wrote, "I would like to talk to my daughter. She is severely autistic. I want to hear what life looked like from her eyes. To understand her. That would be Heaven indeed."

Crystal wrote, "I am looking forward to holding my sweet baby boy David. He passed away at eight months old, and I can't wait to experience his first words. His first time running. See him grow up in Heaven. And most of all for my son to introduce me to our Savior."

One day soon, there will be restoration. All those aborted babies will be in Heaven. Handicaps will be gone, mental and physical disabilities banished. There will be joy. The Bible says that in His presence there is fullness of joy and at His right hand there are pleasures forevermore (see Psalm 16:11).

C. S. Lewis said, "Joy is the serious business of Heaven." [60]

A place of laughter

In Luke 6:21 Jesus said, "What happiness there is for you who are now hungry, for you are going to be satisfied! What happiness there is for you who weep, for the time will come when you shall laugh with joy!" (TLB).

ONE LAST PEARLY GATES STORY

I heard the story of a man who died and approached the gates of Heaven. Peter (who else?) met him at the gates and said, "Okay, friend, this is how it works.

You need a thousand points to get into Heaven. Tell me all the good things that you have done, and I'll give you points for each item.

The man got a little excited and said, "I was married to the same wonderful woman for fifty years. I never cheated on her, not even in my heart."

"Hmm," said Peter. "That's three points."

"Are you kidding me? Just three points for that?"

"Three points."

"Well," the man went on, "I attended church faithfully every Sunday, went to a midweek Bible study, and faithfully gave my tithes and offerings to the Lord. I even gave off of my gross, not my net."

"Okay," Peter replied. "That's another point."

"How many points do I have altogether?"

"Four . . . so far."

"Let's see . . . I worked in a soup kitchen for years and years. Spent my weekends feeding homeless people."

"Ah," said Peter. "That's two points. You're up to six now."

"Good night!" the man said. "At this rate, the only way I will ever get into Heaven is by the grace of God."

Peter smiled. "That's right. Come right in, my friend. The grace of God is worth a thousand points."

I offer this little parable because people really do imagine there must be a point system for getting into Heaven. Some will say, "If I just do enough good works or live a certain kind of life, it will get me in the door." But the truth is, even if you filled your whole life with good works, you still would fall short of God's holy and righteous standards. In fact, that's what sin means: to fall short or to miss the mark.

And what is that mark? What is the standard that God has set for all humanity? *Absolute, total perfection.*

"Well," you say, "who could measure up to that?"

No one!

That's where Jesus comes in. He was God, and He was man. He lived a sinless life, a life of perfection, and bridged the gap for us when He died on the cross and carried our sins. He died in our place, taking our punishment, paying our penalty. Then He rose again from the dead, opening the door of Heaven to all who would receive His offer of complete pardon and forgiveness, receiving Him as Savior and Lord of their lives.

The only way that I ever will walk the streets of New Jerusalem and explore the wonders of the new Earth will be by the grace of God and the willing sacrifice of Jesus Christ:

> May you have grace and peace from God who is, and was, and is to come; and from the sevenfold Spirit before his throne; and from Jesus Christ who faithfully reveals all truth to us. He was the first to rise from death, to die no more. He is far greater than any king in all the earth. All praise to him who always loves us and who set us free from our sins by pouring out his lifeblood for us. He has gathered us into his Kingdom and made us priests of God his Father. Give to him everlasting glory! He rules forever! Amen! (Revelation 1:4–6 TLB)

THREE TAKEAWAY TRUTHS

- It's vital to remember that the New Jerusalem is a real city—a city where all believers can finally "feel at home."
- As amazing as all the other sights of the new Heaven and new Earth are, Jesus Himself will be the main attraction.
- Christ's payment for the forgiveness of sins is the only way to be admitted to this eternal city.

CHAPTER TWENTY-SEVEN
Come, Lord Jesus!

Then he said to me, "These words are faithful and true."
And the Lord God of the holy prophets sent His angel to show
His servants the things which must shortly take place.
(Revelation 22:6)

IN THIS CHAPTER
- How we can experience the blessings of the book of Revelation
- A warning against tampering with the Word of God
- The last words of Jesus recorded in Scripture
- God's standing invitation to all who hear His words

"These words are faithful and true."

I love that sentence. The words come from an unidentified angel in Revelation 22:6 who had been John's tour guide through future glories. After giving the elderly apostle a view of the new Heaven and new Earth, including the New Jerusalem descending from Heaven, he wrapped up the tour with those six words.

The angel spoke regarding the book of Revelation, but speaking as he did on one of the last pages of the Scriptures, he could have said it about the entire Bible. The Word of God is faithful and true.

In today's culture of moral relativism and postmodernism, people question the very concept of truth. They speak of "my truth" or "your truth" but deny the existence of *the* truth.

It wasn't always this way in the United States of America.

Most of our founding fathers believed the Bible to be the Word of God. Even those who were not committed followers of Jesus Christ had, at the very least, a great respect for the Bible. Our judicial system—and really our form of government as a whole—is founded on biblical principles.

Things have changed, haven't they?

Again, people will say, "My version of truth is as valid as your version of truth. How dare you impose your version of truth on me?" Even many of our national leaders seem to have no problem with lying if it advances their agenda.

Wouldn't it be wonderful if you could know that when your president, senator, congressman, governor, mayor, or used car dealer speaks, his or her words are faithful and true?

Thankfully, we do know that about the Scriptures. The words on the pages of your Bible are faithful and true. And the One who is called the Word of God is also called "Faithful and True" (Revelation 19:11). You can depend on Jesus. You can rely on His words. You can entrust your eternity into His keeping.

Here are words from the final chapter of our Bible:

> Then he said to me, "These words are faithful and true." And the Lord God of the holy prophets sent His angel to show His servants the things which must shortly take place.
>
> "Behold, I am coming quickly! Blessed is he who keeps the words of the prophecy of this book."
>
> Now I, John, saw and heard these things. And when I heard and saw, I fell down to worship before the feet of the angel who showed me these things.
>
> Then he said to me, "See that you do not do that. For I am your fellow servant, and of your brethren the prophets, and of those who keep the words of this book. Worship God." And he said to me, "Do not seal the words of the prophecy of this book, for the time is at hand. He who is unjust, let him be unjust still; he who is filthy, let him be filthy still; he who is righteous, let him be righteous still; he who is holy, let him be holy still."

"And behold, I am coming quickly, and My reward is with Me, to give to every one according to his work. I am the Alpha and the Omega, the Beginning and the End, the First and the Last."

Blessed are those who do His commandments, that they may have the right to the tree of life, and may enter through the gates into the city. But outside are dogs and sorcerers and sexually immoral and murderers and idolaters, and whoever loves and practices a lie.

"I, Jesus, have sent My angel to testify to you these things in the churches. I am the Root and the Offspring of David, the Bright and Morning Star."

And the Spirit and the bride say, "Come!" And let him who hears say, "Come!" And let him who thirsts come. Whoever desires, let him take the water of life freely.

For I testify to everyone who hears the words of the prophecy of this book: If anyone adds to these things, God will add to him the plagues that are written in this book; and if anyone takes away from the words of the book of this prophecy, God shall take away his part from the Book of Life, from the holy city, and from the things which are written in this book.

He who testifies to these things says, "Surely I am coming quickly."

Amen. Even so, come, Lord Jesus!

The grace of our Lord Jesus Christ be with you all. Amen. (Revelation 22:6–21)

In Revelation 22:7, Jesus Himself tells us, "Blessed is he who keeps the words of the prophecy of this book."

Revelation not only is unique in that it has its own outline (see 1:19), but it also has its own built-in blessing. Yes, there is certainly a blessing in reading any or the entire Bible. But God says specifically in Revelation 1:3, "Blessed is he who reads and those who hear the words of this prophecy, and keep those things which are written in it; for the time is near."

GOOD TO KNOW

Revelation not only is unique in that it has its own outline, but it also has its own built-in blessing.

God says, "I will bless you when you *read, hear,* and *keep* the words of this book." We went over these three imperatives in the first chapter, but it seems appropriate to review them here, as we draw near the close of this book.

1. Read the Word.

It's a blessing to us as we look at today's headlines and view them from a biblical perspective. But first you have to *read it.* The phrase in Revelation 1:3 could be translated, "Read it out loud."

2. Hear the Word.

But it doesn't stop there. You must also *hear* the words of the prophecy. Jesus would often say, "He who has ears to hear, let him hear!" If you really hear these words, it makes sense out of this crazy world we are living in right now. If you really hear and understand what Revelation is teaching, you realize that events in this day are moving along in accordance with God's plan. You recognize that God is in control, even when things seem chaotic, and that the darkest part of the night is just before dawn. You also recognize that we—God's redeemed sons and daughters—win in the end.

But you must listen to the Word carefully.

Frankly, I don't always do that. Sometimes when I fly and the flight attendant is explaining emergency evacuation procedures, I don't really listen. After noting where the exits are in relation to my seat, I listen passively to their little spiel, maybe flipping through a magazine or dashing off a final text before takeoff. How many times have I heard them tell me that my seat can double as a flotation device if the plane crashes into the water? (Somehow, I've never found that very comforting. There I am, out in the middle of the ocean, holding a seat to my chest. Oh, and they also give you a whistle—which probably alerts all the sharks in the vicinity.)

I remember a particular flight from Miami a number of years ago. I had basically tuned out all the emergency procedures and had become absorbed in a book when suddenly the captain's voice came over the intercom and told us that the plane was having mechanical difficulties and that we needed to prepare for an emergency crash landing.

Immediately the flight attendants began going over the emergency procedures again. This time I listened carefully. Why? Because my life depended on it. For some reason, one of the flight attendants picked me out and said, "I want you to help." Just that quickly, I was deputized. (They didn't give me any little wings to wear or anything like that.) He took me over to the emergency door and showed me how to operate it.

Was I looking at my phone or flipping through a magazine then? Not a chance! I was hanging on his every word. Not only did my life depend on it, but he had also given me the responsibility of helping my fellow passengers, possibly saving their lives. Thankfully, we didn't have to make that crash landing. Whatever the problem had been, it resolved itself.

But it was a good lesson for me. You listen carefully when your life depends on it. And our lives as followers of Christ depend on what we are hearing in God's instruction manual, the Bible.

3. Keep the Word.

The Lord's specific blessing is promised to those who keep what is written in the book of Revelation. It's not enough to just read it. It's not enough to just hear it. You have to *keep* it.

Here's an interesting thought: when the Bible speaks about our future, it often includes an exhortation to live a godly life. God doesn't give us Bible prophecy to tantalize, entertain, or titillate us. Studying Bible prophecy was never meant to be a pastime or hobby. God gives us these glimpses into the future to help us wake up and pay attention to what's going on around us and to exhort us to live godly lives because Jesus Christ is coming back again.

In 2 Peter 3:11–12 the apostle writes: "Since everything around us is going to be destroyed like this, what holy and godly lives you should live, looking forward to the day of God and hurrying it along" (NLT).

Once again, I love what it says in verse 6: "These words are faithful and true." Why should I keep these words?

Because they are faithful. Because they are true.

There is an ironclad guarantee from God Himself that everything in His book is true—every word is trustworthy and reliable.

Why should I keep His Word? Because His coming is near. Verse 7 says, "Behold, I am coming quickly!"

"But Greg," someone might say. "Wasn't this book written a couple of thousand years ago? I guess God's definition of 'quickly' isn't the same as mine."

It reminds me of when my wife and I are going somewhere, and I will say, "Are you ready?"

"Yes," she will say, "I'm ready."

To me, *ready* means that we are walking out the door, getting into the car, and driving away. To my wife, *ready* is a relative term. It may mean that she has to put a couple of things away or maybe run upstairs and grab her sweater. I've concluded that we simply have different definitions of the word. To me, ready means *ready*. To her, it means *almost (but not quite) ready*.

So what does Jesus mean when He says that He is coming quickly? Actually, the Greek word translated *quickly* has less to do with how soon He will come and more to do with the suddenness of the event when it occurs. John is recording a series of events stacked closely together like dominoes. Once the first domino falls, the rest will follow in rapid succession. Once it begins, it will be fast—so be ready.

GOOD TO KNOW

The Greek word translated *quickly* has less to do with how soon Jesus will come and more to do with the suddenness of the event when it occurs.

4. Do His work.

Jesus said, "Behold, I am coming quickly, and My reward is with Me, to give to every one according to his work" (Revelation 22:12).

As followers of Jesus Christ, we will make sacrifices. We will have to lose some things and let some things go. We most certainly will face some form of persecution. We will endure some hardships. But we can also be sure of this: God keeps careful records, and He promises to reward us for our faithfulness.

Remember this: Life today on Planet Earth is as good as it ever will be for a nonbeliever. That's because they don't have the hope of Heaven and the new Earth. In fact, judgment awaits them.

On the other hand, life today on Planet Earth is as *bad* as it will ever be for the believer. No matter what you might be going through right now, you can be confident that if you're a Christian, the best is yet to come.

In the Beatitudes Jesus said,

> "Blessed are those who are persecuted for righteousness' sake, for theirs is the kingdom of heaven. Blessed are you when they revile and persecute you, and say all kinds of evil against you falsely for My sake. Rejoice and be exceedingly glad, for great is your reward in heaven, for so they persecuted the prophets who were before you." (Matthew 5:10–12)

Notice that the word *blessed* is used twice, to emphasize the generous blessing of God for the persecuted. Another way to translate it would be, "Double blessed are the persecuted" or "Happy, happy are the persecuted." In fact, this word *rejoice* could be translated, "Jump and skip with happy excitement." I love that picture! It reminds you of the happiness and excitement of a child who will simply jump for joy. The Scriptures are saying, "When you are persecuted, wear it as a badge of honor."

In the process of doing our Lord's work on Earth, the Scriptures encourage us to be faithful. Galatians 6:9 says, "Let us not grow weary while doing good, for in due season we shall reap if we do not lose heart."

Don't be weary in reading your Bible and seeking to live by what it teaches.

Don't be weary in praying for your family, friends, and country.

Don't be weary in sharing your faith with others.

Don't be weary in serving the Lord with the gifts that God has given to you.

Don't be weary in helping others with provisions and resources that God has given to you as a steward.

Don't be weary in these things. In due season, at the right time, you will reap a harvest from that faithful service if you don't lose heart or give up.

Sometimes we do get tired. Sometimes I get tired *in* the Lord's work, but I never get tired *of* the Lord's work. So when you're tired, take a break. Rest. Recharge. Then go back to work again. Even Jesus took breaks and time off periodically. On one occasion He said to His disciples (from the old King James Bible), "Come ye yourselves apart into a desert place, and rest a while: for there were many coming and going, and they had no leisure so much as to eat" (Mark 6:31 KJV).

As Vance Havner said, "If we don't come apart, we will come apart!"

The point is that we must never get tired of what God has given us to do. It's a great privilege to do our best for Him in the strength that He gives us.

When we read about reaping in due season, we're reminded of what else Paul says in Galatians 6. He tells us,

> Do not be deceived, God is not mocked; for whatever a man sows, that he will also reap. For he who sows to his flesh will of the flesh reap corruption, but he who sows to the Spirit will of the Spirit reap everlasting life. (verses 7–8)

These verses are usually quoted in an aggressive fashion, like, "You'd better wise up and stop doing that bad stuff, because the Bible says that you will reap what you sow!"

That's true. But we need to understand the rest of the verse too. Yes, if you sow to the flesh, if you disobey God, then you will reap the consequences. But if you sow to the Spirit, you will reap life everlasting. In other words, what you are and what you do today will determine what you will be tomorrow—and for eternity.

In Revelation 22:10–11, the angel gave John these enigmatic words: "Do not seal the words of the prophecy of this book, for the time is at hand. He who is unjust, let him be unjust still; he who is filthy, let him be filthy still; he who is righteous, let him be righteous still; he who is holy, let him be holy still."

> **GOOD TO KNOW**
>
> What you are and what you do today will determine what you will be tomorrow—and for eternity.

Obviously, God is not encouraging wicked people to do wicked things. In fact, this is more of a warning. I like the way Charles Swindoll paraphrased it in his commentary on Revelation: "You wrong-doers, go ahead and keep doing wrong. Just see what happens. And all unclean sinners, keep rolling in the mud. Just ignore God's offer of cleansing. You've seen what's in store for you. As for you righteous and holy saints, keep practicing righteousness, keep being holy—and you'll get your reward in due time."[61]

In verses 18–19 of chapter 22, the apostle gives a sobering, specific warning to anyone who would tamper with the book of Revelation:

> For I testify to everyone who hears the words of the prophecy of this book: If anyone adds to these things, God will add to him the plagues that are written in this book; and if anyone takes away from the words of the book of this prophecy, God shall take away his part from the Book of Life, from the holy city, and from the things which are written in this book.

In other words, "Don't mess around with the book of Revelation." This is talking about a person who would deceptively disobey, disregard, distort, or dilute the Scriptures. Who are we to edit God's very words? It's not the job of our culture to make the Scriptures conform to its ever-shifting standards. No, the Bible is absolute truth and the very bedrock upon which we built our nation. When we stray from its commandments, counsel, and principles, we do so at our peril. We don't need to conform the Scriptures to our culture. We should be conforming our culture to the Scriptures.

How would a person add to or take away from the Word of God? One way would be to disobey it. You hear it and say, "I know what the Bible is saying here, but I'm not going to do it. I don't care. I'm going to do what I want to do."

I've even had people tell me, "I don't agree with what the Bible is saying. I like some parts of the Bible, but I disagree with *this* part."

That's an example of taking away from God's Word—just removing from your sight the parts you don't like, don't agree with, or don't intend to obey.

Another way to take away from the Scriptures would be to simply disregard them—to disregard and ignore them altogether. When you hear a sermon, you just tune it out.

Yet another way of adding to or subtracting from the Bible would be to distort the Word. In other words, someone might twist a particular Scripture verse to accommodate their life choices. People do that all the time. Instead of an *exegesis*, which means going to the text, letting the text speak for itself, and properly interpreting it, they will do an *eisegesis*, which means imposing their own views on the text. In other words, *Here is what I believe, and I'm going to twist these verses or stand them on their head to make them support my views.*

This is what the Devil did in his attack on Jesus during the temptation in the wilderness. Satan quoted the Bible. Can you imagine that? The Gospel of Matthew tells us that "the devil took Him up into the holy city, set Him on the pinnacle of the temple, and said to Him, 'If You are the Son of God, throw Yourself down. For it is written: "He shall give His angels charge over you," and, "In their hands they shall bear you up, lest you dash your foot against a stone"'" (4:5–6).

Satan was quoting from Psalm 91, but he was twisting the Scriptures out of their proper context. Satan was taking a legitimate Scripture verse, pulling it out of context, and seeking to bend it to his own evil purposes. By doing so, he was both adding his own spin to the verse and subtracting its original application.

FAMOUS LAST WORDS

Here are the final verses of the book of Revelation—which also happen to be the final verses of the New Testament and the final verses of the Bible:

> He who testifies to these things says, "Surely I am coming quickly."

> Amen. Even so, come, Lord Jesus!

> The grace of our Lord Jesus Christ be with you all. Amen. (22:20–21)

"Surely I am coming quickly" are the last recorded words of Jesus in the Scriptures.

Last words, of course, are very significant.

If you knew for sure you would die today and leave this planet, what would your last words be?

Sometimes people don't know what their last words will be, because death may come suddenly and unexpectedly. But there are people on their deathbeds who know their time has come and have enough strength left for one final statement.

On March 14, 1883, the communist leader Karl Marx died. His housekeeper came to him and said, tell me your last words, and I will write them down. Karl Marx replied, "Go on, get out! Last words are for fools who haven't said enough!"

We will now go from Karl Marx to Groucho Marx, the comedian. His last words were, "Die, my dear? Why that's the last thing I'll do."

Nostradamus, who was known for predicting the future, got it right at least one time. His last words were, "You will not find me alive at sunrise." That was true.

Pablo Picasso's last words were, "Drink to me. Drink to my health. You know I can't drink anymore."

The Roman Emperor Julian, having attempted to reverse the official endorsement of Christianity by the Roman Empire, said with his final breath, "You have won, O Galilean."

The last words of believers are frequently very different from the last words of nonbelievers. When young Stephen, the first martyr of the church, was being stoned to death by an angry mob, he cried out, "Look! I see the Heavens opened and the Son of Man standing at the right hand of God!" (Acts 7:56). Then he went on to say, "Lord Jesus, receive my spirit" (verse 59), and "Lord, do not charge them with this sin" (verse 60).

The final words of the preacher John Wesley were, "The best of all is, God is with us."

Pastor and Bible commentator F. B. Meyer died saying, "Read me something from the Bible, something brave and triumphant."

In contrast, the last words of the revolutionary Pancho Villa were, "Don't let it end like this. Tell them I said something."

Jesus said something. Here are His last words: "Surely I am coming quickly."

In reply, the apostle John offered a prayer: "Amen. Even so, come, Lord Jesus!"

When someone says something that you agree with, you say "Amen." John was saying, "Yes, Lord. You are coming quickly!" Let it be. So be it.

I love it that one of the last verses of the entire Bible is an invitation:

> And the Spirit and the bride say, "Come!" And let him who hears say, "Come!" And let him who thirsts come. Whoever desires, let him take the water of life freely. (verse 17)

Come. That's one of God's favorite words.

In the face of judgment on Earth, God commanded Noah to build an ark. And when it was built, God said, "Come into the ark" (Genesis 7:1).

Moses, standing in the midst of people who had turned away from God in the worship of the golden calf, cried out, "Whoever is on the LORD's side—come to me!" (Exodus 32:26).

God Himself said to Israel, "Come now, and let us reason together. . . . Though your sins are like scarlet, they shall be as white as snow; though they are red like crimson, they shall be as wool" (Isaiah 1:18).

Later in the book of Isaiah, God said,

> "Come, all you who are thirsty,
> come to the waters;
> and you who have no money,
> come, buy and eat!
> Come, buy wine and milk
> without money and without cost." (Isaiah 55:1 NIV)

To the men who wanted to know where Jesus was staying, He simply said, "Come and see" (John 1:39). Later in His ministry, He said, "Come to Me, all you who labor and are heavy laden, and I will give you rest" (Matthew 11:28). Near the end of His time on Earth, He lifted His voice at a great feast in Jerusalem and said, "If anyone thirsts, let him come to Me and drink" (John 7:37).

This is the heart of God. He is calling out to humanity, saying, "Come! Come to Me!"

And what will happen if we come? Our spiritual hunger will be satisfied, and our spiritual thirst will be quenched.

Again, Revelation 22:17 is an *invitation*. It isn't a summons. It isn't a decree. It isn't anything forced. It's not "Come to Me—or else!"

"Whoever desires, let him take the water of life freely."

God is saying, "If you want a drink from the water of life, the living water that will save you from Hell and from a wasted life on Earth, just come on and take it. If you don't want it, you don't have to. This is an offer I extend to all of humanity."

GOOD TO KNOW

When God says, "Come," it is an invitation.

Deep down inside, every one of us is thirsty and hungry for something more in life. This is something this world simply cannot give us. It won't come through a relationship. It won't come through our possessions. It won't come through our accomplishments or fame. It won't come through some exhilarating experience. All these things will leave us empty. We are hungering and thirsting, deep down inside, for God Himself.

A doctor named Robin L. Smith wrote a book called *Hungry: The Truth About a Satisfied Soul*. She writes about those who feel an emptiness after experiencing great success and calls it "being hungry for the high note." She maintains that Michael Jackson and Whitney Houston, who both died early deaths, weren't killed by drugs per se. Rather, they were striving to hit the high note again. [62]

In fact, shortly before Whitney Houston's death, she said, "I'm going to hit that high note again." [63]

In the eyes of the world, these two entertainers enjoyed unparalleled success. Michael Jackson's record *Thriller* is one of the top-selling records of all time. Whitney Houston also enjoyed international success.

So you hit a high note. You're at the peak of life. But what then? You can't hold that note, and you can't stay on the peak. You're not as successful as you once were, and you can't bear that. That's why so many of these super successful people end up strung out on drugs or alcohol.

But drugs aren't the real issue. Alcohol isn't the real issue. The real issue is emptiness.

When you think about it, God could have chosen many different ways to wrap up the Bible. He chose to end it with an invitation to anyone who feels empty and thirsts for something more than they've ever found in life.

He simply says, "Come."

THREE TAKEAWAY TRUTHS

- When Jesus says He is coming quickly, it means He will come suddenly.
- For nonbelievers, this world is as good as it gets. But for the Christian, the best is yet to come!
- God's invitation for us to come to Him is just that: an invitation. Will you accept it?

Notes

Chapter 3: "Jesus' Words to Suffering Christians"

1. C. S. Lewis, *The Four Loves* (New York: Harcourt, 1960), 169.

2. Cornelius Tacitus, *The Annals: The Reigns of Tiberius, Claudius, and Nero*, Book Fifteen, J. C. Yardley, trans. (New York: Oxford University Press, 2008), 360.

Chapter 4: "The Compromising Church"

3. "Las Vegas History," Las Vegas Convention and Visitors Authority, accessed February 5, 2019, https://www.lvcva.com/stats-and-facts/history-of-las-vegas/.

Chapter 5: "A Sick and Dying Church"

4. Charles R. Swindoll, *Insights on Revelation* (Grand Rapids, MI: Zondervan, 2011), 69–70.

Chapter 6: "Jesus' Message to Last Days Believers"

5. Elisabeth Elliot, *Keep a Quiet Heart* (Ann Arbor, MI: Servant, 1995), 90.

6. C. S. Lewis, *The Business of Heaven: Daily Readings from C. S. Lewis* (New York: Harcourt, 1984), 228.

Chapter 7: "The Church That Made Jesus Sick"

7. The Free Library, "The Emperor's New Clothes," by Hans Christian Anderson, accessed May 25, 2021, https://andersen.thefreelibrary.com/Andersens-Fairy-Tales/1-1.

8. G. Campbell Morgan, *A First Century Message to Twentieth Century Christians: Addresses based upon the Letters to the Seven Churches of Asia* (Eugene, OR: Wipf and Stock Publishers, 2004), 203.

9. Robert Boyd Munger, with Dale and Sandy Larsen, *Commitment: My Heart—Christ's Home* (Westmont, IL: InterVarsity Press, 1994), 13.

Chapter 8: "What Heaven Will Be Like"

10. Mark Hitchcock, *The End: A Complete Overview of Bible Prophecy and the End Days* (Carol Stream, IL: Tyndale, 2012), 125.

Chapter 9: "Why We Were Created"

11. Lesley-Ann Jones, *Freddie Mercury: The Definitive Biography* (London: Hodder & Stoughton, 2011), 163.

12. Lesley-Ann Jones, 5.

Chapter 10: The Four Horsemen of the Apocalypse

13. Billy Graham, *Storm Warning* (Nashville: Thomas Nelson, 2010), 30.

14. As quoted in Billy Graham, *Till Armageddon: A Perspective on Suffering* (Waco, TX: Word Publishing, 1984), n. p.

15. James Gerstenzang, "'Nuclear Winter' Seen Killing More Than Atomic Blasts: After U.S.-Soviet War, Famine Would Peril Entire Population of World, Scientists Say," *Los Angeles Times,* September 13, 1985, http://articles.latimes.com/1985-09-13/news/mn-22647_1_nuclear-war.

16. David W. Wiersbe and Warren W. Wiersbe, *C Is for Christmas* (Grand Rapids, MI: Baker Books, 2012), 179.

Chapter 12: "Apocalypse Now"

17. Omri Ron, "Why do some Christians believe coronavirus is an apocalyptic prophecy?" *The Jerusalem Post*, March 26, 2020, https://www.jpost.com/International/Why-do-some-Christians-believe-coronavirus-is-an-apocalyptic-prophecy-622425.

Chapter 13: "When All Hell Breaks Loose"

18. C. S. Lewis, *The Business of Heaven: Daily Readings from C. S. Lewis* (New York: Houghton Mifflin Harcourt, 1984), 142.

19. C. S. Lewis, *The Screwtape Letters* (New York: HarperCollins, 1996), ix.

20. Cathy Lynn Grossman, "'Protestant' is no longer America's top religious umbrella brand. It's been rained out by the soaring number of 'Nones'—people who claim no faith affiliation," *USAToday.com*, October 9, 2012, http://www.usatoday.com/story/news/nation/2012/10/08/nones-protestant-religion-pew/1618445/.

Chapter 14: "Light in a Very Dark Place"

21. C. S. Lewis, *Letters to Malcolm: Chiefly on Prayer* (New York: Houghton Mifflin Harcourt, 1992), 123.

Chapter 15: "Overcoming the Devil"

22. John Phillips, *Exploring Revelation: An Expository Commentary* (Grand Rapids, MI: Kregel, 1987), 160.

Chapter 17: "Who Is the Antichrist?"

23. As quoted in Adrian Rogers, *Unveiling the End Times in Our Time: The Triumph of the Lamb in Revelation* (Nashville: B&H Publishing Group, 2013), 161.

24. J. Dwight Pentecost, *Will Man Survive* (Grand Rapids, MI: Zondervan, 1971), 93.

Chapter 18: "The Mark of the Beast"

25. "The Doomsday Clock," *The Bulletin of the Atomic Scientists: 75 Years and Counting,* accessed June 2, 2021, https://thebulletin.org/doomsday-clock/timeline/.

26. Mark Hitchcock, *Who Is the Antichrist? Answering the Question Everyone Is Asking* (Eugene, OR: Harvest House Publishers, 2011), 103.

27. Meghan Neal, "'Human barcode' could make society more organized, but invades privacy, civil liberties," NY Daily News.com, June 1, 2012, http://www.nydailynews.com/news/national/human-barcode-society-organized-invades-privacy-civil-liberties-article-1.1088129#ixzz2sHkdnf5H.

28. "Gorbachev Says Sept 11 Victims Didn't Die in Vain, (IF . . .)" *Free Republic.com,* October 26, 2001, http://www.freerepublic.com/focus/news/557277/posts.

Chapter 19: "Things to Do Before the End of the World"

29. Charles Haddon Spurgeon, *Sermons on the Last Days* (Peabody, MA: Hendrickson Publishers, 2009), 162.

Chapter 20: "America and Armageddon"

30. "Dictionary of Science Quotations," s.v. "Marcellin Berthelot Quotes," *Today in Science History.com,* http://www.todayinsci.com/B/Berthelot_Marcellin/BerthelotMarcellin-Quotations.htm.

31. C. S. Lewis, *The Business of Heaven: Daily Readings from C. S. Lewis* (New York: Houghton Mifflin Harcourt: 1984), 318.

32. C. S. Lewis, *Mere Christianity* (New York: Macmillan, 1952), 137.

33. As quoted in David Jeremiah, *What in the World Is Going On? 10 Prophetic Clues You Cannot Afford to Ignore* (Nashville, TN: Thomas Nelson, 2008), 189.

34. Ronald Reagan, *The Reagan Diaries* (New York: HarperCollins, 2007), 19.

35. Ronald Reagan, 24.

36. As quoted in David Jeremiah, 194.

37. *The World Factbook 2021,* Washington, DC: The Central Intelligence Agency, 2021, accessed June 2, 2021, https://www.cia.gov/the-world-factbook/.

38. Mark Hitchcock, *Is America in Bible Prophecy?* (Colorado Springs: Multnomah Books, 2002), 20.

39. As quoted in J. P. Toner, *Leisure and Ancient Rome* (Oxford, UK: Blackwell Publishers, 1995), 69.

Chapter 21: "Beauty and the Beast"

40. Dan Vergano, "What if an asteroid were really headed our way?" *USAToday.com,* February 15, 2013, http://www.usatoday.com/story/tech/columnist/vergano/2013/02/15/asteroid-civil-defense/1920553/.

41. Adrian Rogers, *Unveiling the End Times in Our Time: The Triumph of the Lamb in Revelation* (Nashville: B&H Publishing Group, 2004), 191.

42. Brian Hiatt, "Paul McCartney: Yesterday & Today," *Rollingstone.com,* June 18, 2012, http://m.rollingstone.com/music/news/paul-mccartney-yesterday-today-20120618?page=3.

43. Edward M. Bounds, *Heaven: A Place—A City—A Home* (Grand Rapids, MI: Fleming H. Revell, 1921), 125.

Chapter 22: "The Second Coming of Jesus Christ"

44. Warren W. Wiersbe, *The Bible Exposition Commentary: New Testament,* vol. 1 (Colorado Springs: David C. Cook, 2001), 647.

45. Dr. Grant C. Richison, *Verse-by-VerseCommentary.com*, s.v. "Jude 14–15," March 8, 2008, http://versebyversecommentary.com/jude/jude-14-16.

Chapter 23: "Turning the World Right Side Up"

46. Randy Alcorn, *Heaven* (Carol Stream, IL: Tyndale, 2004), 88.

47. Elisabeth Elliot, 20.

Chapter 24: "The Final Judgment of Humanity"

48. E. G. Robinson, quoted in Augustus Hopkins Strong, *Systematic Theology* (Philadelphia: The Griffith & Rowland Press, 1907), 983.

49. Thomas Watson, quoted in *The Westminster Collection of Christian Quotations,* Martin H. Manser, ed. (Louisville, KY: Westminster John Knox Press, 2001), 93.

50. John Wilbur Chapman and Dwight Lyman Moody, *The Life and Work of Dwight L. Moody* (Philadelphia: International Publishing, 1900), 416.

51. Adrian Rogers, *Unveiling the End Times in Our Time: The Triumph of the Lamb in Revelation* (Nashville: B&H Publishing Group, 2004), 243–244.

52. C. S. Lewis, *The Business of Heaven: Daily Readings from C. S. Lewis* (New York: Houghton Mifflin Harcourt, 1984), 142.

Chapter 25: "Heaven and Earth"

53. Randy Alcorn, *Heaven* (Carol Stream, IL: Tyndale, 2004), 88.

54. Charles R. Swindoll, *Insights on Revelation* (Grand Rapids, MI: Zondervan, 2011), 273.

55. Randy Alcorn, 169.

Chapter 26: "The Best Is Yet to Come"

56. Randy Alcorn, *Heaven* (Carol Stream, IL: Tyndale, 2004), 442.

57. Dennis J. Hester, *The Vance Havner Quote Book* (Grand Rapids, MI: Baker, 1986), 109.

58. Randy Alcorn, 242.

59. "How Many People Die Each Day," World Population Review, accessed June 3, 2021, https://worldpopulationreview.com/countries/deaths-per-day.

60. C. S. Lewis, *The Business of Heaven: Daily Readings from C. S. Lewis* (New York: Houghton Mifflin Harcourt, 1984), 19.

Chapter 27: "Come, Lord Jesus!"

61. Charles R. Swindoll, *Insights on Revelation* (Grand Rapids, MI: Zondervan, 2011), 291-292.

62. Robin L. Smith, *Hungry: The Truth About a Satisfied Soul* (Carlsbad, CA: Hay House, 2013), 58-59.

63. "Dr. Robin Smith Says Michael Jackson, Whitney Houston Weren't Killed By Drugs," *TheHuffingtonPost.com,* March 3, 2013, http://www.huffingtonpost.com/2013/03/11/dr-robin-smith-michael-jackson-whitney-houston-death_n_2829735.html.

About the Author

Greg Laurie is the senior pastor of Harvest Christian Fellowship, with campuses in California and Hawaii. He began his pastoral ministry at the age of 19 by leading a Bible study of 30 people.

Since then, God has transformed that small group into a church of some 15,000 people. Today, Harvest Christian Fellowship is one of the largest churches in America and consistently ranks among the most influential churches in the nation.

In 1990 he began holding large-scale public evangelistic events called Harvest Crusades. Since that time, more than 10 million people have participated in these events in person or online around the United States. Harvest Crusades also have been held internationally in Canada, Australia, and New Zealand. More importantly, over 600,000 people have made professions of faith through these outreaches.

Greg is the featured speaker of the nationally syndicated radio program *A New Beginning* and also has a weekly television program on Lifetime, Fox

Business, Newsmax, Daystar, the Trinity Broadcasting Network, and KCAL 9 Los Angeles.

Along with his work at Harvest Ministries, he has served as the 2013 Honorary Chairman of the National Day of Prayer and also serves on the board of directors of the Billy Graham Evangelistic Association. He holds honorary doctorates from Biola University and Azusa Pacific University.

He has authored over 70 books, including: *Billy Graham: The Man I Knew*; *Johnny Cash: The Redemption of an American Icon*; *Jesus Revolution*; and *Steve McQueen: The Salvation of an American Icon*, and his autobiography, *Lost Boy*. Greg's favorite writing project is his work as general editor of the *New Believer's Bible*.

He also has produced a number of feature films and documentaries, including *A Rush of Hope*. He has two films in early production: *Jesus Revolution* and *Johnny Cash: American Icon*.

You can follow Greg's preaching, teaching, and writing at harvest.org.

Greg has been married to Cathe Laurie for more than 40 years, and they have two sons: Christopher, who is in Heaven, and Jonathan, as well as five grandchildren.